JERUSALEM FALLS

JERUSALEM FALLS

SEVEN CENTURIES OF WAR AND PEACE

JOHN D. HOSLER

YALE UNIVERSITY PRESS
NEW HAVEN AND LONDON

For information about this and other Yale University Press publications, please contact:
U.S. Office: sales.press@yale.edu   yalebooks.com
Europe Office: sales@yaleup.co.uk   yalebooks.co.uk

Set in Adobe Caslon Pro by IDSUK (DataConnection) Ltd
Printed in Great Britain by TJ Books, Padstow, Cornwall

Library of Congress Control Number: 2022939275

ISBN 978-0-300-25514-0

A catalogue record for this book is available from the British Library.

10 9 8 7 6 5 4 3 2 1

To my parents,
for everything

CONTENTS

ILLUSTRATIONS

Plates

15. Battle of La Forbie, as drawn in the chronicle of Matthew Paris. © Parker Library, Corpus Christi College, Cambridge
16. Section of Jerusalem's Ottoman Era Walls. © Library of Congress
17. Jerusalem. Public domain

Maps

ACKNOWLEDGMENTS

This is a Covid-Era book. As most scholars will attest, research during a pandemic has been challenging, to say the least, with archives and libraries closed and international travel often impossible. Speaking for myself, I would not have succeeded in this project without the steady support (and editing skills) of my wife, Holly, and the love of my children Gianna, Michael, and Rocco. With the help of numerous resources, including the University of Kansas Watson Library and the Combined Arms Research Library at Fort Leavenworth, I was able to locate materials and meet deadlines despite the worldwide difficulties. I would also like to thank Heather McCallum, Katie Urquhart, and Marika Lysandrou at Yale University Press, as well as my literary agent, John W. Wright, for all their efforts on my behalf.

This book began as a teaching idea. In the spring of 2018, I took over the elective "Deep Roots of Conflict in the Middle East," and decided to orient the lessons around competing claims to Jerusalem: Jewish, Christian, and Muslim. It has been an enjoyable and rewarding journey every iteration, and I thank every student who enrolled in that class over the years, as well as those students in my other elective,

"Warfare in the Age of the Crusades." The environment of the Command and General Staff College has stoked my historical inquisitiveness like no other place I've worked, and a superb and supportive array of colleagues have contributed intellectually to the development of the present book: David Cotter, Gregory Hospodor, Geoff Babb, Jonathan Abel, William Kautt, John Kuehn, Jeremy Maxwell, Nathan Jennings, David Bornn, Brian Steed, and Benjamin Schneider; a special nod to William Nance and Eloy Martinez, both of whom took the time to sit in on my electives and offer feedback. I also thank my medievalist colleagues far and wide, especially Daniel Franke, Andrew Holt, Matthew Phillips, Laurence Marvin, Jonathan Phillips, John France, Kelly DeVries, Michael Fulton, Thomas Madden, Alfred Andrea, Jessalynn Bird, M. Cecilia Gaposckin, Ilana Krug, Bernard Bachrach, David Bachrach, Mike Livingston, and Wendy Turner.

I have been fortunate to remain in contact with many of the good folks from my days at the University of Delaware, where I received my doctorate in 2005. I thank Christine Heyrman and Gary May for their support of my professional goals, as well as Lawrence Duggan and Michael Frassetto for years of learned personal and professional correspondence. Alexander Pavuk generously reviewed several chapter drafts. And of course, I thank my doctoral adviser, Daniel Callahan, a Jerusalem scholar of the first rank. I hope he is pleased that his former student, who once eschewed the Old City map hanging in his office for Angevin England, has finally turned the other direction: "Go East, young man, Go East!"

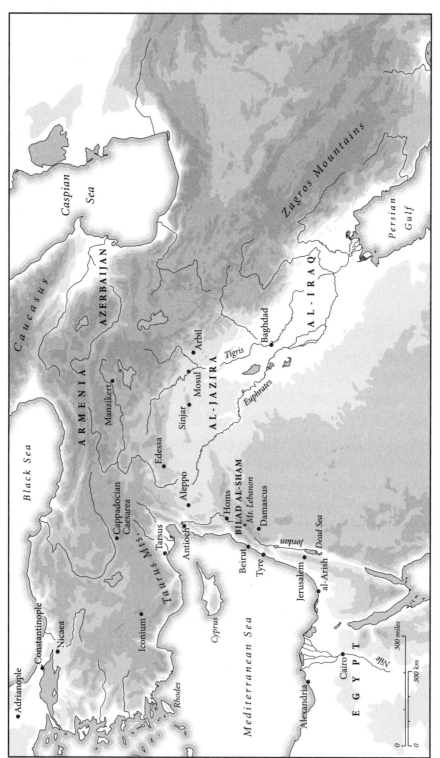

Map 1: The eastern Mediterranean in the Middle Ages

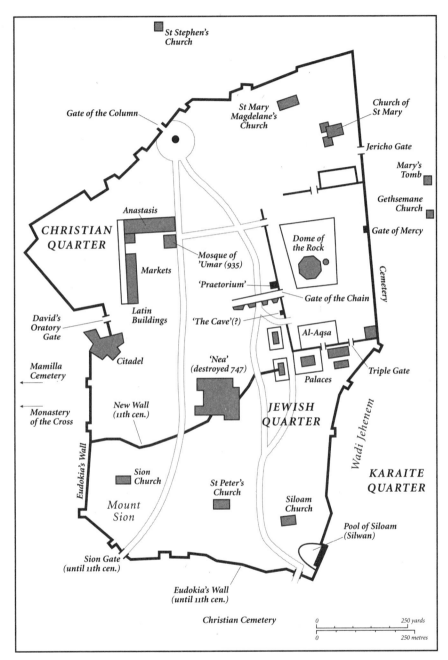

St Stephen's
Church

Gate of the Column

St Mary
Magdelane's
Church

Church of
St Mary

Jericho Gate

Mary's
Tomb

Gethsemane
Church

Gate of Mercy

Anastasis

CHRISTIAN
QUARTER

Dome of
the Rock

Mosque of
'Umar (935)

Markets

'Praetorium'

Gate of the Chain

Latin
Buildings

'The Cave'(?)

David's
Oratory
Gate

Al-Aqsa

Citadel

'Nea'
(destroyed 747)

Palaces

Triple Gate

Cemetery

Mamilla
Cemetery

Monastery
of the Cross

New Wall
(11th cen.)

JEWISH
QUARTER

Wadi Jehenem

KARAITE
QUARTER

Eudokia's Wall

Sion
Church

St Peter's
Church

Siloam
Church

Mount
Sion

Pool of Siloam
(Silwan)

Sion Gate
(until 11th cen.)

Eudokia's Wall
(until 11th cen.)

Christian Cemetery

0   250 yards

0   250 metres

Map 2: Jerusalem in the early Muslim period

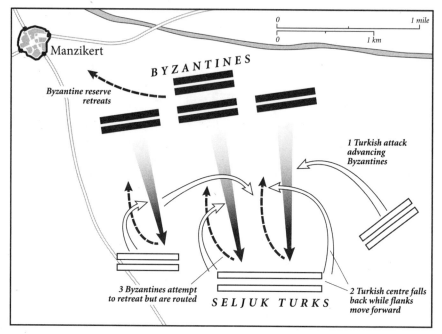

Map 3: Battle of Manzikert

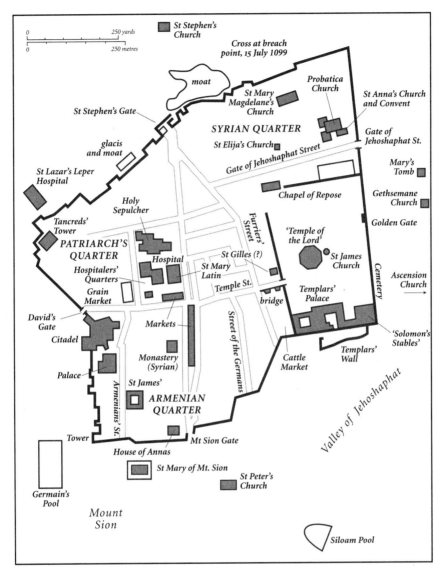

Map 4: Jerusalem in the crusader period

The following labels appear on the map:

0 250 yards
0 250 metres

St Stephen's Church

Cross at breach point, 15 July 1099

moat

Probatica Church

St Mary Magdelane's Church

St Anna's Church and Convent

St Stephen's Gate

SYRIAN QUARTER

Gate of Jehoshaphat St.

glacis and moat

St Elija's Church

Mary's Tomb

Gate of Jehoshaphat Street

St Lazar's Leper Hospital

Chapel of Repose

Gethsemane Church

Holy Sepulcher

Furriers' Street

Golden Gate

Tancreds' Tower

'Temple of the Lord'

PATRIARCH'S QUARTER

Hospital

St Gilles (?)

St James Church

Ascension Church

Hospitalers' Quarters

St Mary Latin

Cemetery

Grain Market

Temple St.

Templars' Palace

David's Gate

bridge

Citadel

Markets

'Solomon's Stables'

Palace

Monastery (Syrian)

Street of the Germans

Cattle Market

Templars' Wall

St James'

Valley of Jehoshaphat

Armenians' St.

ARMENIAN QUARTER

Tower

Mt Sion Gate

House of Annas

St Mary of Mt. Sion

St Peter's Church

Germain's Pool

Mount Sion

Siloam Pool

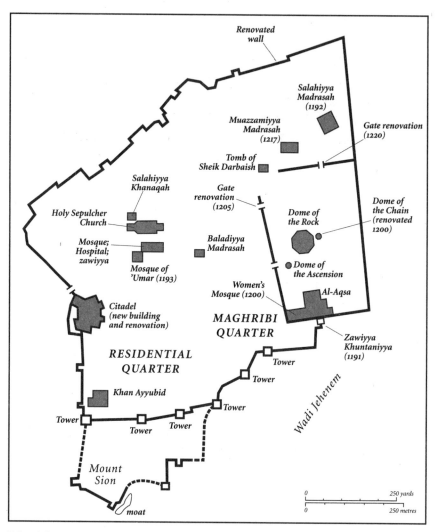

Map 5: Jerusalem in the Ayyubid period

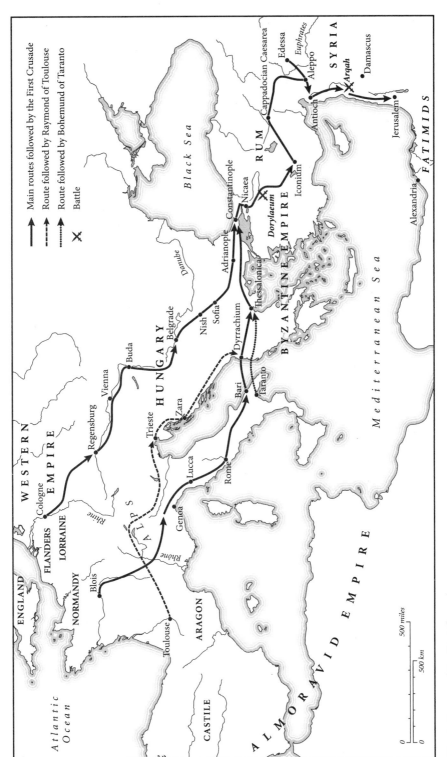

Map 6: Course of the First Crusade

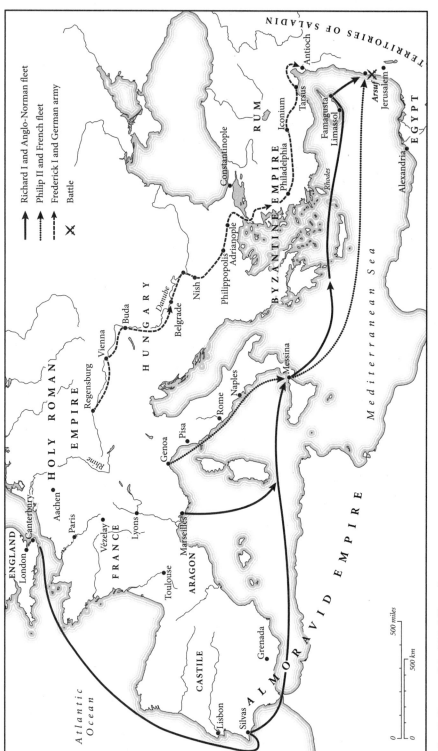

Map 7: Course of the Third Crusade

INTRODUCTION

"Open the gates of victory;
I will enter and thank the Lord.
This is the Lord's own gate,
where the victors enter." (Psalms 118:19–20)

Benjamin passed through the city's strong walls next to the massive Tower of David that stood in perpetual watch over the western gate. He couldn't help noticing the considerable strength of the ancient foundation. Moving further into the streets, he ambled past two hospitals containing knights recovering from battle wounds yet "ever ready to wage war" even as they reclined. He arrived next at the holy places. First, the Sepulchre, full of pilgrims seeking the way of Christ. Second, the Dome, "a handsome cupola." Finally, he reached the Wall that once buttressed the holy Temple and stopped for a while, to whisper a prayer. Thereafter stables, canals, pillars, other tombs, and finally the eastern gates. Traversing the deep valley, he climbed up the mount where the olives grow, from which he saw as far south as beyond the Dead Sea.

Perhaps it happened just this way. Or maybe this Benjamin, Rabbi Benjamin of Tudela, a mid-twelfth-century physician who wrote a travel narrative crisscrossing three continents, did not stroll at all. Perhaps he sprinted, not wishing to linger in a setting so recently and notoriously hostile to men of his faith. Or perhaps he entered with an easy stride only to halt, overawed by the physical traces before him and the deep scars of the past, some visible and others hidden by the ubiquitous stone walls, ruins, and remains within the cityscape. Much of how, and why, Benjamin traveled the world remains obscure, but those who have followed in his footsteps and visited Jerusalem themselves are likely familiar with his multiplicity of impressions, and more.[1]

Jerusalem: it goes, and has gone, by many names: Salem, Hierosolyma, al-Quds, Bayt al-Maqdis, "the Holy City," and "the city of peace." The very name of Jerusalem conjures an array of emotions and images, of a distant and almost mythical place steeped in spiritual meaning yet fraught with peril. Ensconced within the walls of the Old City, today's visitors proceed through labyrinthine streets that twist, ascend, and plunge through distinct quarters of densely packed humanity—here under the bright Middle Eastern sun, there in subterranean tunnels. Amid the bustle of the city's everyday life, they might discern a certain gravity, a heaviness that ceaselessly reiterates the seriousness of the place. Prized continuity in this holiest of the earth's cities has routinely been dashed by epochal change. Few locales have been attacked as often and as savagely as Jerusalem, and even in times of peace sectarian strife can turn the city's inhabitants against their neighbors in a moment. This is a book about that seemingly eternal history of glorious and destructive deeds, and the memories that continue to resonate in Jerusalem's streets and in halls of government and houses of worship throughout the world.

With Jerusalem's extensive history stretching through thousands of years, we must pick our steps deliberately if we are to extract meaning from such a massive data set. Accordingly, this book is not a comprehensive history of the city of Jerusalem; that would be a burden very few writers could shoulder with competence. Neither is it a history of medieval Jerusalem—much less the medieval Levant—in all its various aspects; that, too, would be a heavy task. Rather, it is a book about conquest: those "falls," or moments from the seventh through the thirteenth century when possession of the city passed from adherents of one religious confession to another by way of conflict. This book posits that the Holy City's medieval story is highly pertinent to its modern controversies. Although it is common to attribute to the medieval period only a generalized tale of religious strife, these falls can serve as prisms into an alternate, and rather surprising, narrative: the story of concord and resolution.

Can we really speak of concord in the Middle Ages, a period host to holy war and intense religious animosity? Absolutely. Concord is a narrative forgotten in the standard readings of history and, subsequently, in the historical caricatures that inform our collective memories. Many historians seem to have begun with the explosive events of medieval Jerusalem—understandably so, given their notoriety in the public sphere—and then extrapolated from them, imposing a narrative of conflict on the region and period. The flashpoints and controversies, however, can easily overshadow the unseen currents of cooperation that lay beneath. A different way to approach the topic, then, is to put those moments of high drama into context by reading the broad history of the city, let the evidence take the lead, and see how another dimension of the story is revealed. As one scholar has noted astutely, to recover this disremembered narrative we must "learn (and unlearn)" our respective histories.[2]

From early on, siege has been central to Jerusalem's history, despite the city's relatively low strategic position, lying 60 kilometers east of the Mediterranean Sea in the Judean Hills, away from the major trade routes running through Mesopotamia, Egypt, and Arabia, and along the Levantine coast. Its status as a regional capital ensured continuing attention in times of war. The fall of the city to the

Chaldeans in the sixth century B.C. is well known to readers of the Old Testament, resulting as it did in the "Babylonian Captivity" of the Jews, their release by Cyrus the Great of Persia, the subsequent sparking of the Jewish Diaspora in its wake, and ultimately the rebuilding of Jerusalem's walls under the leadership of Nehemiah. Centuries later, another siege proved perhaps even more consequential: Titus's destruction of the Second Temple in 70 A.D., followed by the brutal Roman suppression of the First Zealot Revolt. The event's importance to Jewish history is unquestionable, and it is still commemorated by a day of mourning, Tisha b'Av.

Yet commemoration can take many forms, some more unpleasant than others. Early Christian theologians provided the bridge between this ancient past and its medieval future by judging Titus's deed praiseworthy in the annals of salvation history, deeming it a comeuppance for Jewish complicity in the crucifixion of Jesus Christ, a popular aspect of the "blood curse" accusation that continues to haunt Christian–Jewish relations today. The Temple's destruction was a deed to be remembered, and from the fourth century it was included in weekly liturgical readings exactly 11 weeks after the Pentecost feast—the same week as Tisha b'Av.[3] As they concluded that Jews had lost their rights to Canaan under the Old Covenant, Christian intellectuals seized upon the idea that spiritual ownership of the city had transferred to the Church.

The nature of this possession changed in the early fourth century. Helena, the Christian mother of Emperor Constantine the Great, arrived at Jerusalem, known then by its Roman name of Aelia Capitolina, in 326. There she purportedly discovered the three crosses of Calvary residing within Christ's tomb, which was itself buried under a temple to Venus. By raising a church over this tomb, the Holy Sepulchre, she signaled the Christian theological claim to the old Jewish heritage in a very physical way. That claim endured even after the so-called "fall of the western Roman Empire" in 476, for the city was retained by the eastern, or Byzantine, empire into the seventh century. Under the respective leadership of Emperor Maurice and Shah Khosrow II, the Byzantines and Sasanid Persians established an alliance that brought peace to the Near East.

It did not last long. The assassination of Maurice in 602 by Phocas the centurion shattered the alliance and ignited a war that lasted 26 years. And in 614, the Persians advanced on Jerusalem itself. As chapter one of this book will show, the Persian attack on Jerusalem set the conditions for a later assault by the Arabs in 638 that gave adherents of the new Islamic religion control over the city. Muslim governance of the Holy City continued into the eleventh century, although the adjective is a relative misnomer. The unity of the Islamic faith was always a mirage, and this led to opportunism. Sunni control over the region continued past the Rashidun caliphs and into the Umayyad (based in Damascus) and then Abbasid (in Baghdad) caliphates. However, in the early 970s a rising Shia power, the Fatimids, captured Jerusalem and held it well past the year 1000. Chapter two explores Fatimid rule and the subsequent wars with the Sunni military powers of the eleventh century, including the Seljuk Turks. Turks attacked Jerusalem twice, in 1073 and 1077, the first resulting in a relatively bloodless capture but the second in a massacre of incalcitrant residents.

The onslaught of the Turks into Asia Minor is a well-known factor in the cause of the First Crusade, encouraged by Pope Urban II in a sermon at Clermont in 1095. Just how much it mattered is a cause of intense debate among crusade scholars, but its role and that of other factors as explored in chapter three led to the formation of coalition Christian armies and their march from West to East. At the close of the eleventh century, two separate armies attacked and seized Jerusalem: the Fatimids wrested the city back from the Turks in late 1098, only to surrender the city to the western Christians, broadly referred to as Franks, in the next year. The latter siege is the most infamous in Jerusalem's history; the "original sin" of the Crusades manifested as butchery of the city's defenders, and the memory of this deed has proven durable in the near-millennium since.

However, as will be seen in chapter four, western control over Jerusalem and the broader, so-called "Crusader States" territories surrounding it steadily degraded over the next several decades. At length it was besieged by the Ayyubid sultan and Muslim icon Saladin. Exploiting his destruction of the army of the Kingdom of Jerusalem at the Battle of Hattin, on 4 July 1187, Saladin captured the city that same autumn and returned it to Muslim rule. This endured until 1229, when the Sixth Crusade of Frederick II, Holy Roman Emperor and *stupor mundi* ("wonder of the world"), succeeded in briefly returning the city to Christian rule, as is detailed in chapter five. Scarcely more than a decade later, in 1244, Muslims took it back. In the seventh, tenth, eleventh, twelfth, and thirteenth centuries, then, Jerusalem changed hands in the midst of both intrareligious and interreligious warfare.

The peoples and events of the seven hundred years covered in this book are as numerous as Abraham's grains of sand, and the stories are complex. The study of them has produced millions of pages of scholarship on the history of Late Antiquity and the Middle Ages, Christianity, Judaism, Islam, Persia, Byzantium, Arabia, Mesopotamia, Egypt, medieval Europe, the Levant, and modern geopolitical and religious controversies. This book makes no pretense of being any sort of complete study, or even a robust survey, of the lengthy period in question. Instead, it threads its way through seven centuries with the singular purpose of examining how military change ushered in religious continuity or change in one specific place—a most consequential place—and what modern readers can learn from that story today.

The wars under scrutiny in these chapters are diverse in scope, nature, and context. Some are of course well known; moments like the captures of Jerusalem in 638, 1099, and 1187 even hold places in the popular imagination. Other upheavals, such as those involving the Fatimids or Frederick II, are significantly less well known. A pure history of the conflicts that led to physical transfers of the city would be interesting by itself and has, in certain ways, been attempted in the past.[4] Yet this approach cannot be the limit of our excursion because it would leave out crucial but routinely neglected details about relations between the different faith communities involved.

Lost in the gruesome details and shocking specters of offensive butchery are key developments of rapprochement and detente. The Arab capture of Jerusalem in 638 was followed by decrees of religious concession towards both Christians and Jews. The Shia Fatimids spared the Sunni residents of Jerusalem the sword in the 970s, and the Sunni Turks did the same to their Shia counterparts in 1073. The Franks, even after the massacre of the First Crusade, gradually let Muslims and Jews back into the city and even granted them rights to public prayer. Saladin and his successors drew lessons from the notoriety of 1099 and refused to repay the insult after he captured Jerusalem in 1187, instead restoring Jewish rights and tolerating local Christians. Frederick guaranteed Muslim rights of worship at the top of the Temple Mount (al-Haram al-Sharif); after he departed for Italy, a joint Christian–Muslim army fought together against the more radical Muslim Khwarazmians, who had sacked the city in 1244.

The conclusion to this book draws these and other threads together to make a dual argument. First, in a strictly historical sense a general theme of religious concord and toleration can be found in the story of Jerusalem's medieval sieges. "Toleration" is a problematic word because of its modern meaning, in which individuals or groups are to be respected despite one's profound disagreement with their views. It is too easy to slip into this anachronism by appropriating historical examples that seem complementary while discarding the rest as insufficient.[5] The dominant Arabic word for tolerance, *ihtimal*, was understood as the bearing of burdens—absorbing others' annoyances and having patience, or forbearance, with them. Nonetheless, in practice medieval Muslims were encouraged to point out the errors of others and render moral judgments on them.[6] In a similar vein, one scholar has dubbed Latin Christian (or "Frankish") tolerance of local, eastern Christians in the period as "rough," insofar that it was a practice and not an ideology. In other words, crusaders and settlers in the Latin East did not see tolerance as intrinsically virtuous, to be pursued for its own sake; rather, to be tolerant was to allow diversity when it advanced economic or political purposes. In the Middle East, unlike Europe, societies were highly permeable, and people of different ethnicities and religions regularly flowed in and out of towns and cities. Moreover, the ownership of those towns and cities frequently changed, and thus their inhabitants were bound by local laws more episodically.[7]

Tolerance in this book, then, refers to the existence of default multicultural communities: those times when, in Jerusalem, people of minority creeds and backgrounds were "put up with" by local rulers and religious majorities for specific, practical reasons.[8] This may not seem morally satisfactory to modern audiences at all. Still, traditions of grudging allowances, especially over long durations, tell us much about interfaith and interpersonal relations, and these are important components to the history of peoples and places.[9] In Jerusalem specifically, this practical sort of tolerance often enabled freer expressions of religious devotion and enduring Jewish, Christian, and Muslim communities over centuries.

History is not inevitable. Pluralistic societies in Jerusalem were the result of careful decisions made by informed, savvy military and political leaders acting in the perceived best interests of themselves and their communities. That their choices were sometimes heinous and shocking should not be difficult for modern minds to grasp, given twentieth and twenty-first-century genocidal horrors that demonstrate that we humans are not immune to such impulses today.

The second principal argument is that, to the misfortune of all involved parties, the positive elements born from such a rough tolerance have been almost wholly de-emphasized in modern histories of the period and in modern political discourse in general. Rather, previous treatments have tended to imagine the past as a story of the unending, and unendable, clash of civilizations: claim versus competing claim.[10] Those choices that were charitable should be easy to salvage from the past, but instead, modern memories have been constructed on the backs of only partial histories, flawed retellings that omit acts of tolerance that enabled diversity of worship. Customized versions of the city's history also suit particular political goals, in which different interest groups push claims of ownership and control based on it. It has not been a purely academic question because of the high stakes involved. As a result, both the remembering and the letting go of even the distant past have proven a major challenge on all fronts.

One way forward, therefore, is for historians to study, interpret, and disseminate the rest of the story: then, for readers to consider and—with any luck—internalize this fuller picture. The idea here is not to "use" history to demolish one version of the past in order to push another: nor is it to make history "usable" for those policy makers and activists wishing to advance modern policy agendas. Instead, the point is to offer a different interpretation, one that admits and locates the place of violence in medieval Jerusalem on the one hand but situates and contextualizes it on the other.

Whether or not that context matters will be up to the readers. For some, the story may seem too long and convoluted, extending as it does across a vast array of peoples, most with unfamiliar names and participating in heretofore obscure events. I have therefore tried to present the history in an accessible fashion for nonspecialists. Conversely, some scholars may wish for greater depth on certain topics, where specificity has been sacrificed in favor of accessibility. Striking a balance between the two is a challenge for historians everywhere, and I have made my best attempt here.

For still others, historical accuracy or presentation is, itself, utterly beyond the point—they know what they know, and no manner of explanation can possibly excuse a given event in a place of such extreme political and religious sensitivity, especially one committed in the name of a rival faith or ideology. The total disregard of inconvenient historical details has led, in the past, to adversarial parties talking past each other. Yet historians cannot bow to fatalism. In this particular case, in fact, the history of the city actually provides a way forward. Real accord between bitter religious enemies was reached in the Middle Ages, and not just once but multiple times across centuries, in diverse contexts and in the midst of near-constant warfare. It is therefore arguable that entrenched contemporary interests are not, despite their heated and seemingly intractable qualities, permanent barriers to peace. The first step is for readers to simply learn about *how* medieval compromise came about— beyond that, one can only hope that informed reflection and discussion will eventually seed future solutions.

I

ISLAM AWAKENS
614 AND 638

"Jerusalem was captured." This short, solitary notice appears in the *Chronicle of 640*, a compilation of early sources by a Jacobite priest named Thomas, who probably scribbled his notes somewhere near the 1036-meter mountain of Mardin in southeastern Turkey.[1] As evidenced by the remains of a Roman fortress on its summit, that prominence was no stranger to conflict. As for Thomas, his reference to Jerusalem is a curious understatement of what had occurred in 614, when a besieging Persian army collapsed part of its northern wall and sacked the city. Its curtness sits in stark relief from battle accounts elsewhere in his compilation, where killings and the enslavement of Christian monks by other Arab or Persian forces are noted in due course. Perhaps his brevity here was a consequence of the quality of his source material.

Or perhaps the magnitude of the event required no further explanation beyond a simple expression of fact. The Jacobites were, and remain, a branch of Orthodoxy that had broken off from the Syrian Melkites, the dominant strain of Chalcedonian belief. Jacobite liturgy is that of James the Just, apostle to Jesus Christ and early leader of the Christian community in Jerusalem. Yet beyond this connection, the significance of that city clearly transcended such discrete ties among divisions of the faithful. Its contemporary preeminence had been fixed by Helena, the mother of Constantine, herself, and while the accounts of her recovery of the True Cross remain dubious in the eyes of skeptics and historians alike, no doubt the tale had reaffirmed the place of the city in the memory of believers living in the seventh century. That the Persians absconded with that very cross in 614 could only have reinforced that memory further.

We are fortunate, however, that our knowledge of this particular sacking of the city is enlivened by more robust Syriac and Greek source material than what Thomas offers.[2] Illuminating many aspects of the highly destructive 614 siege, these sources also reveal details about some Jewish–Christian tensions from the period that contributed to the animus between the two faiths, which had been growing since the fourth century. But this is only the beginning of a grander tale. In the wake of the Byzantine–Persian war that produced the sack, Jerusalem's walls were not properly repaired, rendering the city vulnerable to future attacks. And the timing could not have been more unfortunate, for a new power was rising in the south. When Arabs (often rendered as *ṭayyāyē* in Syriac) arrived before the city just a few years later in 637–8, Jerusalem's residents had few means of defending themselves.[3] In this way, a seemingly unrelated Persian attack enabled Islamic control of the Temple Mount and a legitimate claim of ownership of this landmark that remains to this day.

I

The early seventh century was a time of great invasions. In successive swells, the Persians rushed into the east Mediterranean Levant and conquered Syria, Egypt, and eastern Asia Minor; the Byzantines then swept west from Constantinople and drove them back out, only to be pushed out themselves by waves of Arabs from the south. All this occurred within a period of just 36 years.[4]

The Byzantine–Sasanid War of 602–628 was the grand setting. It was precipitated by the murder of the Byzantine emperor Maurice in 602 by followers of a usurper, Flavius Phocas. Maurice had helped end the previous 572–591 war between the great two empires by ensuring the succession of the Persian Khosrow II to the throne. Now, the killing of Khosrow's benefactor and father-in-law (Khosrow had married Maurice's daughter, Maria) encouraged him to intervene, and war began anew in Mesopotamia. In its midst, Phocas's short reign came to an end in 608 when the exarch of Africa, Heraclius, was proclaimed Emperor Flavius Heraclius Augustus. Eventually, the usurper was executed. Nonetheless, the war raged on and, from 611 onward, gradually shifted from campaigns of periodic raiding and scattershot attacks to full-scale warfare in the regions surrounding Byzantine-controlled Jerusalem in Palestine.[5] Heraclius soon found himself on the back foot, steadily losing territory in the face of increasingly intense attacks from Khosrow's general, Shahrbaraz, whose name means "wild boar of the empire."

The Siege of 614

Shahrbaraz moved against Jerusalem in January 614. The attack came from the west, from Caesarea Maritima, Herod the Great's famous harbor lying astride the Mediterranean Sea, which had been captured the previous autumn of 613.[6] The general moved his forces towards the city and, upon arriving, sent subordinates around its walls to reconnoiter its defenses.[7] According to the account of the Armenian bishop Sebeos, one of the earliest sources for the war, negotiations had actually taken place well before this campaign commenced. These seem to have gone rather well in fact, and war had been averted initially through a two-part deal. Its terms reveal the city leaders' recognition of the precariousness of their situation. They offered a customary bribe of gifts and probably coins to Shahrbaraz and his subordinates but also made a curious request: that a small Persian garrison be quartered within Jerusalem's walls. Or so claims Sebeos; it easily could have been the reverse, with Shahrbaraz insisting on the garrison himself. At any rate, the deal was struck, a Persian attack avoided, and peace was maintained for some months.[8] Jerusalem was now under the rule of the Persians, not the Byzantines.

Youth will be served, but in 614 youthful vigor and restlessness proved to be the city's downfall. Apparently resenting its presence and, likely, the imperial control of Persia in general, some of Jerusalem's youth attacked and murdered members of the Persian garrison. That sparked a larger riot and led to fighting among the city's population itself. Sebeos notes that the fighting eventually coalesced into religious hostility and violence between the Christian and Jewish residents. He does not give the precise cause but notes that because the Christians were in the demographic majority of a city with a probable population of about 50,000 people, the Jews were outmatched and killed in large numbers.[9] Meanwhile, Shahrbaraz, who had before now abided by the negotiated deal, moved his army eastward from Caesarea and besieged Jerusalem in response to the treacherous elimination of his garrison.[10]

The city was thus struck by warfare from within and without, with battle lines that blurred alongside the religious strife. We have a rather dramatic account of it in the testimony of a purported witness to the events, the Palestinian monk Antiochus Strategos of Mar Saba (Saint Sabbas, south of Jerusalem). Strategos teases some details missing in Sebeos's account. The youth who rebelled against the Persian garrison are identified as rival factions, or gangs, known from their clothing as the Blues and the Greens. These had moved into Jerusalem and were busily committing acts of theft, violence, and property destruction—against each other as well as the city residents and local churches—long before the Persians arrived in country.[11] Thereafter, Strategos's chronology becomes confused, but it seems that Zachariah, the Patriarch of Jerusalem, attempted to negotiate the aforementioned peace terms with Shahrbaraz, prompting these gangs to turn against Zachariah as the city's de facto leader. Threats and warnings evidently preceded the violence, so the murder of the Persian soldiers was not a complete surprise.[12]

Strategos also adds nuance to the consequences of the murders. Shahrbaraz did not attack immediately but rather moved his forces to blockade Jerusalem while repeatedly demanding that Zachariah surrender the city outright. The patriarch refused, possibly missing a real chance to avoid the carnage that was to follow. Strategos questioned the decision, but evidently some monks later told him while they all resided in captivity together that angels had been seen on the city towers, brandishing burning lances and shields. Zachariah took this as a sign that God was with the Christians and would aid them in repulsing any attack. Correspondingly, Zachariah sent a monk (and future deputy patriarch) named Modestus out through a rear gate to Jericho, with orders to rally the Byzantine garrison there. How Modestus eluded capture is an unknown but impressive feat, given the Persian encirclement. Having refused further entreaties from the Persians and calling for reinforcements, the patriarch set about the defense of Jerusalem.[13]

Following weeks of threats and demands, the Persian siege entered a new phase on 15 April: blockade gave way to direct attack and assault. Over the course of about three weeks, Shahrbaraz's forces applied steady pressure against Jerusalem's fortified circuit. They utilized two principal tactics. First, miners (or sappers) dug tunnels towards the city with the goal of getting under portions of its stone wall.[14] It would then be propped up with timbers smeared with fat or pitch; once set alight, the wood would disintegrate and collapse the stones above it. Second, while the miners slowly moved forward, archers shot antipersonnel missiles at Jerusalem's defenders. The Persians constructed special siege towers, topped with artillery, which allowed them to shoot at not only the battlements but also directly into the city quarters. Other engines were apparently constructed and utilized, though they go undescribed in the sources. At length, Modestus returned with the Jericho garrison, but once they spied the scale of the siege and the progress made by the Persians, they quickly turned tail and fled.[15]

On the twenty-first day, the wall collapsed from one of the Persian mines. A breach of this type must have been an extreme spectacle to observe and a horrible event to experience. As the sappers' wooden supports were consumed so too was the support for the wall, and gravity took over: stones, mortar, wooden structures like staircases or hoardings, and soldiers atop the battements plunged down in a heap of rock and a cloud of choking dust. Into the breach would then pour attackers, charging across the rubble to eliminate the disoriented defenders. Once the Persians had gained entry, a full sacking commenced, probably on 19–22 May, although the dates are uncertain.[16] It was a destructive spectacle of the sort not seen in Jerusalem since the days of Titus in the first century. As with many premodern sieges, the event progressed in predictable and gory fashion.

The Massacre

The defenders first had to be rooted out and eliminated, following which the attackers could deal with the noncombatants. Persians poured into the city through the breach in the wall while Jerusalem's residents scrambled to run and hide in churches, caverns, and cisterns. Most of them were swiftly located and massacred:

> For the enemy entered in mighty wrath, gnashing their teeth in violent fury; like evil beasts they roared, bellowed like lions, hissed like ferocious serpents, and slew all whom they found. Like mad dogs they tore with their teeth the flesh of the faithful . . .[17]

Strategos cast the Persians as destruction incarnate as they sacked the city. Infants, the elderly, women, and even those who surrendered were cut down with glee; some of the clergy were decapitated. At length, the looters actually ran out of people to kill. Although the obvious hiding places had been cleared, residents had found all sorts of nooks and crannies within the city's narrow streets and tunnels. There was apparently a lack of enthusiasm for rooting them out, and also a lack of energy: "For when the Persians had entered the city, and slain countless souls, and blood ran deep in all places, the enemy in consequence no longer had the strength to slay."[18]

Thus followed a clever trick, which sparked a chain of events and transformed the siege of 614 from a commonplace sacking to an event of enormous interreligious consequence. Shahrbaraz made an offer to the huddled survivors: "Come out … fear not … by me is granted peace."[19] They emerged from the shadows and were interrogated one by one. Those with expertise in architecture or construction were led away to Persia as slaves. In the words of John the Persian, a Nestorian monk who composed his work far away in the Mesopotamian village of al-Kosh (home of the ancient prophet Nathan), "they took into captivity both small and great with prideful insolence."[20] Those who remained were thrown into the Mamilla pool, west of the city gates, and left to die. And many did just that, for hundreds if not thousands of people were piled on top of each other in a suffocating mass of inhumanity.[21]

But Strategos's tale does not end there. Following this internment, those Jerusalem Jews who had survived the ordeals of the siege "conceived a vile plan." They offered to ransom the Christians, paying the Persians to secure extrication from the hole. A single condition was stipulated: anyone so ransomed must deny Christ's Incarnation and convert to the Jewish faith. The prisoners refused, but the Jews ransomed them anyway—and once each individual's freedom was secured, murdered them. Strategos likened the event to the New Testament: just as Judas betrayed Jesus for 30 pieces of silver, so too did the Jews pay silver in order to kill Jesus's followers.[22]

It is a sordid tale, one that carries potential for rancor and controversy among even modern audiences. Is it true? One has to trek through the extant source material to get a bead on the question. A later seventh-century source, the so-called *Khuzistan Chronicle*, provides a different perspective outside that of the West-Syriac and Armenian Christian texts, and it mentions no ransoming of Christians.[23] Sebeos does not mention it either, although he does claim that before the siege commenced Jews were rappelling down the walls of Jerusalem to join the Persians—while this may have indeed happened, it slots into the familiar anti-Jewish trope of Jews as traitors.[24]

This is from the Christian perspective, of course; for Jews of the time, another view prevailed: that of resistance. The trend lines had been against Judaism for some time in Byzantium. Across the diaspora in the eastern Mediterranean, many synagogues had been destroyed in the fifth century, and in general Jewish communities were increasingly subjugated under Christian laws and regulations during the reign of Emperor Justinian (527–565); in Palestine, there were attacks on Jews in the Samaritan revolts of 529 and 556.[25] Byzantine civil and military arrangements had not eliminated Jewish hostility towards Constantinople, as evidenced by a general revolt in Syria and Mesopotamia as recently as 610. And after Jerusalem's fall in 614, Jews were actively courted by the Persians and perhaps encouraged to join in with attacks on the cities of Acre and Tyre.[26] These events occurred within the context of a general Jewish opposition to Emperor Heraclius, whose officials routinely monitored synagogue services for anti-imperial sentiment.[27]

Thus the story of the Jerusalem Jews' supposed defection in 614 seems reasonable and even likely. But one has to move into the next century, several generations later, to find texts corroborating the far more controversial story of the ransoming. Around the year 750, an astrologer named Theophilus of Edessa, who worked in the court of the Muslim Abbasid caliphate, wrote about the ransoming and subsequent killings. His own work has disappeared but was evidently excerpted by several later writers, including the Byzantine monk Theophanes the Confessor (d. 818) and the two Jacobite patriarchs: Dionysius of Tel Mahre (d. 845) and Michael the Syrian (d. 1199).

Theophanes added the detail that each Jew ransomed Christians "according to his means"; in other words, it was not a collective ransom but rather a case-by-case process. In this fashion Theophilus's accusation—that the Jewish hatred for the Christians led to their ransoming of and then killing them—was transmitted all the way into the twelfth century.[28]

In a separate tradition, the story appears in other sources and in a different context. In his annals, the patriarch of Alexandria, Eutychius (d. 940), raises the story in connection with Emperor Heraclius's return to and liberation of Jerusalem in 630. On his journey there, he was approached by Jews from Tiberias and Nazareth. As a gesture of goodwill, he signed a treaty with them promising their safety under his rule. However, upon arriving at the holy city he learned the story of the ransomed Christian victims in the Mamilla pool; thereafter, the local clergy asked him to round up all the Jews in the area for execution. Heraclius initially refused, on the grounds of his recent agreement, but the Melkite monks in the city begged and entreated him, eventually promising that in exchange for this "gift" they would perform a fast, abstain from eating eggs and cheese, and petition God to forgive the emperor for what would surely be a most bloody deed.[29] Heraclius consented, and so the alleged massacre of Christians was mirrored by a massacre of Jews. Eutychius remarks that the Egyptian Copts maintained the fast, although the Syriacs and Melkites did not. Indeed, the latter renewed their consumption of cheese and eggs upon learning of Heraclius's death in 641![30]

The emperor would go further still. In what has been called an attempt to impose religious uniformity, Heraclius ordered the forced conversions of Jews everywhere through baptism.[31] The most famous indication of this is a Greek dialogue dating to the 630s, which purports to record a conversation between a Jew named Jacob and some compatriots. Jacob had been baptized against his will but nonetheless came to accept Christ, and in the dialogue he urges his friends to follow his lead.[32] An imperial order from 31 May 632 specifically instructed the prefect of Africa to baptize all Jews on that continent: how widely this order was carried out is disputed. One Christian witness to it, the theologian Maximus the Confessor, opposed the practice. Residing in Carthage at the time, he worried that those compelled to adopt a religion might not truly believe.[33] Meanwhile, far away in western Europe, the *Chronicle of Fredegar* related that Heraclius requested the Merovingian king, Dagobert, to likewise order the baptism of all Jews in Francia, where they had been in a much more vulnerable state since the collapse of the western Roman government. That story had legs—it was later recopied by Ademar of Chabannes, the "mad monk" of Saint-Cybard (d. 1034), whose writings were fairly obsessed with matters of the Cross and the eschatological role of Jerusalem. Concerning that city specifically, Heraclius forbade entry to Jews into either it or its surrounding area.[34]

To deny that some Jewish violence against Christians occurred would be a hard task indeed, based on the range of sources, Heraclius's various retributions, and the maintenance of the commemorative fast. Motivations, however, may have been varied. One can imagine it as occurring purely in a military context, with Jews joining Persian armies essentially as mercenaries and helping them besiege or sack Jerusalem. Whether or not local Jews also ransomed and then murdered the captive Christians in the Mamilla pool is a related but separate question. Going further, it is debatable whether the execution of prsoners of war was permissible or even justified according to the laws and customs of the day.

How, then, have modern historians treated this incident? Prior to World War II, there seems to have been a rough agreement that something along the lines of ransoming and subsequent killing *did* happen, although its magnitude and lurid details were questioned. In the years after, the tenor changed, and attention shifted from a debate over the event's historicity to its context: that is, of the Jewish experience in early seventh-century Palestine, which seems decidedly oppressive. Heraclius's predecessor, Phocas, had also allegedly ordered forcible baptisms of

Jews. In Antioch, localized Jewish violence against Christians (which included the decapitation of its patriarch) erupted in retribution for the Jews having been expelled from that city in 592–593, among other grievances.[35] As the twentieth century dragged on, however, historians grew increasingly more reluctant to acknowledge even these—perhaps justifiable—acts of vengeance.[36] Today, the possible ransoming and killing of Christians in the 614 capture of the city remains an elusive topic in the history of Christian–Jewish relations.

The Numbers

How many people died in the sack of 614? The numbers differ according to sources. The Pascal chronicle, a very early account roughly contemporaneous with the event, claims that "many thousands of clerics, monks, and virgin nuns" were slaughtered.[37] The nun reference corresponds with Strategos's story of how a monastery of 400 nuns on the Mount of Olives suffered a mass rape by the Persian soldiers.[38] Sebeos, writing two generations later, puts the number at 17,000 dead and 35,000 captured and led away into captivity; the latter included Patriarch Zacharias, who had dared to hold the city against Shahrbaraz and, by extension, Khosrow himself.

Strategos's much higher death toll must be carefully considered because of his proximity and specificity. By his own admission, his number is second-hand. He claims to have spoken with a certain man named Thomas, who was on the scene to count the dead alongside the other survivors. They found some corpses around the streets and others stuffed into nooks, crannies, caves, and houses. Strategos then recorded the body count testimony for each specific location, such as inside church buildings like Sts. Cosmas and Damian and the monastery of Anastasis, in and around the city gates, on the Mount of Olives, the Mamilla pool, around Golgotha, up and down the length of the city walls, and, finally, in various grottos, gardens, caves, wells, and cisterns. All told, the figure reached 66,509 dead.

Finding such precise figures in medieval texts is uncommon because they are typically rounded off to the nearest thousand. Arguably, this encourages greater confidence in the source itself. Archeological discoveries bolster this testimony. These include an excavated 12-by-3 meter cave at Mamilla, in which was discovered a small chapel with plastered walls and a mosaic floor. The cave lies 120 meters west of Jerusalem's Jaffa Gate; inside were hundreds of human skeletons along with 30 oil lamps and 130 coins, one of which dates to the reign of the Emperor Phocas. Mamilla, along with six other sites (one southwest, and two north, of Damascus Gate; a cistern south of Jaffa Gate; and at the Protestant and Greek Orthodox cemeteries at Mount Zion), provide interesting physical corroboration of the sense, and some of the details, of Thomas's testimony.[39]

Strategos's figure only increased over time. Theophilus of Edessa pegged the number of dead at the conveniently rounded total of 90,000. His number stuck: it is subsequently found in the work of Theophanes the Confessor, Michael the Syrian, the *Chronicle of 1234*, and also the later Syriac chronicle of the physician and writer Bar Hebraeus.[40] One can then track it through successive centuries, but suffice to say it has a long reach. Leaping to the 1800s, the number was repeated in César Famin's history of Christian foundations in the Near East; his passage was thereafter excerpted by none other than Karl Marx and Friedrich Engels in their own notes.[41] More recent research, however, has cast aspersions on this number given what we know about the relative urban centers of Palestine at that time and a Jerusalem population that was probably less than half of Theophilus's figure.[42]

The Spoils of War

Once all active resistance had ended and the residents were rounded up or killed, the Persians set about sacking the city. Details abound in the contemporary texts. John the Persian wrote of how they "laid waste the city of Jerusalem." Sebeos notes that soldiers repositioned outside the walls, after which churches and other buildings within the city were destroyed by burning. The Pascal chronicle reports the particular burning of the church containing the Holy Sepulchre, the purported burial chamber of Jesus and site of his Resurrection, as well as other buildings.[43]

Such destruction was customary after the successful seizure of a city by force of arms, and the effect must have been extensive. Perhaps, though, it was not as complete as recorded in the sources. So far, archaeologists have found only scattered physical evidence of destruction from that specific period, and at least one historian has argued that its level did not really transcend that which was customary in other cities sacked in the period.[44] Much later, in the tenth century, Eutychius of Alexandria remarked that the destruction was still evident years after the siege. In early 630, Emperor Heraclius journeyed to Damascus and brought along Modestus, who had attempted to rally the Jericho garrison against the besiegers. Together, they solicited and collected monies for the reconstruction of the Jerusalem churches.[45]

In the midst of the destruction, the Persians also plundered the city and carried away what treasures, monies, and possessions they could find. They did not get everything. In anticipation of the breach, some residents hastened to hide their wealth from the invaders. One excavation has discovered a cache of 264 gold coins in the City of David area (south of the Temple Mount), which had been carefully wrapped in cloth and hidden in the wall of an administrative building complex, which itself resided on a busy paved street filled with shops. That building seems to have been deliberately targeted for destruction, and, when its walls collapsed, the coins were buried underneath the rubble until found in the twenty-first century. Called the Givati Hoard, all of its coins date to the reign of Heraclius and to before 614.[46] Doubtless other such stashes survived the looting and were collected sometime in the aftermath, but it is clear that Jerusalem was systematically picked apart by the occupiers. Various gold and silver items were stolen and melted down.

Infamously, the Persians also seized certain priceless Christian relics. Most prominent among these was the "True Cross," the wood upon which Jesus had been crucified, reportedly discovered by Helena in the early fourth century.[47] Locating it necessitated a search, however, for the Jerusalem clergy had cleverly hidden the cross before the walls were breached. To find it, the Persians arrested Patriarch Zachariah and then tortured his clergy until they revealed its location.[48] A much later account, that of the great Muslim writer al-Tabari, offers some interesting details that may or may not be true: that the cross lay in a gold chest that was buried underneath a vegetable garden, and Shahrbaraz unearthed it with his own hands. He then carried the cross, along with the precious metals, monies, and other treasures, back to the Persian capital of Ctesiphon 56 kilometers south of Baghdad, Iraq.[49]

Shahrbaraz was not the only Persian to obtain a portion of the "True Cross." Another was Yazdin of Karka de Beth Slouq, Emperor Khosrow's financial minister and governor of most of northern Iraq. A convert to Christianity from the Persian monotheistic-dualistic faith of Zoroastrianism, Yazdin was in Jerusalem some time after the city's sack. According to the *Khuzistan Chronicle*, Shahrbaraz grabbed most of the wood of the cross but not all of it, and Yazdin was later able to obtain the remainder.[50] He did this not so much to oppose Khosrow or Shahrbaraz's designs but rather as an attempt to increase his own influence—and therefore that of Christianity itself—at the Persian court. In this telling, as Philip Wood has argued, the confiscation of the relics was not so much about a Zoroastrian attack on Christianity but rather an attempt to relocate the center of the latter's world from Jerusalem to Ctesiphon. Hence, the chronicle dubs Yazdin as no less than "a new Constantine" himself.[51]

A Jewish City Once More?

Despite the horrors of the 614 sacking and a partial breach of its walls, Jerusalem itself survived and was not reduced to a smoking residue. Not everyone had died, and those who remained in residence would now be governed by their new Persian overlords. If, as the sources claim, the bulk of the Christian community had been either executed or marched into Persian slavery, then the remaining people would have consisted mainly of Jews, individuals and families of other, non-Christian confessions, as well as itinerant visitors and merchants. It seems particularly clear that Jews remained in the city because Sebeos claims that Khosrow personally ordered them expelled at a later date.[52] This tradition appears again in the much later account of Bar Hebraeus: "At first they treated the Jews in a peaceful fashion, and then they carried them off finally to Persia."[53]

But before that expulsion we find a curious two-to-three year gap in which a possible appointed Jewish governor appears in the literature. There is a chance, which has been more or less accepted by scholars, of a small Jewish movement in this period to restore the Temple in Jerusalem, the so-called "Third Temple." By the seventh century, Tiberias had become the principal center of Jewish teaching and learning, but of course Jerusalem remained important for reasons of heritage and theology.[54] One interpretation would see the course of events as therefore intentional: that the Jews joined with the Persians to expel Christians from Palestine—or at least extirpate their political control—and leave a vacuum to exploit. Another reasoning would take the events as incidental: a happy eventuality that permitted Jews to fill a political void. In either case, it appears that at least some Jews acted out messianic impulses.

Complicating these interpretations are tantalizing suggestions in evocative but historically suspect apocalyptic literature written around the time of the Sasanid conquest. Two texts in the genre are germane: a poem by the Hebrew liturgical poet Eliezor ben Qalir, and the *Book of Zerubbabel*, which is an anonymous text recounting a vision given to one Zerubbabel of the Last Days.[55] Adherents of this view lean on these texts and hold that a Jewish exilarch ("King of the Exiles," a head of the Jewish Diaspora) named Nehemiah ben Hushiel was placed in charge of Jerusalem as governor until the Persians reclaimed control after about three years.[56] The dating of these sources is uncertain, and other factors probably preclude any real governmental power on the part of the Jews, so the theory has not won wide acceptance.[57]

In any case, we are thus presented with two competing narratives of the events of 614. In the first (Christian) version, the Jerusalem Jews were complicit in the siege and aided and abetted the killing of its Christian population during the sack; once Byzantium regained the city, they were expelled and their lives forfeit on grounds of their duplicity. In a second (Jewish) telling, Byzantium's anti-Jewish policies in Syria and Palestine sparked legitimate resistance, with many Jews favoring the invading Persians as more likely to respect their lives and traditions. In return for their military assistance, the Jews received control, albeit temporary, over Jerusalem for the first time in ages but were then betrayed and expelled by the Persians within a few years.

The apocalyptic texts also tie into a very real historical event: the second expulsion of the Jews from Jerusalem, this time by the Byzantines in 630. The *Book of Zerubbabel* reads:

> He will come against the holy people of the Most High, and with him there will be ten kings wielding great power and force, and he will do battle with the holy ones. He will prevail over them and will kill the Messiah of the lineage of Joseph, Nehemiah b. Hushiel, and will also kill sixteen righteous ones alongside him. Then they will banish Israel to the desert in three groups.[58]

The "he" referenced in the apocalypse is Heraclius. His armies would go on a counteroffensive and by the mid-620s were driving deep into Persian territory. Following that ultimately successful war against Persia, the emperor would return south to Jerusalem to set matters straight. The tenth-century historian Agapias, the bishop of

Manbij, noted a cosmic event during this time: a solar eclipse, of which "half of the disc was eclipsed and the other was not."[59] Light, yet darkness—the emperor was coming, both liberation and retribution were to follow.

Heraclius Strikes Back

The fall of Jerusalem was but one component of the wider Byzantine–Sasanid war. Following Jerusalem's sack, Persian armies invaded Egypt and completed their conquest of it by 621. In 622, Khosrow directed his attention towards Constantinople itself and launched a full-scale invasion of Asia Minor. This coincided with an equally dangerous development: a joint Avar–Slavic assault on Constantinople that broke through the "long wall" (Anastasian) that lay some 60 kilometers west of it in the summer of 623. Attacked on two fronts, Heraclius desperately negotiated to end the Avar threat first, which allowed him to concentrate on the Persian threat the next year. He ordered the mobilization of Roman units at Caesarea in Cappadocia (modern-day Kayseri, Turkey). As the troops mustered there, north of Antioch, Khosrow interpreted the move as the prelude to a southerly move into Syria and Palestine to liberate the holy places. Instead, the emperor attacked northeast against the main Persian line of advance and took Khosrow's army by surprise, eventually driving the emperor himself from the city of Ganzak.[60] It was a stunning turnaround for the Byzantines, who had been on their heels for years.

The Persians responded in force, sending three armies—one of them commanded by Shahrbaraz himself—to block the Byzantine advance into Persia. Heraclius defeated all three while simultaneously moving to avoid encirclement and, by the winter of 625, nearly captured Shahrbaraz himself. But he did not destroy these armies, which regrouped in early 626 for another invasion of Asia Minor, forcing Heraclius back on the defensive. One, led by the general Shahen, invaded from Armenia but was intercepted by Heraclius and destroyed. A second, led by Shahrbaraz, advanced to Chalcedon and burned it, then paused as it awaited a massive Avar and Slav attack on Constantinople itself. Despite Heraclius's successes on the field, the second front against his capital had been reopened.

The combined siege of Constantinople commenced in late July 626 with attacks on the land and sea walls of the city. These were countered by the Byzantine defenders and petered out a week or so into August. Credit for the victory was given to the Virgin Mary, who purportedly intervened to assist in the destruction of Slavic ships off the Golden Horn and Persian transports crossing the Bosphorus River. In the face of significant losses, Shahrbaraz elected to withdraw.[61] Heraclius had survived yet again and regained the initiative.

In 627, the emperor made what would be his final offensive against the Sasanid Empire and marched east with between 25,000 and 50,000 soldiers at his command.[62] He conducted a formal alliance with the Turkic Khazar forces in eastern Anatolia and, together, they besieged and sacked the city of Tiflis (modern-day Tbilisi, Georgia). In September, they advanced into the Sasanid province of Atropatene (in northern Iran), then destroyed a Persian army led by the general Rahzadh in northern Mesopotamia.[63] This ultimately led to victory in the war, as later sketched in a tenth-century treatise of the Byzantine Emperor Constantine Porphyrogenitus ("born in the purple"):

> Thereafter, when the emperor Heraclius marched against Persia, they [the "Iberians," referencing eastern Georgia] united and campaigned with him, and as a result, through the dread inspired by Heraclius, emperor of the Romans, rather than by their own strength and power, they subdued a great number of cities and countries of the Persians. For once the emperor Heraclius had routed the Persians and had forcibly brought their empire to an end, the Persians were easily defeated and mastered, not by the Iberians only, but by the Saracens as well.[64]

In the midst of Heraclius's successful campaigning came the end of Khosrow II. He was arrested by a conspiratorial group composed of his own first-born son, Kawadh-Siroes (Siroy), along with two of Sharbaraz's sons and one of his generals, as well as a number of other Persian officials. They were all supported by Heraclius, who saw an opportunity to end by subterfuge what might have been more costly with further warfare. Once deposed, Khosrow was executed by the Persian version of a modern firing squad on 23 February 628. Subsequent negotiations resulted in a peace treaty, by which Persia promised to release all their Byzantine prisoners and evacuate occupied lands (including Syria and Palestine).[65] In this way the True Cross was likewise recovered: as noted in the *Short History* of Patriarch Nicephoros of Constantinople (d. 828), Heraclius "made a fervent plea concerning the Holy Cross," and it was returned to him.[66]

Heraclius's campaigns into Persia in the 620s have attracted some modern attention. They were swift, stunning, and decisive marches into the heart of Sasanid territory and, perhaps more striking, conducted in the context of his crumbling outer empire and in the face of what seems like insurmountable odds. Practitioners of what modern military professionals would call "operational art and design" could learn much from his ability to maintain and maneuver his forces across vast expanses of difficult terrain and engage, defeat, and destroy multiple field armies on both the offense and defense.

But equally striking is a strategic question poignantly asked by the historian Benjamin Isaac: why did Heraclius invade Persia instead of first liberating Syria and Palestine? Isaac considers three possibilities. First, Heraclius may have simply been imitating previous Byzantine campaigns: in the 570s its armies had campaigned to the Caspian Sea, and in the 580s to Media and the River Tigris. Second, he may have been waging what strategists would today call a war of "exhaustion," in which the aim ideally was to ravage Persian lands and destroy the Sasanid capacity to wage war. Third (and the interpretation that Isaac prefers), the southern provinces were simply not a top priority and that imperial policy privileged its honor, majesty, and religion first: "it was more important to humiliate the enemy than to disarm him."[67]

Another possibility flows from Isaac's fleeting mention of religion. Could it be that Heraclius attacked Persia principally to recover the True Cross from Ctesiphon? This is unlikely. No source substantiates such an interpretation, despite their clear interest in the abduction of the relic and their joy in its safe return. Not even George of Pisidia, a poet and deacon at Hagia Sophia who had been commissioned by Heraclius himself to compose a record of the Persian campaigns, mentions the cross directly.[68] The relic's importance seems to have been magnified in a military sense only during, and then after, its safe return to Jerusalem.

That is not to say that devotion played no role at all. In some contemporaneous literature, the Byzantine–Sasanid War is couched in quite Biblical terms.[69] There is also the depiction of the *Restitutio crucis*, as narrated by later, embellished texts, involving Heraclius's return of the cross to Jerusalem. In an overt imitation of Christ on Palm Sunday, he descended into the city from the Mount of Olives. His attempt to enter the Golden Gate on Jerusalem's eastern side, however, was first rebuffed by a rockslide that covered it and then by an angel who admonished him for the pomp and circumstance of his royal train. Chastened, Heraclius dismounted and entered Jerusalem barefoot, then returned the cross to the sepulchre church.[70] The role of the Golden Gate is especially noticeable and alludes to the Second Coming, not only in Christian eschatological conceptions but Jewish and Muslim ones as well, and the gate's importance would be signaled again just eight years later during the Arab conquests.

What followed was the development of what Averil Cameron has called "the cult of the cross." After its return to Jerusalem, the True Cross became central to Heraclius's mystique and appeared rather frequently in coins, poems, homilies, and liturgical ceremonies.[71] The emperor knew it held political power as well, and in 635 he transferred the relic from Jerusalem to Constantinople, where it served to bolster his image.[72] Heraclius's restoration of the cross was also commemorated in a feast on 14 September the *Exultatio*. It was celebrated both east and west, and for a long time. Ademar of Chabannes mentions it, and, later, a Coptic priest named Abu al-Makarim (d. 1208) related a story of the "Fast of Heraclius," which was still being celebrated in 1186 to commemorate the emperor's liberation of Jerusalem.[73] It remains on the Orthodox liturgical calendar today, celebrated on the same date.

But some have taken this symbolism too far. Periodically, one reads histories attempting to cast the Byzantine campaigns of the 620s as holy wars or even proto "crusades." Certainly some later sources describe them in religiously charged terms. Severus ibn al-Muqaffa, the bishop of Hermopolis Magna (fl. 950s), wrote that "by the grace of Christ, he marched against them, and slew Chosroes, their misbelieving king."[74] But such comparisons are facile and have been roundly critiqued by historians of both Byzantium and the Crusades.[75] Mischaracterization of the war's nature, however, does not preclude a sense of a specific recovery mission on the part of Heraclius himself.

Preparing for the Next War

The theft and return of the True Cross dominates the headlines, then and now, but what of the most pressing military concern: Jerusalem's walls? The Persians had collapsed a portion of the wall to gain entry in 614, but none of the written sources indicate on which side they breached it or at what width. Jerusalem's walls have been built and rebuilt many times over its long history, most famously after 445 B.C. in the days of Nehemiah. After their massive (though not total) reduction in the Roman sack of 70 A.D., the walls were not immediately rebuilt; legions who were camped in the vicinity constituted the principal arm of defense, allowing funds to be spent elsewhere.

Sometime after 300, construction began on new fortifications, and this work sped up during the reign of Constantine. Most of this circuit was modest in thickness, about three meters.[76] These walls were later improved, with very active construction activity particularly on the southern side of the current Old City between the fourth and sixth centuries. There, a particular portion of the southern wall and one of its towers is believed to have been refurbished between 447 and 460. In the Byzantine period, the walls extended much further south, encompassing Mount Zion, and were partially built on top of a rocky scarp.[77]

The Persian breach, however, was almost certainly in the north. In the south, the improved walls were newer and stronger. The eastern side was protected, as always, by the steep incline of the Kidron Valley to the Herodian walls of the Temple Mount, and the Tower of David guarded the western side. The Persian breach appears to have occurred near the present-day Damascus Gate, where a wall collapse is indicated by excavated piles of rubble as well as ceramic evidence dated to the period.[78] This was a critical weakness: without a strong field army in close vicinity, the city's defensive perimeter was its best defense against future raiding attacks and outright invasions. Repairs were thus a vital concern, no matter who controlled the city. Nearby Byzantine forces, such as those at Jericho, still constituted a potential threat to retake the city. Following the Persian example, later sieges in the eleventh and twelfth centuries also saw concentrated mining efforts on the northern side: the army of the First Crusade over-topped it in 1099, and Saladin's coalition attacked it severely in 1187, leading to the city's capitulation.

There is no specific textual evidence of wall reconstruction during the 16 years of Persian control (614–630). Sebeos does report an order from Khosrow "to rebuild the city," and this possibly included some repairs of the circuit.[79] But excavation indicates, to the contrary, that the northern breach was likely not repaired until the eighth century. Instead, the gap was transformed into a dump of rubble and garbage that may have reached over four meters high.[80] One could imagine the garrison's repairs, then, to have constituted little more than collecting stones from the rubble and heaping them into a mound between the intact vertical sections of wall and the gate. Such a pile could easily be guarded against unauthorized entry of individuals or small groups, and as it happened there seem to have been no major or even minor assaults against the city during Persian rule.

For the Byzantines, money was tight and other priorities existed. Heraclius spent little time consolidating military and political gains in the Levant.[81] He appointed a treasurer, not a general, named Theodore Trithourios, to command the Byzantine army in Syria. He was not entirely unskilled, for he had defeated an Arab force at the Battle of Mu'ta in September 629.[82] But Theodore was mostly expected to attend to the vital matter of army pay, in both wages and allotments of rations. These required Heraclius to borrow heavily and confiscate gold and silver from private interests.[83] The emperor personally attended to a series of minor adjustments related to army structure and administration, but it appears he made no major reforms.[84]

The emphasis on the army, and not construction of physical defenses, must be understood within the context of Byzantium frontier strategy. Although many fortified towns existed in Syria and Palestine, they were too geographically dispersed to form any real network of defense. Consequently, topographical features like mountains and rivers often served as practical fall-back areas for defending soldiers, and forward fortresses were lightly garrisoned. Instead, the majority of resources were allocated to the field armies, which continued their training and even conducted winter cavalry training in the 630s.[85]

Nor can we assume that Heraclius paid for Jerusalem's walls out of personal funds. Too many fortifications required upkeep and garrisoning, and a shrinking economy resulted in his pulling back from many of these entirely. Moreover, it was customary for private parties to shoulder some of the burden by partially paying for walls and towers.[86] And there was also the matter of Jerusalem's churches and associated religious buildings, which required repairs of their own.

These took precedence over fortifications, and Sebeos's description of Heraclius's entry into the city says nothing about its defenses:

> He set it [the True Cross] back up in its place, and put all the vessels of the churches in their places, and distributed alms and money for incense to all the churches and inhabitants of the city. He himself continued his journey directly into Syrian Mesopotamia in order to secure his hold over the cities of the frontiers.[87]

Six years would pass between Heraclius's entry and the next siege of Jerusalem, which came at the hands of Arab armies in 637–8. When the Arabs arrived they did not attempt to penetrate the city walls but rather sat down to blockade it. One of our earliest sources of that event, the compiler al-Azdi al-Basri (d. 796–97), notes that the garrison sallied out of the gates once or twice but were driven back inside.[88] Its eventual surrender on favorable terms, however, suggests that the defenses were not strong enough to withstand a serious direct assault.

The 614 sack of Jerusalem has long flown under the radar, but its religious and military contours hold tremendous importance for understanding later affairs. It illustrates the dispositions and antagonisms of the local Jews and Christians and their practical roles vis-à-vis the Holy City. The hostilities in the early seventh century manifested in military alliances and accusations (both real and purported) of oppression, treachery, and murder. It reveals their respective messianic expectations as well. On the one hand, those Jewish plans to rebuild the Temple were quickly dashed; on the other, Heraclius's triumphant entry into the city in 630 recalled images of Christ's Passion and ties into apocalyptic themes in which the return of the True Cross foretold Christ's return as well.[89] Like the more infamous crusader siege of Jerusalem in 1099 during the First Crusade, the brutal dimensions of the event have left physical scars on the city landscape and vestiges of defeat and disgrace that are still painful to modern believers.

In strictly military terms, the Persian collapsing of a portion of the wall left the city more vulnerable to attack. Any rebuilding was lackluster; construction does not appear to have improved after Heraclius's arrival in 630, and the walls were not formally repaired until the 700s. The Byzantine–Sasanid war had also left the region around Jerusalem weak and unstable. Heraclius attended to the maintenance of his forces in Palestine and Syria, but these were themselves uneven and poorly sustained; moreover, he remained reliant on local allies for frontier defense. In short, the events of 614 set the conditions for the arrival of the Arabs a generation later and the momentous changes they would bring. As John the Persian recalled with despondence, "No man escaped from the hand of the children of Esau."[90]

II

In 708, a Syrian Orthodox scholar named Jacob of Edessa busied himself by compiling an annalistic record of important events. It remains unfinished, for Jacob—who one scholar has called "one of the greatest polymaths to ever write in Syria"—died in that same year before completing his work.[91] The text closes with an account of a total eclipse of the sun, which seems an apt and poetic image for an author's final words. Yet some time later, an anonymous continuator of Jacob's work took up his quill and added what he must have deemed a necessary coda:

> In July there was a sign, and that was stars that shot or moved about in the air, which some men call falling stars. And they appeared in every part of the sky, moving about quickly and rapidly the whole night from the southern to the northern quarter, a thing never heard of before since the creation of the world . . . And the outcome of events showed that these shooting stars denoted the Arabs, who at this time entered the district of the North and slew and burnt and destroyed the district and its inhabitants.[92]

In dramatic and cosmic terms, then, he announced the arrival of the Arabs. West-Syrian apocalyptic literature from the period speaks in dreadful tones about the conquests: those undergoing oppression from the "Ishmaelites" or "sons of Hagar," under which, "happy are you who have not remained alive at this time."[93] This literary gravity seems fitting, given that the movement of Arab tribes into Palestine, Syria, Egypt, Persia, and regions beyond was not only a critical development for contemporaries but would become an event of world-historical proportions.

It is impossible to quantify the full historical impact of the Arabs or even the short- and long-term consequences of the Arabic invasions of the early seventh century, though many have tried.[94] They set the basis for the explosion of Islam onto the world stage and subsequent centuries of its dissemination across three continents. The conversion of heritage Christian domains in North Africa, Egypt, and the Levant was not immediate but took considerable time, for while the Arabs waged holy war they did not initially do so with the express purpose of converting the world to Islam.[95] Into the eighth century, Islam represented but one faith in a sea of diverse confessions in the Near East: a Christianity that was anything but unified, Jewish communities, and Zoroastrians, among others.

In geographical terms, the conquest of what amounted to over half of the expanse of the old Roman Empire was swift, and by the close of the 600s only a portion of territory in and around Asia Minor remained in Byzantine hands. By the 700s, Muslim converts dominated the Maghrib and had pushed into Spain; meanwhile, south of the Red Sea Arab vessels tracked past the Horn of Africa and arrived on the Swahili coast. From an economic perspective, an old theory once held that the invasions caused a drastic downturn in Europe by severing its connection to the wealthy eastern districts, although this has long been rejected.[96] In the east, meanwhile, the savvy Byzantines ably established new and profitable relationships with the caliphs and other local Muslim leaders. Clearly, however, the trade landscape had changed alongside the political upheavals that accompanied the seizure of Byzantine lands and the outright Arab conquest of Sasanid Persia following the Battle of al-Qadisiyya in 636.[97]

Narrowing the focus to Jerusalem, few events have been as consequential to religious history as the Arab capture of the city. Less than eight years after Heraclius's triumphant parade through the Golden Gate, the city fell under siege again and surrendered to the forces of 'Umar ibn al-Khattab, the second caliph ("successor") after Muhammad's death.[98] The conquest enabled the construction of two buildings crucial to the history of Islam and, in the modern age, nearly a century of divisive relations not only between the conquest and Judaism but also between peoples and governments, as well as periods of intense warfare between the state of Israel and its Arab neighbors. The al-Aqsa mosque, which sat as the *qibla* (the direction of Muslim prayer) before it was reoriented towards Mecca, and the Dome of the Rock, a shrine built on top of the purported location of Abraham's aborted sacrifice of Isaac, remain two of the most important Islamic sites in the world. Situated within the massive Herodian-era walls of al-Haram al-Sharif, itself under the guard of the Israeli government since 1967, these two sites serve as natural loci for religious and political conflict. Forgotten in the more recent controversies, however, has been the counterintuitive role of religious toleration that existed during and after the initial conquest of Jerusalem in 638.

To the Battle of Yarmuk

As we have seen, a host of governance issues consumed Heraclius's attention in the 630s. His restoration of the True Cross in Jerusalem and subsequent formulation of anti-Jewish policies constituted only a portion of his schedule. Other holy sites, including a multiplicity of churches and monasteries, demanded his attention, but there were foreign policy challenges as well, including the expatriation of resident Persian soldiers and the establishment of a firm border with the Sasanids. He was certainly aware of the general threat the Arabs posed and knew about Theodore's defeat of the soon-to-be-famous Muslim general Khalid ibn al-Walid, the so-called "sword of Islam," at the Battle of Mu'ta in 629. He also had personal knowledge of the region from his travels and seemingly good intelligence on enemy movements.

But beyond alerting the locals to the threat and, later, leaving Jerusalem and moving north to establish a base in Antioch, Heraclius had little time to concentrate on defense. It was not until 634 that he was able to turn his attention fully to his southern defenses, those borders of Palestine and Syria that lay dangerously close to new Arab militancy.[99] To bolster the numbers of regular Byzantine forces, which he still had trouble paying, Heraclius continued the tradition of allying with local Armenian and Arab tribes. While the former were generally reliable, the latter were not; divided into fractious groups that included nomadic Bedouins as well as Christian Arabs, they were prone to desertion and even liable to switch sides in a rapidly changing political environment.[100] Moreover, northern Arabia itself had not so long beforehand descended into sectarian conflict. Following the death of Muhammad in 632, various Arab factions refused to follow his successor, the First Rashidun ("rightly-guided") Caliph Abu Bakr as-Siddiq. These Arabs opposed the exactions of the Medina government, resulting in the so-called Wars of Apostasy (alternatively, the Ridda Wars, *Hurub al-Riddah*).[101]

In any case, it was these motley forces, stretched as they were between far-flung fortifications and cities, that constituted the first and second-level Byzantine defenses against Arab incursions.[102] Local leaders had to blunt the spear's tip. In early 634, while Heraclius was busy attending to other preparations, the Arab military attacks into Palestine and Syria began in earnest. The reasons behind Arab incursions were multifaceted, but surely one aspect was the importance of Jerusalem.[103] The city was the former *qibla* for a reason:

al-Haram al-Sharif had purportedly played host to Muhammad's "Night Journey" (the *Isrā*) from Mecca to "the farthest mosque" (identified as Jerusalem) and his subsequent ascension to heaven to meet with God and the prophets (the *Mi'rāj*). Whether or not Jerusalem was the primary motivation is probably unknowable, but it must be factored into the early Arabic interest in the Levant.[104]

Initially, the first aggressive movements seem to have had the complexion of what Robert Hoyland has dubbed "banditry": small-scale raids of villages outlying the larger population centers. These eventually attracted the attention of some local Byzantine governors, who assembled forces that were nonetheless routed and destroyed in the summer of 634 at the battles of Dathin (near Gaza, February), Ajnadayn (northwest of Hebron, July or August), and near modern-day Rabba, Jordan. In the fall of 634, the Arabs besieged and captured the city of Bosra in southern Syria, and by the year's end the biggest prize thus far, Damascus, fell into their hands. General raiding accompanied these principal battles and continued to the end of that year.[105]

Sometime in the midst of these actions Heraclius specifically instructed his brother, Theodore, to avoid open battle with the Arabs until reinforcements could arrive.[106] The losses through 635 likely confirmed his anxiety about the chances of local levies and garrisons against competent Arab veterans. That said, Heraclius may actually have considered abandoning Syria and Palestine altogether. Given the successful Arab penetrations, the initiative was certainly against him, and his prospects were daunting. Indeed, in his *Futuh-al-Sham* (Book of the Conquests), the writer al-Azdi notes that a flood of refugees fleeing Arab attacks in the south had arrived at Heraclius's headquarters in Antioch. At length, entreaties from Christians in Caesarea and Jerusalem persuaded the emperor to mount a counter-offensive.[107] This required marshaling regular units and moving south before more population centers fell to the invaders.

In the spring of 636, the emperor sent soldiers to succor the south. An army of regional forces was already operating there under the command of the Armenian general Vahan, and the reinforcements were intended to bolster his numbers in the face of increasingly successful and daring Arab attacks. Heraclius further added to these numbers with an expeditionary force led by the treasurer, Theodore Trithourios, master of the eastern armies (*magister militum per Ortientem*). Theodore's ranks, which constituted the imperial field army (*comitatus*) and were filled with regular Byzantine soldiers, gradually decreased in size as they moved south, for Theodore assigned some of his men to garrison duty in cities they passed en route. Other components of this army included a Ghassanid force (a non-Muslim Arab client state of Byzantium) led by their king, Jabala ibn al-Ayham, and more Armenians. Once the different components formed a coalition, Vahan evidently held supreme command.[108]

After nearly two months of maneuvering and some minor clashes in July 636, the Byzantine coalition finally engaged in full and open battle with the armies of the Rashidun caliphate. These were led by the general Abu 'Ubayda ibn al-Jarrah. Tall, thin, and a bit of a hunchback, Abu 'Ubayda had personally fought alongside Muhammad several times, including at the Battle of Badr in 624, which had kicked off the latter's war with his tribe, the Quraysh, in Mecca.[109] He was joined by Khalid ibn al-Walid (who commanded the cavalry) and Hashim ibn 'Utba ibn abu Waqqas (the infantry), as well as other principals.[110] One notable leader was 'Amr ibn al-'As, another Companion of Muhammad and the man credited by the writer Muhammad ibn Sa'd (d. 845) with the later Rashidun conquest of Egypt.[111] Absent was Caliph 'Umar himself, who remained in Medina.[112]

The details of the famous Battle of Yarmuk, which climaxed after many days of fighting on 20 August 636, are hotly contested, and problematic source material has not helped.[113] There are allegations of infighting among the Byzantine commanders; Nicephoros's *Short History* alleges treason on the part of Vahan, and a legend emerged that his soldiers proclaimed him emperor (over Heraclius) during the contest.[114] But the broad contours are reasonably known. The

Byzantine camp lay on the north side of the River Yarmuk, a tributary of the River Jordan east of the Sea of Galilee that angles to the southwest through the Golan Heights. At one point the tributary splits into heavily ravined branches (up to 200 meters in elevation), and it was on the north side of this split that the Byzantines made their initial camp. They eventually sent forces across the northerly ravine, called the *Wadi 'l-Ruqqad*, on an old Roman bridge—the only crossing in the area—and onto a flat plain beyond. A second camp was established on this plain. To the Byzantine right (west) were more ravines; to their front, the Rashidun armies. It was here that both sides prepared to fight for Syria.[115]

Disaster struck. The Byzantines advanced through a series of ambushes laid by the Muslims as they retreated to a better position.[116] When the formal fighting began, Muslim cavalry first outflanked the left end of the Byzantine ranks, thus cutting them off from any escape eastward. Elsewhere, the coalition's infantry and cavalry became somewhat jumbled while repositioning under fire and a slaughter ensued. When evening ended the action, some of al-Walid's cavalry managed to sneak behind the Byzantine camp and secure the bridge over the *Wadi 'l-Ruqqad*. As a result, the Byzantines found themselves fully enveloped with ravines on two sides and Arabs on the other two sides. Upon realizing they were trapped, some of the allies defected into the Muslim ranks while others fled by running or riding down the steep ravine only to be crushed to death when they fell. Still others waited for sunrise and then surrendered, but Abu 'Ubayda wanted no prisoners, so they were killed upon sight.[117] Those remnants who managed to escape were tracked relentlessly and either captured or killed. Of an original army numbering perhaps 15,000–20,000 soldiers, few had survived.[118] Much later, Agapias remarked that so great was the slaughter that the corpses, together, "formed a bridge that one could walk on."[119]

Not long after the battle, an anonymous writer heard of the event and thought it fit to scribble some notes while the memories were still fresh. The text, recorded on the first folio of a codex containing the Gospels of Mark and Matthew, is fragmentary and difficult to read. Its editor postulates that the writer was a low-born priest or monk living in close proximity to the battle, thus offering a fascinating glimpse into how an outsider saw and interpreted the shifting tides around him. We read of the coming of the Arabs and their destruction of villages, killing of residents, taking of slaves, and theft of olive oil and cattle. Breathlessly, "the Romans chased them," but "on the twentieth of August . . . a great many people were ki[lled of] [the R]omans, [s]ome fifty thousand."[120]

At that the account abruptly ends, leaving out the aftermath. In the wake of the triumph at Yarmuk, Abu 'Ubayda moved his forces westward into Palestine and advanced on the remaining fortified cities. Fred Donner has dubbed this the "third phase" of the Arab invasions, with the first being the early raids and the second the events around Yarmuk.[121] Without an army to defend it, the frontier was wide open for conquest. One by one the Byzantine cities fell. In a show of defiance, Caesarea held out until 640, relying upon its coastal location to resupply the garrison. Emesa (modern-day Homs) survived for a while before it, too, surrendered that year.[122] Certainly, a larger city could individually withstand attacks for a time, if, as Walter Kaegi has observed, it possessed good walls and a strong-willed commander.[123] In 638, Jerusalem had neither.

Sometime after 790, long after Yarmuk, an Armenian *vardapet* (a doctor of dogma) named Lewond pondered the magnitude of the Arab victory:

> The Ismaelites, thus enriched by the pillage of the treasures of the Greeks, and having plundered those who were massacred, returned to their country full of joy. Thereafter, they reigned over Palestine and Syria, imposing taxes on the land and on the churches of the holy city of Jerusalem. Consequently, Palestine and Syria ceased to pay tribute to the Greek emperor, since the Greek forces were no longer capable of resisting Ismael. Ismael was already ruling over Palestine.[124]

Military historians are fond of locating "decisive battles" in the past, victories so momentous that they decided the course of a conflict in one swift stroke. Within this framing device, surely the Battle of Yarmuk merits consideration for inclusion. The destruction of the Byzantine field armies meant that the invading Arabs faced no stiff resistance, save that of the garrisons within certain fortified cities.

Heraclius knew these garrisons were doomed. He wrote a series of letters to his governors in the region and, although ordering garrisons to maintain their posts, he forbade them from meeting the Arabs in open battle. Any field activities were to be in the form of scorched-earth tactics in advance of the Arab push. As Byzantine soldiers looted and pillaged their own villages and towns, the emperor left Antioch for Constantinople, never to return. He was not alone: citizens fled along with the army, so much so that the victorious Arabs would discover empty houses in Damascus and elsewhere.[125] Matters of finance and strategy precluded further imperial involvement in the region; a theological dispute with Patriarch Sophronius, whom the emperor had placed in charge of Jerusalem, did nothing to improve his inclinations towards further involvement there.[126]

At the time of his departure, Heraclius famously uttered a final message to Syria: "rest in peace."[127] However, he might as well have added Jerusalem to his valediction. It was only a matter of time before the Holy City came under siege. While the disaster at Yarmuk, along with the fall of Emesa and Damascus, all but guaranteed it, Arab eyes had been on the city for a while. According to al-Azdi, the general 'Amr ibn al-'As had been moving towards Jerusalem prior to his linking up with comrades at Yarmuk and even sent letters demanding its people surrender and convert to Islam.[128]

Following a robust occupation of Damascus and Emesa, Abu 'Ubayda finally set his sights on Jerusalem itself. If the compilations of al-Azdi and also the later historian and geographer, al-Ya'qubi, are to be believed, the general was not overly concerned with the city's defenses.[129] Had Abu 'Ubayda been worried, one suspects he would have not intentionally reduced his combat power as he did, by remanding a division of soldiers apiece at those other cities and sending 'Amr ibn al-'As to Aleppo. Dispatching messengers and obviously full of confidence, Abu 'Ubayda demanded that the Jerusalemites surrender. Should they not, he warned, he would bring to them "men who loved death better than they did life, wine, and hog's meat."[130]

Here, we are left wanting for exact details as provided by contemporary sources. The most specific account is that of the Abbasid historian and judge, al-Waqibi, who died nearly two hundred years after the siege. He speaks of an original striking force of 5,000 soldiers arriving at Jerusalem, which was followed by reinforcements later. The city residents placed catapults on the walls, rejected initial Arab overtures of peace, and then barraged the attackers from above with projectiles. Four full months passed, he claims, in which fighting occurred every day.[131] Al-Azdi, writing two-and-a-half decades before al-Waqisi, presents the claim that the residents sent two desperate sallies issued from their gates, both of which were quickly beaten back. With no major adversary in the vicinity and time on his side, Abu 'Ubayda finally arrived in person and organized a stout blockade of the city.[132]

One cannot help but wonder at the Arabs' lackluster effort to take the Holy City. They never seem to have directly attacked the gates or walls. Proper reconnoitering should have revealed the weakness on the northern side, where the Persians had broken through and the breach had yet to be fully repaired. A direct attack might have led to penetration and swift victory, but in any event one was not undertaken. Perhaps they never intended a direct assault. In the early years of the incursion into Syria, Caliph Abu Bakr had actually commanded his generals to avoid attacking cities until ordered.[133] Even when they did attempt sieges the dominant tactic was blockade, which tended to work well: Aleppo and Antioch fell quickly, as did numerous small towns; Emesa surrendered just as Abu 'Ubayda and Khalid ibn al-Walid considered storming it.[134]

Abu 'Ubayda's blockade at Jerusalem may have simply been a "far blockade," in which soldiers did not fully encircle the city but rather encamped within view of the gates, preventing ingress and egress until the garrison surrendered. Such a method is described at the Arab siege of Damascus in 634, where five Muslim generals positioned their forces outside five respective gates. And even though, there, one of them eventually stormed and took a gate after some months of siege, the breakthrough occurred simultaneously with a surrender agreement from the garrison.[135] Of course, without a Byzantine army in the area of operations and most cities having already fallen (save Caesarea, which was also under siege) the Arabs had time on their side.

From Sophronius's perspective, however, the situation could not have been worse. With Damascus and Homs occupied and Caesarea under siege, Jerusalem essentially stood alone. The breach in the northern wall was a weakness that could be exploited at any moment. No doubt the defensive tactics his garrison employed—sallies, artillery, archery—were designed to keep the Arabs at a distance from it. And Sophronius had keen memories of the Persian attack in 614, which he himself had lamented in verse.[136] Further, he knew well what a sack implied and described the brutality of their war in a sermon from 634, when he himself was under siege in Bethlehem.[137] With a weakened circuit, small garrison, and no relief army in sight, there was no choice but for Jerusalem to negotiate.

'Umar ibn al-Khattab

At this point, the second Rashidun caliph enters our story. Al-Ya'qubi relates that, during the siege, Abu 'Ubayda wrote to 'Umar ibn al-Khattab, who was south in Medina, about the victory at Yarmuk and the spoils it produced. 'Umar responded that the booty should remain undivided until the general had conquered Bayt al-Maqdis, that is, Jerusalem.[138] The city would not fall, however, until 'Umar himself arrived.

Who was 'Umar ibn al-Khattab? Tall, thin, and with a wispy beard, he commanded respect more from his demeanor than his physique.[139] 'Umar was originally opposed to the new religion brought by Muhammad and there is a story that he once grabbed his sword and set out to kill him. On his way to do so, he encountered two converts to Islam: his own sister and her husband. 'Umar accused them both of heresy, slapped his sister across the face, and knocked out his brother-in-law. Tempers eventually cooled, and after some discussion she gave him one of Muhammad's prophecies to read, the 14th verse of Sura Tā Hā: "I am God, and there is no god but I, so serve me, and observe acts of prayer to remember Me."[140] 'Umar then journeyed to Muhammad's house anyway but, instead of attempting to kill him, converted to Islam and followed his subsequent order to go and make his conversion public. Now a follower, 'Umar swiftly proved his worth in battle, fighting in nearly every engagement of Muhammad's campaigns and even taking command of some company-sized raids.[141] His interests ranged widely; interestingly enough, like two other famous generals, Julius Caesar and Napoleon Bonaparte, he was keenly interested in calendars and personally established the Muslim system of dating events from Muhammad's 622 *hegira*.[142]

'Umar's behavior stayed somewhat rough and tumble later in life. As his successor Caliph 'Uthman ibn 'Affan reputedly told Abu Bakr, "his private is better than his public," meaning that he was a man of deep devotion who yet remained a little wild in leadership roles.[143] For instance, following the death of Muhammad 'Umar insisted to crowds that he had not actually died but was only away for 40 days, like Moses, in order to speak to God, and that he would soon return and punish anyone speaking prematurely of his death. This caused a stir among the faithful, so much so that Abu Bakr had to intervene and declare with certitude that, yes, Muhammad had really died.[144] Despite such outbursts, Abu Bakr himself, as he lay on his deathbed, named 'Umar the second Rashidun caliph.

'Umar was also a man with a messianic title. As noted in Patricia Crone and Michael Cook's controversial book, *Hagarism*, he was given the title *al-Faruq* ("the Redeemer"): some say by Muhammad himself, others, by some Jewish observers.[145] This has been fraught interpretative territory in past decades. Although much writing on Islam has sought to de-emphasize (or even suppress) the messianic features of Muhammad's message, this runs counter to the textual evidence in Qur'an and *hadith*, in which "imminent eschatology" featured significantly. The question of whether or not it was a central tenet has been undergoing some debate.[146] So, did this title refer to 'Umar's role in the judgment of humankind, or rather, as is commonly understood in Sunni tradition, a more banal sensibility of knowing truth from lies?

There is more to our digression here. From his sources, al-Tabari offers different versions of a story about 'Umar's travels north of Jerusalem, prior to his entry into the city. In one, at a long-gone town called Jabiyah, astride the Golan Heights, 'Umar is said to have encountered a local Jew:

> 'Umar asked the Jew about the false Messiah, for he was wont to ask about him a great deal. The Jew said to him: "What are you asking about him, O Commander of the Faithful? You, the Arabs, will kill him ten odd cubits in front of the gate of Lydda."[147]

Two things here catch the eye. First, the gate of Lydda was a place in Jerusalem of many names, including the Gate of Mercy and the Golden Gate. As with Christianity and Judaism, this site holds tremendous significance for Islamic eschatology. It is where Jesus Christ will supposedly enter the city one day, perhaps—depending on the Muslim confession—accompanied by a holy warrior known as the *Mahdi*. Here the second reference attaches: at the Golden Gate, he/they will defeat the *dajjal*, the antichrist or "false messiah" related by al-Tabari, ushering in the sorting of believers at the Dome of the Chain. This latter structure, which often goes unnoticed by modern tourists in Jerusalem, is a smaller, open-air octagonal building lying just east of the Dome of the Rock, between it and the Golden Gate. It is to be a place of judgment, the Final Judgment. Interestingly, and in seeming accordance with this context, Al-Waqidi's history posits 'Umar speaking about nonbelievers burning in hell on Judgment Day.[148]

So whether or not 'Umar was truly thought of by early Muslims as a messianic figure, his person is nonetheless tied to a decidedly messianic place in the Holy City. And that sensibility cannot be divorced from modern attitudes regarding holy spaces there. The Golden Gate, one of only two eastern entrances into Temple Mount, is today impassable, sealed by stones placed there in the sixteenth century by the Ottoman emperor Suleiman the Magnificent. Yet it remains a contested space, with controversy arising there as recently as 2019.[149] At the very least, Muslim expectations of End Times, such as they were, coincided with a period of tremendous symbolism in that regard, given the Jewish attempt to rebuild the Temple after 614 and Heraclius's (aborted) triumphal entry into Jerusalem through the Golden Gate. Moreover, to several non-Muslim authors, the dramatic regional convulsions of the Arab conquest in general were seen as portending the apocalypse itself.[150]

To go back a step, how was it that 'Umar ibn al-Khattab came to Jerusalem in the first place? Certainly his generals Abu 'Ubayda and 'Amr ibn al-'As had the situation well in hand, establishing a blockade and fending off garrison sallies. 'Amr may have left at one point to handle a rebellion in Antioch, but afterward he returned to Jerusalem to buttress the siege again.[151] Late in 637, few good options remained for its residents. No Byzantine army would arrive to succor them, so Jerusalem's leader, Patriarch Sophronius, entered into negotiations. Placed in charge by Heraclius, Sophronius had sent the ecclesiastics of Constantinople the *Synodical Letter*, what would become a well-known missive requesting intercessory prayers on behalf of the emperor and against the invading Arabs. He also pleaded, indirectly, with the emperor to campaign south and person-ally repel them.[152]

Sophronius is the explanation for 'Umar's appearance. The patri-arch agreed to surrender the city to the Arabs but on the condition, al-Azdi writes, that the caliph sign the agreement in person. This may well have been a delaying tactic, perhaps undertaken in the hope of taking some pressure off until local garrisons could rally to assist the Holy City. In that sense it partially succeeded because siege oper-ations ceased until 'Umar's arrival.[153] There seems to have been some delay in the Arab response, for the request provoked some consterna-tion in the caliphal court. Would 'Umar's consent to Sophronius's demand give too much honor to the Christians, or, alternatively, might it expedite negotiations and bring a speedier end to the siege?[154]

'Umar settled the debate himself by acquiescing. Gathering his followers, he began the journey to Jerusalem.[155] This was a proces-sion and rather casual in nature, despite Theophanes the Confessor's later complaint that 'Umar "invaded Palestine."[156] He rode on a red camel while reclining in a howdah, a bed of sorts on its hump, from which hung pockets containing flour, dates, and a water jug.[157] Along the way, the sight of several Muslim soldiers dressed in Byzantine attire, consuming rich foods, apparently unsettled him; 'Umar himself was famously austere and, to the end of his life, preferred simple food and traditional clothing over finer trappings. According to one tradition passed along by al-Tabari, as he approached the city he encountered a group of horsemen from Jerusalem: upon receiving a promise of safe conduct, they delivered to him Sophronius's opening terms of surrender.[158] Once he arrived on site, Abu 'Ubayda informed the Jerusalem garrison that negotiations could formally begin.[159]

'Umar's Assurance

The earliest account of the extraordinary February 638 meeting between patriarch and caliph, outside the walls of Jerusalem and on the Mount of Olives, is the lost chronicle of Theophilus of Edessa, whose passages had been copied by later writers.[160] Theophilus relates that Sophronius left the safety of the city and ventured outside the walls to meet the 'Umar on the Mount of Olives.[161] This is rather different from the Arabic source tradition, in which 'Umar agreed to surrender terms while in Jabiyah, sent a garrison to the Holy City, and only afterward rode to Jerusalem himself.[162] It seems unlikely, however, that the patriarch would have traveled so far from his governorship in such hostile conditions, with Arab forces strewn throughout the region.

Accompanied by other notables of the city, Sophronius made two requests that, if satisfied, would persuade him to surrender Jerusalem peacefully. First, the patriarch stipulated the need for treatment comparable to other cities taken by the Arabs.[163] Second, he sought to guarantee Christian rights to their churches, freedom of worship, and retention of local laws. These came with a corollary, one very much in the spirit of Heraclius just a few years before: that Jews be barred from living in Jerusalem.[164] The latter request would essentially codify that Byzantine prohibition in the new political environment of Arab rule.

A contemporary discussion of such diplomatic concessions appears in the *Book of Revenue*, written by the Arab philologist Ibn Sallam. In broad strokes, customs in existence prior to capitulation and agreement were to be maintained in perpetuity. Ibn Sallam relates a story in which some performers from Adhri'at (modern-day Daraa, Syria) put on a show, possibly a dance, with swords and flowers, only to have a clearly unamused 'Umar order them sent away. Abu 'Ubayda intervened, reminding the caliph that they had performed in this way in the time before their surrender: 'Umar therefore relented and allowed the performers to finish their routine. And so on: rights to worship, possession of real estate, payments of rents, and the like were all guaranteed so long as they appeared in the text of peace agreements.[165] This custom presumed the voluntary surrender of the community, however—those who held out and were conquered with force had no certain rights whatsoever.

The consensus of the extant documents is that 'Umar was most ready to agree to Sophronius's proposed terms. For this he is afforded rough respect in the earlier, Christian sources and then extolled as a beacon of generosity and goodwill in the later, Muslim texts. Lewond himself bridged the two, noting that 'Umar "exercised more temperance and indulgence toward the Christian people, presenting himself everywhere as an obliging person."[166] The agreement between the caliph and Sophronius has become known as "'Umar's Assurance."[167]

There is no formal copy of the Assurance itself but rather a collection of its parts strewn throughout narrative accounts of the siege of Jerusalem. Full purported texts within histories have been, unsurprisingly, a hotbed of debate and controversy. Nonetheless, the broad strokes of the agreement were revealed early on. All of Sophronius's requests, and more, were granted initially: 'Umar gave Christian rights not only in Jerusalem but throughout all of Palestine. Jews were henceforth banned from the city, although this stipulation would later change.[168] In exchange, the Arabs took possession of the city and were free to issue the *jizya*, or poll tax, customarily levied on non-Muslim populations. Following the conclusion of negotiations, 'Amr ibn al-'As, the famous general, was named the new governor of Palestine.[169]

Leaving aside the poll tax, three facets of 'Umar's Assurance concern us now. To proceed through them, some recourse to the later documents is necessary. The most commonly cited version of the Assurance is that given by al-Tabari, who died in 923, which he claims to be relaying from reliable sources. While it is impossible to know how faithfully his version replicates the exact agreement, his tendency to prefer sources chronologically closer to the event they describe does offer some confidence.[170] The first plank of the Assurance is the gift to Jerusalem's Christians. It reads:

He has given them an assurance of safety for themselves, for their property, their churches, their crosses, the sick and healthy of the city, and all the rituals that belong to their religion. Their churches will not be inhabited [by Muslims] and will not be destroyed. Neither they, nor the land on which they stand, nor their cross, nor their property will be damaged.[171]

Despite popular assumptions, there were no broad conversion efforts, or Islamization—of either Christians or Jews—in the garrisoned towns during the early years of Arab conquest. Those efforts would come in the eighth century and later. Thus, 'Umar's guarantee of freedom of religion is not so surprising, and similar stipulations are found in other agreements with neighboring towns in Palestine. His tolerance in this regard is interesting, especially given his personal distaste for rival faiths; he apparently refused to even enter Christian churches because the images in their art and sculpture smacked of idolatry.[172] This does not imply that all was accomplished in peace. Whereas matters were largely settled diplomatically in the interior, cities on the Levantine coast experienced a greater degree of violent conquest, and those that actively resisted (such as Caesarea) saw their populations either fleeing or taken away in slavery.[173]

Still, persecution of Christians was not in the general interest of the Rashidun, and the record of named martyrs (some 270, give or take) is from the later Umayyad and Abbasid periods.[174] In other regards, communities adjusted to Arabic language and culture despite their skepticism of Islam.[175] Those liberties pertaining to the physical churches themselves were also broadly, though not always, respected in the centuries following the 638 conquest of the city. When they were violated, it was usually in moments of uncommon zealotry and unusual circumstances such as when the "mad caliph," al-Hakim of Egypt, ordered the Church of the Holy Sepulchre destroyed in 1009. Otherwise, the rights of Christian churches in Jerusalem were generally maintained across the centuries.

In this sense, 'Umar's Assurance has been seen as the first in a tradition of religious toleration in Jerusalem—on the part of Muslims towards Christians—stretching forward centuries from the 600s.[176] In fact, the caliph's grant to Sophronius was renewed in 1458 by the Ottoman sultan Mehmed II, who in the process specifically confirmed 'Umar's Assurance by name. Mehmed's edict was thereafter confirmed by his Ottoman successors into the eighteenth century.[177] In 1757, following long strife between various Christian factions over who controlled what ecclesiastical properties and dispensations and liberties concerning thereof, another Ottoman sultan, Osman III, issued a *firman* (decree) to settle the question forever. Known as the "Status Quo" agreement, it remains in force even today, and 'Umar's role in the process is explicitly mentioned in the standard treatment of the agreement.[178]

A second plank of al-Tabari's copy of the Assurance concerns the Jews: "No Jew will live with them [the Christians] in Jerusalem."[179] Sophronius made this request, quite simply, to keep Jerusalem from becoming a Jewish city again.[180] However, it appears that the prohibition of Jews did not last long because Sebeos speaks of their activity within the city, "after gaining help from the Hagarens for a brief while." He goes on to assert that some Jews assisted in the construction of the first mosque on the mount until being expelled from the site.[181] Later Jewish texts from the tenth century also express gratitude at the Muslim relaxation of the exile.[182] At some point, then, the anti-Jewish stipulation in 'Umar's Assurance was relaxed, and Sebeos marks the year as 641, three years before the caliph died. Some scholars have argued that this was the result of 'Umar relaxing the prohibition personally, for an eleventh-century chronicle alleges that 70 Jewish families were allowed to move back in. An alternative reading is that some Jews had reached a separate agreement with 'Umar altogether.[183] Possibly corroborating any of these interpretations is a remark in the later *Chronicle of Seert*, which claims that Sophronius asked 'Umar to bar the Jews *unless* they bought houses there.[184]

By the tenth century, however, Byzantine texts had considerably simplified what was likely a complex story. The subtleties were completely lost in Emperor Leo VI's military manual, *Taktika* (completed by 908), in which all the Arab victories came through force of arms.[185] Constantine Porphyrogenitus claimed that 'Umar himself besieged and blockaded the city and then "took it by guile" to construct blasphemous Islamic houses of worship.[186] Such hindsight views emphasize only the threats and consequences of invasion and conquest by practitioners of a foreign religion.

What these accounts miss, however, are the short- and long-term subtleties of 'Umar's maneuvering. Although he had won Jerusalem through a lengthy blockade and scant casualties, in the process he granted generous terms to non-Muslims. And he went further by relaxing Heraclius's anti-Jewish disposition—at least in the Holy City—which, while perhaps irking his successors, nonetheless resulted in a higher degree of religious tolerance and cohabitation in the physical city. This social environment would exist over a duration of many centuries. Both this tolerance and cohabitation set the tone for later developments such as the tradition of the "status quo" and, for Jews, later manifestations of Muslim–Jewish tolerance in Jerusalem under the Fatimid and Ayyubid caliphates. This is not the typical image of "conquest" in our modern sensibilities.[187]

Perhaps, though, Constantine Porphyrogenitus had something else on his mind. While complaining about Islamic buildings, he specifically noted their proximity on the Temple Mount. That location, so important to both Jews and Muslims then and now, was in Sophronius's day being used as a garbage dump—a "dung heap" some texts say—and was not mentioned in the surrender negotiations at all. Sophronius himself, as it happens, knew little about Islam's founding, much less the tale of Muhammad's Night Journey, which indelibly placed the location in the heart of Islamic devotion.[188] It would prove to be a sin of omission, of sorts, and one of which 'Umar ibn al-Khattab would take swift advantage.

II

SUNNI AND SHIA
THE 970s AND 1070s

Three things may seem nearly inconceivable to modern readers: that the Temple Mount, a place of such incredible significance and symbolism, once served as Jerusalem's garbage dump; that it once went wholly unmentioned in a political treaty; and that a conqueror essentially acquired it with little effort.[1] In the modern age, of course, Jerusalem and the holy sites attached to the mount lay at the very heart of so many religious and social disputes, geopolitical rancor, and outbursts of violence and war. Yet in 638, Patriarch Sophronius's complete nonchalance towards the former location of King Solomon's Temple enabled its easy acquisition by Caliph 'Umar ibn al-Khattab and its subsequent control by Muslim rulers for the next 461 years.

The caliph took swift advantage of his new possession. Ibn Sallam relates a matter-of-fact tradition about it: "'Umar did not declare the Mosque to be a part of the agreement, because their rights were not attached to it."[2] In other words, the sites on Temple Mount were not included in the protection of Christian churches and foundations, so the entire plateau of Mount Moriah was open for Muslim use and development. 'Umar was very interested in religious instruction. He had, for example, made inquiries of different communities to judge their knowledge of the prophecies and even sent instructors to improve those that were deficient. His efforts in this endeavor were regionally broad: Syria, Mesopotamia, and Yemen.[3] Now, he intended to foster Islamic prayer and learning in the heart of Jerusalem itself.

Once negotiations were complete, 'Umar entered the city and proceeded immediately to the Temple Mount, where he wished to pray. His inappropriate attire apparently caused some consternation: the caliph's clothes were quite dirty from his travels—"filthy garments of camel hair," Theophanes would later complain—so Sophronius lent him a clean robe and loincloth for the occasion, after which 'Umar had them cleaned and returned. Once on the plateau, the caliph ordered that it be cleared and a mosque be built on the site. At this point, Theophanes inserts a story of Sophronius finally realizing the importance of the site and linking the event back to prophecies in the Book of Daniel 11:31: "Armed forces shall move at his command and defile the sanctuary stronghold, abolishing the daily sacrifice and setting up the horrible abomination."[4]

No trace of this first mosque has survived. Traditionally, scholars took the evidence for it from a source known as the Gallic bishop Arculf, from which they argue that it was a poorly built wooden structure holding three thousand worshippers. They have then situated it physically against the southern interior wall of the Temple Mount, thus rendering it the "first al-Aqsa." None of these details can really be confirmed.[5] Two other traditions have 'Umar receiving advice on pinpointing the precise location of the former Temple from a Jewish convert to Islam and, as we have seen Sebeos suggest, of Jews initially assisting in its construction there.[6] In the absence of surviving archaeological traces, it is impossible to know the building's authentic location.

At length, however, it was not 'Umar's mosque that acquired enduring fame and meaning but rather the buildings of the later

Umayyad caliphs: the shrine of the Dome of the Rock, and the al-Aqsa mosque. Both of these buildings still constitute the most important Muslim claims to Jerusalem, and the accusation that modern Israelis are trying to encroach upon al-Aqsa, in particular, is a common refrain of the current Palestinian Authority. Thus the seventh-century sieges of Jerusalem are essential for understanding how Islamic holy sites in that city emerged and why they continue to both inform and confound attempts at modern interreligious concord.

I

The Shrine, the Mosque, and the Walls

The Dome of the Rock is an extraordinary building. Octagonal in shape, with a parapet encircling the stone upon which Muslims believed Muhammad once stood, it is topped with an impressive dome covered centuries later in gold leaf by King Hussein bin Talal of Jordan (d. 1999). Its shape, while often cast as wholly original, was probably based on the dimensions of the Church of the Holy Sepulchre's dome. Historians have endlessly debated the precise reason for its construction.[7] Some local Christians at the time believed the Muslims, at the probable direction of caliph 'Abd al-Malik, were actually building a church, perhaps because of the nearby Church of the Kathisma, which was also octagonal and erected around a stone upon which the Virgin Mary purportedly once sat. A contemporary Christian writer, Anastasius of Sinai, nonetheless objected that al-Malik's structure was no house of God.[8]

Al-Aqsa has a different storyline. Originally a quadrangular structure topped with a dome, built under al-Malik's son, Caliph Walid I, it was destroyed by an earthquake (or, possibly, a series of them) in 747–749, and now only a small section of its southern wall survives.[9] The mosque was rebuilt but then suffered more damage in another earthquake in 1033–34, and, likewise, only a small portion of that structure remains. The version standing today is that which was repaired two years later by the Fatimid caliph al-Zahir, so it is really an eleventh-century structure with other repairs and improvements made over time.[10]

Together, then, the three principal structures on the Temple Mount—al-Aqsa, the Dome of the Rock, and the Dome of the Chain beside it—represent the past and future of Islam. The city itself stood as continuity with the biblical past first and foremost, and secondarily, the mount was where Muhammad purportedly arrived and ascended.[11] Likewise, it is where Muslims expect humanity to be judged in the End Times. The cleansing of the mount and the erection of the holy places plays heavily in Muslim apocalpytic literature from the eighth century onward, and this is evident not only in the buildings themselves but also in the inscriptions upon the Dome of the Rock.[12] The already acknowledged importance of Jerusalem in the days of ʿUmar manifested in beautiful, monumental structures that served as focal points for devotion but also places of contested ownership among the Islamic faithful.[13] For in Palestine the tolerance expressed in the wake of the 638 conquest did not last forever. Indeed, intra- and interreligious violence bloomed in the intervening years between it and the city's next major siege in the 970s.

Strife hit among the Arabs first. The Rashidun had moved beyond Palestine and conquered Egypt in 641, but in the next decade unity began to falter.[14] Controversy over the assassination of the third Rashidun caliph, Uthman ibn ʾAffan, in 656 and his elected successor, Ali ibn Abu Talib, resulted in a civil war called the First *Fitna*. Following a series of battles and arbitrations, the war ended in 661 with a Karijite (commonly understood as simply "rebel") plot and Ali's premeditated assassination at the end of a sword that, according to one account, had been soaked in poison for a month beforehand.[15]

The result was the acceptance of Muhammad's brother-in-law, Muawiyah I, as new caliph and the rise of the Umayyad Dynasty

(661–750). At the time, whatever the devotional emphases of 'Umar on the mount, Jerusalem was still not an important political center, for the capital of the new subdistrict of Arab *Filastin*, in which it lay, was first Lydda and then Ramla.[16] But because the elites of Mecca and Medina refused to accept his authority, Muawiyah probably saw Jerusalem as a powerful symbol that would increase his authority among Muslims outside of Syria. As a result, that is where he chose to declare his caliphate, not his own political capital of Damascus.[17]

Antagonisms between Byzantium and this new Muslim caliphate were another complicating factor. Arab invasions of Asia Minor commenced in earnest under the Umayyads, as soon as 662 or 663, and continued into the eighth century with two major attacks on Constantinople itself.[18] The deteriorating relations between these states trickled down to degrade social relations. Textual references to the conversion of non-Arabs to Islam increase in number during the reign of al-Malik, and this eventually led to consternation over who should hold positions of influence within the Muslim communities as well as in the Umayyad armies: Ethnic Arabs? Or, rather, "cultural Arabs" who swore allegiance to an Arab tribe?[19] Concurrently, those who refused conversion increasingly faced more restrictions and some outright hostility. Coptic Christians, for example, were required to self-identify by wearing seals around their necks and carrying passports.[20] During the caliphates of the Umayyad rulers Umar II (d. 720) and Yazid II (d. 724), groups of Christian pilgrims were tortured and executed for failing to see the light.[21]

Intra-Muslim relations also deteriorated. The emphasis of the Umayyads towards the Syrian region came at the expense of Muslims in Iraq, who were almost completely ignored. Resentment there towards Damascus (and later Harran, which replaced it as capital in time) carried some weight because Iraq was, in fact, wealthier and more populous than Syria and Palestine combined.[22] This was but one component of a host of causes behind the swift fall of the Umayyads in 750, alongside "a confusing mixture of tribal and factional strife, conflicting religious agendas, economic inequities, and raw ambition on the part of the Umayyad elites."[23]

Conspiracies arose, and hopes for new leadership centered on the house of Abbas, those descendants of Muhammad's paternal uncle. One of them, Abu'l-Abbas, was recognized as caliph in the city of Kufa (177 kilometers south of Baghdad), while civil war (the Third *Fitna*) raged in Khurasan (northeast Iran) and elsewhere. Revolutionary forces defeated the last Umayyad caliph, Marwan II, at the Battle of the River Zab near Mosul in 750 and chased him through Syria and into Egypt, where he was at last killed.[24] This ushered in the period of the long-lasting but uneven Abbasid Caliphate (750–1258), which, at its greatest extent, stretched from the Nile to modern-day Afghanistan.

In the midst of these political tensions Jerusalem once again found itself vulnerable. Several local rebellions arose against Umayyad rule during the Third *Fitna*, and Damascus was intent on rooting out all opposition. In the mid-to-late 740s, Marwan II appears to have ordered Jerusalem's walls pulled down to strip away its defenses and, therefore, prevent further rebellious activity there. He had done the same with other towns in Palestine; as we will see in chapter five, much later the Ayyubid sultans of the thirteenth century would replicate the trick in the Holy City to dissuade western crusaders from attempting to seize what they could not thereafter hold.[25] Theophanes the Confessor relates that in 745: "Once he had conquered and taken Emesa, Marwan killed all of Hishan's relatives and freedmen. He destroyed the walls of Heliopolis, Damascus, and Jerusalem, killed many important people, and mutilated the people who remained in those cities."[26]

How extensively Marwan demolished the walls cannot be ascertained. If Theophanes's remark is accurately dated, the event occurred just before the 747–749 quake that destroyed the al-Aqsa mosque and the Umayyad palace complex south of it and completely leveled cities around the Sea of Galilee, such as Tiberias and Antiochia-Hippos (Sussita).[27] Two such events in close chronological proximity frustrate archaeological attempts to distinguish between layers of rubble from the period. Likewise, the rebuilding of the walls may have coincided with repairs to al-Aqsa, carried out by the Abbasids in the 770s–780s.[28] During the reign of Caliph Harun al-Rashid (d. 809), his wife, Zubaida, purportedly spent millions of dinars on fortress construction and then gifted large sums to the three holy cities of Mecca, Medina, and Jerusalem.[29] Still, the latter's peculiar circumstances remained less than ideal amid the swirling of marching armies and dynastic upheaval.

The March of the Shia

The early rule of the Abbasid Caliphate has often been hailed as a golden age for Islam, a time in which Arab society truly flourished. The incredible revenue of the Near East had few, if any, peers in the world, pulled in as it was from the network of communication and trade routes connecting it to East Asia, North Africa, and Europe. That wealth led to an explosion in building, the trade of fine goods, crafts, music, and "one of the most astonishing periods of scholarship in history," centered on the Abbasid capital of Baghdad and other major population centers.[30] In Palestine, the caliphal joining of the Levant with Iraq also led to a broad integration of customs and something of a shared social environment between different religious adherents.[31]

Discontent arose in some quarters against the new rulers in the mid-ninth century. Culturally, the Abbasids were in some ways regarded as a little too cosmopolitan. Diverse belief sets flourished in the midst of the wealth and abundance of the eighth and ninth centuries, and these brought with them some social problems and fracturing among the religious elite. The political green shoots of Shi'ism began to grow in earnest, with significant centers of the confession developing in Morocco, Yemen, and the Caspian littoral.[32] The Shia believe that the fourth Rashidun caliph, Ali, had also been the first imam, a religious leader with divine authority. The sons born from his wife Fatima (Muhammad's daughter), Hasan and Husayn, were the second and third imams, respectively. Seen as rivals to Umayyad power, both sons fell into conflict with Muawiyah and paid with their lives, but in the process Fatima had fostered the bloodline of Muhammad that Shias consider essential for spiritual leadership.[33]

In time, the Shia claim would eventually rival that of the Abbasids. One group of adherents to this different confession, the Isma'ilis, legitimized esoteric interpretation of the Qur'an (as opposed to only literal) and the authority of the imams to do so. They split away from other Shia groups in 765 and became intransigent against Abbasid rule. Operating from the town of Salamiyah northeast of Homs, Isma'ili missionaries traveled throughout the Near East to drum up recruits to their cause. Confronted with such insurgency from within, the Abbasids sought to strengthen their hand. Caliph Mutawwakil (d. 861) embarked on a sort of religious crackdown against all non-Sunnis under his sway. He ordered the destruction of the grave of Husayn, which had swiftly become a Shia pilgrimage site, and also set in place measures to shame religious adherents outside of legal protections: the Christians and Jews (or *dhimmis*). Forced to wear the color yellow on their clothes along with other identifying marks, this was the first time they had suffered such measures from the personal order of a caliph.[34]

Other problematic aspects of Abbasid rule were harder to excise. The caliphate had relocated from Baghdad to Samarra in 836, and, by the time it returned in 892, much political and military strife had undone the regime's legitimacy. Its reliance on non-Arab (especially Persian and Turkish) military commanders and slave soldiers proved tumultuous and hard to unwind. Much later, the famous historian Ibn Khaldun (d. 1406) emphasized the caliphate's alliance with non-Arabs as a theme while looking back:

> They tried to maintain their hold over the government thereafter with the help of Persian, Turkish, Daylam, Saljuq, and other

clients. Then, the (non-Arabs) and clients gained power over the provinces of the realm. The influence of the dynasty grew smaller, and no longer extended beyond the environs of Baghdad.[35]

Turks, Arabs, and others periodically fell into social conflict on the streets of Baghdad. Divisive politics at court did nothing to help, and in 861 a Turk assassinated Mutawwakil. This led to a power struggle between his sons, to whom he had distributed governances across the caliphate, and, ultimately, full-blown war between Samarra and Baghdad. War raged nearly an entire year from February 865 to January 866.[36]

The war had the effect of weakening the Abbasids who, while struggling simply to control affairs close to home, lost power and influence in the peripheries of their caliphate, especially to the west. The most efficacious of the insurgent efforts was that of a Yemenite, Abu 'Abd Abdulla al-Shi'i, and far away from the caliphal power centers of Iraq. Al-Shi'i settled in eastern Algeria in 893 and subsequently converted the Kutama Berbers to Isma'ili beliefs. With a core of Berbers, he set out on military campaigns against the Abbasid adherents in the region, the Aghlabid emirate. As al-Shi'i won victories and gained momentum, the Isma'ili *imam*, 'Ubaydalla Sa'id, made his own way to the Maghrib to capitalize on the potential of this new army, which operated in a much freer environment than it could in proximity to Syria and Iraq. 'Ubaydalla was swiftly identified and captured by the Aghlabids but, in 909, al-Shi'i defeated them entirely and freed the *imam*.[37] In the aftermath, 'Ubaydalla Sa'id declared a new rival caliphate to the Abbasids: the Fatimids.

To trace the story of the Fatimids, it is necessary to leave the city of Jerusalem for a time because their political power was built not there but in Egypt. Over the course of the next six decades, the Fatimids increased their territories by leaps and bounds, eventually carving out a dominion larger than that of their Sunni peers. As Ibn Khaldun succinctly noted in his classic book, *Muqaddimah*, "they took possession of Ifrîqiyah [eastern Algeria, Tunisia, and Libya] and the Maghrib, and then conquered Egypt, Syria, and the Hijâz [western Arabia]."³⁸ These were vast lands, with Egypt sitting as the prize jewel in the middle. Commonly referred to as the breadbasket of the premodern world, Egypt was essentially a personal account with a considerable balance. And it soon became the great prize for a leader named al-Mu'izz li-Din Allah (d. 975): the fourth Fatimid ruler, he was styled Imam-caliph, thus signifying both his claim to authority over Muslims and also his purported descent from the line of Ali.

Yet al-Mu'izz's victory was the final result of a long process in which the Fatimids had invaded Egypt on four separate occasions from 913 to 968, and it was only on the fourth that they succeeded.³⁹ Its occasion was political instability fomented, at its core, by the Abbasid willingness to let others govern Egypt under their banners. These were the Ikhshids, who held power from 935 to 946 but then, for all intents and purposes, lost it to the powerful and cagy eunuch Abul-Misk Kafur, an Abyssinian.⁴⁰ It was Kafur's death in 968 that finally precipitated a general Fatimid invasion.

Two late medieval authors, al-Maqrizi (d. 1449) and Idris (d. 1468), provide strikingly similar narratives of the invasion, each culled and compiled from sources closer in proximity to it.⁴¹ Both follow the activities of Egypt's conqueror, the general Jawhar al-Siqilli ("the Sicilian"), who the Imam-caliph al-Mu'izz had sent to lead the effort. With "a thousand loads of money" and "an innumerable quantity of weapons, horses, and supplies," Jawhar left for Egypt in February 968, and by June the next year sat astride the Nile across from Fustat (Old Cairo). His path had been smoothed considerably by some advanced information operations conducted by Fatimid *da'is*, or missionaries, who distributed white Fatimid banners and sought to convert locals to the Shia cause.⁴²

Jawhar himself shaped the environment by extending an offer of peace and security to the Abbasid vizier in Egypt, Ja'far ibn al-Furat.

(Interestingly, *vizier* translates as "one who bears a burden," a striking connection to the Arabic sense of tolerance, *ihtimal*, or the bearing of burdens.) In a promise known as an *aman*, Jawhar guaranteed safety to their persons, property, and movables, as well as protection from hostile parties.[43] In short order most resistance between Jawhar and the Nile was removed. In June 968, however, two paramilitary groups, one loyal to the recently deceased Kafur and the other to the Ikhshid clan, broke the peace and elevated a rival to challenge Fatimid rule, saying that "between Jawhar and us there remains only the sword." He subsequently engaged them at the al-Jazira island in the Nile Delta and by July had routed the leaders. The decisive action was an amphibious landing conducted by his commander, Ja'far ibn Falah, at the Battle of al-Makhada. The *aman* was restored, and Jawhar went on to found the city of Cairo and build lavish palaces and other facilities there.[44] In the wake of the conquest, Abbasid rule was formally abolished. Its black banners and mode of dress disappeared, replaced with the white variants preferred by the Fatimids. On Friday, 8 July 969, a sermon was offered in Cairo that gave blessings to the Imam-caliph al-Mu'izz, the new "Commander of the Faithful."[45]

All rather interesting context! It is now time to return to the city of Jerusalem, for the Fatimids continued expanding eastward and eventually reached Palestine. The condition of Jerusalem itself was somewhat fraught in the ninth century, when in 842 Bedouin revolts periodically entangled the city and led to the destruction of some churches and once almost the Church of the Holy Sepulchre.[46] Matters stabilized in the tenth century but again local controversies persisted and more churches were damaged during Palm Sunday violence in 938.[47]

The scattered violence, while problematic, did not dissuade people from settling in and improving the city. The Arab geographer al-Maqdisi (d. 991) wrote of the crowds of visitors who filled the streets. Remarking on the quality of Jerusalem's buildings and the bountiful foods found within—enormous grapes! — and "the orange and the almond, the date and the nut, the fig and the banana, besides milk in plenty, and honey and sugar"—the enthusiasm of this native writer is infectious. And he was careful to note to readers the enduring spiritual importance of Jerusalem: while Mecca and Medina are superior, their residents will, nonetheless, "both come to Jerusalem" for the Final Judgment.[48] No wonder that guides for Muslim pilgrimage began to appear in the tenth century, with lists of important sites to visit that included, of course, the Shrine and the Mosque on the Temple Mount but also the Gate of Mercy: yet another indication of the prominence of that apocalyptic site in the first three centuries of Islam.[49]

A cornucopia of tasty delights, then, but not all was so rosy. Al-Maqdisi likewise lamented the omnipresence of other faiths within the city walls. He writes of empty mosques and *madrasas*, the lack of lectures by learned scholars, and "everywhere the Christians and the Jews have the upper hand."[50] Although a number of notable Sunni Muslim teachers had emigrated to the city in the mid-tenth century, their influence seems to have been lacking.[51] The reality is that, despite the long duration of Islamic rule, Jerusalem was a cosmopolitan city in its own right. The tolerances stemming from 'Umar's Assurance had woven themselves into the fabric of city life, and competing religious confessions had not only persevered within the walls but rather strengthened. Correspondingly, secular buildings, such as the old Umayyad complex south of the Temple Mount, deteriorated over the course of Abbasid rule.[52]

Soon after Cairo's founding, Jawhar found cause to extend his lines across the Sinai Peninsula and into the Levant. There was clearly a general Fatimid interest in pushing further into Abbasid territory. Long before, in 953, al-Mu'izz himself said as much. In his second *khutba*, the twice-annual sermons of such import that they could only be delivered by the Fatimid Imam-caliphs themselves, al-Mu'izz beseeched God thus:

Oh God! Support me with Your aid; conquer for me Your enemies with a victory that revives religion and by which the community of Muhammad, lord of the messengers, grows mightily. Provide me with the means to visit his tomb and mount his *minbar*, stay in his house, and perform the pilgrimage to Your sacred house, and with our banners halt at these majestic shrines.[53]

The allusions here are to war and specifically western Arabia and the Red Sea, which, after 969, became real possibilities for expansion.

A more specific cause of Fatimid expansion into Asia, however, was increasing militancy on the part of another rival, the Qaramita, or Carmathians. A splintered Shia community (or communities, as several areas bore the name) in Syria, the Carmathians rejected al-Mu'izz's insistence that they rejoin the Fatimid *da'wa* (calling, founding).[54] They invaded Ramla in the fall of 969, so Jawhar dispatched Ja'far ibn Falah to deal with the threat. A veteran of the Egyptian campaign, Ja'far spent his remaining years ping-ponging around Syria. He was successful in extending Fatimid power and influence over other portions of Syria and in the Levant. Idris writes of his conquest of Homs and, further north, his blockade of Antioch with 20,000 soldiers, which he only aborted when a Byzantine army arrived in relief. Sermons in western Syria extolled al-Mu'izz's name and *da'i*s pushed the Fatimid message around the region.[55]

Yet Damascus remained a persistent thorn in the Fatimid side. Ja'far seems to have captured and lost the city twice. First, Ja'far's initial invasion of Syria resulted in the capture of Damascus in November 969.[56] Second, the city was retaken via the conniving of its Ikhshid ruler, Ibn Tughjl, with the Carmathians and also the governor of Jerusalem, one Muhammad Ishmael ibn al-Sabahi, to whom we shall return. Ja'far was forced to besiege Damascus again.[57] Meanwhile, Carmathian forces continued to amass against him, and in 971 major reinforcements arrived from Bahrain under the command of al-A'sam. A notorious man with a family history of opposing the Fatimids, al-A'sam reputedly once attacked the meteorite stone set in the Ka'ba by Muhammad ("The Black Stone") with a metal rod, bashing cracks into it. Ja'far intercepted these Carmathians outside Damascus but was defeated and killed in the fighting; they hung his decapitated head on a wall afterward.[58] The Carmathians then advanced into Egypt but were defeated by Jawhar outside of Cairo in December 971.

Seizing the initiative after his successful defense of the Fatimid capital, Jawhar went on offense. He ordered his nephew, Ibrahim, to invade Syria full-bore.[59] This invasion was followed by the personal intervention of Imam-caliph al-Mu'izz himself in early 974, and by mid-spring he had routed the Carmathians utterly.[60] It was in this period, 971–974, that the Fatimids seem to have finally acquired the city of Jerusalem for themselves. The event goes unmentioned in the major contemporary histories, presumably because, unlike Damascus, it was taken without a serious fight.

More might be speculated about this silence, however. For the first time in its history, Jerusalem had been exchanged between two Islamic confessions, Sunni to Shia. One might anticipate that such an event would be lamented in Sunni sources, but it was not. One is also tempted to argue that perhaps animosities between the two were not as yet pronounced. Alternatively, it could be asserted that the conquest was less noteworthy because, at the end of the day, the city remained in Muslim hands. On the local level, at least: officially, the Abbasids decried the Fatimid conquests in general and, to humiliate them, repudiated their genealogical line to Ali and posited them instead as descendants of Jews.[61]

The Byzantines Return

According to the account of an eleventh-century Christian physician, Yahya of Antioch, John VII of Jerusalem was in distress in the 960s. His patriarchate there had flourished under Muslim rule and its organizational structure had become more complex; since at least 880 it supervised 25 otherwise autonomous archbishoprics, each with its own geographical boundaries.[62] John's position was thus critical for the survival and flourishing of eastern Christian communities within the Muslim-controlled domains. This situation was permitted by both the Abbasids and then Fatimids in a general sense. However, in the city itself relations between Christians, Muslims, and Jews were not always so rosy. Recalling al-Maqdisi's description of Christians running amok while the mosques sat empty, local grievances were bound to exist within the wider plurality.

In 966, such matters had come to the fore. Arguments among the city's residents suddenly intensified and the local Christians found themselves on the defensive. Burdened by mandatory financial payments (a sort of inner-city tribute) to the city's governor, the aforementioned al-Sabahi, Patriarch John wrote to beg for the assistance of two powerful leaders: Emperor Nicephoros II Phocas in Constantinople and the Abyssinian Kafur in Egypt. Their help did not arrive in time: Yahya claims that civil discontent eventually manifested in a series of riots, which led to the burning of the Church of the Holy Sepulchre and the consequential collapse of its dome. Yahya implicates both Jews and Muslims in its destruction, and the mob seized John himself in the aftermath and burned him at the stake.[63] This event, combined with the scattered attacks on Christians earlier in the 840s and 930s, was a not insignificant interruption of the general assurance of peace levied by 'Umar ibn al-Khattab so long before.

It was, however, an affair involving individual personalities and particular local grievances. And in this sense it was part and parcel of a theme running throughout Jerusalem's history: that it was not military conquest itself but rather poor political relations that produced the bulk of the suffering inside its walls. Much as in 614, there seems to have been Jewish involvement against Christians in the city, though certainly not to the same degree.[64] Moreover, that John simultaneously beseeched both the Byzantines and the Egyptian Sunnis for aid reveals a lot about prevailing diplomatic relations at the time. Whatever the disturbances in the city, he evidently regarded both Muslim and Christian polities as benefactors, or at least potential sources of succor, given the right inducements.

In the wake of John's desperate pleas and subsequent death, help was indeed on the way. John's call to Constantinople in particular was a precursor to the Byzantine reentry into Palestine. It arrived in the form of Nicephoros Phocas, an emperor described in a later century as a holy, pious, virtuous man who aided the poor and downcast and who was "triumphant in all battles"—a literal reference to be sure, for as a commander he won many battles but not necessarily wars. According to the Armenian historian Matthew of Edessa (d. 1144), the emperor advanced south and took several cities in Cilicia: Tarsus, Adana, Mamistra, and Anazarbus.[65] He eventually ended up at Antioch, where al-Maqrizi refers to an encounter between his Byzantine army and the forces of Ja'far ibn Falah in 971.[66] As we have seen, Ja'far moved back south to Damascus and died there, which allowed Nicephoros to prosecute his campaign further into south Syria.

Were the Byzantines now on the cusp of regaining Syria and Palestine? Certainly Nicephoros was as knowledgeable about war as one might hope. At his personal request, an anonymous author composed a tactical manual for him, which specifically notes the proclivity of Muslims ("the arrogant sons of Hagar") to utilize ambushes.[67] In 1915, one historian postulated that Nicephoros had reached Jerusalem itself, but this was clearly a conjecture that other scholars swiftly refuted. Despite the emperor's vigor and the allure of a region fraught with Muslim infighting, he seems to have got no further south than Tripoli by 969.[68] As his contemporary Leo the Deacon wrote, Tripoli was defended too well, so the emperor settled for taking the nearby fortress of Arqa sacking it for nine days before returning north to Antioch.[69]

However, Nicephoros never made it back to Antioch. In December of the same year, he was betrayed by his wife Theophano and nephew John Tzimiskes. According to Matthew of Edessa, after secretly spiriting Tzimiskes back from exile and into Constantinople, Theophano slyly secured the strap to the emperor's scabbard while kissing him. When Tzimiskes burst into the room a short while later, Nicephoros could not draw his sword in time and was cut into three pieces.[70] Or, in Leo the Deacon's telling, John's men smashed out his teeth and then, led by the usurper, split his brain in two and thrust a curved hook into his back; then, to prove the emperor had indeed passed, cut off his head for display, and left the decapitated corpse in the snow for a day.[71] So mocked in life, however, in death Nicephoros lives on. His war booty funded the first monastery established on Mount Athos, Greece (the Monastery of Great Lavra) and a liturgical office is still sung in his name there.[72] The killer, and henceforth Emperor John I Tzimiskes, eventually gathered armies and moved south towards Palestine in three successive campaigns in 972, 974, and 975.[73]

Jerusalem, however, remained out of Tzimiskes' grasp. Matthew copied an astounding letter from the emperor in which he claims to have regained governing control and tributary rights to the Holy City and everything around it.[74] Can this be true? It may have been that the specter of Byzantine power gave such an impression in retrospect, but the reality was quite different. He seems to have had more success than Nicephoros, to be sure; in 975, he marched along the Levantine coast, reaching as far south as Beirut, Sidon, or even Caesarea, depending on the sources.[75] Tzimiskes returned to Constantinople at year's end and died in 976. His exertions brought some security to Antioch by pushing the frontier south, but by the late tenth century the Byzantines had neither the manpower nor the resources to sustain operations as far south as Palestine, much less consolidate gains by garrisoning key towns and fortresses there.[76] However, until the First Crusade, this would be the closest a Christian power came to recovering Jerusalem.

71

An intriguing alternate course of these same events has been reconstructed, most strongly by Moshe Gil: that Jerusalem was indeed conquered, not by the Byzantines but rather by one Alp Tikin, a Turkish commander from Baghdad who allied with the Carmathians and then attacked the Levantine coast, taking Sidon and Acre. Alp Tikin gained further tribal, and Sunni, allies in the region, and these drove off a Fatimid relief force, enabling him to grab Tiberias before finally seizing Damascus in April 975. Arriving in the region, Tzimiskes met with Alp Tikin and the two reached an agreement of sorts, in which the latter was essentially established as a Byzantine subordinate—his conquests, therefore, could be claimed as the emperor's own triumphs. Alp Tikin is then said, in Gil's reckoning, to have conquered the rest of Palestine; after all, Tzimiskes could sensibly write, "We now have freed from servitude to the *Tachiks* [Muslim individuals and/or polities] all of Phoenicia, Palestine, and Syria, and convinced them to enter under Byzantine rule."[77]

The devil is in the details. The later Damascus chronicler Ibn al-Qalansi corroborates that Tzimiskes and Alp Tikin came to an agreement, and the latter indeed campaigned in the area in 974–975. However, Matthew of Edessa is the only source to record the former's letter in its entirety and its claim that Jerusalem came under imperial suzerainty.[78] Matthew's information on the tenth century is rather poor, and his sense of the political tensions between Muslim groups in Syria and Palestine is uninformed.[79] It is strange that other sources make no mention of this, especially John Skylitzes, a high-ranking judicial official personally elevated by the Byzantine emperor Alexios Comnenos. Skylitzes, who wrote as close to an "official" history as can be found for the Byzantine 900s, instead offers that Emperor Tzimiskes advanced as far south as Damascus, restoring rule through either negotiations or war, and then returned home.[80] The historian seems rather concerned with Jerusalem's general condition, writing about the immolation of Patriarch John in 966 as well as the Church of the Holy Sepulchre's destruction at

Fatimid hands in 1009 and its subsequent reconstruction, to which we shall return.[81]

It seems odd, then, that Skylitzes, as well as every other source other than Matthew of Edessa, would neglect to mention something as important as the restoration of imperial power in Jerusalem, whether by proxy or not. Indeed, Leo the Deacon took care to enumerate John Tzimiskes' discovery of holy relics: the sandals of Jesus, the hair of John the Baptist, and a miraculous icon; surely he would have at least mentioned the Holy City had it come back under Byzantine sway. Instead, Leo charts John's course to Damascus, his exaction of tribute there, and then the march back to Lebanon.[82] Going further, in the Arabic sources one would expect at least some measure of Sunni joy in the cessation of Shia rule from the city had Alp Tikin indeed taken it.[83] Skepticism about the purported imperial letter among top specialists of the Fatimid and Middle Byzantine periods—not its authenticity but rather its exaggerations of a conquest that did not occur—has run very high.[84] Ultimately, it is an argument from silence, but a strong argument nonetheless.

However, if Matthew of Edessa's letter is a distortion and Byzantine proxy control in Jerusalem indeed a myth, then the basis of Alp Tikin's purported conquest of the city falls as well. To wit: there was no Turkish conquest of Jerusalem in the tenth century. The city never actually left Fatimid hands following Ja'far's conquest, and in those hands it would remain for another hundred years.

II

Despite continuing Fatimid control of Jerusalem, the fraught civil affairs that had tormented the city from the inside continued into the eleventh century. Still, there was progress on some fronts. The Church of the Holy Sepulchre was partially repaired, with the cupola rebuilt by 976 but other parts remaining without a roof.[85] Moreover, it was in this period during the reign of Caliph al-'Aziz Billah

(975–996) that the Fatimid Empire reached its greatest territorial extent.[86] His reign was also, perhaps, the apogee of religious toleration: understanding his role as the Imam-caliph as being a guide to the whole world, al-'Aziz was happy to allow religious pluralism so long as people remained obedient.

Caliph al-Hakim: an Aberration?

Al-'Aziz's successor was of a decidedly different disposition. Caliph al-Hakim bin-Amr Allah (d. 1031) was ever mindful of his duty of *hisba*: "to command the right and forbid the wrong." Rules and regulations were strictly enforced, men and women were restrained in terms of how they could mix socially, and non-Muslims were forced to wear black clothing and other identifying items.[87] For example, Christians had to wear crosses outside their clothing but this was no mere ornamental jewelry: one cubit wide, one cubit long, and a weight of five pounds![88] Reading through al-Maqrizi's history, however, there seems no rhyme or reason to the caliph's agenda, if indeed he had one. Al-Hakim's orders alternatively reflected both vestiges of tolerant Fatimid sensibilities and purist repressions. Between 1013 and 1014, for example, the caliph ordered Jews entering public baths to wear bells and Christians crosses, but he also relaxed travel restrictions and "Jews and Christians received permission to travel to wherever they wanted."[89]

However, the extensive toleration of the past had disappeared. Soon, al-Hakim's edicts began encroaching on religious customs of Christians, Jews, and even Sunnis. Yahya of Antioch points to a series of events leading up to al-Hakim's greatest depredations. In 1008, the ceremonial use of olive branches and palm fronds in Jerusalem on Palm Sunday was forbidden, and monies from the churches there began to be confiscated.[90] He personally suspended and interrogated several Christian ministers in the city; some were killed via deliberate exposure to the winter elements, and others were forcibly converted to Islam.⁹¹ Yahya reports the destruction of numerous churches and even the exhumation of Christian tombs and destruction of the human remains within.⁹²

But the most infamous deed was yet to come. In 1009, al-Hakim ordered the destruction of the Church of the Holy Sepulchre itself, which since 'Umar's Assurance had withstood two attacks but now faced a reckoning. The governor of Ramla and his team carried out the deed, first stripping the church bare and then tearing the stones down to the foundation, making "the trace of it disappear."⁹³ Confirming Yahya's account was a regional contemporary, Elias, the bishop of Nisibis (today Nusabin, Turkey). Elias offers a condensed account of the event: al-Hakim destroyed the sepulchre church, persecuted Christians, and then destroyed other Christian churches as well as Jewish synagogues across his domains.⁹⁴ Another contemporary, John Skylitzes, the Byzantine author, claims that al-Hakim did these things because he was insane, hence the caliph's later nickname, "the Mad."⁹⁵

What had changed to bring about such events, which were highly at variance with the heritage of Muslim control of Jerusalem's urban population? Insanity can only be a partial explanation. Michael Brett has outlined what seems to have been a threefold agenda that included the strengthening of al-Hakim's direct rule, sound economic maintenance of the caliphate, and, perhaps most importantly, his mindfulness of the *hisba*. As he slashed and burned through his own administration, executing numerous top Muslim officials and confiscating their wealth, al-Hakim streamlined Fatimid governance and centralized power under himself. His more outlandish claims, such as that of his divinity and self-identification as the *Mahdi*, the holy warrior who would defeat the Antichrist inside Jerusalem's Golden Gate, rang suspect with the Sunni locals.

Importantly, under the rule of al-Hakim, Jerusalem—always lurking in the western Christian imagination—came roaring back to prominence when he destroyed the Church of the Holy Sepulchre.

Interpretive clarity for al-Hakim's rule soon emerged in Europe. The reaction to the event can only be described as one of horror. Drawing on pilgrims' accounts of the destruction, two writers in particular, Ademar of Chabannes and Rodolfus Glaber (a monk at the Abbey of St. Benignus, near Dijon), crafted detailed accounts of the event. Glaber blamed it entirely on Jews living in Orleans, saying that they had secretly corresponded with al-Hakim and informed him of a grand Christian strategy to invade his lands from the West and that he ought to destroy the churches in the East to forestall it. In a highly charged passage, Glaber remarks: "Therefore, the devil, driven by envy, sought to pour out the venom of his malice upon the practitioners of the true faith by using his accustomed instruments, the Jews."[96] Ademar adds the detail that Muslims in Spain coordinated with these Jews in the messaging to the caliph.[97] The Jews in Europe, in other words, were conspiring to eradicate a formal Christian presence in the holy land.

In response to these supposed machinations, al-Hakim set about his destructive order.[98] Both accounts seem far-fetched and the purported missives from the West have not survived, if they even existed in the first place. Moreover, there are more proximate and likely causes for the destruction: either al-Hakim's independent plan to strengthen Shia Islam and also tamp down non-Muslim activity, or his unstable personality. Al-Maqrizi's explanation concerns the so-called Holy Fire, the spontaneous sparking of a candle in the sepulchre church at Easter, a miracle still upheld as legitimate by Orthodox Christian believers today.[99] One of the caliph's commanders, Khatkin, told him details about the annual, idolatrous event, at which point al-Hakim ordered the destruction of the church. He ordered his chancery clerk to order a local *da'i* to carry out the deed.[100]

But there is more. Famously, the Roman pontiff of the day, Pope Sergius IV (d. 1012) responded to the event with a letter to the Christian faithful of the West. He reported the news of the sepulchre's destruction and expressed his desire to go to war with the eastern Muslims, to lead an Italian army to the Levant and "kill them all and restore the holy tomb of the redeemer." The authenticity of Sergius's letter has been debated hotly, but if it is real then we see in it elements of a nascent crusading idea nearly a century before the First Crusade commenced in 1096.[101] The letter performs other functions by postulating the inherent evilness of both Judaism and Islam and, by comparison, the peaceful, saving message of Christianity. Both Ademar and Glaber riff on related eschatological themes: that End Times were not far away and al-Hakim was the Antichrist, to whom Jews flocked in the false belief that he was their awaited Messiah.[102]

Thus al-Hakim's destruction of the sepulchre church became a crystallization event in the history of western medieval Christianity. In it, Jews and Muslims were lumped together in an evil collabora-tion, one that portended the end of the world and the Final Judgment. The effect was striking: it brought about a sea-change in Christian–Jewish relations in the West, where social and legal restrictions on Jews grew more common as propaganda about their purported conspiracies in Jerusalem spread. Physical attacks upon European Jewry also increased in size and scope, with a brace of them occurring in the same period of 1007–1012.[103]

Stepping back, however, it seems that a remarkable—and likely unintentional—perversion of a complicated interfaith situation had occurred. The eastern sources, which we should prefer for details of these events, position al-Hakim as a persecutor of Christians, Sunni Muslims, and Jews. He was reviled by many, and his messianic claims rang hollow across the Levant. Yet his trail of destruction was inter-preted in the West as exactly the opposite of reality: he had conspired with Jews to only oppress Christians, and European writers claimed him not as the *Mahdi* who would destroy the Antichrist but rather the Antichrist himself. Of course, Ademar, Glaber, and Sergius were not reading the accounts of Elias of Nisibis, Yahya of Antioch, or John Skylitzes but rather learned of current events via the reports of returning pilgrims amid the winds of rumor and speculation. What we have, then, is a situation in which a widely lamented event was interpreted in radically different ways, and later remembered differently on the basis of what everyone presumed to be the accurate retelling. As the Benedictine writer Guibert of Nogent would note later in his version of Pope Urban II's eventual call for a crusade: "For it is clear that the Antichrist makes war neither against Jews, nor against pagans . . . he will move against Christians."[104]

In the wake of al-Hakim's transgressions, which offended essentially everyone in the affected areas, efforts were made to repair both structures and interfaith relations. Some repairs of the sepulchre church took place in 1012, including the *aedicule* ("little shrine") under the cupola that contained the resurrection tomb. This project was paid for by none other than al-Hakim's mother.[105] Eight years later, the shrine was placed under a formal edict of protection by the local ruler of Palestine, a Bedouin emir named al-Muffarig ibn al-Garrah. If al-Hakim objected to the actions of either subordinates or family members, he did not have time to dispute them for he mysteriously disappeared into the Egyptian desert in 1021, never to return.[106] Negotiations between al-Hakim's successor, al-Zahir, and the Byzantine emperor Romanos III enabled further repairs.[107] These were delayed by the earthquake of 1033–1034, which John Skylitzes claimed "shook for forty days."[108] The quake destroyed many other churches in the city, but by 1048 the rotunda and portico court of the sepulchre church had been rebuilt and the church formally rededicated. In the meantime, evidently there were continuing Christian pilgrimages to the city. Fulk Nerra, the count of Anjou, made four separate trips, two before 1009 and two after, and some believers (including Fulk) acquired stones from the destroyed church structure and brought them back to Europe.[109] Of the repairs, only the rotunda would survive the improvements made by crusaders after the fall of Jerusalem in 1099. Yet its design, albeit temporary, nonetheless managed to influence ecclesiastical structures in the

West in Cambridge and Bologna.[110] Several other churches around Jerusalem were rebuilt in the same period, including the Holy Cross monastery.

The Fatimids and the Others

Turning to Fatimid–Jewish relations, a similar tale of rapprochement emerges in the wake of al-Hakim. On the one hand, there was considerable freedom of worship, and we know of major intellectual communities in Fustat, Jerusalem, Damascus, and Tiberias, where Jewish law was observed on a community level and Jewish schools continued to operate.[111] It was also a time of some religious innovation in Jerusalem in particular, with both Muslims and Jews introducing new rites and observances in what has been called a period of "religious creativity."[112] An interesting way of getting at the details is through the letters from the "Cairo Genizah" collection, which offer lenses into social disputes and reconciliations in these and other cities. While *genizah* typically refers to a depository for discarded prayer books, in the nineteenth century thousands of other sorts of documents were found in Egyptian storerooms in remarkable condition and have henceforth been maintained in the Taylor–Schechter collection at the University of Cambridge.[113]

These documents reveal a panoply of Jewish experience under Fatimid rule. In some places life seems to have been rather tranquil: in others, not so much. One text, the so-called "Egyptian Scroll," describes an incident in 1012 in Cairo, where a Jewish funeral procession erupted in violence. Death sentences were decreed summarily for 23 local Jews. However, their leaders appealed to Caliph al-Hakim, who investigated the matter personally and—in direct contradiction of his typical reputation for intolerance—altered the verdict. Upon discovering that Muslim witnesses had lied about the transpiring events, al-Hakim commuted the sentences and ordered the Jews released.[114] In contrast, a letter from the Jewish community in

Ascalon, dated to 1025, speaks favorably of the governor there and his treatment of them thereof.[115] Pilgrimage of Jews between cities in the Levant remained widespread, and overall, as S.D. Goitein has found, the *genizah* letters do not suggest displeasure with Fatimid rule during the early eleventh century.[116]

This Ascalon missive also makes reference to a group of Jewish Karaites, or those who recognize only the written *Tanakh* (books of the "Old Testament" but in a different order) and not the oral Torah (the *Tanakh* as well as scripture explained in subsequent works such as the Talmud).[117] There was a great deal of strife between these Karaites and the Rabbanites (oral Torah adherents) in Jerusalem at the time, not only related to theological dispositions but also on account of accusations that the Rabbanites were violating the Sabbath, utilizing Muslim courts, and even dabbling in witchcraft. Caught in the middle was Solomon ben Judah, the *gaon* of the *yeshiva* (academy) in Jerusalem who was still negotiating the dispute 10 years later in 1035.[118]

Several of the *genizah* documents concern Solomon and his counterpart in Fustat, Ephraim ben Schemariah. These conversations center on the related issues of authority and finance. Both men confronted challenges to their authority: Ephraim from the envy of Samuel Hakohen ben Abtalion, which led to some intense splintering of the Jewish community in Fustat in the 1020s,[119] and Solomon from a rival, Nathan ben Abraham, who set himself up as a challenger in Ramla and busied himself soliciting Jews in Egypt for support.[120] For his part, Solomon begged Ephraim to settle affairs with his rivals, not only for the relief of the community in Egypt but also for the benefit of the academy in Jerusalem. Here the financial matters intertwine: the Jerusalem Jews were apparently burdened by debts levied by the Fatimid governor, for which some had even been imprisoned. This time, continuing leadership strife in Egypt stymied potential fundraising there for Jerusalem's relief, and Solomon reveals that his own son, Abraham, had been caught up in the mess in Cairo and needed to return home.[121] The nature of these debts is disclosed in another letter from the previous year, 1024, which details the tax and also the petitions by that community to the Fatimid governor for relief.[122] Solomon notes generous donations to the Jerusalem community by the Jewish community in Old Cairo, to the tune of over 29 dinars, 20 of which went to pay off debts in the year 1030.[123]

It seems that these petitioners to the Fatimid governor in 1024 included not only Jews but Muslims and possibly even a Christian. This, and other similar documentation, complicates the social picture, which was not simply a binary and antagonistic *dhimmitude*.[124] One fascinating *genizah* document relates a legal matter, in which a Jewish woman was suspected of sleeping with a Christian doctor: her frequent visits to his office led three Muslim stalkers to alert the authorities. Upon further review, they discovered she was simply seeking to escort him to a remote patient.[125] A comparative case elsewhere indicates that Jerusalem was not an outlier in this regard. In 1050, local Arabs seized control of Damascus and enacted several anti-Jewish stipulations: heavy taxes, and prohibitions on using city wells and the kosher slaughtering of livestock. In response, the Jews sent messengers to the caliph in Cairo, al-Mustansir Billah, seeking redress, which they promptly got. However, Haydara, the new Fatimid governor, threw the caliph's letter away and only agreed to relax the new rules upon payment of a bribe, which was duly handed over.[126]

Such incidents give credence to our argument: that the religious strife in Jerusalem in the tenth and eleventh centuries was predominantly internal and not the result of military conquest. Moreover, the condition of the Jews suggests yet another angle of rough tolerance. It is clear that they were an important element of the city's economy and probably a vital one at that. Jewish connections to the Diaspora (including their own relatives) played key roles in Fatimid trade, so much so that they worked with Muslims "to their mutual advantage."[127] In other respects, Jewish and Muslim rites had enough in common that they respectively flourished in the city. And while conversion between religions were technically forbidden by Fatimid law, such events did happen at the individual level, and perhaps at a greater rate than commonly imagined.[128]

In a similar vein, al-Hakim's strains against the Christians resemble those against the Jews: anomalies, breaks from the status quo agreement that reached back to 'Umar and were thereafter reaffirmed in 1020. More typical was the steady governance of the Fatimid vizier al-Jarjara'i, who had emerged from deadly bureaucratic infighting to become the prime mover of caliphal affairs between 1028 and 1045. In other respects, renewed Byzantine incursions into Syria dictated the peace, and these had allowed Romanos III to negotiate the sepulchre repairs in the first place.[129] To a large extent, conditions in the city were guided by Fatimid–Byzantine economic and political relations. For example, in 1056 Caliph al-Mustansir ordered 3,000 Christians expelled from Jerusalem and the sepulchre church locked, whereupon its treasures were looted by Fatimid officials. This shocking event was not precipitated by deteriorating interfaith relations however, but rather by the Byzantine inability to supply Egypt with grain as promised by treaty.[130]

Other events are probably more indicative of al-Mustansir's personal attitudes towards Christians. One was the German pilgrimage of 1064–1065. In those years, raiders intercepted thousands of travelers from the western Empire as they moved south en masse along the Levantine coast. The caliph ultimately rescued them with a relief army sent from Ramla. He gave them rest and then escorted the survivors to Jerusalem, where they spent two weeks before finally returning to the west via ship.[131] Before that, merchants who had arrived from Amalfi received properties in the Christian Quarter, around the sepulchre church, and residents eventually built a hospital in that district as well.[132]

Of course, anomalies are not meaningless. The suffering of the city's residents under al-Hakim was very real and the destruction significant. Still, a generation after his depredations Jerusalem had returned to its old, bustling self. The famous Bactrian poet and philosopher Nasir Khusraw, whose works are still actively read today, chanced to visit the city in 1047 and wrote a memorable description of it in his book *Safarnama*, the book of travels. He claims Jerusalem's population sat at about 20,000, living among tall churches and pleasant bazaars. Each year, thousands of Muslims went there annually for family circumcisions—Shia, Sunni, and even Sufis had their own mosque at the northern end of the Temple Mount—but Christians and Jews visited the churches and synagogues there, too, and from a variety of locales.[133] There was always a tension, of course, between balancing the needs of the Muslim population against those of rival faiths, but in the meantime, actions like those of al-Mustansir reveal more tolerance between individuals of the three Abrahamic faiths during the Fatimid period than not.[134]

The Turkish Onslaught

Below the surface, however, the city was on a path of steady economic decline. Bouts of famine in Egypt, from whence the Levant received much of its grain, and regional disease outbreaks were real problems in the early eleventh century. While urban activity in Jerusalem continued, as noted by Nasir, the built environment took a beating from accidents and natural phenomena. The Dome of the Rock's cupola collapsed in 1016–1017, with reconstruction not beginning until 1032. Work on the city walls commenced at about the same time, in early 1033, with a new line in the south that pulled back from the Kidron Valley. Ronnie Ellenblum argued that this indicates both a shrinking population and a realization that the old circuit's circumference was simply too big to defend. This meant that Mount Zion was now outside the southern defenses (it remains outside the walls of the Old City today), and builders stripped away stones from its churches for the new fortifications.[135] Subsequent to these projects, the earthquake of 1033–1034 struck and took its toll on the sepulchre church, as noted; then, during Passover in 1034 a nine-meter section of the city wall collapsed for no discernible reason. The building was thus interrupted, and work was suspended again in the 1050s, with the result being that the new walls were not finished until 1063.[136]

Meanwhile, in other Muslim circles the winds of war continued swirling in the mid-eleventh century. As historians of the period know well, there was no appreciable Muslim unity in the mid-to-late eleventh century. Arabs of different persuasions, some in Egypt and others in Iraq and Syria, routinely fought each other; the Turks descended from the north and made various alliances with both, and numerous other lesser actors drew the attention of the leading powers.[137] One threat emerged in Algeria, where the Fatimids embarked on a 10-year war with the Zirgid dynasty.[138] Another, more problematic, contest was in the east. The father and son Abbasid caliphs in Baghdad, al-Qadir Bi'llah and al-Qa'im bi-amri Allah, successively sponsored the martial exertions of the Ghaznavids. These were *mamluks*, or slave warriors, who had served under the Sunni rulers of Iran, the Samanids. Al-Qa'im granted the Ghaznavid general Mas'ud governance over what lands he could conquer, and the Fatimid domains sat squarely within the sights of his Turkish and Afghan army. Unfortunately for Mas'ud, another Sunni army was surging south at the same time: the Seljuk Turks, who defeated him at the Battle of Dandanqan in 1040.[139] Following the loss, Mas'ud—a man of legendary generosity who once donated a thousand dirhams to a poet for every verse he could muster—came to an untimely end when rivals threw him into a well and then sealed it up, burying him alive.[140]

The follow-up to the Ghaznavid losses was a full-scale invasion of the Near East by the Seljuks under the leadership of their two first leaders, Tughrul Beg and Alp Arslan.[141] The former systematically worked his way through targeted regions, starting in 1049 with Diyar Bakr (provinces in Upper Mesopotamia), where he defeated his cousin Ibrahim Yinal in battle and siege. Afterward, in what would become his standard policy, Tughrul had his name pronounced in the *khutba* there, thus demonstrating his authority to the people. The same sequence of events then played out in Isfahan (central Iran) in 1050–1051, Baghdad in 1055, and Tikrit in 1057, after which he marched on Mosul.[142] Yet Tughrul's grip on Baghdad was still too slight. There, a commander of Turkish slave soldiers, al-Basairi, favored Shia interests and emerged as a rival to both Tughrul and the Abbasid vizier, Ibn Muslima.[143]

The hits came quickly. In 1057, Tughrul withdrew to northern Mesopotamia to resupply his army and his enemies struck. First, al-Basairi, funded by the Fatimid caliph, moved north from Basra and entered Baghdad, where the *khutba* was said for his benefactor. Then, al-Basairi funded a revolt among the sultan's Turkish troops and sponsored Ibrahim Yinal to lead it.[144] Tughrul deployed his family to defeat these incursions. His brother, Chagril Beg, had been ruling the eastern portions of the Seljuk domains in central Asia, and now his children became instrumental in the shifting political and military tides. In 1056, Chagril's daughter married al-Qa'im, and in the next year Tughrul turned to her brother, Alp Arslan, for military assistance. In due course he destroyed Ibrahim's forces and then dispatched Ibrahim himself (Alp's first cousin, once removed) by strangling him with a bowstring.[145]

Tughrul Beg died in 1063 without an heir, and so a scrum between his male relatives immediately broke out. It would be his nephew, Sultan Alp Arslan, who emerged victorious and went on to become even more consequential than his uncle. His victory over a Byzantine army at the Battle of Manzikert in 1071 is justly famous and, perhaps, of world-historical proportions. There, the Byzantine army of Emperor Romanos IV Diogenes was cut down by the Seljuks, laying bare the Anatolian highlands for exploitation and precipitating a political crisis in Constantinople. A traditional interpretation of these developments is that they led, along with the fall of numerous Byzantine cities in the 1080s and 1090s, to the "Call from the East":

Romanos's successor, Emperor Alexios Comnenos, requested military assistance from western magnates and also the papacy, which led to the First Crusade.

Much like Yarmuk long before it and Hattin well after, the story of the Battle of Manzikert has been told and retold ad nauseum and analyzed from most possible angles.[146] There is no need to do so again here, where a brief summary will suffice. The Byzantine army, numbering probably between 30,000 and 40,000 soldiers, advanced southeast from Theodosiopolis towards Manzikert, which lies just north of Lake Van in eastern modern-day Turkey. Before arriving, Romanos dispatched a portion of his force towards Khilat (modern-day Ahlat), effectively splitting his army in half, with the more seasoned troops departing towards this secondary objective.[147] He then advanced on the citadel at Manzikert, which appears to have been taken with an independent assault by his Armenian allies.[148]

As John Haldon has explained, well-led Byzantine forces in the mid-eleventh century could be quite capable, but logistical problems and the too-heavy armament of infantry and cavalry proved detrimental. Increasingly a motley collection of militias, mercenaries, full-time regiments (*tagmatas*), and other levees, retainers, and allies, the army had neither the flexibility to match Turkish operational movement and maneuver nor the tactics to reliably engage the masses of enemy light cavalry.[149] The Turks surprisingly arrived outside of Manzikert and repulsed three successive advances of a Byzantine column on the first day of fighting. On the second day, both armies formed ranks and the Byzantines advanced, but the Turks utilized feigned retreats to goad their enemies forward into clouds of arrows. Romanos ordered a retreat, but the Turks attacked his flanks, broke through the right wing, and collapsed the center of the Byzantine army. In the ensuing rout, they killed thousands and captured the emperor himself.[150]

The memory of Manzikert lived on in the Arab world. Poetry celebrated the occasion, which, despite having been ushered in by foreign Turks, was still a signal event in the glorification of mighty deeds against the Byzantines.[151] Much later, other writers interpreted the battle as the first step in the grand effort to expel Christians from the Near East.[152] In practical terms, the victory had lasting effects in territorial acquisition and a corresponding breakdown of Byzantine military and political assumptions regarding their regional security. The Seljuks steadily gained control of border lands as they moved westward. The continuator of the Skylitzes chronicle lamented that, "from this point on, the offspring of Hagar raided the east with impunity and did not cease from ransacking and looting this region day by day."[153] Much of Anatolia had been lost by 1081; the rest largely fell in the decade after.

Alp Arslan did not survive long past this capital success. The Mosul writer Ibn al-Athir provides an account of what can only be described as his pathetic death. One day, the sultan presided over the execution of a captured garrison commander, Yusuf, who dared to denounce him for cowardice as he was being tied to stakes. The proud sultan ordered him released, presumably to meet a more fitting death: but Yusuf then seized the incredible opportunity and hurtled forward in rage. Alp Arslan managed to discharge a single arrow, which missed its target, then ran to attack the prisoner but tripped while coming down from the throne. Yusuf fell on him, stabbing furiously before one of Alp Arslan's servants finally smashed the attacker's head in with a mace. The sultan died soon after from his wounds.[154]

Jerusalem Falls Twice More

Alp Arslan's death led to yet another succession dispute, following which his son, Malikshah, took his place. And it was during Sultan Malikshah's reign that Jerusalem came under attack yet again. The new sultan enabled the militant activities of Turkish generals active in Syria, Mesopotamia, and Arabia: Atsiz Beg and Artuq Beg, two men who would successively capture and then govern the city. In the process, Fatimid-held Jerusalem would fall not once but twice more in rapid succession, the second event featuring a massacre of its garrison *à la* the Persian siege of 614.

In a technical sense, the Fatimids did not wage the struggle against the Turks. The formative rule of al-Jarjara'i set a precedent of powerful viziers who swiftly became the real rulers of the caliphate. A series of detrimental developments led to this change: famines due to low flows of the River Nile, an increasing dependence on Byzantium for grain, and infighting in the Fatimid army ranks between Turks and black African slave soldiers. The latter had become an increasingly potent force, and in the early eleventh century a training school for them opened in Cairo. Along with the Turks, Armenians, and different free-born Berber groups, they formed a component of a very heterodox Fatimid army, which Yaacov Lev has described as a conglomerate of corps differing by specialization, ethnicity, free–slave status, and their loyalty to particular commanders or political leaders.[155]

This leads us back to the reign of Caliph al-Mustansir, who we have already seen protecting the German pilgrims from Turkish raids. The infighting among his army ranks eventually grew beyond his control. His mother, Sayyida Rasad, actually played a formative role in the development of the black contingents. A woman of sub-Saharan African origin, she grew their ranks by tens of thousands via aggressive recruiting. In 1062, however, a certain inebriated Turk encountered a group of them while stumbling through the streets of Cairo. He drew his sword, likely muttered some choice insults, and thus met a predictably sudden end. The incident sparked a virtual civil war between army factions, and thousands of blacks were cut down by Turkish soldiers at the Battle of Qum Rush the next year. This did nothing to settle the issue: Rasad recruited ever more numbers and the interservice rivalries remained.[156]

Needing a better hand to counter both his mother's machinations and the persistent hostilities, in 1073 al-Mustansir solicited the aid of the powerful governor of Acre, Badr al-Jamali. He arrived with an army of Armenian soldiers, was named vizier, ended the factionalism, and thereafter enforced a harsh policy of law and order.[157] Successive military viziers took up this mantle, and as a result the practical workings of the Fatimid state were guided by outsiders, with the caliphs—though still critical spiritual figures—reduced to mere figureheads in a political sense.[158]

In the meantime, Jerusalem fell to the Turks under the command of Atsiz Beg, a Khwarazmian (Turco-Persian) general. As with the Fatimid capture of the city in the 970s, we are once again—and remarkably so, for a city of such prominence as this—ignorant of the exact date Atsiz took it. Vague references in the source material have led to all sorts of different conclusions. In broad strokes, Atsiz seems to have initiated a siege in either 1070 or 1071. This was likely a far blockade, with Turks posted well outside the city gates to control ingress and egress. The Fatimid garrison resisted for a time until its commander (who was Turkish) surrendered on the condition that Jerusalem not be sacked. This occurred anywhere between 1071 and 1073 and seems to have been relatively bloodless; indeed, Atsiz himself was thereafter hired by the Fatimids to suppress some local Bedouin antagonisms.[159] The siege, then, can be reasonably compared to 'Umar's conquest in 638: some sporadic garrison resistance seems likely, but the city surrendered when it became apparent that no hope for succor was imminent. The city was now firmly in Turkish (and Sunni) hands, and in 1075, the *khutba* was said in Jerusalem in the name of the Abbasid caliph, al-Muqtadi.[160]

The next developments were decidedly bloodier. Atsiz set off on an attempted invasion of Egypt but did not stay there long. Screened by Badr's large army patrolling the Nile, which enjoyed resupply from his fleet, the Turks avoided battle but lost sizable numbers of soldiers to desertion while wandering through the desert. At length, Atsiz elected to engage Badr's Armenians but was defeated at Fustat.[161] Retiring to the east, Atsiz apparently got word that some

Jerusalemites had revolted and imprisoned his family in the Tower of David, the massive citadel guarding the city's western wall.[162] He therefore returned to the city, rescued his relatives, and massacred a portion of its population, usually pegged at the round number of 3,000.[163] This second entrance into Jerusalem occurred in either 1077 or 1078 (although confusion clearly reigns because scholars have occasionally placed it in 1073).[164]

Two principal questions spring to mind: how did Atsiz get into the city, and who did he kill there? His combat power had been massively reduced during the Egyptian campaign and his army probably numbered no more than five thousand by the time he retreated.[165] He could not have blockaded the entire city and probably concentrated his forces against a single gate to gain entry. Who did Atsiz kill within the city walls? Ibn al-Athir's account seems to suggest they were primarily Muslims: "Large numbers were killed, even those who had taken refuge in the Aqsa Mosque and the Haram. He spared only those who were in the Dome of the Rock."[166] One can imagine the defenders fleeing as the Turks breached the city gate, and making a last stand on top of the defensible Temple Mount makes sense.

There is a chance, of course, that members of the minority faiths took up arms to oppose the Turkish attack, although it is more likely that Muslims defended the city. Christians at that point resided exclusively in the northwest quarter. Following the earthquake in 1033–1034, they were expected to finance repairs in their sector; the Byzantine emperor agreed to pay for these but negotiations with the Fatimids stipulated that the quarter could be internally fortified provided that Christians lived within—and only within—it. Jews, meanwhile, resided in the northeast quarter, outside the walls of the Temple Mount.[167] If Muslims held the city against him, these demographic placements mean that Atsiz probably entered through the city's western gate, by the Tower of David, and pursued the defenders eastward to the Temple Mount. Moreover, since the Turks ultimately spared those hiding in the Dome of the Rock, we might assume these were only Muslims, as surely non-Muslims encroaching on such a holy site would have been cut down, especially in the heat of battle.[168]

An oft-referenced account of this second Turkish siege is that of the poet Solomon ben Joseph ha-Kohen, who wrote a verse commentary on the attacks in Egypt that utilized both sieges as reference points. As one of just a few Hebrew war poems retelling actual military events (and likewise unique as a Hebrew account praising the Muslim commander, Badr), it is certainly an interesting text.[169] Solomon spoke of the judgment of God upon the Turks for what they had done:

> He also remembered what they had done to the people of
> Jerusalem,
> That they besieged them twice in two years,
> And burned the heaped corn and destroyed the places,
> And cut down the trees and trampled upon the vineyards,
> And surrounded the city upon the high mountains,
> And despoiled the graves and threw out the bones,
> And built palaces, to protect themselves against the heat,
> And erected an altar to slay upon it the abominations . . .[170]

We need not read this passage literally to gain a sense of the destruction. It really only speaks to the first phases of the siege: a general ravaging of the landscape as the Turks arrived and set up their small blockade. The second phase, the entry into the city and the tactics employed there, goes unmentioned, as does the third phase in which the garrison was wiped out. We should also be hesitant of presuming massive damage to the built environment inside the walls. This appears to have been a very bloody but nondestructive affair in which the last vestiges of resistance to Turkish rule were finally eradicated; once again, the *khutba* was said in Jerusalem in the name of the Abbasid caliph al-Muqtaqi.[171]

Whatever the carnage, Atsiz had little time to savor the fruits of his victory. In either the same year or the next (1077–1078), Badr dispatched the Egyptian army to Damascus. In desperation, Atsiz called for aid from a political rival, the emir Tutush, one of the sons of Alp Arslan. Tutush agreeably moved his forces there but upon arriving seized Atsiz and executed him.[172] A later, anonymous Turkish chronicle notes that Tutush "behaved very properly" in this act.[173] For the moment, Jerusalem essentially existed in a political no-man's land.

The tumult of the 1070s apparently induced many Jews and Muslims to leave Jerusalem for more favorable climes. In that decade, a Shafi'i sheikh moved his law school (*madhab*) to Tyre, in modern-day Lebanon, and according to *genizah* documents persuaded the Rabbanite Yeshiva to follow suit. As a result, the bulk of Jerusalem's Jewish population left the city. A much smaller Karaite community was now all that remained.[174]

At this point, Alp Arslan's other former general, Artuq Beg, entered the picture.[175] He had fought not only for the famous victor at Manzikert but also for his son, the sultan Malikshah, and he moved towards the Levantine coast. The history of the well-traveled trustee Ibn al-Azraq (d. 1176), who was located in Damascus for the later part of his life, offers a sparing account. Artuq was in the service of Tutush, and he entered Jerusalem and became its governor on the latter's behalf, also supervising affairs in the surrounding area. Upon his death, Artuq was succeeded in this role by his sons.[176] This was the beginning of the Artuqid Dynasty, which lasted well into the thirteenth century but only held onto Jerusalem until 1098. In that year, the Fatimids, down but not out, returned in a show of force that would surprise the principal actors in both East and West.

Headlines in the West

Meanwhile, these and other Turkish affairs had become known back in the West. Despite the Battle of Manzikert in 1071 and Atsiz's first capture of Jerusalem thereafter, Christian visitors and pilgrims had still been able to visit the Holy City. Knowledge about affairs in the East could sometimes be scarce, but important elements of current events nonetheless flowed into Rome in the 1070s, where Pope Gregory VII (d. 1085) took a keen interest.[177] An embassy from the Byzantine emperor arrived in Rome in the summer of 1073 and reported the Turkish threat in Anatolia, proposing a military alliance to combat it.[178]

In a well-known intellectual prelude to the formal crusade at the end of the century, Gregory began to contemplate the notion of military assistance in the East. Yet it was only the latest in a series of such contemplations. We have already mentioned the letter of Sergius IV: to that can be added, at least, the appearance of sacred war banners and an early "crusading" indulgence in the army amassed against the Normans by Pope Leo IX at the Battle of Civitate in 1053.[179] One historian has likewise emphasized the importance of the Treaty of Melfi in 1059, in which Pope Nicholas II encouraged their reconquest of Sicily from whoever held it, including presumably the Muslims there. Such muscle flexing was regarded by the Mosul historian Ibn al-Athir as a seemingly deliberate sequence designed to defeat Islam writ large.[180]

Gregory's attitude towards affairs in the East is only somewhat revealed by documents in the papal registry. They indicate a growing perception of the need to defend both Byzantium and the Holy Land. In some letters to European leaders, he solicited personnel for a possible military expedition.[181] One letter from Gregory, dated to 27 November 1073, refers to a recent visit to Jerusalem by Isimbard, the abbot of Saint-Lomer (near Chartres), but makes no mention of any reported violence there or even unsettled affairs.[182]

In the following year Gregory's tone increased in severity. In a letter from March 1074, he wrote of the increased pressure of the Seljuks upon Byzantium, of which he had learned from a contact who had "visited the threshold of the apostles." The letter is not so much about Jerusalem as the general state of affairs at and around Constantinople, where the Turks had "slaughtered like cattle many thousands of Christians."[183] Thereafter, his fears ebbed and flowed as 1074 moved on. By September, Gregory had concluded that the Byzantines had improved their position and no longer needed western aid; in December, however, he changed his mind again.[184] Writing to Emperor Henry IV, who was to become his bitter foe during the Investiture Controversy, the pope repeated some of his lamentations and added new concerns.[185] The letter references Armenia, interesting because he may have received a personal visit from the Armenian patriarch Gregory II ("the Traveler") that same year.[186] Gregory now feared the extirpation of whole Christian communities and made the extraordinary offer to personally lead an army of 50,000 soldiers "as far as the sepulchre of the Lord."[187] Here then, Jerusalem firmly enters the equation.

What had changed in the Holy City during 1073–1074? Nothing so dramatic as to raise a pontiff's anxiety to fever pitch. It was in Turkish hands but had been surrendered, as we have seen, without a sack. Valuable research by Shimon Gat has transformed our understanding of life in the city while under this early Turkish rule: far from being a den of suffering, it was (with the exception of the 1077 revolt) peaceful and secure, economically prosperous, and active and diverse in terms of religious worship. Latin sources of the First Crusade, which have been utilized heavily to comment on life in Jerusalem before the western warriors arrived, erroneously describe the situation there as oppressive to Christians. The situation was actually the opposite.[188] And shortly after Atsiz's vengeance, the new church of St. Mary Major arose south of the sepulchre and was dedicated in 1080.[189]

If we reconsider his letters, Gregory VII's animus in the 1070s was based on much hearsay and seems to have been more intense against the Seljuks than the Muslim rulers in Sicily.[190] Because affairs in Jerusalem had been relatively quiet after Atsiz's first conquest, he was thinking primarily of Seljuk depredations against Christians in Asia Minor.[191] His was a general sense of foreboding rather than a targeted response to a threat to the Holy City in particular. He was partially prescient in such thinking, for the Turks did indeed move swiftly across Asia Minor and, starting in the 1080s, western magnates now knew the situation was dire. The Armenian Gregory II appealed again to Rome, this time in a letter, seeking military assistance against the Turks.[192] Moreover, Alexios Comnenos had been personally, and actively, communicating news of the travails while planting the seeds for his eventual call for assistance. One by one Byzantine strongholds fell: Nicaea in 1081, Antioch in 1085, Cappadocia in 1090, Nicomedia in 1094, and the entire western Anatolian coastline by 1094.[193]

That said, it was Gregory's sense of events on the ground that is important. Sense overrode reality and continues to do so today. The general threat of the Turkish conquest notwithstanding, the caliphal grip on Jerusalem up to the 1070s and beyond was not close to the caricature presented in the West during the eleventh century. There was no consistent theme of anti-Christian, anti-Jewish, or even anti-Sunni or Shia oppression. Like many other premodern cities in the Near East, it had experienced periods of unrest, uncertainty, and local strife, but these headlines, despite their exceptional nature, were understood as a ubiquitous part of life.

Pointing to individual events as evidence of interfaith strife in the Fatimid and Artuqid periods can therefore be misleading. Jerusalem experienced revolts in 842 and 938, but in their midst travelers and pilgrims still visited the city and marveled at its unique buildings and features. The burning of the sepulchre church and murder of Patriarch John in 966 was shocking, but we can easily miss that he had called for aid from both Muslim and Christian powers for what was, essentially, a dispute with the local governor. That development was followed by a bloodless Shia conquest of the Sunni-held city, and the church was repaired within a decade of the patriarch's death.

Thereafter, the *genizah* letters reveal the contours of a pluralistic society. Although it is true that the heinous activities of al-Hakim at the turn of the first millennium were destructive in many ways to adherents of all three Abrahamic faiths, they were aberrations lamented by nearly everyone. Later in his reign, Jerusalemites swiftly rebuilt interfaith agreements and set about a restoration. Finally, the Sunni retaking of the city in the 1070s was initially peaceful, with violence only coming with Atsiz's suppression of a Shia move against his family. Thereafter, the city returned to normal functioning.

What do these events tell us? In the main, the history of Jerusalem from the days of 'Umar to the First Crusade was one of social and religious pluralism. Tensions occasionally boiled over and led to violence, but these incidents were nearly always caused by local issues of taxation and governance rather than the killing of people in the name of a particular religion or confession. Western Christians read the Turkish march through Anatolia as a series of campaigns against Christendom itself, but in the Holy City the walls kept most of that noise at bay. Christians, Jews, Muslims, and others continued to work and pray alongside each other in a cosmopolitan environment only periodically interrupted by strife and division.[194] In other words, modern believers in the notion that Jerusalem's history, or medieval history in general, is a tale of eternal religious strife in a grand clash of civilizations should beware of hasty generalizations.

ANKLE-DEEP BLOOD
1098 AND 1099

So far, this book has argued that the broad history of medieval Jerusalem from the seventh through the eleventh centuries was not one of interfaith conflict. It will continue to make this argument through the remaining chapters, which will take us to the end of the thirteenth century. Such a position goes against most modern sensibilities, which tend to conflate Jerusalem and the region around it as one story of never-ending religious strife.

This misconception is not entirely without historical foundation. In a general sense, there were obviously animosities between different faith confessions throughout the Middle Ages, not only in the Near East but in North Africa and Europe as well. Those histories are deep and complex.[1] Violence between Jews, Christians, and Muslims certainly manifested in and around Jerusalem itself, as has been shown. However, in that particular urban center, physical conflict was highly episodic and not the dominant theme, nor anywhere close to being so. Long stretches of time—years and decades—regularly elapsed without major catastrophes or controversies, and those that did occur, such as under al-Hakim, were swiftly recognized by all parties as aberrant and followed by restorative measures. Other incidents, like the murder of Patriarch John or the elimination of the Jerusalem garrison in 1077, were the result of fleeting local disputes, not between whole governments or faith communities but rather individual generals, charismatic leaders, or politicians.

It is perhaps human nature, however, to focus almost exclusively on the exceptional events, and the phenomenon of negativity bias is very real.[2] And in this vein, there is one elephant in the room, a single event universally remembered for its viciousness and lingering effect on memories of Jerusalem's place in the history of violence and warfare: the First Crusade (1096–1099). We cannot help but be fascinated by this episode's complexity and notorious elements. The enduring impression of the event on modern memories of the past comes not from its calling, nor its progress, nor its colorful antagonists. Rather, we most commonly recall with horror the First Crusade's conclusion, the brutal massacres in Jerusalem on 15–17 July 1099. In their wake, the crusaders expelled all surviving Muslims and Jews from the city and, for a time, prohibited their return. Sometimes dubbed the "original sin" of the Crusades, the event seems an irrefutable retort to any portrayal of tolerance in the medieval city. This chapter will argue, however, that it was actually a tragic exception that proves the rule.

I

There are degrees of familiarity with physical places. Jerusalem's Old City residents know the city intimately. Those who have personally visited it learn, to some degree, its streets and tunnels, its quarters and gates. Likewise, those who have traveled around modern-day Israel and the West Bank are familiar with the historical depths of the region, the idea that places of immense significance lie virtually everywhere one walks. But the familiarity drops steeply in the absence of direct experience: those peoples living in the Middle East but with no travel history in these places have a sense of the setting, but only just that. Indeed, it is not uncommon for visiting university students from elsewhere in the Middle East to ask with wonder about what Jerusalem is like, or Caesarea, or Nazareth, or Galilee. Despite their closer proximity as residents of, say, Kuwait, Iraq, or Saudi Arabia, many of these students have neither chanced to visit the city nor really thought about trying to do so in the face of confounding national travel regulations and restrictions.

We would do well to remember that the medieval world was much the same, as illustrated by the lived experiences of locals. For them, Jerusalem was a place with daily encounters and exchanges between people of different ethnicities and religions, a setting where life bustled and, for the vast majority of time, was as "normal" as any other comparable city in the Near East. Visitors like al-Maqdisi, Nasir Khusraw, or Benjamin of Tudela, on the other hand, offer fascinating outsider views in which we can read of their reactions and recollections of time spent there. But the bulk of the Near Eastern population visited neither Jerusalem nor its environs, so its relative familiarity was based on what people had heard or, in rare cases, had read. Even the great invasions within the four hundred years of history covered thus far (by the Persians, Arabs, Byzantines, and Turks) probably represented the first regional forays for most of the soldiers involved.

The armies of the First Crusade are a more extreme example of this unfamiliarity, given the sheer distance between the Levant and northwest Europe. A select few of their number had visited the Levant on pilgrimages, but for the vast majority it was an uncharted place encountered before only in stories, homilies, or scripture. And what a place it would have seemed! Attached to two manuscripts of an anonymous account of the campaign, the *Gesta Francorum* (Deeds of the Franks), is a pilgrim's guide to sites of interest in the wake of the Christian reopening of the region. In Jerusalem sat the houses of Hezekiah and Caiaphas; sites related to Abraham, Solomon, and

Zachariah; the mounts of the Temple, Olives, and Zion; and of course all the places related to Christ's trial, Crucifixion, and Resurrection. Away from the city awaited Zachaeus's tree; Elisha's spring; Mount Tabor, the site of the Transfiguration; the tombs of Isaiah, Jacob, and Lazarus; Bethlehem, Galilee, Jericho, and Hebron.[3] For devout Christians on a first trip to the region, the presence of so many Biblical sites must have been profound.

However, before experiencing such wonders, pilgrims and crusaders alike needed to reach Jerusalem alive. There is no need to offer yet another narrative of the First Crusade from the western perspective; doing so has been a bustling cottage industry for some time.[4] Instead, after commenting on the nature and motivation of the western armies, we will see how newsworthy events in the Levant add pertinent details to an already interesting campaign. What is needed is some sober analysis of the place of the massacres on the Temple Mount within the broad context of the city's history.

The Generation of the First Crusade

In the late eleventh century, Byzantium was under attack from the Seljuk Turks who, as we have noted, had obtained the bulk of important Anatolian cities and coastline between 1081 and 1094. In an escalating response to the threat, Alexios Comnenos petitioned western magnates for military assistance while simultaneously promising rewards and, to some, the possibility of recovering Jerusalem in the process.[5] He eventually directed his diplomatic onslaught towards Rome and the court of Pope Urban II. He found a willing partner: Urban gave a sermon urging a campaign to the East at the Council of Clermont in 1095 to western bishops, who thereafter returned to their dioceses and rallied volunteers for the martial enterprise.[6]

Voila!—supposedly the First Crusade was born. Inconveniently, this narrative is full of elements that deny straightforward explanations. As a result, the foundation of the First Crusade has been told, retold, and analyzed from nearly every conceivable angle. Likewise, it occupies a central place in all major books on the Crusades and is prominent in most surveys of medieval history in general.[7]

Several controversies and disputes surround the generation of the First Crusade, including why it was ordered and what it was, exactly: a holy war, or a new type of holy war, and if so, how new and what type? What was Urban trying to do through his sermon: continue a long-running fight against Islam, fashion an army that could aid Byzantium, defend eastern Christians, recover the Holy City, or a combination of these aims? Going further, what constitutes a "crusade" (a name that arose centuries later) in the first place, and what is the history and theology of its constituent parts? Finally, why did Christians volunteer for the crusade: did their motivations match or depart from Urban's, why or why not, and why does it matter?

As it turns out, discerning the exact reasons why western Christians pledged themselves to a holy war, sewing crosses upon their tunics and becoming *crucesignati* (those signed with the cross), is not so simple.[8] Alas, there seems to have been no single driver for the war. Historians have located multiple causes for participation that are endlessly debated at academic conferences, online, and in print. The spent ink has been prodigious, so much so that answering the simple question of "What caused the First Crusade?" now necessitates a ridiculously long and often convoluted answer. At this point, any scholar proclaiming a sole "reason" that it happened ought to be accused of historical malfeasance.

Two major grand explanations can be dispensed with at once for these were neither righteous Christian armies merely seeking to counter a creeping tide of Muslim *jihadist* aggression nor a barbaric Christian assault on an otherwise tranquil and peaceful Muslim world.[9] Both ideas are nonsense and speak more to the proclivities of their propagators than any historical reality. Blanket explanations and massive generalizations presume that crusaders marched for the exact themes in Urban's sermon (for which we have only testimonies, not an original copy), and there are numerous other possible motivations for the crusade, some more convincing than others.[10] A default position that often appears in more popular discussions is that the crusaders were seeking to enrich themselves. While perhaps a strong motivator for later expeditions, for the First Crusade material gain seems to have been lower on the pecking order of priorities—and once again, any argument for a single cause is suspect.[11] More spiritually attuned soldiers may have felt the need to take vengeance, performed in the name of God, to expel unbelievers from the Holy Land. This was likely not a dominant theme but certainly was a particular motivator for some.[12] To get closer to understanding the war's nature, then, a major emphasis in the literature has been on the people who were drawn to it.

The heritage of Christian pilgrimage was a significant factor. Pilgrims had visited Jerusalem for centuries, with occasional interruptions caused by violent episodes in the city or political interference such as during the reign of al-Hakim. These pilgrims continued doing so all the way up until the 1090s, with one known example actually coinciding with the First Crusade itself.[13] As an "armed pilgrimage," as many historians would dub the enterprise, the crusade was a devotional event of a different sort; William Purkis has called it an "apostolic activity," in which the pilgrim sells his belongings for campaign supplies, picks up his cross, and follows Christ to the Holy Land.[14] These pilgrims acted out of love and charity, sacrificing themselves in the defense of others in a "morally satisfying" venture.[15] Other participants looked back to past efforts in Sicily and Iberia for inspiration and attempted to match the deeds of forefathers there by journeying to the East.[16] Linked to this was Urban's offer of spiritual rewards to those who participated: that if they fought for God in penitence, they would merit the remission of sins. This is the so-called crusading indulgence: fighting for the Church was the same as saying penitential prayers after making a good Catholic confession, so crusading was deemed a meritorious activity.[17]

A general sacralization of warfare smoothed the path of those seeking to fight righteously for God. This phenomenon had deepened steadily since the fall of the western Roman Empire and especially the eighth century. Priests began to perform liturgical rites for armies, hearing confessions on campaign, consecrating war banners, blessing swords, and incorporating saints' relics into weapons and battle standards.[18] The papacy deliberately sponsored warfare, even in contests between Christians, with the two most famous examples being Leo IX watching his recruited army engage the Normans at Civitate and Pope Alexander II's banner flying above William the Conqueror's forces at the Battle of Hastings (1066).[19] However, with sponsorship came limitations. The various "Peace of God" and "Truce of God" movements in France in the tenth and eleventh centuries, in which bishops prohibited collateral damage and limited the days on which warfare could be conducted, are sometimes correlated with crusading opportunism. Given that soldiers seeking military action were stymied from doing so locally, the crusade offered a route to fighting abroad: thrill-seekers and the bored alike could follow Urban's call and ply their trade without episcopal restriction.[20]

Of course, Urban II was not the first pope to consider a military expedition East, and crusades studies are occasionally criticized for unduly obsessing over his sermon. As early as the tenth century, signs and indications appeared of Christian resistance to areas of Muslim occupation, and this is the history that Urban and his predecessors—Sergius IV and Gregory VII, among others—likely reflected upon.[21] Sergius was responding to events surrounding the destruction of the Church of the Holy Sepulchre which, as we have seen, led to the identification of al-Hakim as the Antichrist and the Jews as the pernicious enemies of Christ.[22] The physical setting and the timing both inspired apocalyptic expectations in some people—hopes of the approaching millennium of the year 1000 that, while perhaps not as intense as some have postulated, were nonetheless a very real element of the medieval outlook and partially had provoked great pilgrimages to the East in 1033 and 1064.[23]

So-called "popularist" interpretations seek to position this apocalyptic expectation as a prime motivator for the early crusaders. Gregory VII, like Urban, may have felt the need to defend Byzantium, but he was also responding to Turkish depredations in the Near East and sought to liberate the sepulchre from them. Pilgrims increasingly traveled to Jerusalem, including hordes of monks wishing to remain there and await the return of Christ and the descent of the "heavenly Jerusalem" above the earthly Jerusalem in fulfilment of the Book of Revelation. Western monastic communities increasingly associated their own houses with the city, and the divine office resounded with references to it.[24] Later, Urban may have hit upon apocalyptic themes in his Clermont sermon, and he viewed the Muslims as the necessary soldiers of the Antichrist, against whom Christian warriors must strive.[25] Three different, though linked, elements thus emerge: fear of the Antichrist, expectations of an approaching Final Judgment, and anti-Judaism, the latter of which manifested concretely in the Jewish pogroms in the Rhineland in 1096. These and other explanations and schools of thought have been well-explored in recent literature.

In the end, for the bulk of the participants on the First Crusade, it was all about Jerusalem.[26] Jerusalem was the single crystallizing element that brought all others together in 1095–1096. For those seeking vengeance, it was in Jerusalem that the Mad Caliph's destructive order had been carried out. For those with apocalyptic dispositions, it was where Christ would return, the Tau Cross would rise, and the heavenly Jerusalem would descend. For those seeking the return of formerly Christian lands, who perhaps modeled the future on past Iberian and Sicilian exploits, Jerusalem had been taken from Christians in 638 and was the place to which the Jews had surrendered any claims through their condemnation of Christ. For those seeking penance, spiritual rewards such as indulgences could be earned specifically on the road to Jerusalem; as the *Gesta Francorum* urges, "if any man, with all his heart and mind, really wanted to follow God and faithfully to bear the cross after him, he could make no delay in taking the road to the Holy Sepulchre as quickly as possible."[27] For those who crusaded out of love for God or neighbor, Jerusalem was an ideal location for the dispensing of charity. For the *militum Christi*, the preparatory sacralization of past years—army rites, blessings of sword and banners and campaigns, theories of Just War, the Truce of God—along with the urgings of long-gone occupants of St. Peter's chair, bolstered the legitimacy of the act; the heritage of pilgrimage smoothed the road to the same Levantine destination. For those of practical mindsets, it was Jerusalem that Alexios dangled as an incentive to the western magnates and Urban II, and the city figures prominently in every version of his sermon. Jerusalem was not the goal of every crusade or the sole animating force behind the phenomenon of "crusading" writ large, but in the late eleventh century it was the single element that cut through and clarified, that pierced the din of excitement and outrage, that gave meaning to an audacious plan to set right the state of the world.

Progress of the Crusades

Our interest here is not to retell the story of the First Crusade but rather to observe its progress from the vantage point of the East. While bishops preached the cross and the crusaders prepared and departed for their journey, some important events were taking place in the Levant. In the autumn of 1095, the famous Persian theologian al-Ghazali visited Jerusalem. It was during these travels that he finished his book, *The Revival of the Religious Sciences*, a massive text that united Sufi mysticism with Sunni practice in a comprehensive study of Muslim life and death. It became the most cited Islamic text after the Qur'an and *hadith*.[28] In those days, Jerusalem was still a pluralistic society. Despite the movement of the Rabbanite *yeshiva* and Shafi'i *madhab* to Tyre in the 1070s, plenty of religious activity remained in the Holy City. It hosted visiting religious scholars from all three Abrahamic faiths and had active communities of practitioners and busy schools. The account of a visiting Muslim scholar from Iberia, Ibn al-'Arabi, noted the existence of two *madrasas* and 28 circles of Muslim scholars there on the eve of the First Crusade—a vibrant community indeed. Al-'Arabi also speaks well of local Christians and does not suggest any persecution of them or of Jews.[29]

In the same year, the two sons of the Seljuk emir Tutush quarreled: Ridwan marched on Damascus, held by his brother Duqaq, but ultimately determined that he could not successfully besiege it. As a second option, he turned towards Jerusalem, held by the Artuqids. Ibn al-Athir relates that Ridwan was unable to capture the Holy City—no details are offered in his account, so we cannot know if Ridwan tried to take it and failed or, alternatively, if he judged it similarly impregnable as Damascus.[30] In any case, unbeknown to virtually everyone in the West, then and now, the Jerusalemites saw an army outside their gates in the same year Urban II was preaching his crusade.[31]

The brotherly conflict was not over. Duqaq assembled an army in response to Ridwan's aggression and moved towards Aleppo in the north. The two armies battled each other at Qinnasrin (southwest of Aleppo), and Ridwan's was defeated. Chastened and humbled, Ridwan supposedly consulted with an astrologer who, along with Egyptian envoys promising military aid against Duqaq, persuaded him to ally with the Fatimids. Consequently, Ridwan ordered the *khutba* said in the name of the Imam-caliph in certain portions of his lands.[32] This sparked a conflict with two local Turkish leaders, Yaghisiyan, the governor of Antioch, and Suqman, the lord of Jerusalem. Both were "outraged" by Ridwan's supplications to the Shia; cowed by their anger, he relented and sent apologies to the Abbasid caliph in Baghdad.[33] The incident provides a glimpse into the state of Shia–Sunni affairs on the eve of the First Crusade: some squabbling between Turkish leaders who sensed a need for unity against Egypt, which itself remained a potent political force that deliberately intervened in Levantine and Syrian affairs.

Despite these defeats and diplomatic blunders, in late 1096 Ridwan was still the master of Aleppo. He then made another fateful decision by consenting to release from captivity Kerbogha, one of the warlords who had been imprisoned by his father, Tutush. At the time, Kerbogha was landless; following his release, he hired a force of mercenaries and conquered the town of Harran. Thereafter, he marched on Mosul and took it by November.[34] In command of substantial forces, this Seljuk Turk was now, as it turns out, in an ideal position to thwart the southern movement of the crusaders.

And they were indeed on their way. 1096 was a busy year for the First Crusade and saw the arrival of the first group of western warriors at Constantinople. Alternatively dubbed the "Peasants' Crusade," the "People's Crusade," or, alternatively, the "first wave" of a coherent army deployed in phases, it numbered perhaps 20,000 people, inclusive of about 700 knights and a host of noncombatants.[35] Led across Europe in two separate columns by the minor lord Walter Sans-Avoir (often given as "Walter the Penniless") and the rabble-rousing priest Peter the Hermit, its participants made terrific progress, with some elements achieving a marching tempo of 29 kilometers a day.[36] The columns reached the Byzantine capital on 20 July and 1 August, respectively.[37] The warriors lodged outside in its suburbs, where they eventually grew bored and began rioting, so Alexios sent them into Anatolia where "in a little over ten weeks, they would almost all be dead or enslaved."[38] After committing a series of atrocities against local eastern Christians around Nicaea, some of them captured the castle of Xerigordos. However, they were promptly besieged within it and died there. Others engaged the forces of Sultan Kilij Arslan at the Battle of Civitot on 21 October and were destroyed, with the survivors caught in Civitot itself and killed or captured.[39]

The Peasants' Crusade led to disaster in the West as well. Peter's preaching had partially set in motion local recruiting movements, most notoriously that of Emicho, the count of Flonheim. He recruited soldiers for the crusade but ended up attacking the Jewish community in Speyer in May 1096, then Worms and Mainz; thereafter, he pivoted away from the holy quest and marched to Cologne, Trier, and Metz, capturing the local Jewries and then forcibly baptizing or killing them. As a result, the Jewish Rhineland community virtually ceased to exist.

It seems clear that these forces were driven by both vengeful and messianic sentiments, in which the old blood curse was tied to two notions: the stripping of Jewish inheritance of Canaan (as a consequence of Jewish complicity in the Crucifixion) and the expected return of Christ upon the rescue of Jerusalem.[40] This much was understood in the Jewish sources of the crusade, one of which puts a speech in the crusaders' mouths:

> Behold, we journey a long way to seek the idolatrous shrine and to take vengeance upon the Muslims. But here are the Jews dwelling among us, whose ancestors killed him and crucified him groundlessly. Let us take vengeance first among them. "Let us wipe them out as a nation; Israel's name will be mentioned no more." Or else let them be like us and acknowledge the son born of menstruation.[41]

As we have already noted, these were *western* Christian views, not eastern—the disinheritance argument was not prominent in Jerusalem before the crusades. In Europe, however, these views fused with the preexisting apocalyptic notions sown in the period after al-Hakim's razing of the sepulchre church, both in the sense of the reprisal attacks on Jews in western Europe and the clerical expectations of the years 1000 and 1033, the millennium anniversaries for Christ's birth and death.[42] Yet this train of thought can be pushed too far; we know of manifold other motivations for crusading, and it is a stretch to believe the apocalyptic was the most prevalent.[43] Moreover, whether anti-Judaism was part and parcel with crusading idealism or a byproduct of crusading enthusiasm—or something else entirely—has been a source of debate.[44] Nonetheless, for Emicho's march, at least, the notion of the approaching "End Times" certainly spurred violence against groups deemed as implacable or heretical, such as European Jewish communities, and this motive was reported not only in Hebrew lamentations but also rather widely in Latin sources.[45]

In that same year, 1096, soldiers mustered to form the regular armies of the "First Crusade," "Princes' Crusade," or "the second wave." These necessarily took more time, given that the participants had to make arrangements for their property and movables.[46] Between December 1096 and the spring of 1097, the different contingents began to arrive at the rallying point of Constantinople, where their leaders were welcomed by the Emperor Alexios, whose instructions and counsel they alternatively welcomed, grudgingly accepted, or outright rejected.[47] In May, the Latin–Byzantine coalition army crossed the Hellespont into Asia and marched to besiege the Turkish-held city of Nicaea. It surrendered on 19 June 1097, at which point the crusaders trekked further into Anatolia.

The View from the East

The local Muslim view of the approaching crusaders is difficult to perceive because of the lateness of the Arabic sources. Although Ibn al-Qalansi notes the flow of reports about the crusade's movement into Anatolia, it is unclear whether that news reached very far south, and when.[48] It likely took some time for the fall of Nicaea to become known widely in Syria and the Levant. Once it was, alarms rang out among civilians, although the response further away in Baghdad remained muted.[49] Not so in Egypt, for the Fatimids had a direct line of communication with the crusade leaders very early on. The difference is that, unlike with the Turks, the crusade leaders had taken the initiative to establish diplomatic ties with Cairo as they weaved their way through Anatolia. It was likely not their original idea, however, for during the siege of Nicaea Alexios advised the westerners to send an embassy to Egypt to establish relations and presumably work to safeguard their southern flank should the Levant come into their possession.[50]

Here, the relative attitudes of the crusaders towards different Muslim ethnicities are germane. Outside of intellectual circles, most of the West knew very little about Islam as a religion—the Qur'an would not be translated into Latin until 1143—but there was wider experience with Muslims themselves.[51] Most of that experience was with Arabs, against whom Christians had struggled in Mediterranean conflicts. Although Arabs were certainly viewed as enemies, there seems to have been no special hatred of them; moreover, despite the charged attitudes of the time, political goals could override religious animosities.[52] Likewise, some Muslim knowledge of the West had been evident in Islamic intellectual texts since the tenth century.[53] Popularly, the Franks were regarded as barbarous: zealous and coura-geous, but also dirty and licentious and accompanied by unclean women.[54] On the other hand, the bulk of Muslims' experience with Christians had been with those of the eastern rites, who had prac-ticed their religion while simultaneously respecting Muslim holy sites. Thus Christians could be derided but grudgingly tolerated.[55] All told, it is not so surprising that diplomatic relations were estab-lished between the Fatimids and crusaders. Politically and militarily, the crusade leaders recognized Alexios's suggestion as sage counsel, and they took it.

The diplomatic outreach was efficacious. The crusaders moved from Nicaea and further into Anatolia, where they narrowly avoided destruction at Dorylaeum (near modern Eskişehir, Turkey) on 1 July 1097. From there, the army marched southeast to Heraclea Cybistra (modern Ereğli, Turkey) and then divided into two portions. One, led by Baldwin of Boulogne and Tancred d'Hauteville, advanced south through Cilicia; the other moved first north to Caesarea (Cappadocia) then southeast to Marasch.[56] It was a difficult journey across a harsh, mountainous countryside, and we still do not have a full understanding of how the armies emerged on the other side essentially intact.[57] Both columns eventually arrived outside of Antioch, and it was there that Egyptian ambassadors arrived at the crusader's camp in February 1098.[58]

The purpose of this Fatimid embassy is unclear. An account commonly attributed to the Bavarian abbot Ekkehard of Aura, who missed the First Crusade but participated in the crusade of 1101, noted that "messengers and spies hurried from all parts of the world"; some of these constituted a legation sent to Antioch, who promised an alliance with the Christians if they could expel the Turks from the Holy City.[59] That is one explanation, but the anonymous *Gesta Francorum* and, a few years later, Benedictine monk Guibert of Nogent's paraphrase of it, offer another. In their telling, the Egyptians went to Antioch to scope the size and condition of the western army. Upon seeing the degradation of the starving crusaders outside the city, they held little hope for a strong alliance and indeed there is no mention one was ever made.[60] In any case, the general Egyptian belief seems to have been that the crusaders were working for Byzantium and were therefore potential reliable allies.[61]

A much longer and more intriguing proposal is the one sketched by the Benedictine monk Robert (probably from St-Rémi in Reims, France), whose account of the crusade dates to 1106–1107. In his telling, al-Afdal's envoys objected to the crusaders' use of violence because pilgrims to the Holy Land ought not do such things. Were they to put down their arms and continue to Jerusalem using only "staff and scrip," free passage to the city and worship in the sepulchre church would be guaranteed. This is a fascinating offer suggestive of the broad strokes of Fatimid tolerances toward Christian pilgrims that we have seen, but even were it a true story, Jerusalem was not at that time in Egyptian hands. In any case, the crusaders subsequently declined the offer.[62]

Nonetheless, diplomatic efforts continued and knights returned with the legation to Egypt. Raymond of Aguilers, a participant on the crusade and chaplain to Raymond IV, count of Toulouse, offers an insightful story that has partial credibility.[63] One dubious element is that the Fatimid envoys saw and were moved by miracles visited on the crusaders by the Triune God, but this is likely to be an embellishment. But the second facet tracks with our material in chapter two: the envoys related stories about generous past Fatimid treatment towards Christians and pilgrims. These read like allusions not only to tolerances within cities like Jerusalem but also to the German pilgrimage and the Egyptian efforts to protect it from raiders. As at least a partial result of these assurances, Christian representatives thereafter journeyed with the Fatimid embassy to unknown whereabouts to effect a treaty.[64]

Those Christian knights, perhaps accompanied by an abbot, remained in the Fatimid domains in close proximity to the Armenian vizier, al-Afdal, the son of Badr al-Jamali. Al-Afdal was essentially the ruler of Egypt. The Fatimid caliphs had suffered a succession schism in 1094 upon the death of Caliph al-Mustansir: his eldest son, Nizar, had been assassinated in Alexandria after his younger brother, al-Musta'li, had received the caliphate. In the political chaos, al-Afdal maintained a close grip on the instruments of Egyptian power.[65]

At that point, Jerusalem was held for the Seljuks by the two sons of Artuq, Suqman and Ilghazi, who were accompanied also by some of the extended family members of the Artuqids. We can make some assumptions about the state of the city and its garrison. By the time the Fatimids arrived, some of Jerusalem's combat power had been reduced. The *Gesta Francorum* notes that along with soldiers from Damascus and Aleppo, men from Jerusalem had trekked north (led by Suqman it seems) in a bid to assist Kerbogha's enterprises against the crusaders.

These joined with Ridwan of Aleppo, whose 12,000 men then engaged with 700 knights under the command of Bohemond of Taranto, at the Lake Battle of 9 February 1098.[66] As we have seen, Ridwan and Suqman had had their differences, with the former attacking Jerusalem in 1095 and the latter later reproaching him for his support of the Fatimids. In 1098, however, the march of the crusaders seems to have been enough for the two leaders to ally in response to a common threat. A sentimental interpretation might be that the two men's fathers had once been allies themselves. How the *Gesta Francorum*'s author knew the regional origin of any of the Muslim combatants is an open question; Count Stephen of Blois knew them as well, as evidenced by a letter he sent to his wife from Antioch.[67]

As for Suqman, he was found in the region again in June 1098, leading a Jerusalem contingent in Kerbogha's army. This time, he participated alongside Ridwan's brother, Duqaq, who had fought a foraging crusader group to a draw in December 1097.[68] Neither enjoyed a good experience in the fighting that followed. On 28 June 1098, the besieged crusaders burst out of the Bridge Gate of Antioch and, in a primarily infantry attack, smashed into components of Kerbogha's army and drove them off. Thousands of Muslims fell and the rest fled in a disorganized fashion. Ibn al-Athir notes that Suqman escaped the carnage because he was "stationed in ambush," which probably means that he was positioned in a guard role at the southern end of the St. George Gate of Antioch.[69] This portion swept to the west but was stymied by men under the command of Reynard, the count of Toul. Fleeing the carnage with those troops still under his command, Suqman turned south and hastened back towards Jerusalem.

The Fatimids Retake the City

Suqman arrived in Jerusalem just in time. The Antioch breakout was at the end of June, and the Arabic sources indicate that al-Afdal's army reached Jerusalem sometime in July. That left precious little time to understand the new state of regional affairs. Kerbogha had drawn so many of the urban emirs to his side at Antioch that several Syrian cities, especially those south of Aleppo, were now vulnerable in the wake of his defeat. Should anyone exploit the vacuum in Turkish military power, Suqman, along with his brother Ilghazi, would be forced to fight essentially alone. Worse, his losses at Antioch presumably meant that he now had far fewer soldiers with which to organize a defense of his city.

The siege of Jerusalem in 1098 gets incredibly short shrift from historians, and not just those of the modern sort. The chronicles of the First Crusade offer scant details about it as well. The siege has traditionally played the role of a set-up piece for the arrival of the First Crusade the following year. However, within our limited material for the event lay a number of elements that fit squarely within the overall theme of interfaith toleration and cooperation in the Holy City. Therefore, it deserves a close look from that perspective.

The dizzying machinations of Turkish affairs had left Jerusalem vulnerable. The Artuqids threw in their lot with Ridwan and his former prisoner, Kerbogha, but all three had now been defeated.[70] In July 1098, the Egyptian vizier made his move on the city. The opportunity was simply too good to pass up: news of the events in Antioch had reached al-Afdal, and with the largest Turkish relief army in tatters he swiftly took advantage. Both al-Maqrizi and Ibn al-Qalansi claim that he first sent a message to the Artuqid garrison in Jerusalem demanding its surrender; when this was refused, he assembled his forces and marched east.[71]

Details on the siege proper are scanty. All things considered, Suqman and Ilghazi seem to have led a respectable defense, but the loss of so many soldiers at the Lake Battle and subsequently at Antioch had to have taken a toll. For his part, al-Afdal ordered a steady artillery bombardment: for 40 days, dozens of catapults rained direct fire on the walls as the garrison responded with its own countermeasures. Finally, near the end of August a section of the wall collapsed from the strikes. Faced with a breach and an imminent penetration by Egyptian soldiers, the Artuqids surrendered.[72]

In what we can now safely call a recurring theme, the city fell without further bloodshed. Al-Afdal allowed local Christians to remain residents of the city and observe their rites, even touring the sepulchre church. And then, some gifts: candles and incense for use in that building.[73] Similar mercy was likewise offered to other Muslims: al-Afdal not only gave safe conduct to the Artuqids, allowing them to depart the city in peace, he also did the same for their followers and gave them gifts as well.[74] The western chronicles offer another element: that the vizier allowed some of the Turks to remain in Jerusalem and actually assigned them the defense of the Tower of David on its western side.[75] In classic Fatimid style, he was more than willing to place Turks under the command of Jerusalem's new governor, Iftikhar ad-Daulah, if it provided military advantage. The son of one of Suqman's men even went on to personally serve al-Afdal in Egypt.[76] That these soldiers indeed owed some loyalty to the Fatimids could be argued from the events of the next year, for when Jerusalem fell to the crusaders in 1099 they sought, and received, safe passage to the Egyptian-held city of Ascalon.[77] It was an extraordinarily businesslike progression of events in which very little ill-will can be detected in the sources and certainly no whiff of Shia–Sunni animosities.

This is not to say that bad feelings were entirely absent, however. The chronicler al-Azraq, our chief source on the Artuqid state, is suspiciously silent on the matter, simply jumping to the later crusader siege in 1099.[78] Perhaps this was due to embarrassment or even resentment. He does, however, provide some epilogue for the two Artuqid brothers. Suqman subsequently took control of Diyar Bakr (Upper Mesopotamia), which became the heart of the Artuqid state. His brother Ilghazi went to Baghdad, where the Seljuk sultan Muhammad Tapar made him a *shihna* (military administrator) tasked with informing the sultan about events in Baghdad and the activities of the Abbasid caliph.[79]

At any rate, the siege in 1098 was the third time Muslims had exchanged Jerusalem (along with Ja'far in the 970s and Atsiz in 1073) without a sack. Certainly, there was an opportunity here to avenge Atsiz's massacre of the Shia defenders in 1077. And we ought not to forget that it was al-Afdal's own father, Badr, who was vizier of Egypt during that massacre—the bloody event was surely well-known to him. This makes al-Afdal's restraint all the more inter-esting, especially given his long-term focus on the Turks, not the crusaders, as his principal foe.[80] There is an accusation by Ibn al-Qalansi that al-Afdal was actually a Sunni, which would help to explain his mercy.[81] Of course, he also knew that the crusader army was advancing south towards him and that time was of the essence. Whether al-Afdal spared the Sunni garrison out of benevolence or sheer practicality one can only guess.

His subsequent actions should be considered in the same light. The later report of Albert, a canon from Aachen (Aix-la-Chapelle) claims that an embassy from al-Afdal, numbering 15 men, trekked north as well to announce the expulsion of the Turks from Jerusalem.[82] It evidently offered access to Jerusalem to small groups of pilgrims, but this was rejected by the crusade leaders, who were now at 'Akkar (northern Lebanon) and committed to nothing less than complete possession of the Holy City.[83] It is interesting that the Arabic sources say nothing of this meeting, nor of the earlier embassies sent by al-Afdal to Antioch. Ibn al-Athir, who was well informed about other diplomatic engagements between the crusaders and cities like Tripoli and Shayzar, offers not a whisper.

II

With regard to Jerusalem itself, the key element is the role of the western emissaries. These were the men who had journeyed with the Egyptian embassy, subsequently remained with al-Afdal and, crucially, had witnessed the 1098 Fatimid siege. Ekkehard claims the vizier used them, via a demonstration of his new alliance, to strike fear into the Artuqids and compel their surrender, though this runs counter to the tactical descriptions in all the Arabic sources.[84] The city was taken by assault, not psychological warfare. Following the victory, these emissaries may have spent several more months in Jerusalem; another later source written at Montecassino, *Historia belli sacri*, claims they spent the following Easter (on 10 April, in 1099) praying at the Church of the Holy Sepulchre.[85] This seems like a reasonable notion; indeed, it is hard to believe that the Christian envoys would have spent months in the Holy City without having done so. By mid-May 1099 they had said their farewells to the Fatimids and rejoined the Christian host unharmed.[86]

An Intelligent Operation

This oft-overlooked presence of the western envoys is important: they not only saw the tactics employed by the Fatimids but also knew the exact spots on the wall that were damaged and the specific place where it was breached.[87] In military terms, they were in an excellent position to conduct intelligence collection, and we should assume that they shared the information with the crusade leaders once they rejoined the Christian army.

That army's progress had been delayed after the victory over Kerbogha at Antioch. Because of the summer heat, the crusade leaders elected to remain there for a time, delaying the expedition south.[88] Disagreements and divisions arose among them, most notably with the acrimony between Bohemond of Taranto and Raymond of Toulouse over the possession of Antioch. Bohemond eventually withdrew from the crusade in March 1099 to attend to his new holdings there. In addition, Baldwin of Boulogne had established a state in Edessa in 1097 and probably took power there in 1098; included among his new lands was Saruj (southwest of Edessa), which he acquired via a treaty with the Artuqid ruler Belek, the nephew of Suqman.[89] Meanwhile, hopes of further assistance from Emperor Alexios were dashed when a Byzantine army at Philomelium (modern Akşekar, Turkey) elected to withdraw instead of moving to join the westerners.[90]

During the remainder of 1098, different elements of the army consolidated gains by capturing various fortresses and towns in northern Syria. The central action in that time was the siege of Ma'arra (Ma'arrat al-Numan-an-Noman), which Raymond and Count Robert of Flanders attacked in late November. It was taken on 12 December through the use of a poorly constructed siege tower that nonetheless allowed the crusaders to overtop its southern wall.[91] The march south resumed in January 1099, and the crusaders worked their way down the Levantine coast and engaged at Jabala, Maraclea, Tortosa, 'Akkar, Sidon (where a small company was annihilated by ambushers and others were bitten by poisonous snakes), Arsuf, and Ramla, winning some victories but losing significant numbers of men in the process.

Meanwhile, other later sources written after the crusade by nonparticipants provide potential glimpses into crusader-initiated negotiations with other Muslims in the region. They received supplies, monies, and the services of local guides from the Arab lord of Shayzar in February 1099, who had chosen conciliation instead of resistance to the approaching crusader army.[92] The accounts of Robert the Monk and Baldric, the abbot of Bourgueil, outline an offer from the emir of Tripoli in April and May 1099; he purportedly promised the crusade leaders that he would convert to Christianity if they managed to wrest Jerusalem from Fatimid control.[93]

Once the Christian emissaries rejoined their comrades in Tripoli in May, the crusading army finally decided to move against its principal target and began the direct march to Jerusalem. The gap between their return and the subsequent siege of Jerusalem was less than a month: the remnants of the crusading host left Tripoli on 16 May and arrived before the Holy City on 7 June.[94] Three weeks, then, were available for the incorporation of the envoys' new intelligence into battle planning.

More intelligence was gathered once the host reached Jerusalem. Six days elapsed between the crusaders' arrival and the first attack on 13 June, during which they reconnoitered the city walls.[95] According to his biographer Ralph of Caen, Tancred d'Hauteville took a personal stroll up the Mount of Olives to gaze down on Calvary; there he met a hermit who pointed out local New Testament sites of interest. The hermit offered some advice as well: that the crusaders attack the city immediately, as opposed (presumably) to first creating a thorough blockade.[96] The hermit made this argument again on 12 June, when he descended from the mount and repeated his counsel to all the crusade leaders present; when they balked, on account of insufficient siegeworks, he suggested that only a ladder was needed to get the job done.[97]

And so it was that on the next day, Monday, 13 June, the Christians boldly attacked Jerusalem with a single ladder, which is all they had managed to build with the scarce amount of wood at their disposal. The move was audacious but fraught with difficulty. Jerusalem's city wall was defended by first a dry moat (19 meters wide and 7 meters deep), and then a forewall, a shorter structure (4.5 meters wide and 5 meters tall) that protected the city's main curtain wall from the approach of siege engines.[98] This forewall had been built by the Artuqids and ran north from David's Gate (near today's Jaffa Gate) in the center of the western side of the city; at the northwest corner it turned and ran along the northern side, turned again at the northeastern corner, and then continued some length down the eastern side.[99] The crusaders attacked the northwest section, next to the strong "Quadrangular" tower on their left (subsequently known as "Tancred's Tower").[100] The accounts of Peter Tudebode, a priest from Poitou present at the siege, and the *Gesta Francorum* share many similarities, and both relate that the crusaders broke through the forewall, allowing them to place their ladder against the main curtain wall; the account of Raymond of Aguilers corroborates this.[101] Attackers, including Tancred, scaled up the ladder but were driven back down by the Egyptian garrison and the assault was thwarted.[102]

Two reasons have been given for this "hasty attack." One concerns religious enthusiasm: that being in such proximity to the steps of Jesus Christ encouraged the crusaders' zealous proclivities and they attacked with expectations of divine assistance. Another take concerns the Fatimids: that al-Afdal would soon return to succor his city after hearing news of the crusaders' arrival there, so time was of the essence. Both are possibilities, but there is another potential reason that centers on military intelligence. No doubt Tancred's hermit knew about the Fatimid siege of 1098, and he may have witnessed it personally. After all, the view of Jerusalem from the Mount of Olives is excellent, as any modern tourist posing for a photograph with the famous camel there can attest. It could be that the hermit also knew about the breach al-Afdal's catapults had made in the wall or, perhaps more importantly, the subsequent efforts by the garrison to repair it. But even if our hermit was ignorant, surely the crusader envoys who had traveled with al-Afdal were not. They would have known and transmitted the details of the breached section, which would have been a tactical focus for the 13 June assault.

Indeed, the witness accounts of the siege suggest just such a thing. That the forewall was so easily disassembled with picks indicates its weakened condition. Attacking so close to the tower likewise raises eyebrows. Measuring 35 by 35 meters, the quadrangular structure dominated the northwest corner of the city and was an obvious strong point. Attacking so close to it only makes sense if the wall had been softened. For the later attacks it was no longer so weak: by July, the crusaders had located enough wood to construct a battering ram and siege tower, but the Fatimid garrison had worked hard to restrengthen the northwest defenses in response. These improvements convinced the attackers that assault would be easier further down the line, and they relocated their engines eastward past St. Stephen's gate.[103]

The circumstantial evidence, therefore, helps to explain the hasty attack on 13 June. In all likelihood, the northwest corner and specifically the wall portion east of Tancred's Tower was the same spot the Fatimids breached in 1098. It would have been repaired by the Egyptian garrison in the year thereafter to some extent, but the crusader envoys had witnessed that siege and it is nearly inconceivable that they would have neglected to relay this detail upon returning to their leaders in May 1099. The hermit on the Mount of Olives merely confirmed what was already known, and the hasty attack—what one historian has called a "reckless and ill-prepared assault"—was actually the product of human intelligence collection and an audacious plan to capitalize on previous Fatimid efforts.[104] Moreover, it demonstrated the perils posed by diplomatic embassies, even when conducted by both sides in good faith.

Into Jerusalem

Following the hasty attack, the crusader host settled down for a proper siege. The army was a shell of its former self, its ranks much reduced by the trials and battles along the road, the desertion of allies and crusaders alike, the suffering and starvation at Antioch, and the sieges and battles endured in late 1098 and early 1099.[105] Foraging had been poor, and the growing distance from Byzantine and Armenian territory resulted in scarcer food supplies, which unsurprisingly contributed to weakening and desertion.[106] From a calculated initial strength of 50,000–60,000 Christian soldiers and noncombatants, at most only 14,000 total individuals remained by June 1099.[107] More losses followed as the Holy City came into view. After 13 June, units marched west to safeguard six ships that had arrived at Jaffa four days later. They were subsequently ambushed by 700 Arabs and lost dozens of knights and over a hundred horses. An

Egyptian fleet then arrived at Jaffa, forcing the undefended sailors to burn their ships and haul what wood and supplies they could carry inland to Jerusalem.[108] These materials, along with wood discovered by Tancred in a nearby cave, enabled the crusaders to construct new equipment that included a siege tower, battering ram, and three catapults.[109] A grand procession around the city then commenced on 8 July, led by the clergy accompanying the army, very much in the style of Joshua around the walls of Jericho. While there was no expectation for the "walls to come tumbling down," it did have an important penitential aspect in that all the Christian soldiers were asked to reconcile themselves to their peers in anticipation of the climax of their holy quest.[110]

Once again, the crusaders besieged the city primarily from the north side, while a separate contingent under Raymond of Toulouse also advanced from the south, attacking the Mount Zion Gate. In the north, Godfrey de Bouillon, Tancred, and the two Roberts (counts of Flanders and Normandy, respectively) executed a deception operation. As noted, they built their siege engines on the northwest corner, by the Quadrangular Tower, which compelled Iftikhar's garrison to strengthen the defenses and bolster the supplies there. Then, on the night of 9–10 July, the crusade leaders partially dismantled and shifted the engines from the northwest to the northeast section of the wall. There they busied themselves by rebuilding them and also filling in the moat.[111] Three days later, on 13 July, the attack began. The ram broke through the forewall by the end of the 14th, despite the garrison's attempts to destroy the weapon with naphtha (a form of Greek fire).[112]

This portion of the wall guarded the northern edge of the *Juiverie*, the Jewish quarter of the city. Today, it is known as the Muslim Quarter and is reached by entering the sixteenth-century Herod's Gate.[113] The defenders here, who counted among their number Muslims but also Jews from the residential quarter below, had at best only a single tower on the wall to support their activities.[114] On top of the interior curtain wall, they watched as the crusaders pushed and dragged their last remaining siege tower forward through the fore-wall's new gap to sit astride it and then threw logs and beams down to bridge the gap between the tower's top storey and the stone of Jerusalem's circuit. In what must have been a desperate struggle, archers dislodged their final arrows into the siege tower, while others swung furiously with their melee weapons at those charging across. When the crusaders overtopped the walls at about nine o'clock in the morning, the defenders broke in the face of the assault and fled in different directions: some down the length of the wall west or east, likely some plummeting to their death, and others managing to climb down and into the streets of the *Juiverie*.

From there, the defenders eventually rallied to two main loca-tions. A smaller group, composed of Jews, gathered in the Karaite synagogue but died when it was taken, ransacked, and then burned by the crusaders.[115] The larger group, which appears have been the mass of Muslims along with any noncombatants they swept along while retreating, coalesced on the Temple Mount. They were joined there by another group of Muslims from the south. Raymond of Toulouse, who had struggled against a tenacious Fatimid defense in the tight confines of the Mount Zion Gate area, finally succeeded when the defenders there learned of the breakthrough on the northern side and abandoned their positions. Raymond's Provençals surged into the city and towards the Tower of David, where Iftikhar opened the gate after securing an agreement of safe conduct from the count. Others pushed Muslim defenders east towards the Temple Mount. As the fleeing garrison piled through the gates to that inner fortress, the space began to fill up with people, while others fought the crusaders in the streets in a delaying action to cover the retreat of their fellows.

At this point, most of the crusaders remained outside the city, but gradually more and more flowed inside through the two breaching points. The attackers were funneled, as it were, by Jerusalem's streets, the widest of which were only five meters across, towards the western gates to the Temple Mount: the Gate of Sorrow on its northern side and the Beautiful Gate nearer its center.[116] Given that the crusaders had to press through these gates to enter the Mount, they necessarily were much fewer in number than the thousands of Muslims packed on top of it. They pushed forward anyway, filled with the excitement of the moment or bloodlust (or both) and engaged the front lines of defenders.

Ralph of Caen offers a particularly close view of the fighting.[117] As the attackers pressed, the defenders fought back, some of them discharging arrows from open windows in al-Aqsa mosque. Back and forth they all went, with the crusaders making progress only a step at a time. Meanwhile, their forward push served to compress the defenders and the women and children they guarded: as men were wounded and fell, or even just tripped, the Muslims jumbled together in the tumult. The crush undoubtedly made it difficult to swing swords or thrust spears, and slowly but surely the crusaders cut deeper into the massed humanity. Three hundred Muslims, who seem to have been mostly noncombatants, found a temporary reprieve by climbing on top of al-Aqsa's roof.[118]

The rest were not so lucky and were cut down in the now infamous Jerusalem massacre. How many died is unknown, but the round figure of 3,000 is commonly offered in histories. The deaths of the noncombatants caught in the scrum were a predictable consequence of the city's sacking. Most notoriously, the western chronicles speak of a torrent of human blood that rose to the height of the crusaders' knees or ankles, or, in one account, up to the bridles of their horses. This is obviously a vivid exaggeration (and one likely borrowed from the 14th chapter of the Book of Revelation) that has nonetheless been hard to prove or disprove.[119] The only serious effort to do so beyond pure textual analysis—by actually quantifying the volume of blood spilled by 3,000 corpses, an admittedly macabre task—has essentially been ignored. Whether rivers or puddles, enough blood was spilled to encourage such dramatic impressions.[120]

Luck ran out for those on al-Aqsa's roof the next day. Despite having been given the banners of Tancred and Gaston, the viscount of Béarn, as a sign of protection, in the morning of 16 July crusaders scaled the roof and summarily dispatched them all. Some tried jumping from the roof to escape the blades and presumably either died upon impact or were cut down after landing.[121]

Such was the carnage inside the walls and on the Temple Mount. A limited sack of the city followed, with crusaders sweeping through the residences and robbing, but generally not destroying, them.[122] Substantial debate remains about whether or not there was a comprehensive, general massacre of the remainder of Jerusalem's residents on the third day of western possession. In this telling, with their blood lust diminished and control of both Sepulchre and Temple Mount secured, the soldiers nonetheless took up their weapons again and coldly massacred some 10,000 remaining residents of Jerusalem: men, women, and children. Nonwitness Christian sources make the claim, principally Albert of Aachen, whose account possibly can be substantiated with Hebrew *genizah* letters.[123] The Arabic texts written closest to the event, the so-called Syrian Tradition of authors, do not mention it. Although it might have made strategic sense to remove the possibility of an urban insurgency from surviving residents by simply wiping them out, the argument for this third-day massacre remains somewhat speculative.[124]

The Aftermath

Despite the carnage, much of the garrison and some of the residents survived the siege. Joshua Prawer once wrote of "the complete annihilation of the non-Christian population," but this was simply not the case.[125] Many descriptions of the dead are offered in the Christian, Jewish, and Muslim sources, and they are very often accompanied by numbers. The problem is that the numbers range wildly, from as few as 3,000 to as many as 70,000—these were then inflated in successive centuries as historians, both western and eastern, looked back upon the event from either charitable or cynical perspectives.

Rather than sorting these out in a historiographical fashion as others have already done rather well, it might be wiser to approach the topic demographically: how many people in Jerusalem in July 1099 were there to kill? Under Fatimid rule, the total population of Jerusalem was between 20,000 and 30,000 people, more likely on the lower side of that figure, and included the customary plurality of religious confessions.[126] Iftikhar had ordered the expulsion of the resident Christians, but not all of them left.[127] It is also difficult to gauge the size of the garrison defending it. Following the 1098 siege, al-Afdal, as we have said, allowed the Artuqid brothers to freely depart, along with their supporters; some Turks remained and received Fatimid wages while defending the Tower of David. How many Turks left is unknowable, but the brothers would not have simply left the bulk of their soldiers in Jerusalem. Suqman, in particular, went on to take control of Diyar Bakr and would have needed soldiers to do so. Then, following the siege of 1098, al-Afdal withdrew his army to either Ascalon or Egypt.

Compounding the issue were al-Adfal's diplomatic overtures. By the spring of 1099, al-Afdal was still dangling access to Jerusalem to pilgrims in the offer rejected by the crusade leaders, and as late as mid-May the Christian emissaries were still in Jerusalem. These efforts built upon his earlier efforts at rapprochement, which included his personal assurances for the safe conduct of the crusaders through Palestine and even the provision of supplies to them from Egypt.[128] Had friendly relations been solidified as he sought, a large garrison would have been wholly unnecessary.

In other words, the Fatimids did not take Jerusalem and then stuff it with a massive garrison; rather, they hired some additional help while most of the Turks and Egyptians retired. The vizier's Ascalon army numbered between 10,000 and 20,000 (regular soldiers plus thousands of militia gathered in Palestine) when it finally engaged with crusaders in early August. This was on the higher end of armies typically mobilized by Egypt for field action, which William Hamblin calculated at between 5,000 and 10,000 men.[129] The circumstantial evidence suggests, therefore, that the city was not on a proper war footing until, at most, one month before the crusaders arrived on 7 June. Too many men had been removed from the walls. On the other hand, parts of the city were inherently defensible and did not require large numbers of personnel; for instance, as Fulcher, the priest from Chartres, remarked, the Tower of David could be defended effectively by just 15 or 20 men.[130] One wonders if even the 3,000-strong figure for the garrison is too high.

It is also clear that many Muslims survived the siege. The most prominent were those defending the Tower of David, a point on which the sources concur. Fulcher of Chartres counted these as some 400–500 "Turks, Arabs, and black Ethiopians"—a historically viable snapshot of the customarily heterogenous Fatimid army. This was due to a prior agreement in which the emir had opened the gate to Raymond of Toulouse in exchange for safe passage after the siege concluded.[131] Guibert of Nogent later claimed that the Turks guarding the Tower of David did not even engage the crusaders during the 1099 siege, which might be hindsight exaggeration but certainly conveys the impression of a fairly honored agreement.[132] Raymond ordered the tower's garrison and its commander, Emir Iftikhar, escorted out of the city and to Ascalon on 17 July.[133] These soldiers included both the retained Turks and Fatimid cavalry, which had been sent specifically to the city by al-Afdal to strengthen its defenses by acting in a reserve role—more evidence that the garrison was weak.[134]

Moreover, it is possible that not all of the Muslims caught on the Temple Mount were killed. Fulcher remarks that "not one of them was allowed to live," but he was not in Jerusalem at the time, having remained with Baldwin of Boulogne in Edessa.[135] Other primary accounts throw confusion on the matter. Peter Tudebode noted, "after having overwhelmed the pagans, our men grabbed a large number of males and females in the Temple, killing some, and sparing others as the notion struck them"; both he and the *Gesta Francorum*—probably one copying from the other—relate that these survivors were tasked with piling the corpses into funeral pyres by the city gates.[136] Later accounts are similarly contradictory. Guibert of Nogent claims that these Muslims pressed into labor were killed once the cleaning was complete; Baldric says some were killed while others were sold into slavery, and Robert the Monk stipulates that some crusaders kept young boys and girls who survived as slaves.[137] An older notion held that some Muslim survivors went on to establish a neighborhood in Damascus, but that has now been disputed. Some captured Muslims, like the scholar al-Rumayli, were imprisoned and executed in later months.[138]

What of the Jews? Due to the migration of the Rabbanite Jews to Tyre in the 1070s, the community occupying the *Juiverie* was much smaller, and the *genizah* letters make clear that it was made up primarily of Karaites.[139] A later addition to Baldric's account states that some of them were captured near the Temple Mount and, like the surviving Muslims, pressed into service disposing of the corpses.[140] Several probably died in the synagogue fire, though it is impossible to know the number.[141] Still more were ransomed, and the *genizah* letters indicate that they were released by Raymond of Toulouse because they journeyed alongside Iftikhar, who had surrendered the Tower of David.[142] These Jews are not mentioned in the Christian accounts, which speak only of the Muslim ethnicities. Other Jews managed to escape from the city through unguarded gates during the tumult, journeying to Ascalon on their own. The remainder were ransomed, tortured, or killed. Some might have converted to Christianity and were thereafter granted freedom.[143] Recent research suggests, however, that far more Jews may have survived the siege than previously thought, with possibly up to 400 being ransomed via funds from Egypt in the months afterward.[144]

Therefore, out of a population of 20,000, conservatively speaking, a rough estimate is that about a fifth (4,000) were killed: the 3,000 on the Temple Mount, plus the 300 on the al-Aqsa roof, with the remainder being composed of the small Karaite community and others who had resisted in the streets and on the walls. That number leaps if we accept the occurrence of the third day massacre for which Benjamin Kedar has argued. Without it, however, the number is still significant and the killings in the synagogue and al-Aqsa were certainly cold-blooded. Whatever the method, the intent seems to have been to depopulate the city of non-Christians, by sending away the David tower garrison, ransoming captive Jews, plus either killing or expelling the remaining Muslim residents. Following the crusade's conclusion and the establishment of the Latin Kingdom of Jerusalem, Jews and Muslims were prohibited from living within the city walls, a topic to which we shall return in the next chapter.

Jerusalem was not the only massacre during the First Crusade. We have already noted those in the Rhineland at the start of the Peasants' Crusade. There was another at Ma'arra in December 1098: despite attempts to negotiate a surrender, its garrison was at length eliminated. The apparent reason was booty. In a formal turnover of a city or fortress, the spoils within were divided generally among the leaders; however, when storming into a city, the knights and common soldiers could claim their own share through theft, larceny, or burglary.[145] This behavior, and the other actions that often resulted from it, such as rape and murder, were customarily accorded "the cloak of legality" in western military tradition.[146] It was therefore in the soldiers' interest to get inside fortifications quickly, before matters calmed and order was restored: in chaos there is profit.

This reality raises questions about command and control during the Jerusalem siege. There was no restraint of soldiers entering the city's interior, no discipline, and no order, especially at the southern walls. In a best-case scenario the entry process would have been preplanned before any breach was made. Ralph of Caen admonishes

Tancred on the general issue of planning—perhaps with the benefit of hindsight—by employing the ancient wisdom of Sallust, the Roman historian of the Jugurthine War (112–106 B.C.):

> This leader and soldier [Sallust], expert in what it means to be both a leader and a soldier, said: "Before taking action it is appropriate to take stock. Once having done so, the task should be undertaken properly." It is clear even to the simple folk that it falls to the leader to plan and to the soldier to fight.[147]

Without an operational pause no planning could take place. At the Mount Zion Gate, Raymond urged his men up the ladders once he saw the defense slacken, an increase in tempo that allowed the crusaders to retake the initiative but that also risked a loss of control. Raymond himself may have been negligent in his duties, for Robert the Monk seems to suggest that the count made his way over to the Tower of David in the west while his soldiers marauded eastward to the Temple Mount.[148]

In the north we see a counterexample. A later account has Godfrey immediately sending a squadron of soldiers from the breaching point westward through the city to safeguard the sepulchre church against any potential looting by errant crusaders.[149] If true, these men did not participate in the Temple Mount massacre. Peter Tudebode also speaks of three of Godfrey's men approaching Raymond's southern camp from the Mount of Olives with information that the northern forces were in Jerusalem.[150] Both incidents demonstrate that effective command and control *was* possible even in the frenetic atmosphere. On the other hand, Godfrey himself remained personally involved in the killing, shedding an "incredible" amount of blood.[151]

Without planning, command and control might still have taken place once soldiers gained entrance to Jerusalem's interior. As the Muslim defenders retreated, the situation was more akin to a routed enemy on the battlefield: should one's soldiers maintain contact by pursuing immediately, or pause, reconstitute, and then move forward? The latter would have required moving units into the city interior (either over the walls or through a gate now unlocked from the inside) and then issuing new orders. But this seems not to have taken place. In a situation where soldiers were pouring over the walls in two separate streams, north and south, it would have been extremely difficult for the crusade leaders to restrain their men. Military professionals know well the inherent difficulties presented by pursuit, defined as "completing the destruction of fleeing enemy forces by destroying their ability and will to resist."[152] Indeed, the leaders seem to have joined right in with their men, charging forward and into the fleeing defenders. In this sort of scrum, attempts at communication and the imposition of discipline—sending orders, rallying friends, and identifying foes—was well-nigh impossible.[153]

Judgments

None of this analysis should be read as an excuse for the crusaders' behavior inside the city. As Alan Murray notes, they had committed other massacres, executions, and atrocities on their march south, and these were probably well known among Jerusalem's residents.[154] Indeed, one could argue that this was the First Crusade's *modus operandi*, and such a judgment probably has amplified modern condemnation with the affair, although one could counter that similar massacres had not occurred at Nicaea or Antioch. Nor do we seek to diminish the event's horrific nature. That it was soon recognized as a spiritual reckoning, a second "cleansing of the Temple" (in imitation of Christ having done so by overturning the money-changers' tables) raises modern hackles about the confluence of religion and warfare.[155] The elimination of large besieged populations in such a fashion was not uncommon in the Middle Ages, although it was more common and at a much larger scale in the ancient world and (arguably) the early modern as well.[156] Yet for the victims there was little solace in that they were brutally killed in the context of a long-running custom of siege warfare. One Jewish apocalyptic text compared the event to Pharaoh forcibly drowning Israelite babies in the Nile.[157]

Still, the specter of moral equivalence beckons. The massacre of the First Crusade receives far, far more attention than does Atsiz's in 1077, despite their similar figures. It is not even close; indeed, one suspects that a large contingent of medieval scholars have not even heard of Atsiz, perhaps due to the relative lack of interest in Seljuk studies and dominant preferences for the western sources for the Crusades. Alternatively, as has been argued, the intense scholarly focus on the strict "crusading period" of 1095–1291 has obscured what came before it.[158] The result has been a generalized sense that the significance of Christian versus Muslim interreligious strife trumps that of Muslim versus Muslim intrareligious strife. However if we are honest, Atsiz's deed should inspire equal revulsion: the Muslim lives lost in 1099 were no more or less precious than those lost in 1077.

Yet we also might remember that, in a refrain familiar to modern military professionals, the enemy always gets a vote: one's plans are always conditioned by those of one's opponent. Al-Afdal's strategy had clearly failed. Positioning the Turks as his principal foe, he capitalized on Kerbogha's defeat by capturing Jerusalem in 1098 which, as a result, put him in the crusade's line of sight. In the midst of cordial diplomatic discussions between Latin and Fatimid emissaries, this could only be seen as a treacherous move. Those same Latin envoys provided the crusade leaders with crucial intelligence about the city walls and the condition of its residents. Thereafter, his diplomatic outreach grew more desperate, and he gambled—wrongly—that the crusade leaders would be satisfied with their Levantine gains and a promise of free pilgrimage to the Holy City. His human and material arrangements for Jerusalem's perimeter defense were insufficient to repel the western army, and his relief army at Ascalon was too big to mobilize in time to relieve the beleaguered garrison. Al-Afdal must therefore bear some of the responsibility for the massacre of July 1099. It is no accident that, later in the twelfth century, the Egyptian chancery clerk Ibn Zafir blamed him for losing the city and argued that the Artuqid brothers would have done a much better job against the crusaders than had the Fatimids.[159]

On the other hand, al-Afdal's willingness to engage early and often with the crusader envoys, as well as extend offers to their leaders, speaks volumes about the nature of the interfaith environment of the Levant. We should not write this off as simply a pragmatic attempt at military alliance, although that was obviously an important consideration.[160] Open religious tolerance was part and parcel of the Fatimid way of doing business. And the offer of free pilgrimage, while seemingly trivial from the crusaders' perspective, speaks volumes. The right to enter Jerusalem as pilgrims had been cherished in the past, and the restoration of these rights after al-Hakim's reign had been a key step in reestablishing a vibrant pluralistic community there. The Fatimids had directly intervened in 1064–1065 to protect the German pilgrims from raiders; it can be no surprise, then, that the vizier supposed that a full pilgrimage allowance would satisfy the Latins in the 1090s. Moreover, he could not have known the multiplicity of motivations that drove the crusaders towards their goal. Indeed, as we have seen, even scholars today have trouble sorting the major from minor impulses. For example, no deal would have satisfied the truly apocalyptically minded unless it included possession of Jerusalem itself.

Thus did al-Afdal's offer tie the present with the pluralistic past, and this points to the extremely exceptional nature of the crusaders' "original sin." Simply put, there had been no true sack of Jerusalem since 614, when the Persian army entered, looted the entire city, and executed or enslaved its inhabitants. That is a gap of 485 years, or about twice the lifespan of the United States of America. Some may point to Atsiz's massacre of 1077. While equivalent in mortality, however, there was no subsequent looting of the residences afterwards, and it was intrareligious violence aimed at suppressing a rebellion.[161] It was also a targeted, vengeful response to a very specific slight: the imprisonment of Atsiz's family.

In fact, all of the preceding medieval massacres in Jerusalem had been the result of internal strife. Let us consider them in turn. An attack in 614 had initially been negotiated away: Patriarch Zachariah had a treaty with the Persian army under Shahrbaraz that was nullified when youths in the city murdered the Persian garrison. Only then did the Persians attack, breach the walls, and sack the city. This is rather analogous with 1077: broken terms resulted in mass death. Local Christians were killed during the tumult of 966 and Patriarch John was burned alive, but the core issue was unduly harsh financial levies from Jerusalem's governor, redress against which John petitioned from the Abyssinians. Al-Hakim's widespread murders and persecutions were internal as well: it was a Fatimid city, and as the caliph he personally intervened in religious affairs there. In 1098, al-Afdal breached the wall in a 40-day siege, but when the garrison surrendered he spared everyone's lives and put much of the Sunni Turkish garrison under his pay.

Going further, when internal strife was absent, even military conquest did not lead to massacres. There were none reported when the Rashidun caliph 'Umar ibn al-Khattab took the city in 638, or when the Fatimid Caliph al-Muizz li-Din Allah captured it in the 970s, or when Atsiz first claimed the city in 1073. All of these were blockades with scant fighting that resulted in surrender terms but, unlike the aforementioned, those terms were not broken by recalcitrant residents. In other words, foreign armies did not—and had not since 630—set out with the purpose of conquering Jerusalem and eliminating members of different religions or ethnicities there.

The sieges before 638, in the age before Islam, reveal a rather different theme. The Roman conquest in 70 A.D. caused the destruction of the Second Temple and was followed by pursuit of Jewish zealots then, and later the establishment of the colony of Aelia

Capitolina on the Temple Mount in 129. A temple to Jupiter was built on the site and Jews were forbidden from entering the city except on Tisha B'av. This contributed to the outbreak of the Bar Kokhba revolt (132–136) in which hundreds of thousands of Jews perished.[162] When Constantine and Helena entered the city in the fourth century, the Jewish ban was maintained. In 630, Emperor Heraclius arrived to reclaim Jerusalem from the Persians and embarked on a pogrom against the Jews who had moved in when the old ban lapsed. It expanded widely and led to forced baptisms across the region and beyond. Conquest and forced conversion: this was the heritage of Jerusalem in the period between the lives of Christ and Muhammad.

We have, then, two different epochs. The pre-Islam one is a tale of religious strife and intolerance that fits neatly into modern sensibilities. This is the Jerusalem we think we know. The post-Islam epoch is a rather different tale, however, one in which the three Abrahamic faiths consistently found ways to live, work, and pray side by side. This epoch is really a story of diverse populations in a community, speckled with controversies and periodic upheavals that were nonetheless always followed by mutual reconciliation and "rough tolerance." Its tragedies simply were not ushered in by foreign armies bent on destruction. Some have argued that the western army was designed to destroy Islam or, at the worst, designed for genocidal purposes. Such judgments, even when they do not descend into polemic, entirely miss the point.[163] The fact is that the crusader army was an exceptional anachronism: the only foreign army in five centuries to finish off a conquest of Jerusalem with a massacre driven by antireligious fury. It was shocking precisely because it was so radically against the city's heritage.

For too long, the shadow of its bloody massacre has skewed understanding of the longer duration of Jerusalem's history. By focusing overmuch on the events of 1099, which were the exception to the rule, we have crafted memories of the past in an illogical, emotionally driven, and context-free manner. We can do better by directing our ire from a different perspective: it was awful not only because it was an immoral act but because it undid centuries of interfaith accord that had begun with the rise of Islam. Such details matter when dealing with the horrendous event of 1099. Wielding "Massacre!" as a bludgeon has been a popular means of condemning past actors, religions, and cultures and their present beneficiaries or advancing preferred political and social objectives.

There is a better argument, which is ecumenical, not moral. It drops the accusatory style in favor of the sensibility of lamentation. The 1099 massacre was a sad and regrettable thing, not simply for the people involved but also for the pluralism it impeded, to everyone's detriment. The emphasis on the killing obscures the greater lesson of what was lost: a five-century stretch of accord between competing faith traditions in the most sensitive of places. Those looking for historical ammunition for their partisan positions have preferred—and surely will continue—to repeat the body count. That this view has resonated so strongly, however, only means that we have chosen to privilege it over other interpretative possibilities. An alternate focus on what the Near East lost that year, and how it might possibly be regained, holds greater potential for resolving differences but has not really been tried. It is always easier to use history to denounce the other, but the effect is to remain stuck in neutral, looking through the regrettable "clash of civilizations" lens. We will only see, as Bernard Lewis famously put it, a "struggle between rival systems" that "has consisted of a long series of attacks and counterattacks, jihads and crusades, conquests and reconquests."[164] That is one way to look at the history of the First Crusade, but it is surely a frail and impoverished one.

IV

SALADIN THE MERCIFUL
THE 1100s AND 1187

T he First Crusade, and its aftermath, was the nadir for interfaith relations in Jerusalem during the Middle Ages. It was a complete break from the past, from nearly five centuries in which the dominant theme was accord and resolution within its walls. The damage done went well beyond the massacre. In the aftermath of the siege the city became the center of a newly established state, the Kingdom of Jerusalem, and its new Christian rulers henceforth banned all Jews and Muslims from residing within its walls. It was a total reversal of the pluralistic past and nearly theocratic in nature. It was a return to the days of Emperor Heraclius, who had banned Jews from the city in 630.[1] For Muslims, this was the first time they had suffered such a privation there, to which was added the insult of Frankish occupation of the Dome of the Rock and al-Aqsa Mosque on the Temple Mount. Muslim poets lamented the aftermath of this disaster in evocative and profound tones.[2]

Oddly enough, the conquerors did not enact similar policies around the conquered Levantine regions, neither elsewhere in the kingdom nor in the Crusader States: the counties of Tripoli and Edessa and the principality of Antioch.[3] In those places, there is evidence of better relations between the different faith communities, where the settling crusaders quickly realized that their neighbors, tax payers, and customers could be tolerated under legal and social parameters to everyone's mutual benefit.[4] The particular significance of Jerusalem, then, was what set it apart: its holiness demanded that those rejecting Christ be kept away. Over time, however, the official policy began to wilt, and as the twelfth century progressed more of the excluded populations could be spied within the walls, first as pilgrims or traders, then as settlers granted exceptions, and finally as full-blown residents. Given the multiplicity of holy sites there, it was rather impractical to keep the doors locked forever, especially in regard to Muslims, whose relative access (or lack thereof) was a contributing factor in relations with often antagonistic rulers. Frankish armies in the region, whatever their size, were typically outnumbered, and they regularly sought and maintained amicable communications and diplomatic relations with various Muslim states.

Against this backdrop, a steady desire arose in Muslim communities for the recovery of Jerusalem and the expulsion of its Christian rulers. But who could reasonably attain such feats? The Abbasid caliphs in Baghdad could still raise armies, but they had difficulty projecting power into Palestine and expelling the unwanted guests. The Turks, perpetually fractured in a political sense and still reeling from the blows of the First Crusade, tried in earnest to reclaim lost territories but only succeeded in some cases, most notably at Edessa. The Fatimids, themselves recovering from the loss of Jerusalem and the defeat at Ascalon, entered a slow spiral into military ineffectuality. It was a perfect storm of opportunity, and eventually exploiting it was the famous Ayyubid sultan of Egypt, Saladin: successively overthrowing the Fatimids, overawing the Turks, and out-maneuvering the Franks, he would capture Jerusalem in 1187 and restore in its sensibilities much of the pluralism that had been interrupted in 1099.[5]

I

Consolidating Gains

Those crusaders who remained in the Levant moved swiftly to establish their political control of Jerusalem and also took measures to secure the city. They named Godfrey de Bouillon Defender of the Holy Sepulchre, and he thereafter established his court in the al-Aqsa mosque, which occupied the most prominent spot in the city and was certainly the most impressive and lavish building.[6] As Adrian Boas has noted, being few in number and materially wanting, it is no surprise that the crusaders chose to occupy existing structures instead of replacing them with expensive new buildings. In time, the Frankish settlers made infrastructural improvements to sewage and drainage systems and cleared areas to improve access to the city gates.[7] There was a practical element at work here. Given their precarious position in between so many Muslim polities, to attack the holy sites may have either invited an immediate military response or served to unite the disparate groups together in a general offensive.[8] The situation actually foreshadowed later similar conundrums: Emperor Frederick II faced a similar dilemma when retaking the Temple Mount in 1229, as would the Israelis, centuries later, in 1967.

Accordingly, the Franks made substantial alterations to the three principal holy buildings in the city now in their possession. Starting in 1114, they refurbished the Dome of the Rock, which they referred to as the *Templum Domini*, by installing an altar, candelabra, and mosaics on the interior walls and covering Muhammad's rock with stone slabs. Work in al-Aqsa, which they called the *Templum Salomonis*, was more extensive and took longer to complete. It resulted in a number of entirely new rooms and adjacent buildings appearing in the twelfth century, including granaries, baths, a church, and improvements to the interior layout. These changes facilitated the mosque's new role as first royal palace, and then headquarters of the Poor Knights of the Temple of Solomon, more commonly known as the Knights Templar.[9]

Unsurprisingly, the Franks devoted significant time to the Church of the Holy Sepulchre, which was still in some disrepair since the interruptions of the eleventh century. There was a delay in this construction but by the time it concluded the Franks had tacked on a monastery, complete with cloister; performed work on the *aedicule*, a small chapel under the rotunda, which covered the Resurrection site; and built four new altars plus a new choir and ambulatory. Finally, a new, two-story chapel arose on the southern side to fully incorporate the rock of Golgotha—and the purported spot of the Crucifixion on top of it—inside the church itself.[10] A new mosaic was also installed: depicting both Helena and Heraclius, it visually linked the crusaders' recapture of the city with its Roman heritage.[11] Prelates rededicated the restored church on 15 July 1149, the 50-year anniversary of its capture, and revised the liturgy for the occasion: worshippers chanted "Adore the Lord in His holy house" and marched in a festive procession to the Temple Mount and back.[12] The sepulchre site attracted thousands of pilgrims from abroad during the remainder of the twelfth century, and the city eventually began to bustle with the sights and sounds of a thriving Christian community.[13]

Beneath the veneer of a successful war, the acquisition of towns and territory, and the restoration of holy sites lay serious military problems. Many enemies surrounded the isolated Frankish lands; though roundly defeated, they might have taken solace in the fact that the region had been through this before, when Byzantine armies had moved south under Emperors Nicephoros Phocas and John I Tzimiskes in the tenth century.[14] The Fatimids remained ensconced in Ascalon, which essentially served as a forward operating base for Egyptian soldiers that could be resupplied by land and sea. In terms of sheer army size and combat power, Egypt was the most dangerous threat in the years following 1099. The Turks, still fragmented but beginning to coalesce in the face of the Latin threat, were represented by some familiar faces: the brothers Duqaq and Ridwan (in Damascus and Aleppo, respectively), the Selujk sultan Kilij

Arslan and the Artuqid Suqman and his relatives in Diyar Bakr.[15]
They were down, but not out. Byzantium presented a rivalry in the
north, and while it was not antagonistic per se it was often adversarial. None of these elements were united. The Turks sometimes
joined forces against the westerners, sometimes not. Egypt, which
one might expect to vigorously attempt to regain all its lost terrain,
may have actually preferred having a Christian buffer zone between
it and its Sunni rivals.[16]

Jerusalem also had insecure lines of supply and communication
back to the west. Jaffa was the sole friendly port of entry and an
insufficient one at that in terms of volume and also proximity to the
more northerly territories. Moreover, Fatimid fleets could potentially
disembark soldiers at each Muslim-held port, so the Frankish western
flanks were extremely vulnerable to counterattack.[17] Protection was
another problem. More soldiers were needed to consolidate the gains
made by the First Crusade. Most of the crusading army had returned
to western Europe, with only about 3,000 remaining in the Levant.
These were scarcely enough to safeguard Jerusalem itself, much less
the surrounding area, or to support the conquest of the other coastal
ports, which was a prime goal of the early kingdom.[18] The Franks
desperately needed new means of attracting and compensating
soldiers for regional defense at the turn of the twelfth century.[19]

In response, Pope Pascal II called for another expedition in order
to reinforce the contingents in the Latin East. This effort itself
followed on the heels of earlier recruiting efforts by his predecessor
Urban in Lombardy while the First Crusade was still stuck at
Antioch. New forces from France crossed into Asia Minor in the
spring and early summer of 1101, but rather than directly reinforcing
Jerusalem they split in separate directions. Two contingents moved
east in an attempt to rescue Bohemond—the Danishmends (Turkish
rivals of the Seljuks) had wrecked his army and captured him, after
which they had sent messengers to Antioch demanding its surrender.[20]
These relief forces, however, were destroyed at Merzifon and Eregli.[21]

Two other groups moved south towards Jaffa. Those who took the coastal road were beaten at Eregli and only a group traveling by ship to Jaffa safely completed the journey.[22]

Governance questions also abounded. Landed possessions were key to the administration of the new polities and financing of local defense.[23] Ecclesiastical properties within those domains were likewise important, not only for the propagation of the faith in the Holy Land but for the maintenance of existing churches and monasteries and those new ones that would presumably follow. Dissensions between principals arose almost immediately. In the autumn of 1099, the papal legate Daibert of Pisa essentially blackmailed Godfrey into appointing him Patriarch of Jerusalem, in exchange for the services of the Pisan fleet.[24] Those ships were vital for the protection of the Jaffa port and the maintenance of the Franks' communication and supply lines. But they came at a cost: once Daibert assumed the patriarchate, he became a disruptive force as he pushed a reform agenda. Godfrey only ruled until July of the next year, upon which his brother Count Baldwin left Edessa and journeyed to Jerusalem to become its first Christian king (Baldwin I, 1100–1118). Baldwin first had Daibert expelled from the city and then, when he returned, deposed.[25]

Poor and undermanned though it was, Jerusalem was not always on the defensive in its early decades. Between Godfrey's initial reign and the Second Crusade (1147–1149), the kingdom assembled at least 23 armies that are attested in the sources, which alternatively campaigned, engaged in skirmishes and battles, participated in sieges, relieved beleaguered garrisons, and even helped to build the castle at Montreal.[26] These forces were built from local levies and, periodically, newcomers from the West.[27] Baldwin I moved west in what one historian has dubbed "the coastal strategy": limiting the operational reach of the Fatimid navy by seizing every possible port on the Levantine coast.[28] One by one its harbors fell into friendly hands. He captured three early in his reign (Arsuf and Caesarea in 1101, Acre in 1104), and he acquired Beirut and Sidon in 1110 as well.[29]

1. Easily the most prominent feature of modern Jerusalem, the Dome of the Rock is a shrine that covers the site where Muhammad purportedly ascended to heaven. The Dome of the Chain, a clear model of the larger shrine, is thought by Muslims to be the place of the Final Judgment of mankind.

2. Aerial view of the Temple Mount. The ancient walls of this plateau of Mount Moriah comprise some of the holiest sites on earth. One can spot the small Dome of the Chain, just to the east of the Dome of the Rock, al-Aqsa mosque, and the large expanse of the former Temple grounds. To the southeast of al-Aqsa, just outside the walls, lie the remains of an old Umayyad palace.

3. The *aedicule*, in the Church of the Holy Sepulchre. Located within the rotunda of the church in Jerusalem, this "little shrine" purportedly contains the tomb—and Resurrection site—of Jesus Christ. The location was revealed to Empress Helena in the early fourth century and in it she supposedly found the wood of the three crucifixes of Mount Calvary. The tomb, and the pieces of "the true cross," formed important bases for Christian claims to the city during the Middle Ages and beyond.

4. The name Mosque of Omar is misleading: named in honor of 'Umar ibn al-Khattab's reported prayer near the Church of the Holy Sepulchre, the current building dates not to the seventh century but the twelfth. 'Umar is renowned as a tolerant leader who permitted Christian and Jewish residency in Jerusalem even after he had conquered it in 638.

5. The Madaba Map, at Saint George in Jordan. This sixth-century floor mosaic was discovered in the late nineteenth century and is an important cartographic representation of the Middle East during early Byzantine times. Jerusalem, represented in oval form, is prominent, and one can spy the white line of the Cardo, the main street running north to south through the city, parts of which are still visible in the modern Jewish Quarter.

6. The Church of the Holy Sepulchre was alternately built, destroyed, and rebuilt throughout the Middle Ages, which explains its variety of architectural features. The *aedicule* ("little shrine"), containing the purported tomb of Jesus Christ, lies under the larger dome, and the main entrance is through the visible twin arches.

7. Caliph al-Hakim bi-Amr Allah. Popularly dubbed "the Mad Caliph," this Shia Imam-caliph of Fatimid Egypt was notorious for his treatment of subjects in the Levant. Persecuting Sunni and Shia Muslims, Eastern Christians, and Jews alike, he is responsible for the destruction of the Church of the Holy Sepulchre in 1009.

8. Despite its name, the Tower of David in Jerusalem dates to medieval, not Old Testament, times. The fortress served as an anchor for the western defenses of the city and resisted numerous attacks until its destruction in the thirteenth century. It was thereafter rebuilt, and today it houses the Tower of David Museum.

9. The Fortress at Shayzar, land of Usama ibn Munqidh. Shayzar, in modern-day northern Syria, was the home of the Banu Munqidh family. Its most famous member was Usama, the ambassador who visited Jerusalem in the mid-twelfth century and maintained professional relationships with the Jerusalem aristocracy and the Knights Templar.

10. Zion Gate, Jerusalem. The capture of Jerusalem by the army of the First Crusade in 1099 is sometimes referred to as crusading's "original sin." Once the Franks overtopped the walls in the north and broke through Zion Gate on the south wall of the city, they proceeded to eliminate all resistance in the city, including non-combatants. This massacre has overshadowed a broader story of interfaith accord before and after the siege.

11. The Western Wall. The wall, or *Kotel*, is the largest synagogue in the world. Of Herodian construction, it anchors the southwestern side of the Temple Mount and has served as a formal site of Jewish devotion since at least the twelfth century. Visible above the wall is the golden Dome of the Rock (left) and the al-Aqsa mosque (right), indicating the proximity of Jewish and Islamic holy sites in Jerusalem.

12. The Horns of Hattin. Occurring on this site (pictured in 1934) on 4 July 1187, the Battle of Hattin was a watershed moment in Sultan Saladin's career. His near-total destruction of the army of the Kingdom of Jerusalem left the Holy City vulnerable to attack, and three months after the battle he entered it in triumph.

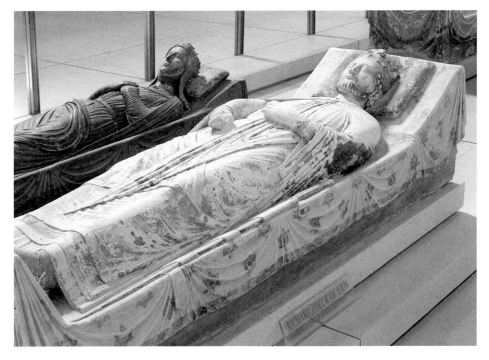

13. Effigy of Richard the Lionheart at Fontevrault Abbey, France. Richard I was one of the principal leaders of the Third Crusade. He and his allies found success against Saladin at nearly every turn, prying away the port of Acre from him and winning at the Battles of Arsuf and Jaffa. The Treaty of Jaffa, concluded between the two rulers in 1192, permitted the reopening of the Church of the Holy Sepulchre.

14. Emperor Frederick II meets Sultan al-Kamil. In an extraordinary event in 1229, the excommunicated Frederick (left) and al-Kamil agreed to a new Treaty of Jaffa. It confirmed Frankish possession of Jerusalem but also guaranteed the Muslim right to prayer on the Temple Mount. The legacy of this arrangement, in some measure, remains today in current interfaith agreements in the city.

15. Battle of La Forbie, as drawn in the chronicle of Matthew Paris. In 1244, Franks formed a coalition with Muslim soldiers from Damascus, Homs, and Kerak to fight against the Muslims of Egypt and their Kwarazmian allies. The event belies claims of an eternal Christian-Muslim antagonisms in the crusading period—when the need arose, leaders of both persuasions found ways to work together.

16. Section of Jerusalem's Ottoman Era walls. A view along the northern side of Jerusalem's walls, as they appeared in the 1940s. The walls of the city were built and rebuilt many times during the Middle Ages, and most of today's structure was built during the reign of Suleiman the Magnificent. Earlier portions, however, remain visible in some places, and archeologists have excavated others.

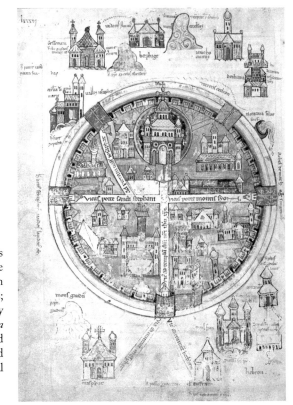

17. Jerusalem. There were several maps of the Holy City created in the Middle Ages, and they typically appeared in manuscripts containing historical works; this one appears in a twelfth-century manuscript of Robert the Monk's *Historia Hierosolymitana*. These were idealized and typically symmetrical in appearance and thus were likely not meant as practical guides for pilgrims.

Jerusalem was also attacked several times in the following decades. Twice, the city was spared a direct assault. A Fatimid army from Ascalon moved on the city while the Franks were occupied with the siege of Tyre in 1124. The Jerusalem residents rallied: led by just a few soldiers, they grabbed weapons and marched out against them. A standoff ensued and the Fatimids eventually departed, although the Franks managed to kill a few of them in pursuit.[30] Much later, in a somewhat surprising move, a descendant of the old Artuqid family returned to attack the city in November 1152. Timür-Tash of Mardin, the son of Ilghazi (and nephew of Suqman), marched first to Damascus and then south towards Jerusalem in a long column. His advance scouts made it to the Mount of Olives, but the kingdom's army, which was stationed in Nablus to the north, took the main body by surprise. Some Franks ambushed the column as it moved through the narrow, mountainous roads towards the River Jordan while others blocked the fords there and killed those who had crossed or watched as others drowned in its waters. Cut off from its advance units and unhorsed in the hills, the Artuqid force lost perhaps five thousand men in the defeat.[31]

The only one of these attacks that actually reached the city was earlier in 1152. In that year, King Baldwin III became embroiled in a territorial dispute with his mother, Melisende (the wife of King Fulk V) that erupted into a civil war. In the course of events, she retreated from Nablus to Jerusalem and barricaded herself in the Tower of David. Baldwin encamped outside and proceeded to besiege it, and an artillery exchange went on for days until Melisende relented.[32] She surrendered the city, with little blood having been shed on either side.

The Return of Safe Conduct

Returning to the early Levantine sieges, some interesting comparisons and contrasts can be made with the taking of Jerusalem in 1099. Acre withstood an initial attack in 1103 but finally fell the next year in a joint land and sea effort, with Genoese and Pisan fleets contributing to the latter.[33] In the process, however, those Italians also partially sacked the city: Albert of Aachen claims they killed over four thousand people while stealing gold, textiles, and livestock from within its walls.[34] There are two points of interest here. First, if Albert's numbers are accurate, they represent more people than were killed in the sack of Jerusalem in July 1099. Historians who harp on the unique bloodiness of that event would do well to think about this. Arguably, the sack of Acre could be read as worse. Most of Jerusalem's victims fell the day of the breach and in the heat of battle, with only 300 perishing after safe conduct was violated on al-Aqsa's roof: whereas at Acre the city was surrendered but, in a violent mood swing, the attackers applied the sword to a whole docile population anyway.[35]

Second, and more important to the general subject of sacks, Baldwin I was apparently outraged at the Italians' behavior, for it violated the safe conduct oath he had sworn to Acre's leaders.[36] That oath assured residents they could leave the city in peace, taking their possessions with them. Outside of the charged climate of the First Crusade, then, one sees a Christian leader striving to limit violence during the acquisition of a city. This would not be the last time Frankish soldiers disobeyed orders in this way, which raises other questions about military discipline and effective command and control.[37] Yet Baldwin's attitude was representative of a broader Frankish willingness to negotiate with Muslim polities when it suited them. He captured Sidon in 1110 and granted terms to everyone in the city; while some Muslims departed, many remained living there in safety. That same year Baldwin's men sacked Beirut, but in that case Ibn al-Qalansi notes that its governor had not parleyed but attempted to flee the city.[38] When Tripoli fell on 12 July 1109, after a seven-year-long effort by Raymond of Toulouse, the townsfolk were tortured and enslaved and the city was looted; the count, however, did grant safe conduct to its governor and garrison, who escaped to

Damascus. In the same year, Tancred took Banyas after guaranteeing the lives of everyone there.[39] In this he treated the Turks the same as he had the Byzantines, whose safety he also guaranteed in 1103 when he seized Latakia from them.[40]

There is a distinct theme that emerges: that early Latin warfare in the East generally followed the same rubric as in the West. As Jim Bradbury suggests—following a long line of consensus on the matter—"when surrender terms were agreed, the defeated could expect that they would be carried out."[41] This was true even in the case of the Jews; the major Jewish populations in Tyre (1124) and Ascalon (1153) were spared because those cities were surrendered, not taken by force.[42] When terms were refused, however, inhabitants could expect to suffer harsh penalties. This was Muslim custom as much as Christian. In an account of the *Continuation of William of Tyre*, after attacking Jerusalem in 1187 Saladin's men managed to scale the northern wall and plant several banners there, at which point the city's commander, Balian, the lord of Ibelin (on the Levantine coast, between Jaffa and Ascalon) finally offered terms. Saladin's response is telling: "Why do you seek to surrender the city and make peace? You can see my banners and my people on the walls. It is too late. As you see, the city is mine."[43] Although Saladin famously relented and allowed Balian to ransom the lives of some of Jerusalem's inhabitants, this was a departure from the norm.

This reality reinforces the sack of Jerusalem as an exceptional event. On that occasion, the crusaders had approached the city and attacked almost immediately, without offering terms to the garrison. They then spent another month gathering supplies and constructing siege engines while still not talking to the city governor, Iftikhar ad-Daulah. So far as we know, neither did the Fatimid garrison send envoys to the siege camp, only spies.[44] It was highly uncommon for a medieval army to attack a city without first demanding its surrender; likewise, it was unusual for a defending garrison not to seek terms. Rushing into the fight meant neither side could lay out expectations or set conditions. Following the First Crusade, however, Frankish armies communicated with the garrison commanders at most cities and fortresses they attacked in the Levant. In other words, once removed from the emotional and once-in-a-lifetime proposition of rescuing the tomb of Christ, western leaders were broadly in favor of sparing residents who would provide revenue from taxes, or, in the case of captured garrison troops, ransom, even if those of a different faith.[45] Privileging those moments of atrocity outside the context of each particular event therefore offers a distorted picture of how sieges were conducted in the period, a time in which diplomacy was very common and more crucial to conflict cessation than the annihilation of populations.[46] This was a sort of rough tolerance but of an unexceptional sort because it was part and parcel with standard ways of doing business.

A New Jerusalem Community

Diverse populations could be tolerated in the coastal cities, so long as Christian governance there was maintained, but this was not the case in Jerusalem. Following the conquest in 1099, the city was depopulated and its demographics were one-dimensional. Crime ran high and there were not enough remaining westerners to properly staff the city and maintain law and order while simultaneously defending its walls. A proper city market that could attract regional merchants would not be arranged until decades later, but even if one had existed enthusiasm would have been tamped down due to the recent bloodletting and expulsion of non-Christians.[47] Franks occupied the Christian Quarter around the Church of the Holy Sepulchre and those eastern Christians who had remained relocated south of the Tower of David (today's Armenian Quarter). Of the many who left of their own accord, they flocked to the coastal towns, where life bustled in the old manner.[48] Later, by 1116, Baldwin I partially solved his population problem by reaching out to surrounding areas. Specifically, he invited eastern Christians (principally Melkites and Jacobites) from lands east of the River Jordan to relocate to Jerusalem. They came in droves, settling in the former *Juiverie* that had been depopulated in 1099 and building a number of churches there.[49]

Gauging the size of the Jewish and Muslim populations in the city is trickier. Both were formally banned by edict, on the basis that their presence polluted the holy sites and could not be tolerated. Following this, the law deemed both groups a second class of residents.[50] We do not know when this edict was promulgated, although it was probably very soon after 1099. Later, the canons of the Council of Nablus, which was called by the Jerusalem patriarch, Warmund, and Baldwin II in 1120, specified laws pertaining to interfaith relations. If, as it has been argued, these canons were not just rhetorical but laws actually put into practice during the twelfth century, they represent a further indication of separation: neither Jews nor Muslims could adopt Christian style attire, Christian–Muslim couples would be mutilated, and any man raping a woman (Muslim or Christian) would be castrated.[51] The rules reveal the Frankish disdain towards any carnal relations with Muslims, but on the other hand there was no systematic attempt to convert local Muslims to Christianity in the early decades of Latin rule, despite the appearance of occasional individual cases in the sources.[52]

These overt references in the literature obscure, however, undercurrents of a more diverse society. It seems clear that within 20 years the initial edict banning residency seems to have lost much of its force. And in general, earlier notions that the crusaders established a sort of apartheid state, in which the westerners lived apart from easterners in a protocolonial model, have now been seriously challenged.[53] Frankish society, even in post-1099 Jerusalem, was more pluralistic than once thought.

The case for the early return of Muslims to Jerusalem is a circumstantial one. There are no formal counts of Muslim residents in

Jerusalem early on, but they were clearly out and about in its streets. In the second decade of Christian rule, Muslim mourners appear in 1118, watching the funeral procession of Baldwin I. Then, in 1120, his successor Baldwin II issued an edict permitting the entrance of Muslim merchants into the city tariff free.[54] We may suppose that such tax relief promoted a more vigorous trade between Franks and Muslims living in surrounding communities.[55] Thus, just two decades after the brutal conquest and legal prohibition on Jews and Muslims, the latter began to physically reappear. The kingdom eventually established trading regulations with neighboring Muslim polities. These specified customs rates both from exported products to "pagan" territories and import into the kingdom, such as salt fish from Baghdad and flax from Damascus. One duty rate distinguished between licorice imports from "Syrians" (meaning eastern Christians) and "Saracens."[56] Turcopoles, the descendants of Turks who served as archers in Frankish armies, had usually been Christianized but some seem to have remained Muslim.[57] This was all part and parcel of the westerners learning to live with—and profit from—their Muslim neighbors on a daily basis.[58] Such norms were generally abhorred back in western Europe, where Muslims were still seen as unreasonable infidels and worthy of condemnation in a stark contrast to evolving attitudes in the Latin East.[59]

More evidence of this legal lapse is then found in the 1130s with the fascinating example of Usama ibn Munqidh, the notable diplomat whose memoirs provide insight into Frankish–Muslim relations in the years before the Second Crusade. Usama's father and uncle were the successive emirs of Shayzar. When a Byzantine army under Emperor John II Comnenos besieged it in 1138, Usama journeyed to Jerusalem to secure an alliance with the Frankish kingdom in response. Such compacts were more common between Christian and Muslim governments in the period than a bystander observing crusade and *jihad* might imagine.[60] Usama returned to the Holy City several times between 1138 and 1144.[61] At other times, however, he opposed their rule, and his memoirs describe numerous occasions on which he personally fought against the Franks, thus illustrating the fluidity of the political landscape and the strange bedfellows it often produced. Medieval historians have wisely taken Usama's many anecdotes with a grain of salt, for some seem like wild exaggerations or invented stories used to draw distinctions between what he saw as civilized Muslims and barbarous Franks, but recently some of his descriptions have been verified with outside sources. He is thus worth a closer look for the information he relays about life in Jerusalem in the mid-twelfth century.[62]

From Usama's memoirs, it is clear that some Islamic worship was tolerated in Jerusalem by the late 1130s. In one of his many stories, Usama, who was probably a Sunni, tells of his visit to the al-Aqsa mosque, in which he spoke to some Templar friends.[63] They allowed him to utilize a small adjacent church (which Usama says had once been a mosque itself) for his prayers, and not just once.[64] On one particular occasion, a Frank disrupted his prayers by repeatedly forcing him to face towards the east, instead of south towards Mecca—the Templars seized the antagonist, threw him out of the building, and then apologized profusely to Usama for the disturbance.[65]

This is an extraordinary tale on many levels. Usama's diplomatic status likely gained him easy entrance into the *Templum Salomonis*, which by that point was no longer the royal residence but rather the Templar headquarters.[66] Foreign dignitaries received uncommon treatment, and Usama's connections were of the highest order. He knew both Nur al-Din and Saladin and spoke to them on multiple occasions, as well as Fulk V, who was king of Jerusalem from 1131 to 1143. On one occasion he traveled to Jerusalem alongside the emir of Damascus, a natural ally of the kingdom. Damascus had opposed the militant efforts of the emir Imad ad-Din Zengi, who captured Edessa in December 1144 and precipitated the Second Crusade.[67] William, the Archbishop of Tyre and voluminous history writer, explains the situation from the Damascene perspective:

The governor [of Damascus] at once dispatched envoys to the king of Jerusalem. Most earnestly he begged in conciliatory words that he and the Christian people would lend their aid and counsel against a cruel enemy, equally dangerous to both kingdoms. Lest he might seem to be boldly soliciting free aid from the king and his nobles, with little hope of return, he promised to pay twenty thousand pieces of gold per month for the necessary expenses of the enterprise.[68]

This was hardly the first alliance between Frankish and Muslim forces in the Levant. In 1108, not even a decade after the conclusion of the First Crusade, Edessa and Mosul fought together against Antioch and Aleppo at the Battle of Tell Bashir; as with Zengi, this also occurred within the context of inter-Turkish fighting.[69] In such situations, the Franks ignored potential alliances with Muslim states at their peril. Diplomatic ties likewise explain Usama's casual banter with Fulk, as recounted elsewhere in the memoirs: he wrote, "I used to visit frequently the king of the Franks [Fulk] . . . on account of the fact that King Baldwin [II] . . . was under obligation to my father."[70]

But to return to al-Aqsa, status does not necessarily explain Usama's proclamation of friendship with Templar knights. This image runs counter to most popular understandings of that military religious order, which routinely appears in books and media productions as the most zealous, violent, and anti-Muslim holy warriors of them all. Some tempering is probably needed: the friendship here was probably of a more formal nature (*suhba* in Arabic), or what Shlomo Goitein has coined a commercial friendship.[71] Usama may have regarded the Templars as trusted brokers with whom he could be reasonably honest; in a corporate sense, there is evidence that the military religious orders approached Christian–Muslim nonmilitary relations with reason and pragmatism, not unbridled religious animosity.[72] Indeed, he had many reasons to hate the Franks in general: his favorite son and also his brother had died at their hands, and at one point they robbed his family after they arrived in Acre. He may have actually regarded killing Franks as somewhat akin to hunting, in that it was a pastime fit for a man of his status.[73] These experiences, combined with the Frankish possession of Jerusalem, probably made for a transactional relationship, not something like the western modes of friendship (*amicitia*) as understood in the crusading period, that is, bordering on brotherly love.[74]

Nor does status fully explain the provision of a prayer space—on the Temple Mount, of all places—to a visiting dignitary. And, in fact, it seems that Usama was not the only Muslim to pray there. The travel guide of John of Würzburg, a priest who visited Jerusalem between 1160 and 1170, offers a most curious tale of Muslim prayer in that space:

> In the Temple, at the altar which stood in the open air, distant from the Temple more than twenty-two paces, Zacharias, the son of Barachias, suffered martyrdom, and upon this altar the Jews in the Old Testament used to offer turtle-doves and pigeons. It has since then been changed by the Saracens into a sun-dial, and may be seen at this day, and is noticeable, because, even at the present day, many Saracens come to it to pray, as it points towards the south, the direction in which they pray.[75]

This short passage is counterintuitive. Modern readers can be forgiven for broadly supposing that the Franks, following the blood-bath of 1099 and outlawing of Muslims from the city, would not tolerate their prayers within its walls at all, much less on the Temple Mount. And yet here they were doing just that. John's report is corroborated by the Persian writer al-Hawari, who himself prayed on the Temple Mount in 1173.[76] Such apparent tolerance on the part of the Latin Christians might not be so surprising. Centuries earlier, in 638, Patriarch Sophronius had been similarly nonplussed about Muslim interest in the site. More importantly, however, this passage demonstrates that freedom of worship in the 1160s was no longer restricted to men of rank or position (if indeed it ever was).

The belligerent Frank who confronted Usama offers another angle into the complexity of crusade-era Jerusalem. According to the Templars, he was a newcomer who did not understand the cultural differences of the local peoples.[77] Usama himself makes the point about how longer association with Muslims bred familiarity and, perhaps, tolerance. The latter is unspoken but seems implied. Even then, this newcomer did not object to, or try to prevent, the prayer itself, only the direction in which Usama prayed. All told, this story demonstrates how, at least on an elite level, there could be cordial relations between Franks and Muslims in Jerusalem and the granting of religious exemptions, and in the most revered of locations, at that.

Ordinary Muslims, such as merchants and pilgrims, make less of an impression in the sources. John of Würzburg seems to indicate their presence. Noting the general Muslim distaste for the cross erected on top of the Dome of the Rock; he writes, in the present tense, "nevertheless they respect this Temple, because they adore their creator therein."[78] Moreover, each Palm Sunday the Golden Gate in the eastern wall of the Temple Mount was opened "to a procession and to the whole people, whether they be citizens or strangers."[79] He lists the various nations of peoples abundant in the city, and in addition to such groups as English, Armenians, Georgians, and Caphetirici (who may have been Ethiopians) he mentions Egyptians, whom he distinguishes from the Copts.[80] Because this passage follows a remark on the maintenance of Christian facilities, the assumption in the literature has been that these were also Christians but this is not explicitly stated.[81] Local interpreters are sometimes spotted as well, and while some were converts to Christianity others may not have been.[82] These are surely vague references.

A clearer example was in the massive, 3,344 square-yard Hospital of St. John in Jerusalem, the facility run by the Knights Hospitaller. Its roots run back to a hostel operated under the permission of the

Fatimid Caliph al-Mustansir, a very interesting connection indeed.[83] As we may recall, he had given aid to Jewish claimants in Jerusalem and also assisted the German pilgrims in 1065. An attested 1182 edict of the expanded hospital states that anyone could receive care there, whatever their origin, status, or sex, and the edict specifically states that "pagans" (Muslims) were included.[84] Presumably, these had been in the city proper or its immediate environs before admittance into the wards, a further indication of at least their itinerant presence. Using these multiple accounts, then, we can determine that there were Muslims in Jerusalem in the 1110s to the 1180s, with the vast majority being visitors and merchants, not residents, who nonetheless had the right to utilize the hospital and pray on the Temple Mount. This Hospitaller facility also welcomed Jews, who are likewise specified as admissible in the 1182 document.

How many Jews utilized this service, or were even seen in Jerusalem at the time, is hard to gauge. Unlike the larger and active Jewish population in places like Acre, Jewish presence in the city between 1099 and 1187 seems to have been virtually nonexistent.[85] When noted in histories and travel accounts they are generally in single digits; for example, just one Jew is detected living there in 1146.[86] During his well-known travels through the region in 1167–1173, Benjamin of Tudela was assiduous in counting Jews wherever he found them, perhaps to help western Jews locate hospitable lodgings during their pilgrimages to sites in Mesopotamia.[87] He counted only four Jewish families in Jerusalem, engaged in the profession of dyeing cloth. Located south of the Tower of David, these seem to have lived there under some special agreement that allowed them to rent lodgings on an annual basis.[88] While four families may have constituted several dozens of people, they remained a tiny number in proportion to the larger population and certainly far less than the 3,000 Jews Benjamin counted living in Damascus to the east.[89] A few years later, the rabbi Petahyah of Regensburg visited and found, once again, only a single Jew in residence.[90]

While residency was light, some allowances for visitation seem to have persisted. Benjamin himself had been able to enter the city freely and made no mention of interference from any local authority. One can therefore assume that, by the 1160s, Jewish passage through the city was permitted and occasional, temporary lodging was possible. Moreover, he notes a crucial detail: that Jews also continued to worship in the city, and at no less than the Western Wall itself:

> In front of it [Dome of the Rock] you see the western wall, one
> of the walls which formed the holy of holies of the ancient temple,
> it is called gate of mercy and all Jews resort thither to say their
> prayers near the wall of the court yard.[91]

Despite the confusing inclusion of the Gate of Mercy, which lies at the other side of the mount, this reference has traditionally been seen as the first reference to prayer at the Western Wall.[92] The most famous medieval Jew of them all, the philosopher Maimonides (d. 1204), probably prayed at the same spot when he undertook a three-day pilgrimage to Jerusalem in October 1165.[93] It is unclear whether or not such prayers were sanctioned or even tolerated by the Franks or whether they were performed in such a manner so as to avoid suspicion. Nonetheless, these travelogues of Usama, John, and Benjamin—a Muslim, Christian, and Jew—testify that by the 1160s both Muslims and Jews were saying their traditional prayers at their respective holiest locations.[94] This was more a reflection of, not a contrast to, the general religious freedom offered to Muslims and Jews in the surrounding cities, towns, and villages in the kingdom of Jerusalem at large.[95]

Learning to Live Together

Interestingly, many remarks on Jerusalem's population center not on religion but rather ethnicity. In a well-known passage, Fulcher of

Chartres remarks on how, in the Levant, God transformed the West into the East through the settlement of the Franks:

> He who was a Roman or a Frank is now a Galilaean, or an inhabitant of Palestine. One who was a citizen of Rheims or of Chartres now has been made a citizen of Tyre or of Antioch. We have already forgotten the places of our birth; already they have become unknown to many of us, or, at least, are unmentioned. Some already possess here homes and servants which they have received through inheritance. Some have taken wives not merely of their own people, but Syrians, or Armenians, or even Saracens who have received the grace of baptism.[96]

This cultural transformation chimes with John of Würzburg's rundown of the different ethnic groups active in the city. Jerusalem was steadily morphing from a Latin-dominated, sparsely populated city to a diverse landscape of peoples: a product of what one scholar has called the "multicultural experience and awareness of the crusaders."[97]

This was particularly true regarding eastern Christians and especially Armenians, who had much greater influence than other groups. Indeed, both Baldwin I and II married Armenian princesses, and Armenians congregated in the cathedral of St. James the Great inside the city. Christianized Turcopoles were present in Jerusalem's armies, albeit to a much lesser extent than in, say, Antioch.[98] Other eastern rites maintained their own churches as well; it has been estimated that Latin churches constituted only 55 percent of the total in the city during the twelfth century, while 28 percent were Orthodox and 17 percent were of other eastern denominations.[99] Scholarly opinion now holds that the Latin–Eastern Christian relationship was complex but, while animosities were evident, there was significant accord in interfaith relations. This was especially true among the people, so much so that churches were sometimes shared, albeit less so in upper ecclesiastical circles.[100]

This should not imply that any of these groups were accorded equal, or even fair, treatment in the city and kingdom of Jerusalem. Visitors and residents could well complain about Frankish laws, and there were two prominent rumors of Muslims entering the city simply in order to assassinate local Christians.[101] This is an urban manifestation of the broader attacks against pilgrims on the roads to Jerusalem, which had precipitated the creation of the Knights Templar in the first place. Much debate has swirled about whether eastern Christians were considered a separate and/or lower class than the Franks. There was simply too much variation in legal and policy norms as well as individual lived experiences over time and too many distinctions between groups—ethnic, religious, and political—to draw blanket conclusions, so attempts to do so have been heavily criticized.[102]

Moreover, these hints and allegations of interfaith contact and apparent exemptions, reduced taxes, or cordial relations do not resemble the sorts of pluralistic societies found in Jerusalem in earlier periods. The Jewish component is the most strikingly different because Jews were broadly absent there between 1099 and 1187: not really part of the city fabric and never found directly engaging with Frankish jurisprudence, the city market, or members of other religions. Still, some families eventually rented lodging in the city and plied their trades there and Jewish prayers were said at the Western Wall. Muslims seem to have been broadly tolerated for reasons entirely of practicality: their money and goods were needed, and periodic alliances with the principalities from which they traveled served Jerusalem's political interests.[103] Public Islamic prayer was conducted in at least two places on the Temple Mount, which means that Muslims could be found near the Dome of the Rock and in close proximity to the Frankish places of worship, refurbished and newly built there. Sex and marriage between Christians and Muslims, however, was forbidden, demonstrating the limits of the intermingling. The experiences of Usama ibn Munqidh are revealing but, as examples of elite contact, can only be pushed so far. Eastern Christians did much better, as we have seen. This all constitutes incremental forward progress from the most common image of the crusaders in Jerusalem: that of the frenetic massacre, enslavement, and ransoming of 1099.

II

In any discussion about medieval tolerance, it is impossible to avoid the subject of the founder of the Ayyubid dynasty in Egypt, the sultan Saladin. For centuries, he has been celebrated by both East and West as a model of medieval generalship and statesmanship, cast as a gentleman with chivalric qualities. Dante gave him a place of honor in *Inferno*, in which he spends eternity wandering in Limbo rather than being tortured for his heresy in the sixth circle of Hell: "solitary, set apart, Saladin."[104] By the time Saladin caught Voltaire's admiring eye, he had been cast essentially as a Frenchman of taste and distinction in seventeenth-century France: "nimble ... valiant, generous, liberal, courtly."[105] His legend has attracted substantial scholarly and popular attention, and in 1898 none other than Kaiser Wilhelm II of Germany laid a wreath at the sultan's tomb in Damascus. He had been, essentially, adopted as a European hero.[106]

Saladin's reputation was enhanced from the very start by three fawning medieval biographers, whom Hillenbrand has called his "spin doctors," who extolled his virtues in contemporary accounts.[107] The reality of Saladin's life is somewhat different from the legend. Those celebrated moments of mercy and tolerance were counterbalanced by others of discrimination, butchery and enslavement, and in this juxtaposition he was arguably no more or less moral than most rulers of his time. This reality is hardly unknown, but the interpretation of it has been interesting.

Broadly speaking, in the West his generous reputation still predominates, but in the modern Middle East this is sometimes

discarded in favor of his more violent tendencies. There, he is celebrated rather as a proponent of *jihad*, a champion of Arab territorial
rights, and a destroyer of infidels and idolaters. For example, current
Palestinian primary and secondary school readings employ only the
jihadi Saladin in their lessons: a powerful Muslim hero who liberated
the Levant from unbelievers and ushered in a glorious epoch through
justified, though violent, means.[108] Yet this is one, and the most
antagonistic, aspect of his reign—emphasizing it, and only it, will do
nothing but provoke division. What if, instead, the lessons added the
sensibilities of the Saladin legend that western readers seem to
prefer? In the eyes of the next generation of students, he might well
become a proud Muslim warrior and liberator, yes, but one who also
allowed Jews to move back into Jerusalem and worship alongside
both Muslims and eastern Christians—the same spirit of accord as
in the Fatimid Caliphate he overthrew.

The Rise to Power

Saladin crept onto the Egyptian scene in the 1160s. A Kurd by birth,
hailing from the Mesopotamian city of Tikrit, he had journeyed to
Egypt with his uncle Shirkuh in 1164 on a mission from the Turkish
sultan Nur al-Din. The recently deposed Fatimid vizier, Shawar, had
requested military assistance in order to reclaim his position, promising significant riches in return (one third of the grain revenues of
Egypt, quite literally a king's ransom).[109] Knowing the economic and
strategic potential of Egypt to his continuing struggle against the
Crusader States, Nur al-Din sent his trusted general Shirkuh to
Egypt to aid and assist. Together, Shirkuh and Shawar began a
campaign against the usurpers in April, and it was effective enough
to procure the reinstallation of Shawar by the end of May. At length,
however, Shawar refused to make good on his financial promises and
ordered Shirkuh to leave Egypt; when he refused, the vizier formed
an alliance with the Franks to drive him out. Together, he and King

Amalric of Jerusalem besieged Shirkuh and Saladin in Bilbais along the Nile. In three months the matter was settled and Shirkuh retired from the area with a promise of safe conduct, 30,000 dinars in his purse, and his nephew Saladin by his side.[110]

Three years later the Kurds were back, once again squaring off against a Fatimid–Frankish alliance in 1167. Whether they fought on behalf of Nur al-Din or for their own ambitions in Egypt is still debated, but in any case Saladin held his first real command. Driving off the Franks in battle south of Cairo, he thereafter held Alexandria for his uncle until peace terms were reached in August.[111] Given the evident strife between the Shia and Sunni principals, Amalric then decided to invade Egypt himself in 1168.[112] Set back on his heels, Shawar begged Nur al-Din's assistance once more, but this would be his final move in a fraught diplomatic career. Shirkuh and Saladin returned and prevented Amalric's forces from capturing Cairo.[113] Despite their adversarial relationship, there is evidence that Saladin and Amalric actually maintained a friendship that dated back to the events in Alexandria, and the former later mourned the latter's death in 1174.[114]

Following Amalric's retreat, Shirkuh finally made his power move: he secured the arrest and execution of Shawar and was subsequently named the new vizier by the Fatimid Imam-caliph, al-Adid.[115] He received all the traditional titles and privileges accorded to the position; like al-Afdal and Badr al-Jamali, he was effectively more powerful than Caliph al-Adid and pulled the major levers of Egyptian power. Upon Shirkuh's death, he was succeeded by his nephew, Saladin.[116]

From that point on, Saladin waged an extremely careful, savvy, and orchestrated rise to power. As a Sunni, he found ways to support the Shia caliph while subsequently building up his own influence. After biding his time, he struck the most consequential military blow in 1169. In that year, the eunuch commander of the Fatimid African corps conspired to ally with the Franks in order to drive Saladin out of Egypt.[117] That force of Nubians, which Caliph al-Mustansir's mother, Rasad, had originally created in the mid-eleventh century, was still a huge, potent defense force barracked in Fustat. The civil war of 1062 had seen them wiped out, only for Rasad to swiftly replenish them. A century later the story would end rather differently. After uncovering the plot, in August Saladin ordered the eunuch executed, and the black soldiers rose up in revolt. In the resulting "Battle of the Blacks," the other elements of the Fatimid army crushed them, killing up to 50,000. He then pursued their wives and children; those who survived were given safe passage across the Nile, where his brother Turanshah wiped them out entirely.[118]

Saladin was now firmly poised to take control of Egypt. Caliph al-Adid died on 13 September, and four days later the *khutba* was said, in both Fustat and Cairo, in the name of the Sunni Abbasid caliph.[119] The Fatimid Caliphate, in which Shia Imam-caliphs had ruled over Egypt and parts beyond since 969, now came to an end. Saladin then pivoted to defeat the Frankish siege of Damietta in October 1169 and spent the next two years cautiously moving forces around Sinai and Gaza to shore up his eastern flank as well as incorporating members of his family into important positions within his new Ayyubid administration.[120]

The seizures of the Levantine ports in the first two decades of the twelfth century, along with a bold invasion of Egypt proper by Baldwin I in 1118, had helped keep the Fatimids at bay during the early history of the Crusader States.[121] Five decades later much had changed. Franks still held the coast, but Saladin began his movements into the region and either defeated or won over Nur al-Din's relatives. Over the course of the 1170s and 1180s, he campaigned against both Turkish and Frankish targets, including Damascus, Homs, and Hama in 1174, Aleppo in 1174–1175, Jacob's Ford in 1179, Beirut in 1182, Mosul in 1182–1183, and several sieges of Kerak. At length, he was able to consolidate power in Syria and add the resources of its emirs to his core Egyptian army.

Enemy Relations

We might pause here and consider Saladin's attitude towards those he conquered. He showed an utter ruthlessness towards the black units, fueled by his need to erode the Fatimid base of military support in order to advance his own political goals. Little has been made of the eradication of their families, an operation that had his full support. If Ibn al-Athir's figures are anywhere in the realm of reality, the families of tens of thousands of soldiers would have been of an equal or higher number. Anne-Marie Eddé has noted that those killed were considered not "thoroughly Arabized or Islamized"—ethnic and religious difference, therefore, made the task easier to contemplate.[122]

Did Saladin treat other non-Sunni demographics similarly? He is typically remembered for tolerant treatment because nearly everyone concentrates only on his capture of Jerusalem in 1187. There are plentiful examples of Saladin's mercy. He spared an infant kidnapped from the crusader camp at Acre, returning it to its mother.[123] After taking Jerusalem, he allowed King Guy's wife, Sibylla, to depart in safety; in 1188, he even released Guy himself from captivity after exacting an oath that the king never again take up arms against him. He captured a Templar garrison at Safad in December 1187 but allowed it to safely depart for Tyre, and in later months he periodically offered similar terms elsewhere in order to effect prompt capitulations.[124]

Yet other examples might be raised in retort. While Coptic Christians and Jews had figured significantly in the Fatimid civil service, Saladin tried to expel them from his new administration in 1172.[125] They, at least, lived to tell the tale: Usama remarks in his memoirs about Saladin's capture of two castles near Irbil; "he took captive all the Christians and Jews," at which point the writer employs a proverb to explain their fates: "stop now the account of those who were killed by passion."[126] A group of captured Franks was executed near Hama in October 1178.[127] Following his victory at Jacob's Ford in August 1179, he executed most of a group of 700 prisoners, many of them Turcopoles, who were deemed traitors to the faith of their fathers.[128]

In 1183, Saladin violated a promise of safe conduct and permitted the execution of captured Franks, although the circumstances of that event were rather extraordinary. In February, Reynald de Châtillon, the lord of Oultrejordain (ancient Moab), had led a daring raid on the Hijaz, in which he assembled a brace of prefabricated galleys at Aylah (modern-day Aqaba, Jordan) and tacked down the coastline of the Red Sea, periodically burning Muslim ships and landing to hit caravans on land. At length, he moved on Medina itself, disembarking and marching to within one day's march of the city, where the plan may have been to steal Muhammad's bones.[129] There they were defeated and 170 Franks taken prisoner, although Reynald himself escaped. His good luck ended in 1187, however, and he was beheaded alongside hundreds of captured Knights Templar and Hospitaller after the Battle of Hattin.[130] On that occasion, Saladin was so keen to execute them that he first purchased their lives from his emirs (50 dinars apiece), which gave him the right to then order their deaths at the hands of otherwise pacifistic Sufis.[131]

Saladin's motivations for both merciful and harsh treatment of prisoners run the gamut of possibilities. A highly skilled politician, he was adept at the diplomatic game, alternatively cajoling or threatening peers, subordinates, and enemies alike; he was often able to swing even steadfast opposition with flattery and generous disbursements of positions, lands (via the system of *iqta*), or lavish gifts.[132] He relied on advice from his personal judges and secretaries and so, as a result, rarely made rash decisions. Strategic considerations were important and sparing a foe at a given moment sometimes served his larger interests. He also had concrete political goals that guided his choices, to some extent.

There were other impulses as well, and by far the most prominent in the literature has been the factor of *jihad*, which had percolated around Antioch during the First Crusade. In the years immediately afterward, Muslim holy war against the newcomers grew in intensity. According to Ibn al-Qalansi, in July 1101 an Egyptian army marched to Ascalon "to prosecute the Holy War against the Franks."[133] Expectations of divinely sanctioned reconquest increased. Nur al-Din had felt them previously, when he was the presumed leader of an Islamic resurgence. As cast by the Muslim intellectuals and poets of his day, this meant no less than to overthrow the Shia Fatimids in Egypt, unify the world's Islamic population, and reclaim Jerusalem from the infidel Franks, in that order.[134] It was Nur al-Din who patronized the writer Ibn 'Asakir, who, at his personal request, wrote the book *Forty Hadiths for Inciting Jihad*.[135]

These burdens subsequently fell on Saladin who, having successfully accomplished the first goal and making some progress on the second, now set about the third.[136] The concept of *jihad* ("struggle") had slowly evolved over time and experienced a steady resurgence of interest in the period of the Crusades. It was most vibrant among the Muslim religious class but by the days of Zengi and the run-up to the Second Crusade had become prominent in military circles as well.[137] Saladin was able to utilize the propagandistic tools of the holy war, which had been institutionalized by Nur al-Din, to increase recruitment of soldiers, aggrandize himself personally, and justify his course of actions to the regional Muslim merchant class and the Abbasid caliph in Baghdad. Jerusalem eventually became the central target in Saladin's *jihad*.[138]

Hattin and Jerusalem

In 1187, the sultan finally set his sights on the Muslim recovery of the Holy City. As usual, Jerusalem was protected not only by its walls, which had been improved in 1116 and also 1177, but also the presence of the army of the Kingdom of Jerusalem.[139] Destruction of that army was a prerequisite to any attempted reconquest of the Holy

City. In late June 1187, therefore, Saladin took what was probably the largest army of his entire reign, numbering between 30,000 and 40,000 soldiers, and marched west from Syria, arriving just south of the Sea of Galilee by month's end.[140] He then crossed the River Jordan and camped at Kafr-Sabt, on a southwest–northeast line between Nazareth and Tiberias. These movements were of course easily detected, and Guy of Lusignan, the king of Jerusalem, ordered his army mustered at Saforie, a well-protected valley to Saladin's east. Saladin traveled there in person on 1 July and offered battle.[141]

Guy dithered as he listened to advisers and considered his options. Refusing battle likely meant the fall of Tiberias but refuse it he did, and that city fell the very next day. Guy then changed his mind and left for Saforie on 3 July to join the army, determined to thwart the sultan's next move. In a strategic sense this was the king's fatal mistake, for he had acted on Saladin's schedule, not his own.[142] His army moved from there eastward but pushed past the last good water supply at Turan and was eventually caught and encircled at the Horns of Hattin, a dormant volcano.[143] The numbers were roughly even but the Franks were in a poor position, lacking water supplies, and so tightly encircled that there was no open path of retreat.[144] Muslim campfires choked the Franks with billowing smoke and archers showered them with arrows. On 4 July, Count Raymond of Tripoli managed a cavalry breakout to the east, but the rest of the army was trapped and either captured or slaughtered when its perimeter collapsed: "they cried out, but there was no one to save them."[145] Guy, utterly exhausted and defeated, was captured while sitting on the ground and has traditionally taken the blame for the loss, for a variety of reasons.[146]

Following the Battle of Hattin, Saladin was in no particular rush to move against Jerusalem. The important strategic targets were the same as the Franks in their post-1099 coastal campaign: the Levantine ports. From early July to early September 1187, he besieged and captured Acre, Sidon, Beirut, and Ascalon in rapid succession. This gave him control of the entire coastline of the eastern Mediterranean from Alexandria in Egypt up to modern-day Lebanon, with only two principal exceptions at Tyre and Tripoli.

Only after Ascalon's fall did Saladin finally turn his attention to the Holy City. He first reconnoitered the city for five days and then arrayed his forces west of the city, opposite St. David's Gate, on 20 September 1187. An archery assault commenced, but after five days of inconclusive fighting he shifted his army to the northern side of the city, assembled artillery devices, and on the 26th began to bombard the wall beyond St. Stephen's Gate. These fires really served as cover for the Muslim sappers moving south, underground. Negotiations began on 30 September, and the garrison capitulated on 2 October.[147]

Coming to an agreement with Balian, Saladin agreed to a monetary ransoming of the Jerusalem residents. The terms can only be described as generous: 10 dinars per man, five per woman, and one per child, with 40 days provided to collect the sums; those ransomed could leave the city in peace with their belongings.[148] Thousands departed in this way, and Saladin graciously exempted thousands more, on the pleading of Balian and the noble Frankish women in the city. More might have been ransomed, but while the Templars and Hospitallers parted with some of their monies to ransom the poor, they evidently kept the rest, their avarice consigning the remainder of the Frankish population to its fate.[149]

The treaty aside, Saladin's personal release of thousands of people unable to pay the ransom speaks volumes about his generosity and has, without a doubt, formed the core of his fine reputation today in both East and West.[150] Moreover, the Ayyubid conquest of Jerusalem is traditionally cast as the return of social and religious tolerance. Despite his promise to "bathe the city in blood," as had the crusaders, Saladin's siege of Jerusalem was nonetheless relatively brief and concluded with the surrender of its Christian garrison instead of a massacre. The contrast with 1099 seems self-evident, and he emerges from the story as a merciful, just conqueror. Yet the combination of interfaith allowances in the 1130s–1180s under the Franks with Saladin's other conduct in 1187 challenge this simplistic judgment.

One must pause and think beyond the popular image. How generous were Saladin's mercies? Although he indeed spared the Jerusalem Frankish population a butchering, he nonetheless enslaved a large portion of its population. They had arguably been left out in the cold by military religious orders, who are the most responsible for their fate. Still, it is reasonable to examine the treatment of these prisoners of war. Few historians write in detail about them beyond noting their number, which seems to have been anywhere between 7,000 and 16,000 people. Saladin gave some of them to his soldiers as gifts, while slavers purchased the rest and thereafter sold them in the regional markets. The incident passes rather lightly in the Arabic sources. Even Ibn al-Athir, the historian whose writings display occasional hostility towards Saladin because of the latter's siege of his home city of Mosul in 1182, was succinct, writing simply that these peoples were taken captive and distributed. Modern biographers of Saladin have followed suit.[151]

Yet this was not simply the taking of prisoners. The women and children were divided between Saladin's soldiers, who took them as wives, concubines, or slaves. The secretary 'Imad ad-Din Isfahani offers a version of their humiliation. Numbering the women at 8,000, he writes:

How many well-guarded women were profaned, how many queens were ruled, and nubile girls married, and noble women given away, and miserly women forced to yield themselves, and women who had been kept hidden stripped of their modesty, and serious women made ridiculous, and women kept in private now set in public, and free women occupied, and precious ones used for hard work, and pretty things put to the test, and virgins dishonoured and proud women deflowered ... turbulent men able to give vent to their passion.[152]

This was not just enslavement: it was forced marriage, concubinage, and rape. Is it the truth, or just hyperbole?[153] 'Imad al-Din's writing is endlessly creative and full of similes and metaphors; in one instance, he offers dozens of these to characterize Frankish women as essentially whores.[154] Again, the question of equivalence rears its head: historians have been more than willing to accept the lurid stories of carnage on the Temple Mount in 1099 and its rivers of blood. In the case of 1187, however, the notion of poetic license has led many general histories of the crusades to ignore this event entirely.[155] One popular history not only neglects it but, incredibly, characterizes the whole taking of Jerusalem as "without a bloodbath, destruction, or hatred," as if forcible marriage and rape involved none of those things![156] This contrasts with perceptions when the tables were turned; the poet Ibn al-Khayyat once lamented the purported rape of Muslims at the hands of crusaders, actions that violated "the sanctity of the womenfolk."[157]

Yet 'Imad al-Din was no ordinary chronicler. He was a friend and companion to Saladin from 1174. Moreover, his work was meant for the sultan himself, recited to him on at least one occasion and available for his perusal, and its flowery language typically does not preclude accurate content.[158] That proximity makes it highly unlikely that he would lie outright, especially when describing an event so clearly related to Saladin's reputation. Depending on one's perspective, then, these forced marriages and rapes of thousands of women and girls either rise to the level of the crusader sack in 1099 or not. It was clearly a brutal process of enslavement and subjugation, albeit one accepted as current practice in the Islamic armies of the time.[159]

Nonetheless, some Latin Christian residents seem to have been spared and even asked to remain in the city, which was permitted so long as they paid the *jizya* and occupied only menial employment.[160] These Christians were evidently still there in 1192, when envoys of the English king, Richard I "the Lionheart," requested that they not be molested.[161] Many eastern Christians remained as well, after humbly requesting a dispensation from Saladin and offering to pay the *jizya*, but theirs was a diverse fate: Arabic, Syriac, and Armenian Christians largely left; the Georgians and Copts were allowed to remain and were, indeed, favored by Saladin; the Jacobites competed with the Melkites for control of now vacant Latin properties.[162]

To return to the narrative, seven days later, on 9 October, Saladin rode into Jerusalem. In retaking the city, he had fulfilled the grandest hopes of the intellectual Muslim class, whose letters, chronicles, and poetry had collectively cried out for restitution. His men immediately set to work purifying the city. They stripped away nearly all of the Christian additions to the Dome of the Rock, including the mosaics, the protective covering of Abraham's rock, and the large cross on the top of its dome; Saladin's nephew Taqi al-Din washed the interior with rose water.[163] Further south at al-Aqsa, workers dismantled the Templars' structural additions to the mosque along with most of those rooms traveled by Usama ibn Munqidh during his prayerful visit there. Two *minbars* (pulpits) became the new prominent interior features, one of which had been built on the order of Nur al-Din for the express purpose of installation in Jerusalem.[164] Clerics removed copies of the Bible and reinstituted Islamic preaching, with the first *khutba* said in both Saladin's and Caliph al-Nasir li-Din Allah's names. Saladin temporarily closed down the Church of the Holy Sepulchre, but he resisted calls to destroy it, perhaps in imitation of 'Umar, who had likewise spared it in 638.[165] One anonymous account claims that the church and Calvary, enclosed within it, was also relieved "of all decoration" in the process.[166]

Around the city, Muslims busily refurbished existing mosques and repurposed certain churches as new ones, and Saladin approved the founding and endowing of a *madrasa* and a hospice for Sufis.[167] Funds were endowed (*waqf*) for their maintenance and for that of the holy sites on the Temple Mount, as well as on the Mount of Olives, and the *qadi* (judge) Baha al-Din Ibn Shaddad took up the role of overseeing it all.[168] In one form or another, that *waqf* has existed ever since, and it was affirmed anew in 1967 following the Israeli capture of the Temple Mount in the Six Day War. Therefore, Saladin's capture of the city enabled his Ayyubid successors to permanently stamp an Islamic presence that has persisted and mirrors the modern day: Muslims on top of the Haram and Jews at the Western Wall below, on the outside looking in.

In the wake of his great victory, Saladin was compared to none other than 'Umar ibn al-Khattab, who had first obtained the holy sites for Islam in 638. His entrance into the city was staged to resemble 'Umar's, and the Spanish traveler Ibn Jubayr wrote that God had given the honor of Jerusalem's first conquest to 'Umar but the reward of reconquering it to Saladin.[169] Inscriptions in the Dome of the Rock deepen that connection in Qur'anic terms.[170] Clearly the two leaders had much in common in political and military terms but the pairing goes deeper and into the eschatological realm. There was apparent fear that the holy sites, especially the rock of Muhammad, were under threat from the Frankish presence on it, and this was spoken of in terms of the approaching Last Hour; Saladin arrived and "broke the cross" in apocalyptic symbiosis with the Qur'anic Jesus at the final judgment and thus fitted squarely into the narrative of an End Times scenario.[171] The comparison calls for a look back at 'Umar's journey to Jerusalem, when he engaged the Jew about the Gate of Mercy and the defeat of the Antichrist beyond it.[172] Reference to that gate is made again in 'Imad ad-Din Isfahani's description of the city, joining the two commanders again in a physical and spiritual sense and, in more modern times, together in Muslim memories.[173]

Saladin himself did not actually spend much time in the Holy City. He was only there from 9–30 October 1187, after which he departed for Acre. He took his army first to besiege Tyre and Hunin in Upper Galilee, abandoning the first and capturing the second, and then, acceding to demands from his emirs, allowed the soldiers to go home to winter quarters. In March 1188 they returned and Saladin marched north to attack Belvoir Castle, which was too strongly defended. Abandoning that siege as well, he regrouped at Damascus and then undertook a lengthy campaign north. Between June and September he captured a number of minor towns and fortresses, but Tyre continued to hold fast and he could not reach Antioch before the commencement of the West's grand counteroffensive.[174]

The Third Crusade

Bad news had been the order of the day in the lead-up to Hattin, and the disaster there had significant effects around the Mediterranean. The Byzantine emperor, Isaac II Angelos, soon pondered Saladin as a possible ally for the defense of his realm, specifically from the German army gathering under the leadership of Emperor Frederick Barbarossa.[175] The Armenians lamented the city's fall, with one poet calling for Prince Levon II to intervene and liberate the city.[176] The defeat struck western Europe particularly hard. Saladin's earlier defeats were reported by merchants and clergy in the Latin East; they, and most prominently the patriarch of Jerusalem, Heraclius, employed biblical language from books like Lamentations to paint a dire picture.[177] Upon hearing about events at Hattin in July, Pope Urban III reportedly died instantly, and his successor, Gregory VIII, subsequently issued the papal bull *Audita tremendi severitate* ("When we heard of the severity") at the end of October 1187.[178] The presumption, which was possibly the cause of poor Urban's demise, was that Jerusalem would inevitably be retaken by Saladin.[179] Certainly, history favored this pessimistic view. The absence of a protective field army has customarily precipitated the city's fall. This had been the case in 638, when (Emperor) Heraclius's army was first wiped out at Yarmuk, again when the Carmathians were defeated outside of Cairo in 971, and yet again when Badr al-Jamali's Armenians were busy quelling strife between the Nubians and Turks in the Fatimid ranks; and finally, once Kerbogha had been defeated and al-Afdal withdrew his army to Ascalon in 1098–1099.

Gregory VIII's bull constituted the formal launching of what became known as the Third Crusade. Christian states in France, the British Isles, Denmark, the Holy Roman Empire, Iberia, Hungary, Flanders, and elsewhere joined in a massive coalition of soldiers that journeyed to the Levant in a piecemeal fashion, arriving at different times between 1189 and 1191.[180] They swarmed to Acre, where the now free Guy of Lusignan began a siege in August 1189 with a few thousand recruits, many of them the ransomed survivors of Saladin's attack on Jerusalem. At Acre arriving crusaders were dropped into a blender: Guy's army encamped between the city's Muslim garrison and Saladin's field army that had arrived to succor them. For nearly two years, the westerners tried to break through Acre's fortifications while fending off attacks from the rear, taking tens of thousands of casualties in the process from combat, starvation, exposure, and disease. At length, the arrival of fresh soldiers under two kings, Richard the Lionheart and especially Philip II "Augustus" of France, led to the successful undermining of the wall and capitulation of the garrison.[181]

Despite the victory, the army that emerged from Acre was hardly an ideal force for snatching back Jerusalem. Philip departed for Europe, leaving Richard to lead a depleted force south along the Levantine coastline. Saladin's army tracked its movements and intercepted the crusaders at Arsuf on 7 September 1191, with the latter eking out a victory and opening the road to Jaffa.[182] By then, however, Richard commanded no more than 10,000 men. Although the First Crusade had taken Jerusalem in 1099 with scarcely more than this, it had the freedom to conduct siege operations in relative security. That would not be the case in 1191, when a potential attack on the Holy City presented two major issues. Saladin could not only cut the crusaders' line of communication and sustainment (westward to Jaffa) but the presence of his field army meant a siege could feasibly result in either another encirclement—Acre, reprised—or, worse, another Hattin.

Saladin was also in a strategic bind. His army had been the difference maker because its proximity prevented Richard from making any serious moves against Jerusalem with his smaller force. Yet Muslim morale was dropping after more than two years in the field; there had already been defections at Acre in 1191.[183] Richard could cause serious problems even with small numbers, and the Frankish naval presence at Acre was now a threat to Egyptian trade. Between December 1191 and September 1192, the sultan worked hard to repair and improve Jerusalem's defenses: Muslim workers, alongside 2,000 Frankish prisoners, dug new protective ditches, repaired the northern wall and some towers, and also elongated the southern circuit to once again enclose Mount Zion within it.[184] Despite these exertions and their expense, by the summer of 1192 Saladin reached the conclusion that a treaty served his interests better than continued war.[185] In a long series of back and forth requests between intermediaries, on 2 September of that same year Richard and Saladin agreed to a three-year arrangement, the Treaty of Jaffa.[186] In broad strokes, the former retained the Levantine coast, the latter the interior, and in a joint Christian–Muslim operation the walls of Ascalon were demolished, preventing anyone from using it as a staging base in the future. Once the negotiators finalized the details, Christian and Muslim soldiers shared a meal together and the Third Crusade came to an end.[187]

Relevant to Jerusalem is the treaty's provision regarding pilgrims. According to his biographer, Ibn Shaddad, who witnessed the event, Saladin proclaimed (through a herald) that "any person from their lands who wishes to enter ours may do so, and any person from our lands who wishes to enter theirs may also do so."[188] Bishop Hubert Walter of Salisbury also secured an agreement for small Christian staffs to reside in the Church of the Holy Sepulchre for maintenance purposes.[189] So it was that the sepulchre reopened and Christian pilgrims worshipped there. The Norman writer Ambroise, who composed a verse chronicle of the Third Crusade in Old French, was part of a company that visited Jerusalem after the signing of the Treaty of Jaffa. Its members kissed the tomb of Christ, visited the Crucifixion site, then Mount Zion and the location of the Last Supper, the Siloam Spring, and the tomb of Mary at the foot of the Mount of Olives.[190] Throughout they seem to have been vocally harassed by Muslim soldiers, but they safely made a circuit of the city: starting in the northwest, moving south outside Zion Gate, around the eastern side of the city by the Kidron Valley, and ending at the northeast corner.

One wonders if these visitors spied any Jews while moving through the city. In the midst of the Third Crusade, while Saladin was himself busy countering the crusaders' moves at the siege of Acre in 1190, he appears to have relaxed the previous legal restrictions on large-scale Jewish residency. According to the writings of Rabbi Yehuda Alharizi, Jews began to move back into Jerusalem in appreciable numbers.[191] Whether Saladin's decree was in writing or simply proclaimed is unclear, and Yehuda's note is uncorroborated in Arabic sources. On an individual level, fair treatment of Jews and Christians can be found throughout Saladin's career. In Egypt, he granted communal autonomy to both after the former petitioned him directly to let them decide strictly Jewish matters among themselves, as they had during earlier Fatimid times. As was typical, Saladin first consulted his own jurists, in this case from the Shafi'i and Maliki schools, who approved the concept with a few exceptions.[192] He was also treated by both Jewish and Christian physicians throughout his reign.[193] Regarding eastern Christians specifically, some elements of the "status quo" sensibility of 'Umar's Assurance remained in force. Those who could afford the ransom remained in the city and retained some ecclesiastical properties, while losing others.[194] Saladin was therefore a key figure in the rediversification of the city's population by amplifying the trend lines of settlement and public devotion that had manifested in the Kingdom of Jerusalem.

The sultan's last visit to the city came in September 1192. Following the cementing of the Treaty of Jaffa, he returned to Jerusalem in order to "prepare the material to restore it, to look to its

173

welfare and to get ready to leave for the Hajj." This was probably when he founded the *madrasa* and also a hospital; Ibn Shaddad was instructed to stay in the city to oversee the construction and administration of both.[195] Saladin then departed, never to return, and died from an unspecified illness in Damascus on 3 March 1193. His named heir in Syria was his son, al-Afdal, who in 1193 endowed a Maliki school (*Madrasa al-Afdaliyya*) to the west of the Western Wall, in the Maghribi district where Muslim Africans resided and visited, of which only traces now remain. A *waqf* ensured a reliable flow of money for its upkeep and use by pilgrims and scholars. The modern demolition of this site remains a point of controversy.[196]

Finessing a Complex Legacy

There is much to ponder here. The Saladin legend that holds him as ever merciful and just should be revised. Indeed, Eddé has declared in no uncertain terms: "Let us refrain, however, from projecting onto him our modern conceptions of openness and tolerance."[197] His soldiers did not sack Jerusalem, and he certainly maintained the best traditions of medieval warfare in terms of giving freedom to a large portion of the population via negotiated ransom or outright release. Yet with his permission, his soldiers also enslaved or otherwise raped and brutalized a huge portion of the population that was unable to secure its liberty. The city's Christian leaders must bear some responsibility as well, for they agreed to the terms that made this possible, and those Templars and Hospitallers who coveted their money more than the lives of the poor are especially culpable. At other moments in his reign, the sultan was pleased to execute prisoners, including not only Frankish garrison troops but Christian and Jewish noncombatants. On the other hand, Saladin also allowed many Christians to remain in residence in Jerusalem and he later reopened the city to pilgrimage and worship at the sepulchre. That he did so primarily in response to military pressures must be noted, but the Arabic sources betray no serious hesitation in this regard; indeed, the biggest sticking point in the Jaffa negotiations was not Christian pilgrimage but rather the ownership of Ascalon.

Attempting to sort these conflicting realities would surely be an effort fraught with bias and cultural partisanship. Historians would instead be wise to consider Saladin a complex figure with attributes that have appealed to different audiences. Modern readers have mined his life story for those parts they prefer and which serve certain (invariably political) utilities and then ignored the rest. Equally important, the focus on Saladin as a dominating and consequential personality— the "great man" view of history—has obscured the contextual story of Jerusalem's history in the 1180s and 1190s. That story is, arguably, bigger and more important than any individual legacy.

For if we can step back and take a broad view, in some aspects the conquest of 1187 actually resembles that of 1099. We routinely remember the differences, but they also have a great deal in common. In both instances, the respective victors meted out harsh treatment to alien believers, whose religious observations in Jerusalem ceased. They then depopulated the city, "purified" the prominent buildings for proper use, and instituted oppressive laws. Afterward, they rebuilt walls in order to protect these hard-won changes. And yet, in both cases the victors also soon relaxed local restrictions, opened access to the city, and allowed rival, "infidel" worship at the holiest sites possible. All this resulted from a shared, practical realization: that the Levant was full of Jews, Christians, and Muslims, and the economic well-being of all required some level of interaction and tolerance of difference. Saladin reached this conclusion quickly, in just a few years, while the Franks obstinately held on a while longer. Perhaps that pushes him ahead of the Baldwins of the world in the line of respectability but ranking in this way is an exercise in triteness, one that obscures the more important lesson. Once the moments of greatest rancor and violence subsided, the future of Jerusalem once again lay along its previous path of religious pluralism.

V

ALLIANCES AND ANTICHRISTS
1229 AND 1244

Richard the Lionheart had failed to recover Jerusalem for Christendom. Yet despite latent disappointment in the situation in the East there was cause for optimism back in the West. Christian armies had directly confronted and bested Saladin three times (at Acre, Arsuf, and Jaffa), thus demonstrating that even the mightiest Muslim commander was not invincible. Moreover, a revised strategy had begun to take hold, one that King Amalric had originally pursued during Saladin's original rise to power: the conquest of Egypt. The core of Ayyubid military power, it provided cash and a substantial block of soldiers for Muslim field armies, and these served as a constant check to Frankish ambitions.[1] A future crusading army might well recapture Jerusalem, but holding it thereafter was rather unlikely in the face of assured responses from the Nile. So it was that crusading endeavors of the thirteenth century sought to capture Egypt as a necessary prelude to any march on Jerusalem itself. Numerous expeditions followed this pattern.[2] The most powerful pope of the Middle Ages, Innocent III (1198–1216), promoted two crusades to the East and under his successors several more expeditions followed. The results were mixed, to say the least.

Yet by 1229 Jerusalem was indeed back in Christian hands. As it happened, the pressure was decisive: while the army of the Fifth Crusade did not actually conquer Egypt it had done well enough to convince the Ayyubid sultan al-Kamil to negotiate with the western powers.[3] The sultan saw a western presence in Jerusalem as potentially beneficial, a bulwark between Egypt and his antagonistic relatives in Damascus. As a result, the Holy City was won not by siege and sack but rather by an agreement between Egypt and the Holy Roman Empire. Entering the city peacefully, Emperor Frederick II claimed the Jerusalem throne but immediately irritated all other parties by splitting control of the city among Christian and Muslim sectors. And soon after the expiration of his treaty the city was inundated with invaders from central Asia, the Khwarazmians, who brutally sacked the city in 1244 and defeated a combined Muslim–Christian coalition army desperate to drive them out. Muslim rule over Jerusalem endured for more than six centuries thereafter, until the dramatic 1917 entrance of the British field marshal, Edmund Henry Hynman Allenby, during World War I.

Frederick's actions in 1229, though broadly unknown in the popular sphere or the bookshelves of diplomats and policy makers, have resounded through the last eight hundred years.[4] He confirmed a running political-religious tradition that had been established in the seventh century and maintained in various formulations thereafter: Muslim prayer on the Temple Mount, Christian prayer in the Church of the Holy Sepulchre, and a tolerated, piecemeal Jewish presence in the city at large. For this, and a great many other things, Frederick—who was once deemed "the most apocalyptic of medieval German figures"—was denounced by the Latin church as the Antichrist.[5] Nonetheless, his arrangements were firmly cemented in the sixteenth century by the Ottoman sultan Suleiman the Magnificent and remained in force until the twentieth century. So it was that medieval conquests, which seem so far removed from the vicissitudes of the modern Middle East, left an indelible stamp on Jerusalem's present status.

I

Affairs in the Levant were decidedly unsettled as the thirteenth century approached. Saladin's sons quarreled soon after his death and Jerusalem changed hands twice in rapid succession during the course of rapidly deteriorating family matters. In 1194, al-'Aziz, the ruler of Egypt, marched against his brother al-Afdal in Damascus; the latter then called for assistance from his uncle, al-'Adil (Saladin's brother), who gathered allies and swiftly marched south from the Jazira to succor him.[6] In a mutual agreement, the brothers essentially split Palestine and Syria between them, with al-'Aziz ending up with Jerusalem and his brother with Damascus.[7] This was the beginning of a long history of quarreling between the Egyptian and Syrian branches of the Ayyubid confederation. In the next year al-'Aziz tried again, but this time the alliance against him was so strong that he fled backwards to Egypt, abandoning his holdings in Palestine entirely, including Jerusalem. Al-Afdal took the city without a fight, simply sending emissaries to demand the surrender of its governor.[8] Al-'Adil established himself in Egypt, surreptitiously as an adviser to his bellicose nephew. Together, they campaigned against al-Afdal, took Damascus, and reclaimed Jerusalem for the Egyptian branch of the family.[9]

Frankish affairs in the Holy Land at the turn of the thirteenth century were likewise unsettled. Jaffa had fallen in 1197, and the security of the other Levantine ports was questionable. Still, the army of Duke Henry of Brabant successfully secured Sidon and Beirut with an army in the same year, making for favorable prospects and perhaps even a move on Jerusalem itself. Aimery of Cyprus married Isabella of Jerusalem to create a Cypriot line for the throne and, backed by Henry's some three thousand Germans, that king might have created some strategic momentum. Instead, the Germans withdrew to Europe and the truce with the Ayyubids was extended to 1204.[10] The latter fortified the top of Mount Tabor, the purported site of Christ's Transfiguration, which has a dominating view of lower Galilee and thus posed a renewed threat to Frankish localities, including the kingdom's capital at Acre.[11]

Pope Innocent III

Innocent III was a transformative pontiff. On his reception of the papal mitre and crown, he remarked that the first was for spiritual things and the second for temporal, "the crown for the *regnum*."[12] His papacy was decisively political in that respect, and in the medieval power swings between papal and secular figures Innocent represents one of the apogees for the former. He dominated several of the rulers of his day, excommunicating King Alfonso IX of León and also King John of England. From John he received England as a fief and, later, he annulled Magna Carta, which sparked a rebellion of the English barons. He openly supported the Welf family of Otto IV for the imperial throne, while simultaneously hedging his bets by acting as the childhood guardian of Frederick Hohenstaufen. Going further, Innocent personally launched numerous crusades and took an active role in their propagation and regulation and after entreaties by St. Francis of Assisi he endorsed the Order of Friars Minor, or the Franciscans.[13] He was thus a monumental figure in high medieval history.

In 1198, Innocent's mind was on Jerusalem, and "he hoped most fervently to aid and recover the Holy Land, considering carefully how he could effectively fulfill this desire."[14] Within six months of his rise to St. Peter's chair the forceful pope was calling for another crusade. That war, known as the Fourth Crusade (1202–1204), infamously went awry. Unable to pay for passage east on Venetian vessels the expedition's leaders agreed to sack the Christian city of Zara (Zadar, modern-day Croatia) as partial payment, a deed for which Innocent excommunicated the Venetians.[15] They continued on nonetheless, eventually reaching, and then sacking, Constantinople. The warriors were brutal and thorough in their tasks: they despoiled and looted houses, palaces, and churches; they greedily stole holy relics; and they made off with precious art and melted down bronze statues. They murdered Byzantines who resisted, and raped women in the streets and in churches.[16] With these heinous acts the Fourth Crusade essentially came to an end, although some army units did eventually reach the Levant to conduct limited operations. In the process, the grand campaign did tremendous diplomatic harm to Latin–Byzantine ecclesiastical relations, which continues, in some measure, to the present day.[17]

Some time elapsed between this debacle and the next major crusading effort to the East, for numerous concerns filled Innocent's schedule. One, of course, was the new situation of Constantinople, which resulted in the election of Count Baldwin of Flanders to the (now Latin) Byzantine throne. While Innocent cheered and personally promoted the political change, he remained concerned about the violent and unstable civil and religious situation there.[18] A second was a threat closer to home, that of heresy: specifically, the stubborn and growing population of dualist "Cathar," or "Albigensian," heretics in Languedoc (southern France). This heresy was not new by any stretch of the imagination, and neither was adherence to it in that region; indeed, the Third Lateran Council had denounced it in 1179.[19] Now, however, Innocent embarked on a course to stamp it out entirely, which led to the so-called Albigensian Crusade of 1209, his second push for a holy war.

In time, however, the reality that Jerusalem remained in Ayyubid hands returned to the fore. One of the most notable church assemblies of the Middle Ages, the Fourth Lateran Council, became one of Innocent's vehicles for propagating his new, and second, crusade to the

East. It commenced in Rome in April 1215 after two years of preparation, and the long wait enabled a massive and thorough, society-wide effort to recruit soldiers and funds for the expedition.[20] Innocent's call to arms, *Ad liberandum*, displays an interesting East–West dissonance in Christian interfaith perceptions and interactions. He called for all Jewish moneylenders to cease the collection of interest on loans and forbade trade of supplies or "any aid, counsel, or favor" with Muslims.[21] Infamously, the canons of Lateran IV announced a host of restrictions on Muslims and Jews generally, including a decree that they dress in distinguishing clothing so that they (or their children, if from mixed marriages) could be more easily spotted.[22]

In reality, interfaith relations in the East were better than these discriminatory prohibitions in Europe suggest, and one reading only histories of the medieval West can easily be led astray.[23] As in prior centuries, there was certainly mistrust, manipulation, and, depending on who was in charge, oppression of other faith communities in the Levant. The Ayyubids levied heavy, nearly extortionate, taxes on the *dhimmi* populations of eastern Christians and Jews.[24] Even so, relations between adherents of the three major faiths in the early thirteenth century continued to follow the customary, if uneasy, path of grudging tolerance. In Egypt, the pragmatic relations of past centuries between political and monied interests remained largely in effect and there had even been some broad strokes of accord between western entities and the next Ayyubid sultan, Saladin's brother al-Adil. These included commercial agreements with Venice and Pisa in 1207–1208, and in 1212 some 3,000 western merchants could be found in the city of Alexandria alone. The bulk of these merchants relocated to Acre in 1216, which gave the savvy al-Adil a measure of advance notice of Innocent's grand designs.[25] Silver poured into the Levant from the West, in what one scholar has dubbed "a period of unprecedented economic exchange with Europe."[26] Thirteenth-century calls to holy war thus sidestepped market realities, in which plenty of people—both Muslims and Christians alike—conducted increasingly lucrative activities that were, perhaps, worth preserving. As one scholar has quipped, "holy war is bad for business."[27]

Jewish Pilgrimage

Meanwhile, Jerusalem remained a popular destination for pilgrims of all stripes, and this was especially notable in the Jewish communities. Those western Jews with enough interest and wealth tended to make the journey, so in the main, pilgrimage was not exactly an institutionalized practice.[28] Correspondingly, somewhat dormant messianic activities percolated anew in the early thirteenth century in the wake of Saladin's 1187 conquest: his decision to allow Jews back into the city sparked eschatological enthusiasm and led to a renewed interest in performing certain rites in the Holy Land.

The most famous of these Jewish pilgrimages was the so-called *aliyah* ("going up") of the 300 rabbis, a group that set out for Jerusalem from Provence in 1209–1210. Led by the head of the *yeshiva* in Lunel, Jonathan ha-Kohen, it had been stoked by messianic rumblings in Yemen as well as the numerical reckonings of the philosopher Maimonides.[29] Years earlier, sometime after 1196, Jonathan had written a letter to Maimonides in which he invited the philosopher to journey again from Egypt to Jerusalem himself, in order to hasten his people's redemption.[30]

The plot thickens. The author Samuel ben Samson, who accompanied Jonathan and wrote about the trip, asserts that the King of Jerusalem, John of Brienne, had personally invited Jews to relocate to Jerusalem, and that this was the practical reason for the pilgrimage of the 300.[31] It is a very curious possibility. John was obviously not in control of Ayyubid-held Jerusalem itself and ruled from Acre. His invitation could be read as either welcoming and conciliatory or, rather, deliberately subversive if the plan was to use pilgrimages to destabilize a Muslim-held polity. Such a plan seems far-fetched in conception. Alternatively, given John's strictly titular status, Prawer doubts that the reference is really to John at all but rather to Jerusalem's Muslim governor. Even if that were so, he readily notes that Jews nonetheless gathered to welcome John of Brienne to Acre in the same year, 1210.[32]

Soon after entering the city through the David gate in the west, Samuel and Jonathan first made their way to the Western Wall and prayed in its vicinity. An arch, perhaps Wilson's Arch, is noted as the entrance to a tunnel system.[33] Samuel also mentions the burning of the red heifer, which is seen by some as a prerequisite to the rebuilding of the Third Temple.[34] In time, these travelers were followed by more Jewish pilgrims, enough of whom ended up staying permanently and thus shifting the local demographics. By 1216, the Jewish community in Jerusalem had greatly increased and numbered three principal congregations from Ascalon, France, and the Maghrib.[35]

The thriving business affairs between East and West and resurgence of visitors to Jerusalem did little to bolster the spirits of western ecclesiastics. Indeed, the plight of Christianity in the Levant seemed as desperate as ever. Jacques of Vitry (d. 1240), the prodigious bishop of Acre, spoke and wrote in tones more akin to the anxieties in Rome. In one of his sermons to pilgrims, he focused more on difference than similarity, alluding to non-Christians in the Levant as "infernal dogs" and "demons and most pernicious inhabitants."[36] Jacques heaped scorn on those cordial relations that did exist, accusing settled Franks in the Levant of not only being soft and living degenerate lifestyles of luxury but also of complicity with the enemy:

A multitude of Saracens would flee from before their fathers, even though they were few; at the voice of their thunder they hastened away; but they feared their cowardly descendants no more than so many women, unless they had some French or other Westerns [i.e. crusaders] with them.[37]

This sentiment accords well with the social bifurcation established in the twelfth century between western settlers who had culturally adapted to life among Muslims and Jews in the Levant and those newcomers who, like the man who had accosted Usama ibn Munqidh at al-Aqsa, maintained their contrariness. Along with cowardice, Jacques condemned the Franks for their infighting, their frequent treaties with Muslim polities, and the periodical interfaith alliances between the two. On the Italian merchants specifically, of whose trade activities he was intimately aware, he complained that they were simply more interested in making money from Muslims than fighting them.[38]

Jacques of Vitry also had little but scorn for the Jews, who he argued had no understanding of the Old Testament, a history of idol worship, and complicity—carrying on, here, the old blood curse charge—in their ancestors' crucifixion of Christ. This latter reference corresponds with his general eschatological persuasion, which had been forcefully thrust back into prominence by the contemporary Italian theologian Joachim of Fiore. Joachim's precise calculations on the contours of the Antichrist's activities, in which he "had moved from unfounded conjectures to science," pegged his coming to some time before 1260, and many eventually identified the emperor Frederick II as this servant of Satan in the flesh.[39] In the meantime, Jacques of Vitry saw a need for crusade in order to counter the machinations of the Antichrist's designs.[40] The Muslims, he claims, only permitted Jews to work in the laboring professions and did not trade with them, as they did with the aforementioned Christian traitors.[41]

This is probably an overstatement. The reality was more akin to the days of Fatimid rule in the tenth and eleventh centuries: a small Jewish population that lived and worked in Jerusalem but were somewhat dependent on funds from relatives and connections in Egypt and the other, more populous Levantine cities.[42] Jacques's assessment of interreligious relations in the early thirteenth century is jaundiced but representative of a general western medieval view, and his depiction of a region split by tensions is akin to those so often held by modern intellectuals today. .

The Fifth Crusade

Meanwhile, Innocent III's call to crusade had not gone unheeded. Recruitment efforts were more widespread than in previous wars, with minute attention paid to the local and diocesan level. Priests were trained to integrate their pastoral messages with crusading themes, and theologians wrote preaching manuals and assembled sermon collections to aid in the effort. Crucially, these centered on the role of crusading in personal salvation (or, particular judgment) and the role of the crusading indulgence.[43] The most famous examples are the model sermons of Jacques of Vitry, which hit on devotional themes of the cross of Christ and tied crusading to Old Testament exemplars: Rahab, Jacob, Joshua, and Elisha.[44] Jacques ably prosecuted the cause of the holy war and preached not only to men but women including, on one occasion, the wives of Genoese soldiers.[45] When Pope Innocent died in 1216, his successor Honorius III took up the mission with gusto, utilizing the bureaucracy of the papal curia and its departments to disseminate materials pursuant to recruiting, taxation, and diplomatic efforts.[46] Two hundred relevant letters survive in his registers, which attest to his intense interest in the endeavor.[47]

The combined efforts were efficacious, though not of the order of magnitude of the crusades of the twelfth century. Several notable magnates took the cross and journeyed East, but they were not from the most powerful states in Western Europe: Henry III of England was only 10 years old; Philip II of France, fresh from his great victory at the Battle of Bouvines in 1214, had already had his crusade and was content to watch the exploits of his son, Louis VIII, against England; and while Frederick Hohenstaufen had taken the cross he never personally participated in the war.[48] Instead, the principal leaders of the Fifth Crusade were such leaders as King Andrew II of Hungary, John of Brienne, Duke Leopold VI "the Glorious" of Austria, King Hugh of Cyprus, and Hermann von Salza, the Grand Master of the

Teutonic Knights.[49] The mustered forces were, combined, somewhere in the range of 13,000–23,000 soldiers at most, a third of the size of the armies of the First Crusade.[50] These soldiers traveled in contingents from both Italian ports and the Low Countries; a significant chunk of the latter were held up after getting diverted in Portuguese affairs and entangled in the siege of Alcácer do Sal, southeast of Lisbon. There, claims of miraculous events made it back to Rome: in the sky a banner bearing the cross had appeared, and a shining heavenly knight had joined in the fight on the ground.[51]

Eventually, the crusaders rendezvoused in Acre, joining Frankish contingents from the army of Jerusalem as well as the military religious orders. However, in accordance with the strategic tradition of the period, this coalition was not bound for Jerusalem, but rather Egypt. It departed Acre on 24 May 1218, made a short stop at Atlit to the south, and finally arrived at the Egyptian shore on the 27th.[52]

According to the English chronicler Roger of Wendover, two signs awaited the crusaders on the Egyptian shore. A total eclipse of the moon served as a portent of success against their adversaries and a sudden salting of the Nile south of Damietta—thereby denying the Muslim garrison in that citadel any refreshment—provided them an operational advantage. They would need every edge obtainable, for Damietta was an exceedingly daunting target: "in the middle of the river Nile ... a high and handsome tower strongly built of stone, from which an immensely thick iron chain was extended across the river to the city which stood on the other bank of it."[53] This structure has not survived, and indeed that space in the Nile Delta has changed dramatically over the centuries from damming, canal alterations, and silting from both those and the shifting shoreline of the Mediterranean Sea. A participant on the Fifth Crusade, the German scholar Oliver of Paderborn, claimed that Damietta's fortifications included three walls and a moat; the giant chain served to block passage down the Nile towards Cairo, the seat of Ayyubid power.[54]

The resulting siege of Damietta occupied the Christian soldiers for the duration of the Fifth Crusade. As they dug siegeworks and thought of creative ways to attack the citadel, including a siege tower mounted on top of galleys, they also weighed the importance of taking it versus marching directly on Cairo itself.[55] Central to this debate was the morale of the men who, long encamped before Damietta, grew frustrated by their lack of progress and the nonaggressive tone of the campaign in general. Two offensive actions resulted from the tedious climate, both aimed at the camp of the new sultan of Egypt, al-Kamil, southwest down the Nile. The first (in May) came to nothing when al-Kamil refused battle and remained in camp. The second (in August) was a substantial force led by John of Brienne, as well as the cardinal legate Pelagius and Jacques of Vitry. It elicited a Muslim response, and the result was a crushing defeat at the Battle of Fariskur on 29 August 1218, in which between 2,000 and 4,000 crusaders perished alongside several of their leaders.[56]

Jerusalem: Refused

This defeat did not end the crusade, however, and the Christian–Muslim negotiations before and after it are interesting, especially in reference to the status of Jerusalem. Despite Fariskur, crusaders remained entrenched around Damietta and had even strengthened their circumvallation of the citadel, and the defeat in battle did nothing to change that fact. Lower than expected flooding of the Nile also foretold a poor farming season and possible famine for the Ayyubid subjects. With time not on his side, in September 1219 al-Kamil offered to cede control of Jerusalem to the Christians in exchange for their departure from Egypt. The deal included not only Jerusalem but monies for its reconstruction, the return of the piece of the True Cross captured by Saladin at Hattin, and the return of other castles west of the River Jordan, plus an annual payment of 15,000 bezants—a rent payment for the castles of Kerak and Montreal, which were to remain in Muslim hands.[57] A second, similar offer was made some time after the fall of Damietta, in August 1221, when the sultan's strategic situation was even more desperate, and he may have even returned the True Cross independently in an apparent show of good faith.[58] Here was a strategic victory served on a platter, and yet the crusaders rejected both offers.

Why were these stunning deals turned down? The reasons are complicated but all center on the notion that Jerusalem, by itself, no longer held the allure it once did. Opinion in the army split over the terms.[59] John of Brienne wanted to accept the deal: more strategically minded than others, he saw how it achieved both the ends of the crusade and his own personal interest, which was the acquisition of his lost capital. Others, such as Pelagius and the Italian leaders, saw his transparency for what it was. From their perspective, Kerak and Montreal sat east of the Jordan and were therefore essential regional defense pieces. Without them, Jerusalem could simply be retaken by Muslim forces in due course. Moreover, the Italians had commercial interests that the Holy City, sitting off the major maritime routes as it did, simply did not serve.[60] The August 1221 deal in particular came after the fall of Damietta and the departure of John of Brienne to Syria in 1220, where he pressed his claim to Cilician Armenia and defended his other lands against attacks from al-Kamil's Ayyubid brother, al-Mu'azzam.[61] Lacking proper military leadership but confidently in control of a major ingress port to the Nile, as well as expecting further reinforcements from the Holy Roman Emperor, Frederick II, Pelagius and others believed the full conquest of Egypt was in sight.[62]

On the other hand, there is also reason to doubt the sincerity of al-Kamil's offers. It clearly served his interests of having a buffer zone of Franks between Egypt and Syria, where the Damascene branch of the Ayyubid dynasty remained a threat. Yet he also knew his proposals would cause dissension within the crusader ranks, divisions that he could exploit in a strategic sense.[63] Moreover, one can further question al-Kamil's good faith because he was not actually in possession of Jerusalem in either 1219 or 1221; that honor was held by al-Mu'azzam. The latter was willing to assist Egypt by sending relief raids, but he was otherwise quite worried about the crusaders' success, so much so that he took drastic measures of his own.

In a dramatic move, while the Christians were bolstering their siegeworks at Damietta in 1219 al-Mu'azzam ordered the demolition of Jerusalem's defensive walls. His logic was that the Christians would be less interested in an indefensible city, which, even if retaken, could not be held for long. (Whether known to him or not, the Umayyad caliph Marwan II had pulled the same trick, as we have seen, in the 740s.) In Ibn al-Athir's interpretation of events, a looming envelopment beckoned: recent incursions of Mongol forces from the east and the Fifth Crusade in Egypt raised the prospect of a vise slowly closing on Palestine, and Jerusalem's destruction was designed to forestall it.[64] According to al-Maqrizi, the entire circuit of walls and all of the towers were pulled down, with only the Tower of David surviving.[65] This was likely due to the strength of its construction, for 20 years later another Muslim force was only able to demolish it with great difficulty. The demolition caught other structures in its path. Oliver of Paderborn claims that al-Mu'azzam considered destroying the Church of the Holy Sepulchre but ultimately stayed his hand.[66] St. Mary on Mount Zion was not so lucky. It had been given over to eastern Christians by Saladin in 1187 but was now destroyed in 1219.[67] The various Ayyubid improvements to the Temple Mount, including new fountains for washing and drinking, two new *madrasas*, and assorted architectural flourishes, survived. But as Hillenbrand has noted, despite Jerusalem's religious significance no Ayyubid ever tried to make it their capital. Moreover, both al-Mu'azzam's reduction of its walls and al-Kamil's later relinquishing of the city to Frederick II in 1229 illustrate that political expediency was more important than anything.

Word of the demolition spread quickly. John of Brienne knew about it and personally informed Frederick II in a recently discovered letter: "they destroyed the holy city of Jerusalem."[68] Jacques of Vitry claims that the action provoked a reaction from Christians in Georgia, who threatened al-Mu'azzam with war as a result.[69] Certain Orthodox prelates also suspended pilgrimages for eastern Christians due to the overall tensions of the Fifth Crusade.[70] Muslims likewise despaired, with men, women, and children reportedly shaving their hair at the top of the Temple Mount in anguish. One poet lamented, "the rest of my tears overflow"; another, "Mecca should cry for it, because [Jerusalem] is its sister."[71]

Going further, al-Mu'azzam expelled most of the city's population. This included some of the Jews, who had returned to Jerusalem in growing numbers since Saladin's conquest in 1187. The three congregations there were active, and in 1211 *genizah* letters show some of their members soliciting monies from Egypt for the restoration of a synagogue (probably the old Karaite synagogue destroyed during the First Crusade in 1099). Al-Mu'azzam himself had a Jewish physician named Abu Zikhri, but such interpersonal relationships did not deter his expulsion order. Those Jews who were not expelled left voluntarily, many for Acre, because they evidently feared the insecurity of a defenseless city in the face of potential Frankish sieges.[72] Some evidently returned by 1221, but evidence of them is slight and the population must have been very small.[73] It was a scene reminiscent of the dangers while rebuilding the city in the wake of the ancient liberation of the Jewish people from the Babylonian captivity: "But they are in great distress, and count for nothing; Jerusalem is but broken walls and charred gates."[74]

In sum, then, al-Kamil's offers to trade a broken Jerusalem for Damietta came to nothing. And despite the enthusiasm for victory in 1221, the Fifth Crusade ultimately stalled during the eventual great offensive towards Cairo. The crusading army became trapped by Ayyubid forces amidst the Nile's water system near al-Mansourah, and in exchange for their lives they "surrendered Damietta without compensation."[75] A poet celebrated al-Kamil's victory, calling the sultan "a Glorious One / Generous in praise, flawless, brave / Handsome in countenance, full of goodness and good actions."[76] Safe in the comfort of twenty-first-century hindsight, it is hard to avoid lambasting the crusaders for squandering the political fruits of effective warfare in the pursuit of final, total victory.

Amplifying the disappointment was the fact that promised reinforcements from the Empire never arrived. In late July 1215, Frederick had been crowned emperor at Aachen. He amplified his already high profile coronation by also taking the cross, after which he listened to a day's worth of crusade sermons by preachers conveniently on the scene at the exact moment required.[77] However, he inadvertently boxed himself in with a promise to depart for the East no later than August 1221. In theory he had plenty of time to participate in the great expedition, given that the first major groups of crusaders, taking both land and sea routes, did not arrive in the East until late 1217.[78] Yet he missed the deadline anyway because of numerous complicating factors, not least his effort to gain recognition of his son, Henry, as his heir.

By the time Frederick's nobles agreed to the succession scheme it was too late.[79] The stakes are revealed in a letter from the Damietta camp, from the summer of 1221:

> Moreover we have long expected the arrival of the emperor and other nobles by whom we hope to be relieved, and on their arrival we hope to bring this business, which has commenced by the hands of many, to a happy termination; but if we are deceived in our hope of this assistance in the ensuing summer, which I hope will not happen, both countries, namely Syria and Egypt, and that which we have lately gained possession of as well as that which we have held a long time, will be placed in a doubtful position.[80]

Deceived they were. Two modest groups of soldiers had sailed from Frederick's lands to Egypt, but by the time they arrived John of Brienne's army was already surrounded.[81]

Frederick II was one of the more dazzling figures of medieval history known as *stupor mundi*, or "the wonder of the world": a modern-style skeptic, he had strong interests in natural science and political theory and authored a book on hunting with birds of prey, which is considered a classic to this day.[82] He was also a lightning rod in imperial–papal relations. Two popes, Gregory IX and Innocent IV, eventually denounced him as the Antichrist himself, a heretic with designs on the desecration and debilitation of the Catholic Church. Frederick gave as good as he got, retorting that Gregory was, in fact, the real Antichrist: a false prophet, and an enemy of peace.[83] However, all those controversies postdated the events at Damietta: in 1221, the major takeaway was his lukewarm interest in the cause for holy war, and he thus received partial blame for the failure of the Fifth Crusade.

II

Yet to some extent Frederick's eye remained on the East. In 1223, he reaffirmed his interest in crusading at San Germano and promised to depart by 1225, along with other stipulations regarding the number of knights and ships.[84] Along the way, Honorius III carefully prodded the emperor forward to the task in a series of negotiations, which culminated in that pontiff helping arrange Frederick's marriage. The bride, Isabella, was the daughter of John of Brienne, and the match had the purpose of more closely connecting Frederick to affairs in the East which would, hopefully, persuade him to finally go there himself. But in a surprise move, at least on the surface, Frederick had instead enlisted the aid of the Syrian barons to abandon John and declare him the true holder of the Jerusalem crown.[85] In 1225, John was deposed from the throne—he lost his kingdom, and Frederick gained an enemy for life.[86]

Frederick II on Crusade

His claims to Jerusalem now solidified, Frederick set out for the East in August 1227 but, infamously, turned back to Sicily on account of a debilitating illness. Contemporary accounts seem to indicate that his sickness was legitimate and not a ruse slyly employed to get out of the war. Honorius's successor in Rome, Gregory IX, cared not a whit and excommunicated the emperor anyway for failing to fulfill his crusading vow. Ernst Kantorowicz sketched an enduring image of a formidable pontiff nonetheless acting with prejudice and ill intent:

> Though an old man he was still strong and handsome ... The wild fire of his youth still burned in the aged man and flared up, now in the ecstatic mysticism of a Francis of Assisi, now in passionate unbridled hate towards Frederick II. [. . .] His weapons and methods were for the most part unattractive ... and produced an ugly impression ... The obstinate old man, drunk with hate, pursued his end with the singleness of airn [iron] to his last hour.[87]

Ad hominem aside, Gregory was within his rights to impose the ban. It seems clear he did so on a purely technical basis: whatever the excuse, the emperor had missed the deadline. Frederick's apparent recalcitrance was amplified by scholarship over the course of centuries, in which he was cast as a reluctant crusader and, worse, a friend to Muslims, willing to sacrifice Christian interests for better relations with them.[88] As Gregory reportedly complained, "he takes more account of the servants of Mahomet than those of Christ."[89]

Yet it was not as if Frederick had shirked his holy war responsibilities wholesale. Back in Sicily, in the midst of what the papacy saw as dithering on the cause of the crusade, Frederick had set about eradicating the Muslim presence. This meant cutting off the island from its line of support from Tunisia by capturing the island of

Djerba off its coast; he thereafter invited North African Jews to move to Sicily.[90] On the other hand, his motivation for these efforts was fairly transparent: he sought to join Sicily with his imperial lands in central Europe, and his overwhelming interest was in that course, not in the affairs of the East. Still, he sought a removal of the excommunication ban on these and other grounds and could legitimately claim to have ridden Sicily of its Muslim population, which had persevered through centuries. Gregory, for his part, refused to relent unless Frederick accepted papal counsel on the political question of imperial expansion there.[91]

The emperor could not abide this delay. On 28 June 1228, Frederick sailed from Brindisi with 70 ships in a dramatic, disobedient start to his long-awaited crusade.[92] Sailing first to Cyprus, where he entangled himself in local politics with King John of Ibelin, he eventually landed in Beirut.[93] From there, he made his way to Tyre, and finally, south to Acre.[94] Discord arose there immediately in certain quarters due to his excommunicated status; and questions about his legitimacy—and the legalities of following a hell-bound monarch—persisted throughout his stay in the East.[95] From Acre, Frederick entered into talks with the Egyptian Ayyubids. He first sent envoys to Nablus to discuss terms with al-Kamil; then, in November 1228 the two leaders met together in Jaffa.

It was an extraordinary event. Not even Richard the Lionheart and Saladin had managed to meet in person, and this was, indeed, the first time a western monarch had sat down with an Egyptian sultan.[96] More astounding is the nature of the negotiations: the two leaders talked by themselves, apparently with no interference by either leader's magnates.[97] Several factors guided their discussion. One was the threat posed by Frederick's army. It was not a huge force, even in comparison to the modestly sized Fifth Crusade. The emperor did have somewhere around a thousand knights, in addition to whatever infantry was transported on the 70 vessels that preceded him to Cyprus.[98] Most of them had arrived in the Levant before

Frederick and those who had not immediately returned West in despair about his absence busied themselves by fortifying Caesarea and Jaffa.[99] These were bolstered by the local forces of the Templars and Hospitallers (who supported his campaign, but not him personally), and the more reliable Teutonic Knights.[100] Overall, however, the military threat to al-Kamil's interests was not great and other contextual elements probably influenced the negotiations more. These included the history between the two leaders, who had been corresponding since at least 1226 in both diplomatic and friendly terms. In December of that year, al-Maqrizi claims the sultan personally invited Frederick to Acre, promising him Levantine ports in exchange for military assistance against his brother.[101] Al-Kamil was effectively prioritizing the need to settle with the crusaders so that he might attend to his Muslim rivals in Syria.

The result of this capital meeting was a new Treaty of Jaffa, to which al-Kamil and Frederick agreed on 18 February 1229. It included several restorations of lands and fortresses to the emperor, including Bethlehem, Nazareth, and Sidon. The Franks and Ayyubids exchanged prisoners and agreed to a truce with a duration of just over ten and a half years.

Jerusalem Reclaimed

The most controversial elements of the treaty concerned Jerusalem. Al-Kamil turned over the city to Frederick, who agreed to maintain an Islamic presence within it in two ways: Muslims retained a court there and, more importantly, retained the right to freedom of worship on the Temple Mount. When the emperor entered the city, he represented himself as a successor to King David (and by extension Jesus Christ) and took the crown of Jerusalem for himself in the sepulchre church. Less coronation and more demonstration of his preexisting rule, based on his familial claims to the throne, the audacious act generated tremendous hostility among the Christian intellectual class.[102] Jewish rights go unmentioned in the treaty. Their residence in the city was apparently forbidden after 1229 but pilgrimage to and worship at the Western Wall persisted into the 1230s and the 1240s.[103]

It all seems a remarkable concession: that a Christian ruler would grant Muslims religious liberties on their most hallowed ground. Frederick likely had little choice in the matter and had to agree in order to secure the rest of the city so easily and without bloodshed. Moreover, the concept of this compromise was not exactly a new idea. Something similar had been proposed back in 1192 during the early negotiations between Richard and Saladin: "Jerusalem shall be ours and you can have the Dome of the Rock."[104] The details of Frederick's and al-Kamil's arrangement differ, depending on the source. Frederick himself spelled out his thinking in a notable letter to his counterpart in England, King Henry III:

> It is provided, however, that the Saracens of that part of the country, since they hold the temple in great veneration, may come there as often as they choose in the character of pilgrims, to worship according to their custom. And we shall henceforth permit them to come, however, only as many as we choose to allow, and without arms, nor are they to dwell in the city, but outside, and as soon as they have paid their devotions they are to depart.[105]

In this telling, the Franks retained a measure of control by regulating Muslim traffic and preventing their residency. It was an illusion. These may well have been words designed to win over Henry to the imperial side, for the English king had spent the previous two years trying to mediate between Frederick and Pope Gregory IX. In April 1229, the papacy exacted a tenth of the English clergy's goods for the prosecution of war against the emperor and then, later in that same month, attempted to extract monies from a recalcitrant English laity.[106] Henry III's indirect support of the papal armies was further compounded by his political ties. He had been in communication with a rival claimant to the imperial throne from the Welf family, to which England had prior connections: Emperor Otto IV had allied with Henry's father, King John, against the French in 1214, only to suffer a decisive defeat at the Battle of Bouvines.[107] In this context, Frederick's letter, which offers an alternate reality vis-à-vis the Temple Mount, seems more a calculated political ploy than an honest reckoning of events in the East.

Indeed, the Muslim perspective was rather different. The limited, controlled, and invitation-only space for Muslim prayer was actually as unrestricted as before. The scholar and Ayyubid ambassador, Ibn Wasil, whose first teaching position was in a Jerusalem *madrasa*, wrote:

The sacred precincts of the city, with the Dome of the Rock and the Masjid al-Aqsa were to remain in Muslim hands, and the Franks were simply to have the right to visit them, while their administration remained in the hands of those already employed in it, and Muslim worship was to continue there.[108]

This is the opposite of Frederick's claim: it was the Franks who could periodically visit but the Temple Mount itself, and the holy sites at the top remained firmly in Ayyubid hands. What was the reality? A letter from Gerold, the patriarch of Jerusalem, seemingly settles the question in favor of Ibn Wasil's interpretation. In a missive full of invective against Frederick, Gerold lamented that the emperor had received the crown "although the Saracens still held the temple of the Lord and Solomon's temple, and although they proclaimed publicly as before the law of Muhammad—to the great confusion and chagrin of the pilgrims."[109]

Despite Frederick's assurances, then, it seems to have indeed been the case that Muslims retained the Temple Mount. This Christian correction of the record thus illustrates that continuity, not change, was the order of the day at al-Aqsa. Al-Maqrizi tells a revealing story in which the emperor actually threw a Bible-toting Christian cleric out of al-Aqsa and warned that any other Franks daring to enter would lose their eyes as a consequence.[110] For those looking to accuse him of pro-Muslim sympathies the proof seemed in the pudding.

The magnitude of Frederick's prohibition was not immediately apparent. Frankish political activity at these sites, such as the former Templar headquarters, had obviously disappeared with Saladin's entrance into the city in 1187. With it went any devotional activities in and around the Dome of the Rock. In the 42 intervening years any formal Christian prayer on the mount had been wiped away. Technically, Christian pilgrims still had a right to visit the locale but they were likely few and far between, and in any case the real draw was not the Dome but rather the Church of the Holy Sepulchre. This seems borne out in the numerous Christian itineraries from the period that have survived. These are essentially travel guides, containing descriptions of various sites of interest for the faithful. Whether or not the respective authors had actually visited the places mentioned is unclear but all the texts center thematically on five similar areas of pilgrim interest: the Mount of Olives, the Church of the Holy Sepulchre, Mount Zion the Jehoshaphat Valley, and, last and decidedly least, the Temple Mount.[111]

For in regard to the latter an odd lacuna exists in these itineraries. Three anonymous texts, all dating to between 1229 and 1265, contain instructions to pilgrims not only on how to get to Jerusalem but also on what to visit, and where, in the city after arriving. All three include brief descriptions of the Temple Mount, the *Templum Domini* and *Templum Salomonis*, and other sites such as the gates leading to it. However, unlike their descriptions of the sepulchre church, none describe the inside of those buildings.[112] Perhaps this was simply because their authors did not visit them, due to Muslim presence on the plateau. More surprising, however, is that neither do these accounts mention that Muslims controlled these sites.[113] A fourth Latin account dating to 1239 purports to list all the territory under Ayyubid control; Jerusalem is not mentioned, which makes sense, but neither is the Temple Mount, which does not. The single nod to any sort of Muslim ownership or restrictions is in a Greek itinerary from 1253–1254, which only mentions that the Golden Gate had been closed with iron.[114] Such accounts cannot be expected to provide full contours of the political-religious landscape, of course, but the absence of caustic remarks or even laments in these travel guides is noticeable. In any event, pilgrims to the Levant of the thirteenth century differed somewhat from those of the twelfth, in that the former were less connected to crusading objectives in Egypt.[115]

Betrayal!

As often happens with compromise agreements, no party was entirely happy with the situation in Jerusalem. Complaints flooded in from all quarters in the wake of Frederick's treaty. Merchants of all stripes in cities like Acre, Damascus, Beirut, and Tyre worried about how the event might destabilize the tenuous—but positive and lucrative—trade relations between Frankish and Muslim communities.[116] The Muslim faithful packed into the Great Mosque of Damascus and filled it with their cries and lamentations.[117] The *muezzin* at al-Aqsa, who was responsible for calling Muslims to prayer, issued an invective against Frederick while the emperor was still in the city, reciting anti-Christian passages and calling out that "God has no son."[118] No doubt Frederick's physical movements spurred other negative reactions: after securing his treaty, he took a guided tour of the Temple Mount and entered both the Dome and al-Aqsa, even ascending the *minbar* in the latter. His guide, the *qadi* Shams al-Din of Nablus, actually forbade the *muezzin* from offering Friday prayers that day, in defer-ence to their honorable guest.[119] Al-Kamil's general deference and religious outreach to Frederick has been characterized as essentially earnest by at least one scholar but it unsurprisingly read poorly in the minds of contemporary observers.[120] In Damascus, the Ayyubid sultan al-Mu'azzam instructed his best preacher, the renowned intellect Sibt ibn al-Jawzi, to attack al-Kamil for his parleys and denounce him as a traitor, which he was more than happy to do: "O shame upon the Muslim rulers!"[121]

Things were no better from the Christian perspective. Patriarch Gerold judged Frederick's conduct deplorable and called him despicable and wicked.[122] On Gerold's personal orders, Peter, the archbishop of Caesarea, journeyed to Jerusalem and placed the entire city under interdict, which incredibly banned all church services from being held in this holiest of Christian cities. This earned Frederick the wrath of the Christian pilgrims who, unlike their Muslim counterparts on the Temple Mount, now had no sanctioned place to pray.[123]

Compounding the overall negative impression was Frederick's prior history with Muslims living in Christian lands. Earlier in the 1220s, he had solved the problem of a latent Muslim insurgency in Sicily by rounding up most of the belligerents and deporting them to a colony in Lucera, on the Italian mainland. An Islamic governor ruled over this fortified city, assisted by religious advisers, while the Muslims farmed and raised horses for Frederick's army.[124] And in a fascinating move, he did not even attempt to convert them to Christianity, which won him not only continuing poll tax payments (similar to the Islamic custom of *jizya*) but also their loyalty. They became his personal standing army, and one Muslim bodyguard even accompanied him to Jerusalem in 1229.[125] Frederick could well be accused of personally providing for the wellbeing of Muslims in both Italy and the Holy Land, which from a spiritual perspective were the two most important regions of Christendom.

That the emperor brokered the Treaty of Jaffa while excommunicated only compounded the feelings of betrayal, as did the nature of his departure from the Holy Land. He redistributed the lands secured in the treaty to those who had supported him, namely the Teutonic Knights, and dispossessed the Templars and Hospitallers.[126] He had backed the Teutonic order from early on in his reign by contacting it immediately after taking the cross, granting it gifts and privileges and working very hard to get papal backing for their order.[127] Frederick then traveled from Jerusalem to Acre, where Philip of Novara says he "was unpopular with all the people" as well as with the Templars and Hospitallers.[128] According to Gerold, they reignited their conflicts by informing him of their plan to retain soldiers in Acre for the defense of the city. Frederick responded that this was unnecessary because of the peace with al-Kamil; they retorted that there were other dangerous Ayyubid actors and forces in the region but could not ultimately convince him. At length, he denied their request and forbade any soldiers from remaining, but the people of Acre declined to obey any orders from a sullied excommunicate like him.[129]

This led to a bit of nastiness in which Frederick, as the saying goes, went out on a bad note. The emperor besieged the Templar quarter in Acre, ordered its knights expelled on pain of death, and had his bailiff whip any soldiers who lingered in the streets, as well as some visiting Dominican and Franciscan brothers.[130] In opposition, Gerold and his ecclesiastical company placed the city under interdict. Frederick seized Acre's defensive weaponry and carried it away on his ships and destroyed the other vessels in the harbor, thereby rendering the city and its people trapped and defenseless. At length, he himself slipped away in a galley, but not before some of the angrier residents spotted him and "pelted him with tripe and bits of meat most scurrilously."[131]

Amid the high drama of an emperor fleeing the Holy Land in a flurry of ecclesiastical invective and food fighting, it is worthwhile to step back and appreciate the significance of Frederick's compromise, ill received as it was. Jerusalem had now changed hands several times since the early seventh century, and in every one of those cases Muslim prayer on the Temple Mount had been maintained. 'Umar cleaned and sanctified the place when Sophronius freely gave it to him in 638, and the Umayyads established al-Aqsa and the Dome of the Rock there afterward. Sunni worship was the rule until the 970s when the Fatimids captured the city, but they did not make the spot exclusive to Shia devotions. In the flip-flops of the eleventh century— the Sunni Atsiz in 1073 and 1077, and the Shia Fatimids in 1098— no one excluded the other's confession from the spot. Following a hiatus after the massacre of 1099, Muslims were praying on the spot again by the 1130s. It was once thought that in 1229 the Franks, now back in control for the first time since 1187, again prohibited Muslims from living in the city; alternatively, as Ibn Wasil alleges, al-Kamil himself ordered them to depart. It seems, however, that this never actually happened, for other Arabic sources indicate that Muslims lived there from 1229 onward.[132] Islamic devotions were therefore a near constant feature of the Temple Mount, at both dome and mosque, for seven medieval centuries. Crucially, these had been allowed not only by Muslim rulers but also by the Christian kings of Jerusalem.

All this being the case, the deeper meaning of Frederick's action is easy to overstate. From his friendship with al-Kamil and other related matters, he is sometimes cast as a "precursor to modern tolerance," especially since so much of the evidence comes from Arabic sources— and is thus thought freer of imperial propaganda. This is probably not the case, however. James Powell has argued for the immense role of propagandistic efforts on all sides: eastern writers demonstrating how a Christian king might see the error of his ways, and western writers amplifying his dealings with Muslims in order to denounce his antipapal measures.[133]

In any case, since 1229 Muslim worship on the Temple Mount has been interrupted just twice due to warfare, and that only slightly. The first occasion would be in 1243, as we shall soon see. The second was not until the elapse of seven more centuries, in early July 1967 during the Six Day War.[134] In other words, the Muslim right to worship survived throughout a stretch of nearly 1,400 years—from 'Umar's acquisition of the city to the present day. It is, in fact, one of the most enduring traditions in the history of Jerusalem and one that has been successively ratified by Muslim, Christian, and Jewish politicians in several different centuries and a diverse array of historical contexts.

The Truce Expires

As he sailed from Acre, Frederick II named two men the custodians, or *baillies*, of the kingdom of Jerusalem: Balian of Sidon and Garnier l'Aleman.[135] In a shifting political landscape, these Syrian barons could at least look forward to a measure of peace with the Egyptian Ayyubids over the next decade. It was fleeting, however, because the kingdom was only one piece in a puzzle involving the other Latin states and the interests and possessions of the military religious orders.

By negotiating with al-Kamil, the Franks had aligned with the Egyptian branch of the Ayyubids, but after al-Kamil's death in 1238 alliances shifted in a curious manner. The politics are complicated but center on four actors. Al-Kamil had two sons: al-Adil II, who took control of Egypt from his father, and al-Salih Ayyub. The latter initially accepted this arrangement, as well as the rule of the third actor, al-Kamil's brother (for casual readers, unhelpfully named al-Salih Isma'il) in Damascus. In 1240, however, al-Salih Ayyub ousted his brother with the help of the fourth actor, al-Nasir Da'ud, a former lord of Damascus, and now controlled Egypt himself.[136]

These events have a backstory that involves Jerusalem. Frederick II's 1229 Jaffa treaty had a term of ten years, five months, and forty days, and this expired in the fall of 1239. Despair percolated as the end date drew near. Pope Gregory IX, figuring that by the time masses could be assembled Jerusalem would be lost once more, issued a letter to all Christians lamenting the city's fall.[137] The Franks moved swiftly to reconcile their defensive situation with the new threat environment. Calls for a renewed crusade had been ongoing since Frederick's departure from Acre, and preparations for what would become known as the Barons' Crusade were active in the late 1230s. However, some of its forces ended up diverted to the aid of Constantinople instead and only small contingents ended up in the East. One, led by Count Theobald of Champagne, arrived in Acre in September 1239: it marched to fortify Ascalon but was defeated in November by an Egyptian army and limped back north to Jaffa without several captured and imprisoned magnates.[138]

Also in November, the resident Franks began to rebuild the city's defensive walls. The construction included a new citadel on the western edge, which incorporated the Tower of David.[139] But they, too, had waited too long: in the same month, al-Nasir Da'ud, now the ruler of Kerak, made two power moves. First, he imprisoned his cousin, al-Salih Ayyub, and then he moved against Jerusalem and besieged the Tower of David from the city's western side.[140] For three weeks, the Muslims assaulted the tower, perhaps using artillery against it, while the small garrison put up a desperate fight.[141] With no relief armies on the horizon its members surrendered the tower in exchange for their lives. In the aftermath, al-Nasir sent his miners forward, and they proceeded to crack its mortar, pry out its iron bindings, and tear it down stone by stone:

> Thus was destroyed the Tower of David which had stood there ever since it was first built until that day, in times of peace and war, of heathens and Jews, of Muslim Saracens, of Christians and all kinds of people.[142]

The Tower of David had directly experienced, yet survived, numerous sieges, from the assault of Atsiz in 1077 to the sack of 1099.[143] After taking fire from Baldwin III's catapults in 1152, it was refurbished by King Amalric in the late 1160s: he added towers, forewalls, and a ditch and barbican to offer further protection. It could supposedly hold thousands of people in its late twelfth-century condition, and in 1219 the stronger citadel had ably resisted al-Mu'azzam's demolitions of the rest of the city.[144] But 1239 was its swan song, and the structure's return to grandeur would have to wait until the fifteenth century, during Ottoman rule.[145] In the meantime, Jerusalem had fallen yet again.

Treaties negotiated on the strength of the crusaders' military presence proved the way forward. In August 1240, Count Theobald struck two agreements, one with Damascus and the other with al-Nasir, that returned Jerusalem and several other cities, including Tiberias, Ascalon, and Bethlehem, to Frankish control, and also authorized the release of some prisoners.[146] A letter from Hermann of Perigord, the Templar Master, overstates the deal by claiming that God "has restored to the Christian power the whole of the country entire," but it was, in any case, successful in restoring the Holy City itself.[147] Theobald then departed the East, in advance of the arrival of the second major contingent of crusaders in October 1240. Led by Earl Richard of Cornwall, Frederick II's brother-in-law, this force had to choose carefully amid a revised threat landscape. His role was to conclude a third treaty with the final principal, the now free al-Salih Ayyub in Cairo. Its terms granted the return of the remaining French prisoners taken in 1239; the treaty was confirmed in April 1241, the men were returned, and by mid-August Richard was sailing back west, having first fortified Ascalon as a bulwark against future Egyptian aggression. Muslim control of the Temple Mount, as decreed by Frederick II, was reconfirmed.[148] For the moment, Jerusalem was safe.

The Khwarazmian Factor

Lost in all the niceties of the treaties and truces was the reality of the situation: with neither the Tower of David nor city walls for protection, Jerusalem remained virtually defenseless against future moves by either branch of the Ayyubids or their allies. The latter were particularly dangerous. Sultan al-Salih Ayyub, who now had some security against Damascus by virtue of his agreement with Richard and alliance with al-Nasir, moved to further consolidate his position in the period of 1241–1244. He barracked a new unit of mamluks in Egypt and hired Sunni, Turco-Persian Khwarazmian mercenaries from central Asia to guard his lands in northern Mesopotamia.[149]

The Khwarazmians were especially terrifying to all concerned, and one Christian source seemingly ranked them as more dangerous than the Ayyubids, for they "destroyed all sorts of people—heathens, Muslims, Jews and Christians—without distinction."[150] The name Khwarazmian applied to a loose coalition of soldiers made up largely of Kurds, Oguz (related to the Pechenegs and originating near the Aral Sea), and Qipchaks (from the Altai mountains in central Asia).[151] Through a representative to Innocent IV, who had become pope in 1243, Frederick II himself offered to fight the various Muslim forces in the East, but only in exchange for a removal of his excommunication ban. This superficial offer was promptly refused, and in any case Innocent blamed the emperor for causing the problems in the first place, fomenting, as he had, discord between not only Christian interest groups in the Levant but also among his own subjects and magnates in Europe.[152] Among the Muslims, the situation was dangerous enough to rupture the agreement between Kerak and Cairo: in 1243, "dissension broke out again between the princes," and al-Nasir allied instead with the Damascene Ayyubid al-Salih Isma'il. Together, they made a fairly astounding offer to the Franks: in exchange for military assistance against the Khwarazmians, Christians would not only be guaranteed Jerusalem but also control of the Temple Mount itself.[153]

It is useful to pause here to comprehend the relative gravity of this event. On the one hand, to surrender the holy places on top of the mount for even a short time must have been a tremendous sacrifice. After all, by that point it had been an exclusive Muslim possession for 56 years, and Islamic prayer had been permitted there for several decades before Saladin's liberation of the city. On the other hand, Jerusalem was still without walls, and it lacked a robust garrison to boot. Yet even in these precarious circumstances, it seems that the Christians, unlike in 1099, had been reasonably respectful towards the Muslim holy sites.[154] The hope was that this would continue even if the mount's ownership changed hands. Moreover, the Muslim lords must have surely known that any Christian possession of the city could only be temporary—and indeed they would have been prescient because it was reconquered the very next year.

In August 1244, the Khwarazmians reminded everyone of their presence in the most spectacular way possible: by taking and sacking Jerusalem. Their attack, in fact, was the most savage in centuries. Not since 614, when the Persians took the city from the Byzantines, had there been such brutalization of the local population and destruction of the city's built environment. The *Rothelin* author notes that it took place in three stages. First, the Khwarazmians attacked the city several times in succession, attriting the defenders and ultimately killing about 2,000 of them. The residents then appealed to their Muslim allies in Damascus and Homs for help, but as it was slow in coming many of them faced the hard choice of whether to stay or go. A group of about 6,000 decided the danger was too great and sneaked out of the city, attempting to reach the Mediterranean coast to the west. Some were caught and either killed or enslaved by local Muslim forces while the rest were intercepted on the Ramla Plain by Khwarazmian riders and cut to pieces. Only 300 survived the ordeal.[155]

The city was now emptied of its residents, but a few remained to take the brunt of what happened next. According to Ibn al-Furat, the Khwarazmians entered and put every Christian man inside to the sword, sparing none, and then enslaved all the women and children.

They ransacked the sepulchre church and destroyed the aedicule tomb inside it, and from its other tombs in the floors and walls they extricated and burned the bones. Afterward, they "purified" the Temple Mount in an unspecified manner and then departed for Gaza.[156] In the words of William of Châteauneuf, the Grand Master of the Hospitallers:

> Young men and virgins they hurried off with them into captivity, and retired into the Holy City, where they cut the throats, as of sheep doomed to the slaughter, of the nuns, and aged and infirm men, who, unable to endure the toils of the journey and fight, had fled to the church of the Holy Sepulchre and Calvary, a place consecrated by the blood of our Lord, thus perpetrating in His holy sanctuary such a crime as the eyes of men had never seen since the commencement of the world.[157]

In a stroke, the Khwarazmians had done what no other Muslims had attempted since the days of "the mad caliph," al-Hakim, in 1009. They tore asunder the old assurance of 'Umar ibn al-Khattab and violated the Christian sites in the city that had largely persevered over two centuries (apart from a few repossessions ordered by Saladin).

The Khwarazmian sack ensured that the exclusion of Muslims from the Temple Mount had lasted only a single year, from the summer of 1243 to the summer of 1244. If one accepts that a similar loss occurred between 1099 (the crusader sack) and 1138 (Usama ibn Munqidh's first appearance in the city), then Muslims had been denied the right to pray on al-Haram al-Sharif for a maximum total of 40 years during the Middle Ages. In quantitative terms, this is a paltry sum. Today, in 2022, Muslims retain exclusivity on the plateau, in the tradition begun by 'Umar in 638, so by subtracting these 40 years, that right to pray has existed for 1,344 years—or 97 percent of all Islamic history.

Back in the crusading era, for the third time Christians had failed to hold Jerusalem against Muslim assault, but other regional Muslim actors now found themselves in a similarly tight spot. Still hemmed in on two flanks between the Khwarazmians and Egyptians, they doubled down on their treaty with the Franks and, in 1244, recommitted to a military alliance with them.[158] The coalition is fascinating for its interreligious complexion. Three Islamic polities joined: Damascus, led by al-Salih's uncle, al-Salih Isma'il; Homs, led by the Kurd al-Mansur Ibrahim; and even Kerak, led by al-Nasir Da'ud who had, just four years previously, assisted the Egyptian sultan's expulsion of his own brother.[159]

Politics makes for strange bedfellows, indeed. According to Ibn al-Furat, Damascus wanted the Homs soldiers because they had a successful track record against Khwarazmians in previous encounters. Together, al-Salih and Ibrahim reached out to the Franks for both infantry and cavalry support, but negotiations were somewhat obtuse. Some of the Franks, for their part, requested support from Damascus and Homs in accordance with previous treaties guaranteeing Frankish retention of lands. It now seems that the Franks and Muslims agreed to two separate treaties. The first, in early 1244 and concluded between the Syrians and only the Templars, granted to the latter the whole of Jerusalem and lands west of the Jordan River. The second brought in the rest of the Frankish principals, including the Hospitallers, and thus boosted the combat power of the alliance. It likewise granted Jerusalem but only if the coalition managed to conquer Egypt first.[160]

It was all sorted in time and in early October 1244 Ibrahim met with the Christians in Acre and enjoyed the hospitality of the Templars for an evening. Thereafter, he, his retainers, the Templars and Hospitallers, and soldiers from the kingdom's army traveled south to Gaza, where they joined with the men of Damascus and Homs. Once there, Ibrahim reached out to al-Nasir and successfully procured his military support as well, although not his personal participation.[161] Al-Nasir himself certainly had his own issues with the Franks. Not only had he destroyed the Tower of David in 1239, but in 1242 he had raided Bethlehem; that provoked a Frankish sacking of Nablus in response, but in the same year he actually teamed with some Knights Templar to defeat an Egyptian expeditionary force near Gaza.[162] The common menace of the Egyptians motivated all concerned groups to unify for the sake of expediency.

So it happened that on 17 October 1244, a coalition of Christian and Muslims leaders assembled a grand army to destroy the Khwarazmian menace and, by doing so, cut the legs out from under the Egyptian Ayyubids. However, the resulting clash of arms at the Battle of La Forbie—a fascinating, interfaith moment virtually unknown outside of specialist circles—was more nadir than apogee.[163] The total force was impressive for its time: up to 5,000 soldiers for the Syrians and 9,000–12,000 for the Franks.[164] Give such numerical disparity, it is remarkable but not surprising that all the coalition soldiers rode under Christian standards: the Franks on the right wing, men from Damascus and Homs in the center, and those of Kerak on the left. In what may be propagandistic flair, both Ibn al-Furat and al-Maqrizi claim that priests blessed the Muslims with the sign of the cross and, in the former's telling, gave them wine to drink.[165] These Arabic accounts thus skewered the anti-Egyptian Muslims with apostatic rhetoric, on the basis of which they could subsequently celebrate their justified destruction.

Indeed, it was a poetic beginning to a tale of disaster. The Khwarazmians crashed into the allied left wing, which crumbled as the Muslims fought each other, "just as if they had not been followers of the same law."[166] The center, under Ibrahim, held out a little longer but was also routed. Meanwhile, the Christian right appears to have fared somewhat better, driving off much of the Egyptians, but the remainder held fast and, with the Khwarazmians, eventually encircled the Franks and captured or killed most of them.[167]

La Forbie was a strategic disaster. Out of an army of several thousand coalition warriors, only a few escaped and some 800 were captured.[168] The losses among the military religious orders were particularly devastating: only 10 percent of the Knights Templar survived, 8 percent of the Hospitallers, less than 1 percent of the Teutonic Knights, and the leper knights of the Order of St. Lazarus were wiped out entirely.[169] Following the annihilation, the orders withdrew to their customary strongholds in Acre, Atlit, Montfort, and the Galilee region to lick their wounds and recuperate.[170] The loss of so many soldiers meant that recovering Jerusalem was now out of the question for local Christian forces. Damascus and its allies were likewise powerless to prevent future strategic designs on Cairo.

The attempt to regain Jerusalem had failed and future efforts would repeatedly do so again. Given the destruction of the kingdom's army, military success in the East could now only be achieved via the traditional route: more crusades. These were abject failures. The Seventh (1248–1254) and Eighth (1270) Crusades, led by the pious king Louis IX of France, both came to disastrous ends, with Louis being captured in Egypt in the former and then dying from sickness in Tunisia in the latter.[171] Despite other attempts in the fourteenth and fifteenth centuries, the so-called "Later Crusades," no western army would again enter Jerusalem until that of General Allenby on 11 December 1917.

The New Becomes Old Again

There followed yet another shifting of Muslim alliances. With the Christians in retreat, al-Mansur Ibrahim of Homs got his payback against the Khwarazmians in May 1246, crushing their army before his own city. The survivors fled and received the aid of al-Nasir, the lord of Kerak, who had not been at La Forbie himself and now found himself needing soldiers. This was an opportunity. Previously so antagonistic to the Damascenes and all their allies, al-Salih, the sultan in Egypt, now saw a chance to eliminate the dangerous threat of the zealots themselves, who had grown so powerful in such a short time. Together with Ibrahim's men, a joint army of Homs and Cairo smashed most of the remaining Khwarazmians in Gaza in September 1246. In March of either 1247 or 1248, the Egyptian sultan was in Jerusalem, distributing alms and making arrangements for the reconstruction of its walls.[172] Work was sporadic and incomplete, however, and it would fall to Suleiman the Magnificent to finish the job in the 1500s.[173]

As our story nears its conclusion in the mid-thirteenth century, Jerusalem had been reduced to rather desperate straits in a Near East that was inexorably changing in complexion. The military power of the Franks had been largely broken at La Forbie and Frankish-held towns in the kingdom declined in number. They were steadily reconquered, first by the Ayyubids and then by their successors, the Burji Mamluks, led by the general Baybars.[174] In the 1260s, Baybars captured Nazareth, Arsuf, Atlit, and Jaffa; he also invaded Asia Minor, captured Antioch, and ended the Mongol threat from the East at the Battle of Ayn Jalut.[175] In the course of these events, Jerusalem's political role in the region was virtually nonexistent. By 1268, its population sat at only some 2000 people: 1700 Muslims, 300 Christians, and, reportedly, no Jews at all—a hollow shell of its former self.[176]

A dreary image, indeed, but deceptively so. The lower population figures come from a report by Nahmanides, a famous Catalonian Jewish scholar who had made his way to Jerusalem in 1268. Once there, he proceeded to help rebuild the community, which had not been exiled by any law but rather had fled the approach of the Mongols.[177] The result was the Ramban Synagogue, built on Mount Zion, which, after a lengthy hiatus during the Ottoman period, remains in use today.[178] Jews thereafter returned to live and worship in the city, albeit in small numbers. As for the Christians, who were in an increasingly precarious position, allowances for continuing pilgrimages to the Holy City were confirmed in a series of treaties with the Mamluks. One brokered in 1272 by the Lord Edward (the future Edward I of England) set a truce for 10 years, 10 days, and 10 hours.[179] Once that decade elapsed another truce was concluded between the Mamluks and Templars.[180] More deals with the Mamluks followed in the fourteenth century and trade continued between them and the West. However, a more permanent peace, whatever the conditions, proved elusive in the run-up to the final expulsion of the Franks from the Levant, at Acre in 1291.[181]

As the thirteenth century drew to a close, therefore, a circle had seemingly been completed. Jerusalem's society was returning to its state during the days of 'Umar in the seventh century: small, poor, and sparsely populated but, nonetheless, religiously diverse. The city remained vulnerable to attack, and indeed, in 1299–1300 the Mongol soldiers of the Ilkhanate territories may have entered it during the course of their war against the Egyptian Mamluks.[182] Soon after, however, a remarkable event took place within the city. In 1317, famine struck Jerusalem hard, and as its wells dried up the residents came together in common cause. Muslims, Jews, and Christians alike made their way outside and, together, prayed earnestly for rain. And rain it did, two days later—a fitting image for Jerusalem's pluralistic heritage.[183]

CONCLUSION

"If the past has lessons for the future anywhere on the face of the earth, Jerusalem is the place."

So wrote Rashid Khaladi, the Edward Said Professor at Columbia University in 1992, and the sentiment is undoubtedly true. But the nature of those lessons may not be what he and others have supposed.[1] The bulk of studies on the Arab–Israeli conflict, written by historians, political scientists, policy makers, ambassadors, and even heads of state, have centered specifically on the last two centuries, often neglecting the Middle Ages entirely or dispensing with that period in one or two summarizing chapters.[2] This has been a poor and even dangerous course. So many interpretations of the city's history end up being superficial treatments that either foster or buttress ignorant and jaundiced memories of the past, through which individuals, peoples, governments, and interest groups make claims about respective rights in, and to, the city on grounds of historical legitimacy that can only ever be partial.

These claims are often predicated on time and tolerance. In any given telling, a claim is usually based on how long "we" have possessed Jerusalem, or when we acquired it, or at what moments we took it back; and going further, how while in control "we" treated non-Jews, non-Christians, and/or non-Muslims better than they treated us when the roles are/were reversed. Such claims are usually accompanied with indictments of the other side—while "we" were seeking solutions "they" disrupted the status quo by seizing control through a morally suspect use of violence, discrimination, and intolerance. These are historical and ethical arguments. As this book has hopefully illustrated, however, in the Middle Ages there was no one who was universally tolerant, no single faith confession that displayed greater political morality while in a position of power.

However, what the preceding chapters strongly suggest is that a dominant theme of medieval Jerusalem's history is one of military conflict leading to gradations of rapprochement. This consistently enabled a diverse ethnic and religious community. Karen Armstrong has noted that, "for centuries, Jews, Christians, and Muslims were able to live together there."[3] It is an obvious point, albeit one that requires deeper pondering. This coexistence was not happenstance but rather the result of deliberate choices made by an array of commanders, political and religious leaders, and visitors and neighbors who made self-interested and practical (and, yes, often grudging) choices in order to thrive and survive. The result was diversity of religious worship and a measure of a pluralistic society over exceedingly long stretches of time. In short, there are no entities that can lay sole claim to proper, "tolerant" treatment of religious minorities because this was actually the norm. An examination of the major points of dispute in the medieval period, despite having been employed in the past as means of distinguishing between good and bad actors, really illustrates that Jerusalem's medieval people and rulers consistently sought ways to coexist.

Interfaith Relations

The end of Byzantine rule over Jerusalem in 638 was a watershed moment in that it set a pluralistic tone that has endured to the present day. Caliph 'Umar and the armies under his command could have easily overpowered Patriarch Sophronius's defenders, captured the city whole, and established a purely Islamic city. Instead, 'Umar negotiated a surrender and thereafter issued his Assurance, which established the basis for the tolerance of the three Abrahamic faiths: Muslims worshipping on the Temple Mount, Christians retaining rights to their churches, and, soon after, the relaxing of physical and devotional prohibitions on Jews. It was a pleasant notion that played out thematically over the next seven centuries, albeit at times with some difficulty.

From 638 to the eleventh century, a Jewish/Christian/Sunni/Shia community persevered through the swirls of warfare outside Jerusalem's walls, between Umayyads, Abbasids, Carmathians, Fatimids, and Seljuks. The common myth of a medieval Middle East as a sectarian region dominated by a Muslim majority has been exposed by Jack Tannous, who has shown that one can only understand the growth of Islam in the region by including the context of the other faith communities living there.[4] There were no pogroms against anyone until the reign of al-Hakim, and the episodes of violence against Christians had more to do with internal politics than religious strife. Even after the year 1000, members of the Abrahamic faiths experienced hardships but always rallied back towards repair and reconciliation. Disgust with the Mad Caliph was nearly universal, and his own mother worked hard to repair the damage his policies inflicted. The coming of the Turks represented a new threat, but one that is easy to overstate. Karaite Jews remained in Jerusalem while the Rabbanite *yeshiva* moved to Tyre in the 1070s, but that, too, demonstrates a fascinating continuation of the theme: they left upon the suggestion of a Muslim, Shafi'i sheikh, who had already moved his *madhab* there, so even in flight there was interfaith cooperation. When the Egyptian vizier al-Afdal took back Jerusalem from the Sunnis in 1098, he maintained the tolerant and multifaceted Shia, Sunni, Jewish and eastern Christian community he found there. Four hundred years, then, of living together.

This arrangement was dramatically sundered by the First Crusade, which no doubt did enormous damage to pluralism by expelling Jews and Muslims outright. But as we have seen, those prohibitions did not last long. By the 1130s Muslims could again pray on the Temple Mount, and by the 1160s Jewish visitors could pray at the Western Wall. Conflicts and confusion remained. Usama bin Munqidh's memoirs illustrate the tensions between newcomers, who had trouble processing the existence of Muslim devotions in a Christian city, and old-timers who knew that coexistence demanded a measure of tolerance, even if it was only in the name of profit.[5] Still, despite the brief interruption during the early formation of the Crusader States, from the mid-twelfth century forward the trend lines were in the direction of both minority and majority ethnic and religious groups visiting, worshipping, and then living in the city, and this continued into the fourteenth century and beyond.

Property destruction occurred alongside the occasional bouts of violence, and there is no point in denying that it happened under everyone's watch. The Umayyads pulled down the city walls in the mid-eighth century. Bedouins destroyed churches in Jerusalem in the mid-ninth century; more were harmed in 938. The Fatimids presided over the burning at the stake of Patriarch John VII, the toppling of the sepulchre church's dome, and the reviled desolations of al-Hakim. Crusaders burned down the Karaite synagogue and converted the Muslim holy sites for Christian use. Saladin then destroyed some of their churches and/or replaced them with mosques and *madrasas*. His Ayyubid successors demolished Jerusalem's walls again, the church of St. Mary of Zion, and then expelled Jews and Christians from the city. In the thirteenth century, the army of Kerak destroyed the Tower of David, and the Khwarazmians sacked the city and massacred its Christian residents. They then destroyed the Church of the Holy Sepulchre, as had Caliph al-Hakim the Mad in the eleventh and, before him, the Muslim and Jewish rioters of 966; the Fatimids also looted it in 1056. No medieval possessor of Jerusalem had clean hands, and to center only one faction as deliberately demolishing physical structures of the other is to distort.

The above sounds terrible when combined into a simplistic narrative. Some have plucked from it certain events in order to argue a given political position: Christians did worse deeds than Muslims, or vice versa. This is common and holds tremendous power because certain audiences are disposed to the idea that their side has been treated unjustly or has suffered inordinately compared to everyone else. However, neither of these methods provide real avenues towards reconciliation, only continuing rancor. In reality, as these pages have shown, each event occurred within complex contexts. Seizing upon any single transgression in order to generalize about the disposition of its religious adherents can be politically satisfying but can never be considered scholarly. Moreover, the transgressions were actually rather few in number when considered against a timeline of some 700 years, and after every occasion people swiftly moved to rebuild.

There is therefore another way to think about interfaith relations in Jerusalem. As one author has noted, the status and protection of these sites today "hangs suspended like a sword over future negotiations regarding the city."[6] Instead of focusing on guilt for foul deeds, historians, religious leaders, policy makers, and educated readers could emphasize that, despite the litany of offenses, the medieval rulers and communities of Jerusalem themselves consciously preferred and pursued religious pluralism of the sort idealized in 'Umar's Assurance. That trend continued into the early modern and modern periods and was confirmed through a series of Ottoman and Israeli laws. Following the fall of Jerusalem in 1967, the State of Israel issued a law known as the Protection of Holy Places, which states that "The Holy Places shall be protected from desecration and any other violation and from anything likely to violate the freedom of access of the members of the different religions to the places sacred to them or their feelings with regard to those places."[7] These "holy places" were then enumerated in the following years and include, in Jerusalem, the Tomb of the Virgin Mary, the Church of the Holy Sepulchre, the Sanctuary of the Ascension, and the Convent of Dayr al-Sultan.[8] These match those protected in earlier Ottoman protections under Sultans Mehmed II in 1458, Osman III in 1757, and Abdülmecid I in 1852—the so-called "Status Quo" agreement.[9] In some measure, then, the legacy of 'Umar's Assurance has persisted into the twenty-first century.

Wars and Massacres

Yes, some may retort, Jerusalemites generally got along, but the military conquests of the city tell a different story: one of assault, suffering, massacres, and destruction. These events pop out of the history books more than anything else and can draw the eye away from the complicated mosaic of civil relations. In particular, the First Crusade is often singled out as a singularly heinous example of medieval religious violence. Like the occasional persecutions and demolitions of buildings and walls, however, a single war tells only an incomplete story. A quantitative approach is an easy way to approach the problem. Jerusalem was at least attacked 19 times in the period 614–1248 (see Appendix), and that seems like a lot. As usual, however, context is needed to interpret the statistics.

Of these 19 attacks on Jerusalem, 14 of them were muted in one way or another, giving the lie to an impression of constant, destructive conflict across the centuries. Its military history is actually one of relatively modest sieges. Three of the attacks were military offensives that never reached the city walls: Ridwan of Aleppo in 1095 (aborted mid-campaign), the Fatimids in 1124 (driven off by resident skirmishers), and Timür-Tash in 1152 (destroyed on the march). On eight more occasions Jerusalem surrendered either immediately or after blockades that did not produce any sort of mass suffering: Heraclius in 630, 'Umar in 638, al-Mu'izz in 971–974, Atsiz in 1073, al-Afdal in 1098, Frederick II in 1229, Theobald in 1240, and al-Salih Ayyub in 1247–1248. Three more involved intense artillery attacks on the city that prompted capitulation but no mass casualties: the Fatimids in 1098, Baldwin III in 1152, and al-Nasir Da'ud in 1239. That we have emphasized only the worst sieges says more about the modern uses of history than historical reality.

Those worst moments came in the five other falls of the city, but their lessons are not as obvious as supposed. Two of them, narrated in chapter one, belong to the pre-Islamic era in Jerusalem and are more relics of the ancient past than representative of the accord engendered in the Middle Ages. In 614, Persians and Jews enabled the sack of Jerusalem, which was surely a horrific event, and this was followed by Heraclius's peaceful retaking of the city in 630 after triumphing in the Byzantine–Sasanid War. For the latter, the conquest of the city was essentially nonviolent, but its aftermath most certainly was not: the emperor's mass persecution of Jews that resulted in untold executions and forced conversions to Christianity. Outside of individual anecdotes, such things largely went away after Heraclius bid adieu to Syria. This was a turning point: the coming Rashidun armies eschewed such methods and instead ushered in the first era of religious coexistence of all three Abrahamic faiths in the city. We could harp on the destruction or, rather, commemorate and celebrate the paradigm shift: the coming of Islamic rule was a break from the comparative ugliness of the ancient world.[10]

As chapter two then demonstrates, there were no massacres in Jerusalem for the next four centuries. This accomplishment is all the more impressive when remembering that the Shia Fatimids attained possession of the city in the tenth century but did not eliminate, much less persecute, the Sunnis living there. Inter-Muslim violence finally erupted in the third fall of Jerusalem, in 1077, when Sunni Turks under Atsiz killed 3,000 Shia. Here, context matters. Atsiz's first siege in 1073 was a relatively tame blockade that concluded with capitulation but no massacre. He only returned four years later when insurgents imprisoned his family and challenged his authority—his response, while unpleasant to say the least, does not appear to have been driven by religious acrimony. In the aftermath, Shia were not banned from the city, and a pluralistic community persisted all the way up to the First Crusade, even after the Fatimids reclaimed it in 1098 and could have easily taken bloody revenge.

This trend line continued with the fourth example, in chapter three: the crusader sack of 1099. It is easily the most infamous attack in the medieval history of Jerusalem, and incredible amounts of ink have been spilt on it. Moreover, it continues to inflame passions about religious warfare in modern discourse. It was, indeed, out of step with the heritage of peaceful coexistence. But we have focused too much on the blood and not enough on the event's place in Jerusalem's broader story. Even the crusaders could not permanently alter the trajectory of the city's pluralism, which had been cemented by that point with 461 years of interfaith traditions. Given the city's history, it should be no surprise that, less than two generations after the sack, Muslims were back on the Temple Mount, praying towards Mecca.

Chapters four and five covered the remaining violent assaults on Jerusalem. Saladin's in 1187 is justly celebrated as restrained, in that he could have massacred its Christian population but did not. Reasonable discussions should be had about the allegation of mass rape of those who could not pay the ransom price and whether or not the glowing contours of the sultan's legend are legitimate. Still, it is clear that in the aftermath he tolerated an interfaith community of Jews, Muslims, and (eastern) Christians—very much in the vein of 'Umar, to whom Islamic poets compared him specifically. Finally, the sack of the Khwarazmians in 1244 wiped out the remaining Christian population, and Jews likely would have suffered too, had they not already fled the city in advance. The event gladdened no one, and led to a grand alliance between Christians and Muslims that likely surprises those modern readers who presume that East and West have always been at war in a grand clash of civilizations. After that army failed at the Battle of La Forbie, a coalition of forces from Homs and Cairo—the latter of whom had recently hired the Khwarazmians in the first place—crushed what was seen by virtually everyone as a pernicious threat to both political and religious stability.

As with property destruction, these climactic five events tell us that virtually every major interest group contributed to massacres in Jerusalem. The method of employing a particular massacre as the basis of a modern complaint can never prevail in an argument because competing parties can retort with a counterexample. It may be more productive to simply admit that, yes, the history of the city showcases bad actors from every persuasion. Following this are two other, more optimistic conclusions: the bulk of Jerusalem's falls occurred in a restrained, even mundane, fashion; and that the rest did not—could not—transform the city into the exclusive domain of any given faith confession.

The Temple Mount

A common refrain from Islamic authorities today is that al-Aqsa is in danger, which is taken to mean the entire structure of the plateau, that mosque and the Dome of the Rock, and the Muslim right to prayer on the Temple Mount. The latter tradition is, in fact, the most enduring in Jerusalem's medieval story. Muslims have been praying on the Temple Mount since 638, as permitted by medieval Sunni and Shia rulers as well as the Christian kings of Jerusalem. As we have seen, there were only two breaks in this tradition: after the First Crusade (1099–1130s), and then possibly in 1243–1244. In both cases, prayer was, counterintuitively, restored by the Christian kings of Jerusalem. Put another way, over the 1,400 year history of the religion, Islamic prayer has been absent from the Temple Mount for less than 40 years: under 0.03% of those 1,400 years.

This grand heritage has not been interrupted again, but there are fears that could change. These are not entirely without foundation. In 1969, there was an attempt to burn down the al-Aqsa mosque, and plots to blow up the holy sites followed in the 1980s.[11] Corresponding efforts by some ultra-Orthodox Jews to pray on the site, as well as messianic Jewish (and fundamentalist Christian) groups seeking to rebuild the Temple, have not helped.[12] Seemingly giving credence to Muslim suspicions were much publicized visits to the Temple Mount like that of then Prime Minister Ariel Sharon in September 2000, accompanied by Likud officials and the Israeli Defense Forces (IDF) and, afterward, asserting the rights of Jews to visit the area.[13] Likewise, periodic IDF quellings of protests and riots have engendered another measure of discomfiture.[14] The reaction to these perceived slights has been multifaceted: a campaign waged since 1996 by the Islamic Movement in Israel to position "al-Aqsa as the central religious-nationalist symbol of the Palestinian struggle"; The Second Intifada (2000–2005), a period of intense violence and conflict, which carried the alternative name of "the Al-Aqsa Intifada"; protests and riots; and even political rhetoric from world leaders.[15] For their part, the Israelis have consistently maintained that their interest is to keep the status quo, but obviously mistrust runs rampant on both sides.

Some historical comparisons are instructive here. One of the most controversial events of the Six Day War was the Israeli conquest of Jerusalem's Old City and securing of both the Western Wall and the Temple Mount.[16] Firmly in control of the city and with enough combat power to do as he pleased, the Israeli Minister of Defense, Moshe Dayan, could have drastically altered the long-established arrangements. But ignoring the purported urgings of Shlomo Goren, Chief Rabbi of the Military Rabbinate of the IDF, to detonate the Dome of the Rock and al-Aqsa mosque (the veracity of which is still debated today), Dayan, refused. In an address to IDF soldiers, he said:

> We have returned to our holiest site so as never to part with it again. To our Arab neighbors, Israel stretches out its hand in peace ... We did not come to conquer the holy sites of others or to restrict their religious rights, but to ensure the integrity of the city and to live there with others in brotherhood.[17]

For those familiar with the medieval story, this should sound very familiar. Dayan (a Jewish atheist) was acting in the same manner as Frederick II (a Christian) had over six hundred years before him. Dayan himself may have been oblivious to this connection, for he mentions neither Frederick nor the 1229 Treaty of Jaffa in his autobiography.[18] Yet the similarity is unmistakable: at the precise moment when each military leader held supreme power over the city and occupied it with soldiers, both opted to retain Muslim worship on the mount.

Today, Israel has still not moved to claim the Temple Mount for itself, and Muslim prayer remains the only legal sort on the plateau. Not everyone was happy about this in 1229, and many remain unhappy even today. But if read in the spirit of medieval detente that this book has charted, the events in the Old City in 1967 could be substantially reimagined. At least in the sense of religious rights, they do not represent a rupture but rather continuity with a centuries-old tradition in which these rights had been confirmed by Muslims and non-Muslims alike: from 'Umar, al-Mu'izz, and Saladin—but also Frederick, Richard of Cornwall, and Moshe Dayan.

The Western Wall

Because it was granted by both Christian and Jewish governments, there is thus a sturdy Islamic argument for devotional rights on the Temple Mount: on, that is, but not around. There has been an ahistorical tradition running parallel to the al-Aqsa debate that seeks to disinherit the Jews from prayer at the Western Wall. Their devotions, like those of Muslims above on the mount, also date back to the twelfth century, at least, and were confirmed by both Muslim and Christian rulers.

As this book has shown, the notion that medieval Jews only prayed outside Jerusalem until 1800, which is repeated in various publications and statements, is fanciful. Jewish worship there dates back to at least the mid-twelfth century. Benjamin Tudela noted devotions there in the 1160s, and Maimonides probably prayed there in 1165. In 1210, the travelers Samuel ben Samson and Jonathan ha-Kohen prayed there, and Jewish pilgrimages to the spot continued into the 1240s.[19] One of the criticized Israeli demolitions after 1967, the *Madrasa al-Afdaliyya*, had only been endowed in 1193, meaning that Jewish worship at the spot technically predated it.[20] This is not to say, however, that the Western Wall, or even Jerusalem itself, was always central to Jewish devotional activities, and we have seen that other Levantine cities very often held the more vibrant, and populous, portions of their communities, especially in the tenth and eleventh century.

Equally important is understanding how these devotions were made possible: through the dispensations of Christian and Muslim rulers. Prayer there, by a few sparse residents but mostly by visitors, began in either the reign of Baldwin III or Amalric I. Saladin's conquest resulted in a large influx of Jews to this city, where they were tolerated, and this continued through the pilgrimages of the early thirteenth century. The practice continued after Frederick II obtained Jerusalem in 1229. After Jews fled the city in advance of the Khwarazmians and, later, the Mongols, they returned in sparse numbers, as noted by Nahmanides, to the Mamluk-controlled city. Prayer at the Western Wall was, by then, an established tradition. In 1546, the Ottoman sultan Suleiman the Magnificent confirmed it by issuing a decree (*firman*) that Jews had the right to pray at the

Western Wall in perpetuity.[21] This happened, it should be noted, in the wake of an earthquake that same year, in which the Temple Mount was damaged—so even in a time of worry for the Muslim holy sites above, a Muslim ruler nonetheless cemented Jewish rites down below. Subsequently, Jews resided in southern neighborhoods near the Western Wall during the following century.[22] The *firman* remained in force all the way until 1949, when Jordan prevented any and all Jewish access. It proved to be an exceptional and short break: the Israelis retook the wall in 1967 and Rabbi Goren blew the *shofar* on a live radio broadcast. Save for that 18-year gap, Jewish worship at the Western Wall is a historical tradition nearly nine hundred years old, at least.

However, today it seems that many have sought to deny this history or explain it away. The Palestinian Authority has claimed that the Western Wall or, as they call it, the Al-Buraq Wall, is part of al-Aqsa and Jews have no right to it.[23] They are not alone in this claim, which is made by the Waqf itself: that "al-Aqsa" refers not just to the specific mosque first built by Walid I but the entire Temple Mount, above, below, and all around.[24] This dispute exploded in 2016, when UNESCO adopted a resolution that called the Western Wall "the Buraq Plaza," which followed on the heels of assorted moments of calling Jewish heritage sites only by their Arabic names, thereby implying their primary Islamic functions. The technique appears to be part of a comprehensive movement to deny any Jewish connection to the Temple Mount at all.[25] These and other resolutions ultimately led to both Israel and the United States withdrawing from UNESCO entirely in October 2017.[26]

What's good for the goose is good for the gander: if medieval history can be used to validate Muslim claims to al-Haram al-Sharif, then it likewise validates Jewish claims to the Western Wall. As with Frederick and Dayan, accommodations there were proffered and confirmed by non-Jewish rulers. An appeal to medieval tradition, if considered in its fullness, is honest and unifying: as their forefathers agreed to a sharing of Herod's great edifice, so too could contemporary voices confirm the pluralistic accords of the medieval past.

Epilogue: A Path Forward

As noted in its opening, this book is designed neither as a sledgehammer to destroy studies that emphasize Jerusalem's violent past nor as a means of advancing any sort of policy agenda. Rather, it has sought to fill in the gaps of such studies and provide a fuller history of the city, one in which the dominant theme appears to be accord, not antagonism. This interpretation emphasizes not historical rights in and of themselves but rather the avenues by which they were acquired. Crucially, it also centers on the fact that the major interreligious rights and allowances in the Middle Ages were either proffered or confirmed by rulers practicing different religions. In other words, diversity led to community.

Such a conclusion is only possible through a review of the contexts of the military, political, and religious history of medieval Jerusalem across the period, and here it arose from a consideration of a certain set of archaeological and textual materials. This study has focused on Jerusalem itself, but further inquiry into interfaith trends in the broader Near East across the same stretch of centuries would no doubt add further layers of meaningful context.[27] Diverse communities existed elsewhere in the region. In cities like Acre, Tyre, Cairo, and even Damascus, hints of interfaith problem solving can be spotted in the period following the seventh-century Arabic conquests. Whether or not Jerusalem was exceptional in its pluralism will need to be determined through further inquiry into the broad history of such places. Moreover, future studies could likely find more connections between the medieval world and modern controversies that this book has not addressed.

The fuller the historical inquiry, then, the better. Nothing shocking there, but in the case of Jerusalem most treatments have lacked both breadth and width. In this sense, periodization can be problematic because while the history of, say, religious customs in the eleventh century tells us one story, the history of both religion and warfare in the tenth through twelfth century reveals others. Partial histories, especially when written from partisan perspectives and for activist purposes, neglect elements that suggest the counternarrative and help feed the rhetorical contests seen on news broadcasts. In these, advocates make divisive claims based on historical precedence, in the full knowledge that they each have built-in audiences who are already favorably disposed towards their interpretation. This approach sells books and wins applause in different quarters but has not, and likely will not, produce any winners.

Historians look to the past and ought not to be in the business of prescribing solutions, but it is well within the disciplinary ethic to suggest that past preludes can be useful for thinking about contemporary issues in new ways.[28] The medieval narrative both validates and nullifies historical claims for every party, in both reassuring and uncomfortable ways. In the end, what Jerusalem was, then, is what it remains: a city for all.

APPENDIX: ATTACKS ON AND
EXCHANGES OF MEDIEVAL JERUSALEM

Chapter	Year	On Offense	On Defense	Result
1	614	Shahrbaraz	Zachariah/Byzantines	Taken; massacre
1	630	Heraclius	Sasanid Persia	Surrendered
1	638	'Umar ibn al-Khattab	Sophronius/Byzantines	Surrendered after blockade
2	971–4	al-Mu'izz li-Din Allah	Carmathians/Abbasids	Surrendered
2	1073	Atsiz Beg	Fatimid Caliphate	Surrendered after blockade
2	1077	Atsiz Beg	Shia revolutionaries	Taken; massacre
3	1095	Ridwan of Aleppo	Artuqid dynasty	Attack aborted
3	1098	al-Afdal Shahanshah	Artuqid dynasty	Surrendered after assault
3	1099	Godfrey de Bouillon *et al*	Fatimid Caliphate	Taken; massacre
4	1124	Fatimids	Kingdom of Jerusalem	Attack aborted
4	1152	Timür-Tash	Kingdom of Jerusalem	Attack aborted
4	1152	Baldwin III	Queen Melisende	Surrendered after assault
4	1187	Saladin	Balian of Ibelin	Surrendered after assault
4	1195	Al-Afdal ibn Salah ad-Din	al-Malik al-Aziz Uthman	Abandoned to attackers
5	1229	Frederick II	al-Malik al-Kamil	Acquired via treaty
5	1239	al-Nasir Da'ud	Kingdom of Jerusalem	Surrendered after assault
5	1240	Theobald of Champagne	al-Nasir Da'ud (Kerak)	Acquired via treaty
5	1244	Khwarazmians	Kingdom of Jerusalem	Taken; massacre
5	1247/1248	al-Salih Ayyub	Khwarazmians	Surrendered

NOTES

Introduction

1. *The Itinerary of Rabbi Benjamin of Tudela*, trans. and ed. A. Asher, 2 vols. (New York: Hakesheth, 1938), I.69–72.

2. Paul E. Chevveden, "The Islamic View and the Christian View of the Crusades: a New Synthesis," *History* 93:2 (2008): 199.

3. Israel Jacob Yuval, *Two Nations in Your Womb: Perceptions of Jews and Christians in Late Antiquity and the Middle Ages* (Berkeley: University of California Press, 2008), 37. For more on the general topic, see Lawrence E. Frizzell and J. Frank Henderson, "Jews and Judaism in the Medieval Latin Liturgy," in *The Liturgy of the Medieval Church*, ed. T.J. Heffernan and E.A. Matter (Kalamazoo: Medieval Institute Publications, 2001), 187–214. Interestingly, there was no parallel *adversus Christianos* tradition in Jewish literature; see Robert Chazan, "Crusading in Christian-Jewish Polemics," in *The Medieval Crusade*, ed. S.J. Ridyard (Woodbridge: Boydell Press, 2004), 34.

4. For example, Eric H. Cline, *Jerusalem Besieged: From Ancient Canaan to Modern Israel* (Ann Arbor: University of Michigan Press, 2005); and even more broadly, Gary L. Rashba, *Holy Wars: 3,000 Years of Battles in the Holy Land* (Philadelphia and Newbury: Casemate, 2011).

5. As in, arguably, Amy-Jill Levine, "Epilogue: Sites of Toleration," in *Tolerance, Intolerance, and Recognition in Early Christianity and Early Judaism*, ed. O. Lehtipuu and M. Labahn (Amsterdam: Amsterdam University Press, 2021), 291–303.

6. Jacob Lassner, *Jews, Christians, and the Abode of Islam: Modern Scholarship, Medieval Realities* (Chicago and London: University of Chicago Press, 2012), 177-8. Indeed, in general "the medieval Muslim felt superiority and condescension towards Christians"; see Carole Hillenbrand, *The Crusades: Islamic Perspectives* (Edinburgh: Edinburgh University Press, 1999), 267.

7. Christopher MacEvitt, *The Crusades and the Christian World of the East: Rough Tolerance* (Philadelphia: University of Pennsylvania Press, 2008), 21–3.

8. Defining "minority" in the period is tricky because groups' situations often changed and there were no fixed categories, but for a working concept based on power see the introduction in C.A. Vidal, J. Tearney-Pearce, and L. Yarbrough (Ed.), *Minorities in Contact in the Medieval Mediterranean* (Turnhout: Brepols, 2020), 11–30. On other aspects, see N. Berend (Ed.), *Minority Influences in Medieval Society* (London and New York: Routledge, 2021).

9. For various aspects, see the essays in M. Gervers and J.M. Powell (Ed.), *Tolerance and Intolerance: Social Conflict in the Age of the Crusades* (Syracuse: Syracuse University Press, 2001).

10. The notion of a "clash of civilizations," popularized first by Bernard Lewis and then Samuel Huntington, has somehow survived scathing academic critique and remains common in the popular imagination. See, for example, the essays in E. Qureshi and M. Sells (Ed.), *The New Crusades: Constructing the Muslim Enemy* (New York: Columbia University Press, 2003).

Chapter I Islam Awakens: 614 and 638

1. "A Chronicle Composed AD 640," in *The Seventh Century in West-Syrian Chronicles*, trans. A. Palmer (Liverpool: Liverpool University Press, 1993), 10, 17.

2. See for overviews Sebastian P. Brock, "Syriac Sources for Seventh-Century History," *Byzantine and Modern Greek Studies* 2 (1976): 17–36; and Sebastian P. Brock, "Syriac Historical Writing: a Survey of the Main Sources," *Journal of the Iraq Academy, Syriac Corporation* 5 (1979): 1–30. See also Michael Philip Penn, *Envisioning Islam: Syriac Christians and the Early Muslim World* (Philadelphia: University of Pennsylvania Press, 2015).

3. Penn, *Envisioning Islam*, 57–9. On other meanings of the word, see Jack Tannous, *The Making of the Medieval Middle East* (Princeton: Princeton University Press, 2013), 525–31.

4. A tidy, albeit partial, blow-by-blow list is provided by the close contemporary Jacob of Edessa; see E.W. Brooks, "The Chronological Canon of James of Edessa," *Zeitschrift der Deutschen Morgenländischen Gesellschaft* 53 (1899): 323. There is a debate underway in the field about the words "Byzantine/Byzantium" and their pejorative and anachronistic uses, as the people of the time referred to themselves not as Byzantines but rather "Romans." Given that specialists have yet to agree on a replacement, this book retains the terms. For an interesting take, see Panagiotis Theodoropoulos, "Did the Byzantines Call Themselves Byzantines? Elements of Eastern Roman Identity in the Imperial Discourse of the Seventh Century," *Byzantine and Modern Greek Studies* 45:1 (2021): 25–41.

5. John Haldon, *Warfare, State and Society in the Byzantine World, 565-1204* (London: Routledge, 1999), 14. See also Jon Seligman, "The Hinterland of Jerusalem during the Byzantine Period," in *Unearthing Jerusalem: 150 Years of Archaeological Research in the Holy City*, ed. K. Galor and G. Avni (University Park: Penn State University Press, 2011), 361–83.

6. According to the much later account of Agapios, bishop of Manbij; see Agapios, *Kitāb al-'Unvan: Histoire universelle écrite par Agapius*, trans. A. Vasiliev, 2 vols. (Paris: Firmin Didot, 1909), II.1; English translation Agapius, Universal History, *Tertullian.org*, trans. R. Pearse, https://www.tertullian.org/fathers/agapius_history_02_part2.htm; accessed March 3, 2022.

7. "Antiochus Strategos' Account of the Sack of Jerusalem in A.D. 614," *English Historical Review* 25:99 (1910): 504.

8. *The Armenian History Attributed to Sebeos*, trans R.W. Thompson (Liverpool: Liverpool University Press, 1999), 68–9.

9. Leah Di Segni and Yoram Tsafrir, "The Ethnic Composition of Jerusalem's Population in the Byzantine Period (312-638 CE)," *Liber Annus* 62 (2012): 412.

10. *Armenian History*, 69.
11. On their history, see Alan Cameron, *Circus Factions: Blues and Greens at Rome and Byzantium* (Oxford: Oxford University Press, 1976).
12. "Account of the Sack of Jerusalem," 503–5. This source has a tricky lineage, for Strategos did not write it but rather gave his testimony to someone else, who recorded it in Greek; this was then copied into Arabic and then Georgian. Because the original Greek version is not extant, this Georgian copy is all that survives.
13. "Account of the Sack of Jerusalem," 505–6.
14. On the construction of the walls at this point, see Shlomit Wekler-Bdolah, "The Fortifications of Jerusalem in the Byzantine Period," *ARAM* 18–19 (2006–2007): 85–112.
15. "Account of the Sack of Jerusalem," 506.
16. On the dates, see Robert G. Hoyland, *Seeing Islam as Others Saw It: A Survey and Evaluation of Christian, Jewish and Zoroastrian Writings on Early Islam* (Princeton: Darwin Press, 1997), 126 n. 35.
17. "Account of the Sack of Jerusalem," 506–7. See also *Armenian History*, 69.
18. *Armenian History*, 69; "Account of the Sack of Jerusalem," 507.
19. "Account of the Sack of Jerusalem," 507.
20. John the Persian and Rabban bar ʾIdta, *The Histories of Rabban Hormizd the Persian and Rabban bar-ʾIdta*, ed. and trans. E.A. Wallis Budge, 2 vols. (London: Luzac, 1902), I.252, line 1275.
21. "Account of the Sack of Jerusalem," 507–8.
22. "Account of the Sack of Jerusalem," 508. He also accuses the Jews of burning down more buildings once the Christians had been led off into captivity.
23. "Chronicon anonymum," in *Chronica minora, pars prior*, ed. I. Guidi (Leipzig: Otto Harrassowitz, 1903), 23.
24. *Armenian History*, 69.
25. See in general Nicholas de Lange, "Jews in the Age of Justinian," in *The Cambridge Companion to the Age of Justinian*, ed. M. Maas (Cambridge: Cambridge University Press, 2005), 401–26.
26. A reference to Acre ("Ptolemais") specifically is found in the *Dialogue Jacobi nuper baptizati*, which reports that, in the wake of the Persian invasion, local Jews killed several Christians and burned down their churches; see Vincent Déroche, "Doctrina Jacobi Nuper Baptizati," *Travaux et mémoires* 11 (1991): 181–2.
27. John F. Haldon, "Seventh-Century Continuities: the *Ajnād* and the 'Thematic Myth,'" in *The Byzantine and Early Islamic Near East, Volume III: States, Resources and Armies*, ed. A. Cameron (Princeton: Darwin Press, 1995), 410.
28. See *Theophilus of Edessa's Chronicle and the Circulation of Historical Knowledge in Late Antiquity and Early Islam*, trans. R.G. Hoyland (Liverpool: Liverpool University Press, 2011): 64 (Michael the Syrian) and 65 (*Chronicle of 1234*); for Dionysius, see *Seventh Century in West-Syriac Chronicles*. For numerous recent studies on Theophanes, Theophilus, Agapius, and other narrative sources of this period, see M. Jankowiak and F. Montinaro (Ed.), *Studies in Theophanes, Travaux et mémoires* 19 (2015); see in particular the essays by Muriel Debié and Robert G. Hoyland on further debate over the identity of "Theophilus" and his role as a primary source for the later authors. An older treatment is Ann S. Proudfoot, "The Sources of Theophanes for the Heraclian Dynasty," *Byzantion* 44 (1974): 367–439.
29. Eutychius, "Annals," trans. R. Pearse <https://www.roger-pearse.com/weblog/eutychius-annals-my-posts-containing-the-translation/>, II.18.5–6; accessed January 14, 2021.
30. Eutychius, "Annals," II.18.6.
31. That is the typical explanation. The later account of Severus bin al-Muqaffaʿ, the Christian bishop of Hermopolis Magna (fl. 950s) claims that Heraclius had a dream in which a "circumcised nation" would conquer his lands so, assuming this meant the Jews,

NOTES to pp. 19–23

he ordered them baptized to eliminate the threat. That nation turned out to be the Arabs instead; see "History of the Patriarchs of the Coptic Church of Alexandria," trans. B. Evetts, in *Patrologia Orientalis*, 4 vols. (Paris: Firmin Didot, 1907), II.492–3.

32. Jacob's forced baptism, which occurred after he unsuccessfully tried to pass as a Christian while incognito, is described in Déroche, "Doctrina Jacobi," 217–19. For Maximus's letter, see Robert Devreesse, "La fin inédite d'une lettre de saint Maxime: Un baptême forcé de juifs et samaritains à Carthage en 632," *Revue de sciences religieuses* 17.1 (1937): 34–5. On both Maximus and the dialogue of Jacob, see Pieter W. van der Horst, "A Short Note on the Doctrina Jacobi nuper baptizati," in *Studies in Ancient Judaism and Early Christianity* (Leiden and Boston: Brill, 2014): 203–8.

33. Walter E. Kaegi, *Heraclius: Emperor of Byzantium* (Cambridge: Cambridge University Press, 2003), 216–17.

34. See for context Stefan Esders, "The Merovingians and Byzantium: Diplomatic, Military, and Religious Issues, 500-700," in *The Oxford Handbook of the Merovingian World*, ed. B. Effros and I. Moreira (Oxford: Oxford University Press, 2020), 347–69; and also Mark R. Cohen, *Under Crescent and Cross: The Jews in the Middle Ages* (Princeton: Princeton University Press, 1994), 44; Daniel F. Callahan, *Jerusalem and the Cross in the Life and Writings of Ademar of Chabannes* (Leiden and Boston: Brill, 2016), 52–3. Contemporary references to the expulsion of the Jews from Jerusalem are *Armenian History*, 70; and Theophilus of Edessa, as excerpted by Michael the Syrian and the *Chronicle of 1234* (in *Theophilus of Edessa's Chronicle*, 64–5) and Dionysius of Tel Mahre (*Seventh Century in West Syrian Chronicles*, 128).

35. One could take the story further back into the fifth century, to the militancy of Barsauma the Monophysite, a Byzantine effort to restrain his and others' destructive impulses in 423, followed by a swift return to anti-Jewish actions in 438; see G.W. Bowersock, "Polytheism and Monotheism in Arabia and the Three Palestines," *Dumbarton Oaks Papers* 51 (1997): 4.

36. For a review of the literature, see Elliott Horowitz, "'The Vengeance of the Jews was Stronger than Their Avarice': modern historians and the Persian Conquest of Jerusalem in 614," *Jewish Social Studies* 4:2 (1998): 1–39.

37. *Chronicon Pascale, 284-628 AD*, trans. M. Whitby and M. Whitby (Liverpool: Liverpool University Press, 1989), 156.

38. "Account of the Sack of Jerusalem," 509.

39. Gideon Avni, "The Persian Conquest of Jerusalem (614 c.e.)—An Archaeological Assessment," *Bulletin of the American Schools of Oriental Research* 357 (2010): 35–40. Strategos specifically notes that those captured were confined within "the reservoir of Mamel"; see "Account of the Sack of Jerusalem," 508.

40. *Theophilus of Edessa's Chronicle*, 64–5; *Seventh Century in West-Syriac Chronicles*, 128. For Bar Hebraeus, see *The Chronography of Gregory Abû'l Faraj, the Son of Aaron, the Hebrew Physician, Commonly Known as Bar Hebraeus: Being the First Part of his Political History of the Word*, trans. E.A.W. Budge, 2 vols. (London: Oxford University Press, 1932).

41. César Famin, *Histoire de la rivalité et du protectorat des églises Chrétiennes en Orient* (Paris: Firmin Didot, 1853), 10; Karl Marx and Friedrich Engels, *Gesamtausgabe (MEGA), vierte Abteilung: Exzerpte, Notizen, Marginalien*, ed. M. Neuhaus et al (Amsterdam: International Institute of Social History, 2007), 354.

42. See, for example, Seth Schwartz, *The Ancient Jews from Alexander to Muhammad* (Cambridge: Cambridge University Press, 2014), 149.

43. *Histories of Rabban Hormizd the Persian*, I.252, line 1273; *Armenian History*, 69; *Chronicon Pascale*, 156.

44. See Doron ben-Ami, Yana Tchekhanovets, and Gabriela Bijovsky, "New Archaeological and Numismatic Evidence for the Persian Destruction of Jerusalem in 614 CE," *Israel*

234

Exploration Journal 60:2 (2010): 217–18; and the first chapter of Yuri Stoyanov, *Defenders and Enemies of the True Cross: The Sasanian Conquest of Jerusalem in 614 and Byzantine Ideology of Anti-Persian Warfare* (Vienna: Austrian Academy of Sciences Press, 2011). On the Byzantine-era paved street running through the area, see Yana Tchekhanovets, "Ring with Resurrection Scene from Umayyad Jerusalem," *Electrum* 26 (2019): 177–85; and on shops and commerce there, Yana Tchekhanovets, "Recycling the Glory of Byzantium: New Archaeological Evidence of Byzantine-Islamic Transition in Jerusalem," *Studies in Late Antiquity* 2:2 (2018): 215–37.

45. Eutychius, "Annals," II.18.6–7.
46. Doron ben-Ami et al., "New Archaeological and Numismatic Evidence," 204–21.
47. Nearly every source records this: see *Chronicon Pascale*, 156; "Account of the Sack of Jerusalem," 510; *Armenian History*, 69–70; *Theophilus of Edessa*, 64–5 (for Theophanes, Michael the Syrian, *Chronicle of 1234*); *Seventh Century in West-Syriac Chronicles*, 128 (for Dionysius of Tel Mahre); Nikephoros, *Short History*, trans. C. Mango (Washington D.C.: Dumbarton Oaks Research Library and Collection, 1990), no. 12; and *Histoire Nestorienne inédite (Chronique de Séert), première partie*, trans. A. Scher (Paris: Fermin Didot, 1907), 556.
48. *Armenian History*, 69.
49. Abu Jaʿfar Muhammad ibn Jarir al-Tabari, d. 923. See *The History of al-Ṭabari, Volume V: the Sāsānids, the Byzantines, the Lakmids, and Yemen*, trans. C.E. Bosworth (Albany: State University of New York Press, 1999), 318. Much has been written about al-Tabari, but see the concise summary in Abd al-Aziz Duri, *The Rise of Historical Writing Among the Arabs*, ed. and trans. L.I. Conrad (Princeton: Princeton University Press, 2014), 69–71.
50. "Chronicon anonymum," 23.
51. Philip Wood, *The Chronicle of Seert: Christian Historical Imagination in Late Antique Iraq* (Oxford: Oxford University Press, 2013), 211–3. And besides, generalizing the Sasanids as simply a Zoroastrian power is not without issue; see Garth Fowden, *Before and After Muhammad: the First Millennium Refocused* (Princeton: Princeton University Press, 2013), 110–11.
52. *Armenian History*, 69–70.
53. *Bar Hebraeus*, 94.
54. De Lange, "Jews in the Age of Justinian," 410–11.
55. Robert Hoyland, "Sebeos, the Jews, and the Rise of Islam," in *Medieval and Modern Perspectives on Muslim-Jewish Relations*, ed. R.L. Nettler (London and New York: Routledge, 1995), 91–2.
56. Nehemiah ben Chusiel ben Ephraim ben Joseph. For a popular account of this view, see Meir Loewenberg, "When Iran Ruled Jerusalem," *Segula: the Jewish History Magazine* (January 2013): 37–8.
57. Averil Cameron, "Blaming the Jews: the Seventh-Century Invasions of Palestine in Context," in *Travaux et mémoires 14* (2002): 62–3. Moreover, these books offer an alternate anti-Persian attitude, which Bowersock has claimed "overshadowed the Muslim conquest" itself; see "Polytheism and Monotheism," 9. In any case, the Persians would have still seen to the maintenance of local administration and provided monies for the city's self-defense; see Leif Inge Ree Petersen, *Siege Warfare and Military Organization in the Successor States (400–800 AD): Byzantium, the West, and Islam* (Leiden and Boston: Brill, 2013), 393.
58. "Sefer Zerubbabel," in *Trajectories in Near Eastern Apocalyptic: a Postrabbinic Jewish Apocalypse Reader*, ed. J.C. Reeves (Atlanta: Society of Biblical Literature, 2005), 59. For a survey of the corpus at the time, see Avraham Grossman, "Jerusalem in Jewish Apocalyptic Literature," in *The History of Jerusalem: The Early Muslim Period, 638-1099*, ed. J. Prawer and H. Ben-Shammai (New York: New York University Press, 1996), 295–310.

59. Agapius, *Universal History*, II.192.

60. James Howard-Johnston, "Heraclius' Persian Campaigns and the Revival of the East Roman Empire, 622–630," *War in History* 6:1 (1999): 14–6.

61. Howard-Johnston, "Heraclius' Persian Campaigns," 18–22. See in general Martin Hurbanič, *The Avar Siege of Constantinople in 626: History and Legend* (Cham: Springer, 2019).

62. Kaegi, *Heraclius*, 159.

63. Howard-Johnston, "Heraclius' Persian Campaigns," 22–5. For a recent study of these campaigns, see Andrew Harris, "'Save thy people and bless thine inheritance': Consolidation of Gains, the Roman-Persian War, and the Rashidun Conquest, A.D. 622-637" (Master's thesis, School of Advanced Military Studies, 2020), 13–28. The best analysis of the campaign's operational details is Kaegi, *Heraclius*, 159–73. An older narrative is Norman H. Baynes, "The Military Operations of Emperor Heraclius," *United Service Magazine* 46 (1913): 526–33 and 659–66, and issue 47 (1913): various, non-contiguous.

64. Constantine Porphyrogenitus, *De administrando imperio*, ed. G. Moravcsik, trans. R.J.H. Jenkins (Washington D.C.: Dumbarton Oaks Center for Byzantine Studies, 1967), 206–7.

65. Kaegi, *Heraclius*, 174–8.

66. Nikephoros, *Short History*, no. 15. There has been some debate over who returned the cross to Heraclius and whether or not it was, indeed, a fake; see Constantin Zukerman, "Heraclius and the Return of the Holy Cross," *Travaux et mémoires* 17 (2013): 197–218.

67. Benjamin Isaac, "The Army in the Late Roman East: the Persian Wars and the Defence of the Byzantine Provinces," in *The Byzantine and Early Islamic Near East*, 132–7.

68. Jan Willem Drijvers, "Heraclius and the *Restitutio crucis*," in *The Reign of Heraclius (610-641): Crisis and Confrontation*, ed. G.J. Reinink and B.H. Stolte (Leuven: Peeters, 2002), 182; James Howard-Johnston, *Witnesses to a World Crisis: Historians and Histories of the Middle East in the Seventh Century* (Oxford: Oxford University Press, 2010), 20. On other aspects, see Ioannis Vassis, "George of Pisidia: the Spring of Byzantine Poetry?" in *A Companion to Byzantine Poetry*, ed. W. Hörandner, A. Rhoby, and N. Zagklas (Leiden and Boston: Brill, 2019), 149–65; and Mary Whitby, "George of Pisidia's Presentation of Emperor Heraclius and His Campaigns: Variety and Development," in *The Reign of Heraclius*, 157–74.

69. For example, a poem about Alexander the Great dating to the 620s–630s, which utilizes allusions to Heraclius and Khosrow; see "A Discourse Composed by Mar Jacob upon Alexander, the Believing King, and upon the Gate which He made against Agog and Magog," in *The History of Alexander the Great, being the Syriac Version of the Pseudo-Callisthenes*, ed. and trans. E.A. Wallis Budge (Cambridge: Cambridge University Press, 1889), 191–7. On the poem, see Brock, "Syriac Sources for Seventh-Century History," 35.

70. Drijvers, "Heraclius and the *Restitutio crucis*," 185–6. For Strategos's account, see "Account of the Sack of Jerusalem," 516. There is also a passing reference to Heraclius in Jerusalem in the ninth-century *Liber sastitatis*, Isho'dnah of Basra's biographies of 140 monastics in northern Mesopotamia; see *Les livre de la Chasteté composé par Jésusdenah, évêque de Baçrah*, ed. J.B. Chabot (Rome: Ecole Française de Rome, 1896), 57.

71. Cameron, "Blaming the Jews," 69–73. A gold coin dating to Heraclius's reign was recently found while excavating in Tel Aviv; it features the emperor on the obverse and Golgotha on the reverse; see Stuart Winer, "Building Project Unearths Ancient History in Tel Aviv Suburb," *Times of Israel* (August 18, 2021).

72. Nikephoros, *Short History*, no. 18; Paul Stephenson, "The Imperial Theology of Victory," in *A Companion to the Byzantine Culture of War, ca. 300-1204*, ed. Y. Stouraitis (Leiden and Boston: Brill, 2018), 41–2.

73. Callahan, *Jerusalem and the Cross*, 51; *History of Churches and Monasteries of Egypt, and some Neighbouring Countries, Attributed to Abû Salih, the Armenian*, ed. and trans. B.T.A. Evetts (Oxford: Clarendon, 1895), 39–40.
74. "History of the Patriarchs of the Coptic Church of Alexandria," I:498. Severus's information here is inaccurate, for Khosrow died not at Heraclius's hand but rather on the order of his son, Kawadh-Siroes, in 628.
75. See, for example, Warren Treadgold's scathing review of Geoffrey Regan, *First Crusader: Byzantium's Holy Wars* (New York: Palgrave Macmillan, 2003), in *Catholic Historical Review* 90:1 (2004): 94–5. On Byzantine notions of holy war, see George T. Dennis, "Defenders of the Christian People: Holy War in Byzantium," in *The Crusades from the Perspective of Byzantium and the Muslim World*, ed. A.E. Laiou and R.P. Mottahedeh (Washington D.C.: Dumbarton Oaks Research Library and Collection, 2001), 31–9.
76. Katharina Galor and Hanswulf Bloedhorn, *The Archaeology of Jerusalem: From the Origins to the Ottomans* (New Haven and London: Yale University Press, 2013), 114, 129, 131.
77. Yehiel Zelinger, "The Line of the Southern City Wall of Jerusalem in the Early Periods," in *Ancient Jerusalem Revealed: Archaeological Discoveries, 1998-2018*, ed. H. Geva (Jerusalem: Israel Exploration Society, 2019), 285–8; W. Harold Mare, *The Archaeology of the Jerusalem Area* (Grand Rapids: Baker, 1987), 247; Kathleen M. Kenyon, *Digging Up Jerusalem* (New York: Praeger, 1974), 267. See also Frederick Jones Bliss and Archibald Campbell Dickie, *Excavations at Jerusalem, 1894-1897* (London: Committee of the Palestine Exploration Fund, 1898), 307–8.
78. Jodi Magness, "Archaeological Evidence for the Sasanid Invasion of Jerusalem," in *City of David Studies of Ancient Jerusalem, the Eleventh Annual Conference*, ed. E. Meiron (Jerusalem: Megalim, 2010), 50–51.
79. *Armenian History*, 70.
80. Magness, "Sasanid Invasion of Jerusalem," 50; Jodi Magness, "The Walls of Jerusalem in the Early Islamic Period," *The Biblical Archaeologist* 54:4 (1991): 212.
81. Harris, "Consolidation of Gains," 28–30.
82. Walter E. Kaegi, *Byzantium and the Early Islamic Conquests* (Cambridge: Cambridge University Press, 1995), 35–37, and on Mu'ta, 72.
83. John F. Haldon, *Byzantium in the Seventh Century: The Transformation of a Culture* (Cambridge: Cambridge University Press, 1990), 48.
84. John Haldon, "Administrative Continuities and Structural Transformations in East Roman Military Organisation, c. 580-640," in *State, Army and Society in Byzantium: Approaches to Military, Social and Administrative History, 6th-12th Centuries* (Aldershot: Variorum, 1995), V:18.
85. Haldon, "Administrative Continuities," V:17. For background on Byzantine armies, see Conor Whatley, *Procopius on Soldiers and Military Institutions in the Sixth-Century Roman Empire* (Leiden and Boston: Brill, 2021).
86. Kaegi, *Early Islamic Conquests*, 50–51 and 60–61.
87. *Armenian History*, 90.
88. *The Fotooh Al-Sham, Being an Account of the Moslim Conquests in Syria, by Aboo Asma'il Mohammad bin 'Abd Allah al-Azdi al-Bacri*, ed. E.W.N. Lees (Calcutta: Baptist Mission Press, 1854), 38. On al-Azdi's date, reliability, and relative freedom from bias, see Suleiman A. Mourad, "On Early Islamic Historiography: Abū Ismā'īl Al-Azdī and his Futūḥ Al-Shām," *Journal of the American Oriental Society* 120:4 (2000): 577–93.
89. See Gerrit J. Reinink, "Heraclius, the New Alexander: Apocalyptic Prophecies During the Reign of Heraclius," in *The Reign of Heraclius*, 81–94.
90. *Histories of Rabban Hormizd the Persian*, I.253, line 1277.
91. Tannous, *Making of the Medieval Middle East*, 86. This Jacob should not be confused with Jacob Baradaeus of Edessa, who lived in the sixth century.

92. "Chronological Canon of James of Edessa," 324. This particular passage was excerpted from the chronicle of Michael the Syrian. For more on Jacob, see Brooks, "Chronological Canon of James of Edessa," 100–102.

93. From the *Apocalypse of Pseudo-Methodius* (c. 690-691) and the "Edessne" apocalyptic fragment (c. 683); see *Seventh Century in West-Syrian Chronicles*, 14–5.

94. The literature is vast. A well-reviewed recent effort to chart Arabic history is Tim Mackintosh-Smith, *Arabs: a 3,000-Year History of Peoples, Tribes, and Empires* (New Haven and London: Yale University Press, 2019); see also Philip K. Hitti, *History of the Arabs* (London: Palgrave Macmillan, 2002), which is now into its 10th edition; and Albert Hourani, *A History of the Arab Peoples* (Reprint, Cambridge, MA: Harvard University Press, 2002). For the conquest specifically, see Hugh Kennedy, *The Great Arab Conquests: How the Spread of Islam Changed the World We Live In* (Philadelphia: Da Capo Press, 2007)

95. As seen via the incorporation of non-Muslims into military ranks and the absence of mass conversions; see Robert Hoyland, *In God's Path: The Arab Conquests and the Creation of an Islamic Empire* (Oxford: Oxford University Press, 2015), 56–63.

96. The theory was originated by the Belgian historian Henri Pirenne (d. 1935). Arguments over "the Pirenne thesis" are by now well-trodden and common fodder in introductory medieval history surveys, but see Fowden, *Before and After Muhammad*, 38–9, for a broader assessment and some pertinent citations.

97. See Sayyid Muhammad Yusuf, "The Battle of al-Qadisiyya," *Islamic Culture* 19 (1945): 1–28; and, on formations and tactics there, J.W. Jandora, "Developments in Islamic Warfare: the Early Conquests," *Studia Islamica* 64 (1986): 101–13.

98. Efforts to see the conquest of Jerusalem as an original plan of Muhammad have been unconvincing; see, for example, Abdallah Ma'rouf Omar, *Jerusalem in Muhammad's Strategy: The Role of the Prophet Muhammad in the Conquest of Jerusalem* (Newcastle-upon-Tyne: Cambridge Scholars Publishing, 2019), and his review of the literature on 119. On the caliphs post-Muhammad, see in general Wilferd Madelung, *The Succession to Muhammad: A Study of the Early Caliphate* (Cambridge: Cambridge University Press, 1997).

99. Kaegi, *Early Islamic Conquests*, 63–4, 76–7.

100. Kaegi, *Early Islamic Conquests*, 52, 62–3.

101. On the Ridda Wars, see Fred M. Donner, *The Early Islamic Conquests*, rev. ed. (Princeton: Princeton University Press, 2014), 82–90. Still useful is Ilyās Shūfānī, *Al-Riddah and the Muslim Conquest of Arabia* (Toronto: University of Toronto Press, 1973), which argues that this was not a separate war but rather one front of many in an ongoing war, with Byzantium constituting another. For more specialized studies, see Henry Rosenfeld, "The Social Composition of the Military in the Process of State Formation in the Arabian Desert," *Journal of the Royal Anthropological Institute of Great Britain and Ireland* 95:1 (1965): 75–86.

102. An older but thorough survey of Arab movements into the broad region is René Dussaud, *La pénétration des Arabes en Syrie avant l'Islam* (Paris: Geuthner, 1955). On roads, communications, and defense networks, see John Haldon, "Information and War: Some Comments on Defensive Strategy and Information in the Middle Byzantine (*ca.* 660-1025)," in *War and Warfare in Late Antiquity*, ed. A. Sarantis and N. Christie (Leiden and Boston: Brill, 2013), 373–93.

103. On Arab strategy during these invasions, see Petersen, *Siege Warfare*, 430–32.

104. On the other motives for invasion, see Donner, *Early Islamic Conquests*, 96–8. For the Night Journey, the reference is *Al-Qur'an*, 17.1: "Glory to God / Who did take His Servant / For a Journey by night / From the Sacred Mosque / To the Farthest Mosque / Whose precincts We did / Bless, in order that We / Might show him some / Of Our Signs: for He / Is the One Who heareth / And seeth all things." On Arabic historical

understandings of the event, see Vinay Khetia, "The Night Journey and Ascension of Muhammad in *Tasfir* al-Tabari," *Al-Bayān* 10:1 (2012): 39–62; and more recently Tamar M. Boyadjian, *The City Lament: Jerusalem Across the Medieval Mediterranean* (Ithaca and London: Cornell University Press, 2018), 34–6.

105. Hoyland, *In God's Path*, 42–5. On these early encounters: for a largely Byzantine perspective, see Kaegi, *Early Islamic Conquests*, 83–100; and for the Arab perspective, see Donner, *Early Islamic Conquests*, 112–27. For an older view, Philip Mayerson, "The First Muslim Attacks on Southern Palestine (A.D. 633-634)," *Transactions and Proceedings of the American Philological Association* 95 (1965): 155–99.

106. Kaegi, *Early Islamic Conquests*, 110–11.

107. Muhammad ibn Aballah al-Azdi al-Basri, d. 797; *Fotooh Al-Sham*, 20.

108. Kaegi, *Early Islamic Conquests*, 119; Kaegi's assessment contradicts an earlier interpretation that saw Theodore as supreme commander; see John W. Jandora, "The Battle of the Yarmūk: a Reconstruction," *Journal of Asian History* 19:1 (1985): 9. For a lightly-sourced study of troop types, tactics, and generalship at Yarmuk, see Md Saifuz Zaman, "Yarmouk—the Necessity of Studying the Battle in Early Medieval Military Historiography," *Journal of Military and Strategic Studies* 16:2 (2015): 160–78.

109. Muhammad ibn Sa'd, *The Men of Medina (Volume 1)*, trans. A. Bewley (London: Ta-Ha, 1997), 237. On Ibn Sa'd's works, see Duri, *Rise of Historical Writings*, 40.

110. Kaegi, *Early Islamic Conquests*, 120. Donner lists the principals and participating Arabs at Yarmuk; see *Early Islamic Conquests*, Appendix C. In addition, for Arab women who fought at Yarmuk see Rana Mikati, "Fighting for the Faith? Notes on Women and War in Early Islam," *Journal of Near Eastern Studies* 78:2 (2019): 206–7. For army formations, see Harold W. Glidden, "A Note on Early Arabian Military Organization," *Journal of the American Oriental Society* 56:1 (1936): 88–91.

111. For a near-contemporary account of the conquest of Egypt by 'Amr ibn al-'As, see the account of John, the Coptic bishop of Nikiu in *The Chronicle of John, Bishop of Nikiu, Translated from Zotenberg's Ethiopic Text*, trans. R.H. Charles (London and Oxford: Text and Translation Society, 1913), 180–84. Originally written in Coptic, then translated into Ethiopic, the chronicle receives close study in Phil Booth, "The Muslim Conquest of Egypt Reconsidered," *Travaux et mémoires* 17 (2013): 639–70; and also Daria Elagina, "The Textual Tradition of the Chronicle of John of Nikiu: Towards the Critical Edition of the Ethiopic Version" (Ph.D. thesis, Universität Hamburg, 2018).

112. *Armenian History*, 101–2. On 'Amr ibn al-'As, see Muhammad ibn Sa'd's description in *Men of Medina*, 305.

113. The claim that the Byzantine army numbered a hundred thousand soldiers, for example, in the *Khuzistan Chronicle*; see "Chronicon anonymum," 31. Donner has attempted to sort the various reconstructions in different groupings of source material and remains the best treatment of the subject; see *Early Islamic Conquests*, 128–46.

114. Nikephoros, *Short History*, no. 20. Essentially accepted in Hoyland, *In God's Path*, 46, but disputed in Kaegi, *Early Islamic Conquests*, 120.

115. Paraphrased from the account of Muhammad Ibn 'Umar al-Waqidi: *The Conquest of Syria, Persia, and Egypt by the Saracens, Containing the Lives of Abubeker, Omar and Otham, the Immediate Successors of Mahomet*, trans. S. Ockley (London: R. Knaplock, 1708), 235.

116. Nikephoros, *Short History*, no. 20.

117. The treatment of prisoners of war, particularly on the question of whether to ransom or execute them, was uneven in the early Islamic period, owing to discrepancies between the opinions of jurists, Qur'anic verses, and the customs and history of marshal practice, as well as the opinions of writers such as al-Tabari; see Lena Salaymah, "Early Islamic Legal-Historical Precedents: Prisoners of War," *Law and History Review* 26:3 (2008): 521–44.

118. The best account of the battle is Kaegi, *Early Islamic Conquests*, 120–40; see n. 23–5 for his critique of the other available narrations and their historiographical shortcomings.
119. In *Theophilus of Edessa's Chronicle*, 101.
120. *Seventh Century in the West-Syrian Chronicles*, 1–4, text 2–4. The text names the spot as "Gabitha," which has been understood as referring to Yarmuk.
121. Donner, *Early Islamic Conquests*.
122. Hoyland, *In God's Path*, 47; Kaegi, *Early Islamic Conquests*, 146.
123. Kaegi, *Early Islamic Conquests*, 108.
124. *History of Ghevond: the Eminent Vardapet of the Armenians (VIII Century)*, trans. Z. Arzoumanian, 2nd ed. (Burbank: Western Diocese of the Armenian Church of North America, 2008), 49.
125. Daniel J. Sahas, "The Seventh Century in Byzantine-Muslim Relations: Characteristics and Forces," *Islam and Christian-Muslim Relations* 2:1 (1991): 6.
126. Heraclius was a supporter of monothelitism, which held that Jesus Christ had only one will, as opposed to two (human and divine). Sophronius denounced monothelitism as heresy, perhaps embarrassing the emperor in the process. The scene is sketched in Eutychius, "Annals," II.18c.2–3; see in general Daniel J. Sahas, "Why Did Heraclius not Defend Jerusalem and Fight the Arabs?" *Parole de l'Orient* 24 (1999): 79–97.
127. See the assorted versions of Heraclius's bidding Syria "adieu," in *Theophilus of Edessa's Chronicle*, 106–109. For the cultural, social, and economic impact on the Arab conquests on Byzantium, see John F. Haldon, *Money, Power and Politics in Early Islamic Syria: A Review of Current Debates*, ed. J.F. Haldon (Farnham: Ashgate, 2010), 1–20.
128. *Fotooh Al-Sham*, 21–2.
129. Ahmad ibn Abi Ya'qub al-Ya'qubi, d. 897. Al-Ya'qubi wrote a work of universal history up to 872, so his focus was not only on Arabs but an assortment of peoples in the Near East and even the Chinese; see Duri, *Rise of Historical Writing*, 64–7.
130. Othman Ismael Al-Tel, "The First Islamic Conquest of Aelia (Islamic Jerusalem)" (Ph.D. dissertation, University of Abertay Dundee, 2002), 162; *Fotooh Al-Sham*, 37. The reference to pork is a possible indication that Jews were still not permitted in the city, due to Heraclius's ban in 630. The *Chronicle of 1234* claims that Abu 'Ubayda arrived after Caliph 'Umar, not before; see *Theophilus of Edessa's Chronicle*, 116. On more recent appreciation for al-Azdi's reliability, see Mourad, "On Early Islamic Historiography," 578–9.
131. Abu Abdullah ibn 'Umar Muhammad ibn Waqid al-Aslami, d. 823; Al-Waqidi, *The Conquest of Syria*, 243–6. On al-Waqidi as a historian, see Duri, *Rise of Historical Writing*, 37–9.
132. *Fotooh Al-Sham*, 37.
133. See Donner, *Early Islamic Conquest*, 117, 122 (Palmyra), and 129 (Bosra).
134. Donner, *Early Islamic Conquest*, 150, 138
135. Donner, *Early Islamic Conquest*, 131, 137.
136. Hoyland, *Seeing Islam*, 68.
137. Demetrios J. Constantelos, "The Moslem Conquests of the Near East as Revealed in the Greek Sources of the Seventh and Eighth Centuries," *Byzantion* 42 (1972): 329–30. For his sermons, see *Homilies: Sophronios of Jerusalem*, ed. and trans. J.M. Duffy (Washington D.C.: Dumbarton Oaks Medieval Library, 2020).
138. From the Hebrew *Beit Ha-Miqdash*; see Milka Levy-Rubin, "Why Was the Dome of the Rock Built? A New Perspective on a Long-Discussed Question," *Bulletin of the School of Oriental and African Studies* 80:3 (2017): 453; and Al-Tel, "The First Islamic Conquest of Aelia," 163. The said spoils were divided afterward in Jabiyah; see Muhammad Ibn Sa'd, *Kitab at-Tabaqat al-Kabir, Volume III: The Companions of Badr*, trans. A. Bewley (London: Ta-Ha, 2013), 218.

139. Al-Waqidi, *Conquest of Syria*, 119. Thanks here to Ben Beller and Ryan Bicek.
140. *Al-Qur'ān*, 266.
141. *Companions of Badr*, 205–6, 209–10.
142. Duri, *Rise of Historical Writing*, 21.
143. *Companions of Badr*, 152.
144. Steven Shoemaker, *The Death of a Prophet: The End of Muhammad's Life and the Beginnings of Islam* (Philadelphia: University of Pennsylvania Press, 2012), 179–80.
145. Patricia Crone and Michael Cook, *Hagarism: The Making of the Islamic World* (Cambridge: Cambridge University Press, 1977), 5. For one reference to *al-Faruq*, see *History of al-Ṭabarī, Volume XII: the Battle of al-Qadisiyyah and the Conquest of Syria and Palestine*, trans. Y. Friedmann (Albany: State University of New York Press, 1991), 189.
146. On eschatology, see Shoemaker, *Death of a Prophet*, 120–83 and especially 169; for a partial retort, see Averil Cameron, "Late Antique Apocalyptic: A Context for the Qur'an?" in *Apocalypticism and Eschatology in Late Antiquity: Encounters in the Abrahamic Religions, 6th–8th Centuries*, ed. H. Amirav, E. Grypeou, and G. Stroumsa (Leuven: Peeters, 2017), 1–19.
147. *History of al-Tabari, Volume XII*, 189. This may well have been during a different journey, not in 638 but earlier, in 635–6. Sorting out the chronological and descriptive issues in the accounts of 'Umar's various trips to Syria is Othman Ismael al-Tel, "'Umar ibn al-Khattab's Visits to Bayt al-Maqdis: a Study on Its Reasons and Objectives," *Journal of Al-Tamaddun* 12:1 (2017): 79–91.
148. Al-Waqidi, *Conquest of Syria*, 250. On the Dome of the Chain, see Galor and Bloedhorn, *Archaeology of Jerusalem*, 164.
149. The Jerusalem Islamic *Waqf*, the trust that manages the structures on the Temple Mount, attempted to renovate it into a place of Muslim prayer; the Israeli police locked down the site with gates and made arrests.
150. Sahas, "Seventh-Century in Byzantine-Muslim Relations," 12–15.
151. According to the later account of al-Balahuri (d. 892); see *Kitâb futûḥ al-Buldân of al-Imâm abu-l 'Abbâs Aḥmad ibn-Jâbir al-Balâhuri*, trans. P.K. (New York: Columbia University Press, 1916), I.213. On his method, sources, and works, see Ryan J. Lynch, *Arab Conquests and Early Islamic Historiography: The Futuh al-Buldan of al-Baladhuri* (London: I.B. Tauris, 2020).
152. Sahas, "Why Did Heraclius not Defend Jerusalem?" 81–2.
153. As noted in the early-ninth-century account by Abi 'Ubayd al-Qasim Ibn Sallam, *The Book of Revenue: Kitab al-Amwal*, trans. I.A.K. Nyazee (Reading: Garnet, 2005), 153–5.
154. *Fotooh Al-Sham*, 39. The later accounts of al-Balahuri, al-Waqidi, and then al-Tabari's compilation, repeat the tradition in this same spirit; see *Kitâb futûḥ al-Buldân*, 213; *History of al-Tabari, Volume XII*, 190; al-Waqidi, *Conquest of Syria*, 247–9, 255.
155. There is debate over whether 'Umar was in Medina at the time or, rather, already in Jabiyah; al-Balahuri claims it was the latter in *Kitâb futûḥ al-Buldân*, 213.
156. *Theophilus of Edessa's Chronicle*, 114.
157. "Chronicle of 1234," in *Theophilus of Edessa's Chronicle*, 116; see also al-Waqidi, *The Conquest of Syria*, 250. On the howdah, see J.M. Kistler, *War Elephants* (Lincoln: University of Nebraska Press, 2007), 136. On the use of camels in warfare at the time, see Louise E. Sweet, "Camel Raiding of North Arabian Bedouin: a Mechanism of Ecological Adaptation," *American Anthropologist* 67:5 (Oct 1965): 1132–50.
158. *History of al-Tabari, Volume XII*, 190.
159. *Fotooh al-Sham*, 39.
160. On the location, see Daniel J. Sahas, "The Face to Face Encounter between Patriarch Sophronius of Jerusalem and the Caliph 'Umar ibn al-Khaṭṭāb: Friends or Foes?" in *The Encounter of Eastern Christianity with Early Islam*, ed. E. Grypeou, M. Swanson, and D. Thomas (Leiden and Boston: Brill, 2006), 37.

161. *Theophilus of Edessa's Chronicle*, 115.
162. As typified in the *History of al-Tabari, Volume XII*, 193–94; it likewise appears in Eutychius, "Annals," II.18c.7, who is contemporaneous with al-Tabari. Agapias, another contemporary of al-Tabari, utilized the earlier Theophilus account instead; see *Theophilus of Edessa's Chronicle*, 115.
163. *Kitâb futûḥ al-Buldân*, 213.
164. According to the transmissions of Theophilus in the chronicles of Michael the Syrian, Agapias, Dionysius of Tel Marhe, and the *Chronicle of 1234*; see *Theophilus of Edessa's Chronicle*, 115–17, and *Seventh Century in West-Syriac Chronicles*, 161–2. Agapias later added details specifying that any Jew found in the city would be punished and his property seized.
165. Abi 'Ubayd al-Qasim ibn Sallam, d. 837; see Ibn Sallam, *Book of Revenue*, 153–5.
166. *History of Gevond*, 105–6.
167. Which is distinct from the more-famous "Pact of Umar" that has been misattributed to 'Umar ibn al-Khattab but in reality dates to the tenth century or later.
168. *Theophilus of Edessa's Chronicle*, 117. These seventh-century fragments from Theophilus stand opposed to the claim that no details for the Assurance predate the ninth century; see, for example, Mahmoud Mataz Kazmouz, "Multiculturalism in Islam: the Document of Madīnah & 'Umar's Assurance of Safety as Two Case Studies" (Ph.D. thesis, University of Aberdeen, 2011), 160, which is an otherwise interesting examination of the Assurance in its context. The absolute rejection—somewhat polemical—by Abd al-Fattah El-Awaisi does not deal with the question of Theophilus; see "Umar's Assurance of Safety to the People of Aelia (Jerusalem): a Critical Analytical Study of the Historical Sources," *Journal of Islamic Jerusalem Studies* 3:2 (2000), 47–89 and especially 76–7.
169. *Fotooh al-Sham*, 40. The literature on *jizya* and other forms of Muslim taxation in the period is massive, but for a foundational document see the *Kitab al-Kharaj* of Abu Yusuf Ya'qub Ibrahim al-Ansari al-Kufi, who died in 798 and references 'Umar's decisive role in many pertinent customs: *Taxation in Islam*, ed. and trans. A. Ben Shemesh, 2 vols. (Leiden: Brill, 1958). Two years after the taking of Jerusalem, 'Umar is said to have ordered a census of all his realm and henceforth imposed *jizya* on the entire Christian population there; see Tannous, *Making of the Medieval Middle East*, 321–2.
170. This being the *isnād*, or "chain of authorities transmitting a report"; see Duri, *Rise of Historical Writing*, 23, 70. Milka Levy-Rubin has further made a strong case that al-Tabari's version of the Assurance is a faithful rendering; see "Were the Jews Prohibited from Settling in Jerusalem? On the Authenticity of Al-Ṭabarī's Jerusalem Surrender Agreement," *Jerusalem Studies in Arabic and Islam* 36 (2009): 63–81.
171. *History of al-Tabari, Volume XII*, 191. On the different Christian churches and religious foundations up to the time of 'Umar, see the listing across Di Segni and Tsafrir, "Ethnic Composition of Jerusalem's Population," 405–54.
172. Tannous, *Making of the Medieval Middle East*, 382.
173. Milka Levy-Rubin, "Changes in the Settlement Pattern of Palestine Following the Arab Conquest," in *Shaping the Middle East: Jews, Christians, and Muslims in an Age of Transition, 400–800 C.E.*, ed. K.G. Holum and H. Lapin (Bethesda: University Press of Maryland, 2011), 155–7.
174. For a recent study, see Christian C. Sahner, *Christian Martyrs Under Islam: Religious Violence and the Making of the Muslim World* (Princeton: Princeton University Press, 2018). On the martyrology texts, see Hoyland, *Seeing Islam*, 336–86. On a more famous text, see the bibliography in David Woods, "The 60 Martyrs of Gaza and the Martyrdom of Bishop Sophronius of Jerusalem," in *Arab-Byzantine Relations in Early Islamic Times*, ed. M. Bonner (Aldershot: Ashgate, 2004), 129–50.
175. Milka Levy-Rubin, "New Evidence Relating to the Process of Islamization in Palestine in the Early Muslim Period—the Case of Samaria," *Journal of the Economic and Social History of the Orient* 43:3 (2000): 261–3.

176. It was utilized by Christian writers in later years to argue against undue restrictions on their communities by later caliphs; see Penn's discussion of the eighth-century *Life of Gabriel of Qartmin* in this regard in *Envisioning Islam*, 120–21.
177. Charalambos K. Papastathis, "A New Status for Jerusalem? An Eastern Orthodox Viewpoint," *Catholic University Law Review* 45:3 (1996): 725–7.
178. L.G.A. Cust, *The Status Quo in the Holy Places* (London: HMSO, 1929), 5. On the protected sites in the eighteenth century and beyond, see Michael Dumper, *The Politics of Sacred Space: The Old City of Jerusalem in the Middle East Conflict* (Boulder and London: Lynne Rienner, 2002), 20.
179. *History of al-Tabari, Volume XII*, 191. 'Umar's prohibition of the Jews remained worthy of mention into the thirteenth century, where it appears in *Bar Hebraeus*, 94.
180. Sahas, "Why Did Heraclius not Defend Jerusalem?," 85.
181. *Armenian History*, 102–3.
182. Hoyland, *Seeing Islam*, 127.
183. Levy-Rubin, "Were the Jews Prohibited from Settling in Jerusalem?," 80–81.
184. *Chronique de Séert*, 624.
185. *The Taktika of Leo VI*, trans. G.T. Dennis (Washington, D.C.: Dumbarton Oaks Texts, 2014), 18.104.
186. *De administrando imperio*, 82–3.
187. Hence the argument in al-Balahuri's history, that Jews and Christians actually preferred to live under Muslim rule; see *Kitâb futûḥ al-Buldân*, 210. But dubbing it, as one study has, "the first Muslim liberation of Jerusalem," as in a great act to rid the Jews and Christians from Byzantine oppression, assigns motives that are, in this writer's view, far too idealistic; see El-Awaisi, "'Umar's Assurance of Safety," 78–9.
188. Sahas, "Face to Face Encounter," 36. The much later fifteenth-century source Mujir al-Din, a Jerusalem local who nonetheless knew little about the city's early history, claims that this dung heap was started by Empress Helena herself, following her destruction of the Roman temple there; see Robert Schick, "Jerusalem in the Roman and Byzantine Periods in Mujir al-Dīn's Fifteenth-Century History of Jerusalem and Hebron," in *Radical Traditionalism: The Influence of Walter Kaegi in Late Antique, Byzantine, and Medieval Studies*, ed. C. Raffensberger and D. Olster (Lanham: Rowman & Littlefield, 2019), 26. By the next century, ignorance of Islam's tenets further declined; see the famous case of John of Damascus, in Pablo Argárate, "Islam from an Eighth-Century Christian perspective," *Orientalia Patristica: Papers of the International Patristic Symposium, April 23 – 27, 2018* (Drohbeta-Turnu Severin: Didahia Severin, 2019): 57–84.

Chapter II Sunni and Shia: The 970s and 1070s

1. In fairness, Heraclius had ordered the Temple Mount cleaned up, but the work was still incomplete upon 'Umar's arrival; see Levy-Rubin, "Why Was the Dome of the Rock Built?," 458. For a contemporary Christian account of the cleaning, see that of the Byzantine ascetic John Moschus in Hoyland, *Seeing Islam*, 64.
2. Ibn Sallam, *Book of Revenues*, 156.
3. Tannous, *Making of the Medieval Middle East*, 274–5.
4. The story is from the excerpted sections of Theophilus in the works of Theophanes the Confessor, Agapias, Michael the Syrian, the *Chronicle of 1234* (see *Theophilus of Edessa's Chronicle*, 114–17) and Dionysius of Tel Mahre (see *Seventh Century in West-Syrian Chronicles*, 161–2). Al-Waqidi's accounts are similar to the Syriac texts; see *Conquest of Syria*, 261–4. For a much later description of 'Umar's reconnoitering and cleaning of the mount, see Ibn Sallam, *Book of Revenue*, 156; and Eutychius, "Annals," II.18c.7; Eutychius's tale that 'Umar exchanged with Sophronius ownership of the sepulchre church for the mount is exceptional.

5. This is due to the fact that "Arculf" is not actually a source but rather was presented as legitimate in the insular works of Adomnán, the abbot of Iona (d. 704) and the Venerable Bede (d. 735); see Lawrence Nees, "Insular Latin Sources, 'Arculf,' and Early Islamic Jerusalem," in *Where Heaven and Earth Meet: Essays on Medieval Europe in Honor of Daniel F. Callahan*, ed. M. Frassetto, M. Gabriele, and J.D. Hosler (Leiden and Boston: Brill, 2014), 79–100. Eutychius's locating it in proximity to the rock of Abraham and Isaac is too late to be authoritative; see "Annals," II.18c.7.

6. See Levy-Rubin, "Why Was the Dome of the Rock Built?," 453, and the scholarship cited there. For the dominant Arabic stories of this first mosque, see *History of al-Tabari, Volume XII*, 194–7.

7. G.R. Hawting, *The First Dynasty of Islam: The Umayyad Caliphate, 661–750* (London: Croom Helm, 1986), 60–61.

8. 'Abd al-Malik ibn Marwan, d. 705; see Tannous, *Making of the Medieval Middle East*, 383–4.

9. Al-Walid ibn Abd al-Malik ibn Marwan, d. 715.

10. Al-Zahir li-i'zaz Din Allah, d. 1036; see Galor and Bloedhorn, *Archaeology of Jerusalem*, 152, 164–6; and Mare, *Archaeology of the Jerusalem Area*, 265–7.

11. On this ordering see Suleiman ali Mourad, "The Symbolism of Jerusalem in Early Islam," in *Jerusalem: Idea and Reality*, ed. T. Mayer and S.A. Mourad (Abingdon: Routledge, 2008), 86–102.

12. See Levy-Rubin, "Why Was the Dome of the Rock Built?," 461–3, for the relevant citations.

13. For a concise survey, see Oleg Grabar, "Islamic Jerusalem or Jerusalem under Islamic Rule," in *The City in the Islamic World*, ed. S.K Jayyusi et al. (Leiden and Boston: Brill, 2008), I:317–27.

14. On the conquest of Egypt, see Maged S.A. Mikhail, *From Byzantine to Islamic Egypt: Religion, Identity and Politics After the Arab Conquest* (London and New York: Tauris, 2014).

15. Ibn Sa'd, *Companions of Badr*, 25–6. On the Kharijites' identity, traditions, and religious zealotry, see Hannah-Lena Hagemann and Peter Verkinderen, "Kharijism in the Umayyad Period," in *The Umayyad World*, ed. A. Marsham (London and New York: Routledge, 2021), 489–517.

16. On the city, see A. Petersen and D. Pringle (ed.), *Ramla: City in Muslim Palestine, 715–1917* (Oxford: Archaeopress, 2021).

17. Muawiyah's reasons are hotly debated; see Jacob Lassner, *Medieval Jerusalem: Forging an Islamic City in Spaces Sacred to Christians and Jews* (Ann Arbor: University of Michigan Press, 2017), 61–72, for a thorough discussion of proposals and possibilities.

18. For an overview, see Walter E. Kaegi, "Confronting Islam: Emperors versus Caliphs (641–c. 850)," in *The Cambridge History of the Byzantine Empire, c. 500–1492*, ed. J. Shepard (Cambridge: Cambridge University Press, 2008), 365–94; and Hélène Ahrweiler, "L'Asie Mineure et les invasions arabes (VIIe – IXe siècles)," *Revue Historique* 227 (1962): 1–32; for excerpts from Arab sources, E.W. Brooks, "The Arabs in Asia Minor (641–750), from Arabic Sources," *Journal of Hellenic Studies* 18 (1898): 182–208. On the first siege, from 674–678, see Marek Jankowiak, "The First Arab Siege of Constantinople," *Travaux et mémoires* 17 (2013): 237–320; for the second, from 717–718, see Rodolphe Guilland, "L'Expedition de Maslama contre Constantinople (717–718)," in *Études Byzantines* (Paris, 1959), 109–33.

19. Hoyland, *In God's Path*, 161–9.

20. Hugh Kennedy, *The Court of the Caliphs: The Rise and Fall of Islam's Greatest Dynasty* (London: Weidenfeld & Nicolson, 2004), 1.

21. Constantelos, "Moslem Conquests," 340–41.

22. Umar ibn Abd al-Aziz and Yazid ibn Abd al-Malik. Hugh Kennedy, *The Prophet and the Age of the Caliphates: The Islamic Near East from the Seventh to the Eleventh Century*, 3rd ed. (London and New York: Routledge, 2016), 100–101.

23. Steven C. Judd, "Medieval Explanations for the Fall of the Umayyads," in *Umayyad Legacies: Medieval Memories from Syria to Spain*, ed. A. Borrut and P. Cobb (Leiden and Boston: Brill, 2010), 89.
24. Marwan ibn Muhammad ibn Marwan ibn al-Hakam, d. 750. Kennedy, *Court of the Caliphs*, 4–10.
25. The Second *Fitna*, not discussed here, took place in 680–692, following the death of Muawiya.
26. *The Chronicle of Theophanes: Anni Mundi 6095–6305 (A.D. 602–813)*, ed. and trans. H. Turtledove (Philadelphia: University of Pennsylvania Press, 1982), no. 422.
27. Galor and Bloedhorn, *Archaeology of Jerusalem*, 166–70. The Zinman Institute of Archaeology at the University of Haifa has sponsored years of research at the site; for updates and publications, see *Hippos (Sussita) Excavations Project*, <https://www.dighippos.com/sussita/index.php/staff/2-eisenberg>; accessed November 8, 2021.
28. Magness, "Walls of Jerusalem," 214–15.
29. Ibn Sallam, *Book of Government*, 142–3.
30. For a survey, see Peter Frankopan, *The Silk Roads: A New History of the World* (New York: Knopf, 2015), 91–5.
31. Marina Rustow, "Jews and Muslims in the Eastern Islamic World," in *A History of Jewish-Muslim Relations: From the Origins to the Present Day*, ed. A. Meddeb and B. Stora (Princeton: Princeton University Press, 2013), 86.
32. *Towards a Shi'i Mediterranean Empire: Fatimid Egypt and the Founding of Cairo, the Reign of the Imam-Caliph al-Mu'izz from al-Maqīrī's Itti'āẓ al-ḥunafā*, trans. S. Jiwa (London: I.B. Tauris, 2009), 2.
33. For a recent treatment of the divergence, see Laurence Louër, *Sunnis and Shi'a: A Political History*, trans. E. Rundell (Princeton: Princeton University Press 2020), although only two of its eleven chapters concern medieval Islam.
34. Abu al-Fadl Jafar ibn Muhammad al-Mu'tasim billah. Kennedy, *Court of the Caliph*, 239–40. This decree thus preceded by centuries the more commonly referenced stipulation of the Fourth Lateran Council that Jews do the same; see in general *Jews and Muslims Under the Fourth Lateran Council: Papers Commemorating the Octocentenary of the Fourth Lateran Council (2125)*, ed. M.-T. Champagne and I.M. Resnick (Turnhout: Brepols, 2018). For more on Mutawwakil's edicts, see Luke Yarbrough, *Friends of the Emir: Non-Muslim State Officials in Premodern Islamic Thought* (Cambridge: Cambridge University Press, 2019), 88–110.
35. Ibn Khaldun, *The Muqaddimah: An Introduction to History, the Classic Islamic History of the World*, trans. F. Rosenthal, ed. N.J. Dawood (Princeton and Oxford: Princeton University Press, 2005), 124. On the Abbasid use of slave soldiers, see Daniel Pipes, *Slave Soldiers and Islam: The Genesis of a Military System* (New Haven and London: Yale University Press, 1981), 131–8.
36. For the sequence of events, see Kennedy, *Court of the Caliphs*, 268–83.
37. Jamil M. Abun-Nasr, *A History of the Maghrib in the Islamic Period* (Cambridge: Cambridge University Press, 1987), 60–62. Ibn Khaldun notes that even the Aghlabids had resisted Abbasid control in some measure previously; see *Muqaddimah*, 124.
38. *Muqaddimah*, 244–5.
39. On the state of the Egyptian military establishment prior to the Fatimid conquest, see Maged S.A. Mikhail, "Notes on the 'Ahl al-Dīwān': the Arab-Egyptian Army of the Seventh through the Ninth Centuries C.E.," *Journal of the American Oriental Society* 128:2 (2008): 273–84.
40. Abun-Nasr, *Maghrib in the Islamic Period*, 66.
41. Al-Maqrizi (Taqi al-Din Ahmad ibn 'Ali al-Maqrizi) was a prolific Sunni author who nonetheless held some Fatimid sympathies due to his own Egyptian origin and a recognition of the caliphate's legitimate bloodline, from which he claimed descent. He leaned on writers such as al-Muyassar (d. 1278/9), al-Tuwayr (d. 1220), al-Musabbihi (d. 1029),

and also the well-known philosopher/historian al-Kindi (d. 961). Idris (Idris 'Imad al-Din), was from a Yemeni Qurashyi family and was a Tayyibi Ismaili *da'i*; he pulled his account from the primary accounts of al-Qadi al-Nu'man (d. 974), who was the official historian of the Fatimids. See *Towards a Shi'i Mediterranean*, 32–3 and 36; and *The Founder of Cairo: The Fatimid Imam-Caliph al-Mu'izz and His Era, an English Translation of the Text on al-Mu'izz from Idris 'Imād al-Dīn's 'Uyūn al-akhbār*, trans. S. Jiwa (London: I.B. Tauris, 2013), 6, 25–8. For their historiography, see Shainool Jiwa, "Historical Representations of a Fatimid Imam-caliph: Exploring al-Maqrizi's and Idris' Writings on al-Mu'izz Li Din Allah," *British Alifba: Studi Arabo-Islamici e Mediterranei*, 22 (2012): On al-Kindi, see Matthew S. Gordon, "Kindi, Al-, Philosopher," in *Medieval Islamic Civilization: An Encyclopedia*, ed. J.W. Meri, 2 vols. (New York and London: Routledge, 2006), I.438.

42. *Towards a Shi'i Mediterranean*, 59, 67.

43. *Towards a Shi'i Mediterranean*, 67–72. On the vizier, see Mathew Barber, "Al-Afḍal B. Badr Al-Jamālī: The Vizierate and the Fatimid Response to the First Crusade: Masculinity in Historical Memory," in *Crusading and Masculinities*, ed. N.R. Hodgson, K.J. Lewis, and M.M. Mesley (London and New York: Routledge, 2020), 55; and on his amenable relationship with the Egyptian Copts, Juan Pedro Monferrer Sala, "'And the Lord will raise a great emir in a land': Muslim Political Power Viewed by Coptic-Arabic Authors, a Case in the Arabic 'Apocalypse of Pseudo-Athanasius' II, in *Minorities in Contact*, 191–210.

44. The survivors fled but were rounded up by the fall of 969, to the tune of some 5,000 militants; see *Towards a Shi'i Mediterranean*, 75–77, 84; and *The Founder of Cairo*, 216–17. On the fighting, see also "Histoire de Yahya-ibn-Sa'id d'Antioche, continuateur de Sa'id-ibn-Bitriq," in *Patrologia Orientalis*, trans. I. Kratchkovsky and A. Vasiliev, vol. 18 (Paris: Firmin-Didot, 1924), 818–19.

45. *The Founder of Cairo*, 220–21. See also Ibn al-Athir's summation of the conquest of Egypt in Ibn el-Athir, *Annales du Maghreb & de l'Espagne*, ed. and trans. E. Fagnan (Algiers: A. Jourdan, 1898), 366–7.

46. Cline, *Jerusalem Besieged*, 157.

47. Cline, *Jerusalem Besieged*, 157.

48. *Description of Syria (Including Palestine) by Mukaddasi*, trans. Guy Le Strange (London: Palestine Pilgrims' Text Society, 1886), 34–7.

49. On Ibn al-Murajja's guide, see Amikam Elad, *Medieval Jerusalem and Islamic Worship: Holy Places, Ceremonies, Pilgrimage* (Leiden and Boston: Brill, 1999), 68–71.

50. *Description of Syria by Mukaddasi*, 37. These evidently included some western Christians, including nuns; see Michael McCormick, *Charlemagne's Survey of the Holy Land: Wealth, Personnel, and Buildings of a Mediterranean Church Between Antiquity and the Middle Ages* (Washington D.C.: Dumbarton Oaks Research Library & Collection, 2011), 76–91.

51. Moshe Gil, *A History of Palestine, 634–1099* (Cambridge: Cambridge University Press, 1997), 330–31. As opposed to Isma'ili study, which flourished; see Abdul Aziz Duri, "Jerusalem in the Early Islamic Period, 7th–11th Centuries AD," in *Jerusalem in History*, ed. K.J. Asali (Buckhurst Hill: Scorpion, 1989), 117.

52. Mare, *Archaeology of the Jerusalem Area*, 275.

53. *Orations of the Fatimid Caliphs: Festival Sermons of the Ismaili Imams*, ed. and trans. P.E. Walker (London: I.B. Tauris, 2009), 133. On their extensive maritime empire, see also David Bramoullé, "The Fatimids and the Red Sea (969–1171)," in *Navigated Spaces, Connected Places*, ed. D. Agius et al., BAR International Series (Oxford: Archaeopress, 2012), 127–36; and, in more detail, his *Les Fatimides et la mer (909–1171)* (Leiden and Boston: Brill, 2019).

54. Michael Brett, *The Fatimid Empire* (Edinburgh: Edinburgh University Press, 2017), 86.

55. *Founder of Cairo*, 241.
56. *Towards a Shi'i Mediterranean*, 84; *Founder of Cairo*, 216 n. 457 and 240 n. 515.
57. *Towards a Shi'i Mediterranean*, 89–94.
58. Abu Tahir al-Hasan ibn Ahmad al-A'sam. *Founder of Cairo*, 252; *Towards a Shi'i Mediterranean*, 90–5.
59. *Founder of Cairo*, 254.
60. *Founder of Cairo*, 266–7.
61. Quoting al-Maqrizi, in Paul E. Walker, "Al-Maqrīzī and the Fatimids," *Mamlūk Studies Review* 7:2 (2003): 91.
62. See in general Milka Levy-Rubin, "The Reorganisation of the Patriarchate of Jerusalem During the Early Muslim Period," *ARAM Periodical* 15 (2003): 197–226 and especially 206–208 on the place of the archbishoprics.
63. "Histoire de Yahya-ibn-Sa'id d'Antioche," vol. 18, 799–802 and 802 for the quotation (my translation). Steven Runciman notes the passage in *A History of the Crusades*, 3 vols. (Cambridge: Cambridge University Press, 1951), I.30. On Kafur, see Joshua Starr, "Notes on the Byzantine Incursions into Syria and Palestine(?)," *Archiv oritentální* 8:1 (1936): 93–4.
64. Starr, "Byzantine Incursions," 94.
65. *Matthew of Edessa's Chronicle*, trans. R. Bedrosian (Sophene, 2020), 8–9. See also C.E. Bosworth, "The City of Tarsus and the Arab-Byzantine Frontier in Early and Middle 'Abbāsid Times," *Oriens* 23 (1992): 278–80.
66. *Towards a Shi'i Mediterranean*, 94.
67. "Skirmishing," in *Three Byzantine Military Treatises*, trans. G.T. Dennis (Washington D.C.: Dumbarton Oaks Texts, 2008), 196–7. For more on Byzantine dispositions towards Muslims in the period, see John Haldon, "Eastern (Byzantine) Roman Views on Islam and Jihād, c. 900 CE: A Papal Connection?" in *Italy and Early Medieval Europe: Papers for Chris Wickham*, ed. R. Balzaretti, J. Barrow, and P. Skinner (Oxford: Oxford University Press, 2018).
68. Starr, "Byzantine Incursions," 92–3. On the invasion, see "Histoire de Yahya-ibn-Sa'id d'Antioche," vol. 18, 823–25; and John Skylitzes, *A Synopsis of Byzantine History, 811–1057*, trans. J. Wortlet (Cambridge: Cambridge University Press, 2010), 259.
69. *The History of Leo the Deacon: Byzantine Expansion in the Tenth Century*, ed. D. Sullivan and A-M. Talbot (Washington D.C.: Dumbarton Oaks Studies, 2005), 122.
70. *Matthew of Edessa's Chronicle*, 9–10.
71. *History of Leo the Deacon*, 137–41.
72. Stephenson, "The Imperial Theology of Victory," 46.
73. *History of Leo the Deacon*, 22.
74. *Matthew of Edessa's Chronicle*, 41–7.
75. Starr, "Byzantine Incursions," 94–5.
76. Denis Sullivan, "Byzantine Fronts and Strategies, 300–1204," in *Byzantine Culture of War*, 284; Haldon, *Warfare, State and Society*, 41.
77. *Matthew of Edessa's Chronicle*, 47. See Moshe Gil's short and long developments of this narrative in "The Political History of Jerusalem during the Early Muslim Period," in *The History of Jerusalem: The Early Muslim Period*, 20–21, and *History of Palestine*, 343–48, respectively. On "tachiks," see Tara L. Andrews, *Matt'ēos Urhayec'i and His Chronicle: History as Apocalypse in a Crossroads of Cultures* (Leiden and Boston: Brill, 2017), 109. A later but vaguer version of Tzimiskes' campaign can be found in *The Chronicle of Michael the Great, Patriarch of the Syrians*, trans. R. Bedrosian (Long Branch, NJ: Sources of the Armenian Tradition, 2013), 157.
78. John Skylitzes and Yahya of Antioch do not mention it; for Ibn al-Qalansi's account (translated into French), see Marius Canard, "Les sources arabes de l'histoire Byzantine aux confins des Xe et XIe siècles," *Revue des études byzantines* 19 (1961): 293–5.

79. Andrews, *Matt'ēos Urhayec'i and His Chronicle*, 110–12.
80. Skylitzes, *Synopsis of Byzantine History*, 295.
81. Skylitzes, *Synopsis of Byzantine History*, 267, 329, 366.
82. *History of Leo the Deacon*, 207–9.
83. This narrative is adopted by Cline, *Jerusalem Besieged*, 158.
84. This skepticism is echoed by Anthony Kaldellis, "Did Ioannes I Tzimiskes Campaign in the East in 974?" *Byzantion* 84 (2014): 235, building off the work of Paul E. Walker, "The 'Crusade' of John Tzimiskes in the Light of New Arabic Evidence," *Byzantion* 47 (1977): 319–21. Warren Treadgold has suggested that the 975 campaign was essentially a shaping operation for future efforts to retake the city; see *A History of the Byzantine State and Society* (Stanford: Stanford University Press, 1997), 512.
85. Robert Ousterhout, "Rebuilding the Temple: Constantine Monomachus and the Holy Sepulchre," *Journal of the Society of Architectural Historians* 48:1 (1989): 69; Daniel Galadza, *Liturgy and Byzantinization in Jerusalem* (Oxford: Oxford University Press, 2018), 119–20.
86. Paula A. Sanders, "The Fāṭimid State, 969–1171," in *The Cambridge History of Egypt, Volume I: Islamic Egypt, 640–1517*, ed. C.F. Petry (Cambridge: Cambridge University Press, 1998), 152.
87. Brett, *Fatimid Empire*, 133.
88. Related by al-Maqrizi, quoted in Paul E. Walker, *Caliph of Cairo: Al-Hakim bi-Amr Allah, 996–1021* (Cairo and New York: American University in Cairo Press, 2009), 83.
89. Quoted in Walker, *Caliph of Cairo*, 85.
90. "Histoire de Yahya-ibn-Sa'id d'Antiche, continuateur de Sa'id-ibn-Bitriq," trans. I. Kratchkovsky and A. Vasiliev, in *Patrologius orientalis*, vol. 23 (Paris: Firmin-Didot, 1932), 487.
91. "Histoire de Yahya-ibn-Sa'id d'Antiche," vol. 23, 488–9.
92. "Histoire de Yahya-ibn-Sa'id d'Antiche," vol. 23, 491.
93. "Histoire de Yahya-ibn-Sa'id d'Antiche," vol. 23, 491–2: "et d'en faire disparaitre la trace."
94. *La chronographie d'Élie Bar-Šinaya, métropolitain de Nisibe*, ed. L.J. Delaporte (Paris: H. Champion, 1910), 140–41.
95. Skylitzes, *Synopsis of Byzantine History*, 365.
96. Rodulfus Glaber, *The Five Books of the Histories and The Life of St. William*, ed. N. Bust, trans. J. France and P. Reynolds (Oxford: Oxford University Press, 1989), 132–5.
97. Daniel F. Callahan, "The Cross, the Jews, and the Destruction of the Church of the Holy Sepulchre in the Writings of Ademar of Chabannes," in *Christian Attitudes Toward the Jews in the Middle Ages*, ed. M. Frassetto (New York and London: Routledge, 2007), 15–16. The accounts of Ademar are provided in Callahan, *Ademar of Chabannes*, 81–4.
98. On these events, see Michael Frassetto, *Christians and Muslims in the Middle Ages: From Muhammad to Dante* (Lanham: Lexington, 2020), 126.
99. Callahan, "Destruction of the Church of the Holy Sepulchre," 16. On the Holy Fire, see Marius Canard, "Destruction de l'Église de la Résurrection," *Byzantion* 35 (1965): 16–43; and Alex Lidov, "The Holy Fire and Visual Constructs of Jerusalem, East and West," in *Visual Constructs of Jerusalem*, ed. B. Kühnel, G. Noga-Bannai, and H. Vorholt (Turnhout: Brepols, 2014), 241–52. *Matthew of Edessa's Chronicle*, 77–9, claims the candles failed to light that year, thereby exposing the miracle as a hoax, upon which al-Hakim's forces entered the city and killed 10,000 Christians.
100. Walker, *Caliph of Cairo*, 75, 78.
101. As quoted in Frassetto, *Christians and Muslims*, 124. Frassetto seems to lean towards the letter's authenticity; see the studies cited therein.
102. Frassetto, *Christians and Muslims*, 128. Ademar tended to see the designs of the Antichrist all around him; see Daniel F. Callahan, "Heresy and the Antichrist in the Writings of Ademar of Chabannes," in *Where Heaven and Earth Meet*, 178–226.

103. See Robert Chazan, "1007–1012: Initial Crisis for Northern-European Jewry," *Proceedings of the American Academy for Jewish Research* 18–19 (1970–1971): 101–17.

104. Guibert of Nogent, *The Deeds of God Through the Franks*, trans. R. Levine (Teddington: Echo, 2008), 39.

105. Martin Biddle, *The Tomb of Christ* (Stroud: Sutton, 1999), 74. Conceptual images of the rebuilding can be found in the Theodore Psalter, which was finished in 1066; see Cecily Hennessey, "The Theodore Psalter and the Rebuilding of the Holy Sepulchre, Jerusalem," *Electronic British Library Journal*, Article 4 (2017): 1–11.

106. Belief in the eventual return of al-Hakim and the truth of his divinity is a core tenet of the Druze faith; see Nejla M. Abu-Izzeddin, *The Druzes: A New Study of their History, Faith and Society* (Leiden: Brill, 1993).

107. Al-Zahir li-i'zaz Din Allah, d. 1035.

108. Skylitzes, *Synopsis of Byzantine History*, 374.

109. See Renana Bartal, "Relics of Place: Stone Fragments of the Holy Sepulchre in Eleventh-Century France," *Journal of Medieval History* 44:4 (2018): 406–21.

110. Galadza, *Liturgy and Byzantinization*, 122; Ousterhout, "Rebuilding the Temple," 70–72.

111. Sanders, "The Fāṭimid State," 166–7.

112. Daniella Talmon-Heller and Miriam Frenkel, "Religious Innovation under Fatimid Rule: Jewish and Muslim Rites in Eleventh-Century Jerusalem," *Medieval Encounters* 25:3 (2019): 203–26.

113. "Cairo Genizah," *Cambridge Digital Library*, https://cudl.lib.cam.ac.uk/collections/genizah/1; accessed May 19, 2021. For a thorough review of the documents and their contexts, see Marina Rustow, *The Lost Archive: Traces of a Caliphate in a Cairo Synagogue* (Princeton: Princeton University Press, 2020).

114. "Cairo Genizah," T-S 8K10.

115. "Cairo Genizah," T-S 13J19.15.

116. Miriam Frenkel, "Pilgrimage and Charity in the Geniza Society," in *Jews, Christians, and Muslims in Medieval and Early Modern Times: A Festschrift in Honor of Mark R. Cohen*, ed. A.E. Franklin et al. (Leiden and Boston: Brill, 2014), 59–66; S.D. Goitein, *A Mediterranean Society: The Jewish Communities of the Arab World as Portrayed in the Documents of the Cairo Genizah. An Abridgment in One Volume*, ed. J. Lassner (Berkeley: University of California Press, 1999), 164.

117. On the distinctions and characteristics of the two groups, see Goitein, *A Mediterranean Society*, 75–7; on their culture, see Meira Polliack, "The Karaites," in *Jerusalem 1000–1400: Every People Under Heaven*, ed. B.D. Boehm and M. Holcomb (New Haven and London: Yale University Press, 2016), 79–81; on some of the work done there, see Miriam Goldstein, *Karaite Exegesis in Medieval Jerusalem: The Judeo-Arabic Pentateuch Commentary of Yūsuf ibn Nūḥ and Abū al-Faraj Hārūn* (Tübingen: Mohr Siebeck, 2011).

118. "Cairo Genizah," T-S 13J33.12. For more on the dispute, see Mark R. Cohen, "New Light on the Conflict over the Palestinian Gaonate, 1038–1042, and on Daniel b. 'Azarya: a Pair of Letters to the Nagid of Qayrawan," *AJS Review* 1 (1976): 1–39. Even so, Marina Rustow has argued that the Karaites and Rabbanites remained cooperative when needed in both public and private life; see *Heresy and the Politics of Community: The Jews of the Fatimid Caliphate* (Ithaca: Cornell University Press, 2008).

119. A. Marmorstein, "Solomon ben Judah and Some of his Contemporaries," *Jewish Quarterly Review* 8:1 (1917): 16–19.

120. "Cairo Genizah," T-S 16.261.

121. "Cairo Genizah," T-S 12J23.11.

122. "Cairo Genizah," T-S 28.18.

123. "Cairo Genizah," T-S 13J13.17.

124. On the term and criticism of it, see Josef (Yousef) Meri, "Critical Reflections on the Study of Muslim-Jewish Relations," in *The Routledge Handbook of Muslim-Jewish Relations*, ed. J. Meri (New York and London: Routledge, 2016), 21.

125. "Cairo Genizah," Or.1080 J93.
126. "Cairo Genizah," T-S 13J26.13.
127. Lassner, *Jews, Christians, and the Abode of Islam*, 198.
128. Alexandra Cuffel, "Conversion and Religious Polemic Between Jews and Christians in Egypt from the Fatimid through the Mamluk Periods," in *Minorities in Contact*, 71–103.
129. Brett, *Fatimid Empire*, 162–3 and 173. The salient account is from *Bar Hebraeus*, X, which also relates that the Fatimids agreed to release thousands of Christian prisoners in Egypt, though their identities and crimes are unclear.
130. Ronnie Ellenblum, *The Collapse of the Eastern Mediterranean: Climate Change and the Decline of the East, 950–1072* (Cambridge: Cambridge University Press, 2012), 188–89.
131. For the narrative see Jay Rubenstein, *Armies of Heaven: The First Crusade and the Quest for Apocalypse* (New York: Basic Books, 2011), 8–12; see also Hans-Henning Kortüm, "Der Pilgerzug von 1064/65 ins Heilige Land. Eine Studie über Orientalismuskonstruktionen im 11. Jahrhundert," *Historische Zeitschrift* 277:3 (2003): 561–92; and Einar Johnson, "The Great German Pilgrimage of 1064–1065," in *The Crusades and Other Historical Essays: Presented to Dana C. Munro by His Former Students*, ed. L.J. Paetow (Freeport, NY: Books for Libraries, 1928), 3–43. For a primary account, see "Annales Altahenses maiores: pars altera auctore monacho Altahensi a. 1033–1073," in *Monumenta Germaniae Historica*, ed. G.H. Pertz, SS, vol. XX (Hannover, 1868), III.815–17; in English, "The German Pilgrimage of 1064–65," in *Pilgrimage in the Middle Ages: A Reader*, ed. B.E. Whalen (Toronto: University of Toronto Press, 2011), no. 38. The interfaith contours are alluded to in MacEvitt, *Rough Tolerance*, 47.
132. See William, Archbishop of Tyre, *A History of Deeds Done Beyond the Sea*, trans. E.A. Babcock and A.C. Krey, 2 vols. (New York: Columbia University Press, 1943), II.241–45. The roots of the Hospital of St. John in Jerusalem will be discussed further in chapter four.
133. *Nāṣer-e Khosraw's Book of Travels (Safarnāma)*, trans. W.M. Thackston (Albany: The Persian Heritage Foundation, 1986), 21 and 32–3. For more on Fatimid treatment of non-Muslims, see Johannes den Heijer, Yaacov Lev, and Mark N. Swanson, "The Fatimid Empire and its Population," in *Medieval Encounters* 21 (2015): 323–44.
134. On the proposed reasons for this, see Shainool Jiwa, "Governance and Pluralism Under the Fatimids (909–996 CE)," in *The Shi'i World: Pathways in Tradition and Modernity*, ed. F. Daftary, A.B. Sajoo, and S. Jiwa (London: I.B. Tauris, 2015), 111–30. See also Luke Yarbrough, "Muslim Rulers, Christian Subjects," in *Christian-Muslim Relations: A Bibliographical History*, ed. D. Pratt and C.L. Tieszen (Leiden and Boston: Brill, 2020), 375–76. On the notion of what "tolerance" meant in the period, see Meri, "Critical Reflections," 26. A popular Arabic handbook stressed the need to prioritize the majority; see Isabel Toral-Niehoff, "Justice and Good Administration in Medieval Islam: *The Book of the Pearl of the Ruler* by Ibn 'Abd Rabbih (860–940)," in *The Good Christian Ruler in the First Millennium*, ed. P.M. Forness, A. Hasse-Ungeheuer, and H. Leppin (Berlin: De Gruyter, 2021), 393.
135. Ellenblum, *Collapse of the Eastern Mediterranean*, 176–7.
136. Ellenblum, *Collapse of the Eastern Mediterranean*, 178–81. On other finds along the walls in general, see Kay Prag, *Excavations by K.M. Kenyon in Jerusalem 1961–1967: Discoveries in Hellenistic to Ottoman Jerusalem* (Oxford: Oxford University Press, 2008).
137. For a tidy summation, see John France, "Egypt, the Jazira and Jerusalem: Middle-Eastern Tensions and the Latin States in the Twelfth Century," in *Crusader Landscapes in the Medieval Levant: The Archaeology and History of the Latin East*, ed. M. Sinibaldi et al. (Cardiff: University of Wales Press, 2016), 146–8.
138. See Michael Brett, "Fatimid Historiography: a Case Study—the Quarrel with the Zirgids, 1048–58," in *Medieval Historical Writing in the Christian and Islamic Worlds*, ed. D.O. Morgan (London: School of Oriental and African Studies, 1982), 47–59.

139. Brett, *Fatimid Empire*, 176–8.
140. *The Annals of the Saljuq Turks: Selections from al-Kāmil fīl-Ta'īkh of 'Izz al-Dīn ibn al-Athīr*, trans. D.S. Richards (London and New York: Routledge, 2002), 43.
141. For an introduction, see Claude Cahen and M. Cahen, "La première pénétration Turque en Asie-mineure (seconde soitié du xi e S)," *Byzantion* 18 (1946–1948), 5–67.
142. *Annals of the Saljuq Turks*, 73–4, 76–7, 99–100, 108.
143. A.C.S. Peacock, *The Great Seljuk Empire* (Edinburgh: Edinburgh University Press, 2015), 49–50.
144. Peacock, *Great Seljuk Empire*, 50–51.
145. On the marriage, see *Annals of the Saljuq Turks*, 103–4; on the battle and execution, 124–25.
146. On its general reputation, see S. Tucker (Ed.), *Battles That Changed History: An Encyclopedia of World Conflict* (Santa Barbara: ABC-CLIO, 2011), 108–10. For a scholarly treatments, see Carole Hillenbrand, *Turkish Myth and Muslim Symbol: The Battle of Manzikert* (Edinburgh: Edinburgh University Press, 2007); and John F. Haldon et al., "Marching Across Anatolia: Medieval Logistics and Modeling the Manzikert Campaign," *Dumbarton Oaks Papers* 55–6 (2011–2012), 209–35 and especially the literature cited in 214 n. 11. For more popular renderings, see David Nicolle, *Manzikert 1071: The Breaking of Byzantium* (Oxford: Osprey, 2013); Brian Todd Carey, *The Road to Manzikert: Byzantine and Islamic Warfare, 527–1071* (Barnsley: Pen & Sword, 2012); and Alfred Friendly, *That Dreadful Day: The Battle of Manzikert, 1071* (London: Hutchinson, 1981).
147. Haldon, "Modeling the Manzikert Campaign," 5–6.
148. Antonios Vratimos, "Revisiting the Role of the Armenians in the Battle of Manzikert," *Reti Medievali Rivista* 21:1 (2020): 2–3.
149. Denis Sullivan, "Byzantine Fronts and Strategies," 288–9; John F. Haldon, "Approaches to an Alternative Military History of the Period ca. 1025–1071," in *The Empire in Crisis? Byzantium in the Eleventh Century*, Institute for Byzantine Research International Symposium 11 (Athens, 2003), 72–3, and a run-down of Byzantine-Turkish victories and defeats in battle on 57.
150. See Paul Markham, "The Battle of Manzikert: Military Disaster or Political Failure?," *deremilitari.org* (2005) https://deremilitari.org/2013/09/the-battle-of-manzikert-military-disaster-or-political-failure/; accessed June 4, 2021; and Łukasz Różycki, "Between the Old and the New: Byzantine Battle Tactics in the Time of the Battle of Manzikert," in *War in Eleventh-Century Byzantium*, ed. G. Theotokis and M. Meško (Abingdon and New York: Routledge, 2020), 9–36.
151. Hillenbrand, *Battle of Manzikert*, 149.
152. Hillenbrand, *Battle of Manzikert*, 227–8.
153. *Byzantium in the Time of Troubles: The Continuation of the Chronicle of John Skylitzes (1057–1079)*, ed. and trans. E. McGeer and J.W. Nesbitt (Leiden and Boston: Brill, 2020), 139; on whether John himself was the author of this continuation, see 5–6. See in general Alexander Daniel Beihammer, *Byzantium and the Emergence of Muslim-Turkish Anatolia, ca. 1040–1130* (London and New York: Routledge, 2017).
154. *Annals of the Saljuq Turks*, 176–7.
155. Yaacov Lev, "Regime, Army and Society in Medieval Egypt, 9th-12th Centuries," in *War and Society in the Eastern Mediterranean, 7th–15th Centuries*, ed. Y. Lev (Leiden: Brill, 1997), 143, 145–7. On the various contingents, see B.J. Beshir, "Fatimid Military Organization," *Zeitschrift Geschichte und Kultur des Islamischen Orients* 55 (1978): 37–49; on the black soldiers specifically, see Abbès Zouache, "Remarks on the Blacks in the Fatimid Armies, Tenth-Twelfth Century CE," *Northeast African Studies* 19:1 (2019): 23–60.
156. Jere L. Bacharach, "African Military Slaves in the Medieval Middle East: the Cases of Iraq (869–955) and Egypt (868–1171)," *International Journal of Middle East Studies*

NOTES to pp. 88–92

13:4 (1981): 482–5. On Rasad, see the various discussions in Delia Cortese and Simonetta Calderini, *Women and the Fatimids in the World of Islam* (Edinburgh: Edinburgh University Press, 2006).

157. Sanders, "The Fāṭimid State," 152–3.
158. Sanders, "The Fāṭimid State," 172. Badr's reign saw the end of the intellectual lineage of Fatimid scholarship as well, with the last major representative being the poet al-Muʾayyad; see Verena Klemm, *Memoirs of a Mission: The Ismaili Scholar, Statesman and Poet al-Muʾayyad fiʾl-Dīn al-Shīrāzī* (London and New York: I.B. Tauris, 2003), 104.
159. 1070 is given in Ibn al-Athir but 1071 by al-Maqrizi; see *Annals of the Saljuk Turks*, 172 n. 42. 1070 is accepted by Taef Kamal El-Azhari, *The Saljūqs of Syria During the Crusades, 463–549 A.H./1070–1154 A.D.*, trans. C.E. Bosworth (Berlin: Schwartz, 1997), 34; 1071 is used in Osman Aziz Basan, *The Great Seljuqs: A History* (New York: Routledge, 2010), 85. See also Johannes den Heijer and Joachim Yeshaya, "Solomon ben Joseph ha-Kohen on Fāṭimid Victory: a Hebrew Ode to al-Mustanṣir Billāh and Badr al-Jamālī Reconsidered," *Al-Masaq* 25:2 (2013): 170. On Atsiz and the Bedouins, see Claude Cahen, "The Turkish Invasion: The Selchükids," in *A History of the Crusades, Volume 1: the First Hundred Years*, ed. M.W. Baldwin and K.M. Setton (Madison: University of Wisconsin Press, 1958), 148.
160. *The History of the Seljuq State: A Translation with Commentary of the Akhbar al-Dawla al-Saljuqiyya*, trans. C.E. Bosworth (London and New York: Routledge, 2011), 46–7.
161. Yaacov Lev, "Army, Regime, and Society in Fatimid Egypt, 358–487/968–1094," *International Journal of Middle East Studies* 19:3 (1987): 352.
162. Steven Runciman reads this—erroneously, I believe—as a Fatimid "recovery" of Jerusalem; see *History of the Crusades*, I.76.
163. Konrad Hirschler, "The Jerusalem Conquest of 492/1099 in the Medieval Arabic Historiography of the Crusades: from Regional Plurality to Islamic Narrative," *Crusades* 13 (2014): 51 n. 37.
164. Basan, *The Great Seljuqs*, 89; El-Azhari, *Saljūqs of Syria*, 43; Paul M. Cobb, *The Race for Paradise: An Islamic History of the Crusades* (Oxford: Oxford University Press, 2014), 84; for 1073, see Joseph Yahalom, "The Temple and the City in Liturgical Hebrew Poetry," in *The Early Muslim Period*, 292. Other outliers are Walter Besant and Edward Henry Palmer, *Jerusalem: City of Herod and Saladin* (London: Chatto & Windus, 1908), 152, who conflate both sieges in 1077.
165. Lev, "Army, Regime, and Society," 352. Ibn Al-Athir speaks of the attrition via battle as well as hostility from local residents, whom his soldiers were abusing; see *Annals of the Saljuq Turks*, 193.
166. *Annals of the Saljuq Turks*, 192.
167. Joshua Prawer, "The Settlement of the Latins in Jerusalem," *Speculum* 27:4 (1952): 491–2.
168. But see El-Azhari, *Saljūqs of Syria*, 44, who sees Jews massacred alongside them.
169. See den Heijer and Yeshaya, "Solomon ben Joseph ha-Kohen," 171–4. Jonathan Decter argues that the small corpus nonetheless reveals Jewish familiarity with the conventions of the genre; see *Dominion Built of Praise: Panegyric and Legitimacy Among the Jews in the Medieval Mediterranean* (Philadelphia: University of Pennsylvania Press, 2018), 11.
170. Solomon ben Joseph ha-Kohen and Julius H. Greenstone, "The Turkoman Defeat at Cairo," *American Journal of Semitic Languages and Literatures* 22:2 (1906): 165, lines 60–68.
171. *History of the Seljuq State*, 46.
172. Taj al-Dawal Tutush. *Annals of the Saljuq Turks*, 197–8.
173. *Akhbār al-dawla al-saljūqiyya*, 52.

174. S.D. Goitein, "Geniza Sources for the Crusader Period: A Survey," in *Outremer: Studies in the History of the Crusading Kingdom of Jerusalem Presented to Joshua Prawer*, ed. B.Z. Kedar et al. (Jerusalem: Yad Izhak Ben-Zvi Institute, 307. Shafi'i is one of the four major schools of Sunni jurisprudence, the others being Hanfai, Maliki, and Hanbali.
175. For a brief accounting of the deeds of Atsiz and Artuq, see Peacock, *Great Seljuk Empire*, 61–5.
176. His account is translated in *A Muslim Principality in Crusader Times: The Early Artuqid State*, ed. and trans. C. Hillenbrand (Istanbul: Nederlands Historisch-Archaeologisch Institut, 1990), 29–30.
177. MacEvitt, *Rough Tolerance*, 48.
178. Peter Frankopan, *The First Crusade: The Call from the East* (Cambridge, MA: Harvard University Press, 2012), 97–8.
179. On the battle, see Charles D. Stanton, "The Battle of Civitate: a Plausible Account," *Journal of Medieval Military History* 11 (2013): 25–56.
180. See Paul E. Chevedden, "A Crusade from the First: the Norman Conquest of Islamic Sicily, 1060–1091," *Al-Masaq* 22 (2010): 191–225; a retort is Daniel P. Franke, "Strategy, the Norman Conquest of Southern Italy, and the First Crusade," in *Warfare in the Norman Mediterranean*, ed. G. Theotokis (Woodbridge: Boydell & Brewer, 2020), 216–218. For al-Athir, see *The Chronicle of Ibn al-Athir for the Crusading Period from al-Kamil fi 'l-Ta 'ikh*, trans. D.S. Richards, 3 vols. (Farnham: Ashgate, 2005), I.13; as well as Paul E. Chevedden's two essays, "The Islamic Interpretation of the Crusades: a New (Old) Paradigm for Understanding the Crusades," *Der Islam* 83 (2006): 90–136; and "The Islamic View and the Christian View of the Crusades: a New Synthesis," *History* 93 (2008): 181–200.
181. At one point he praised Count William VI of Poitou for agreeing to join in; see *The Register of Pope Gregory VII, 1073–1085: An English Translation*, trans. H.E.J. Cowdrey (Oxford: Oxford University Press, 2002), 2.3. On Gregory's increasingly militant language in the 1070s and 1080s, see I.S. Robinson, "Gregory VII and the Soldiers of Christ," *History* 58 (1973): 169–92; and H.E.J. Cowdrey, "Pope Gregory VII and the Bearing of Arms," in *Montjoie: Studies in Crusade History in Honour of Hans Eberhard Mayer*, ed. B.Z. Kedar, J. Riley-Smith, and R. Hiestand (Aldershot: Variorum, 1997), 21–36.
182. *Register of Pope Gregory VII*, 1.32.
183. *Register of Pope Gregory VII*, 1.49.
184. H.E.J. Cowdrey, *Pope Gregory VII, 1073–1085* (Oxford: Oxford University Press, 1998), 484–5.
185. The controversy, or "Contest" as it is sometimes known, involved questions of whether pope or emperor possessed the power to invest bishops with the physical and spiritual tools of their office.
186. On Armenia, see Jacob G. Ghazarian, *The Armenian Kingdom in Cilicia During the Crusades* (Richmond: Curzon, 2000), 81. There is a large literature on the Investiture Contest, but for documents and interpretations see Brian Tierney, *The Crisis of Church and State, 1050–1300* (Toronto: University of Toronto Press, 1988); and Uta-Renate Blumenthal, *The Investiture Controversy: Church and Monarchy from the Ninth to the Twelfth Century* (Philadelphia: University of Pennsylvania Press, 1988).
187. *Register of Pope Gregory VII*, 2.31.
188. Shimon Gat, "The Seljuks in Jerusalem," *Cathedra: For the History of Eretz* 101 (2001): 91–124 (in Hebrew); there is an English version in *Town and Material Culture in the Medieval Middle East*, ed. Y. Lev (Leiden and Boston: Brill, 2002), 1–40. Still, it is clear that there were some appeals by Jerusalem Christians to the West in the ninth to eleventh centuries; see Andrew Jostischky, "The Christians of Jerusalem, the Holy Sepulchre and the Origins of the First Crusade," *Crusades* 7 (2008): 57.

189. Galor and Bloedhorn, *Archaeology of Jerusalem*, 195.
190. This is the argument in H.E.J. Cowdrey, "Pope Gregory VII's 'Crusading Plans' of 1074," in *Outremer*, 33. For a discussion of the three Muslim rulers of Sicily in the 1060s–1070s, see Georgios Theotokis, "The Norman Invasion of Sicily, 1061–1072: Numbers and Military Tactics," *War in History* 17:4 (2010): 387.
191. Cowdrey, *Gregory VII*, 490.
192. Ghazarian, *Armenian Kingdom*, 81; see also Tara Andrews, "Matthew of Edessa (Matt'eos Urhayec'i)," in *Franks and Crusades in Medieval Eastern Christian Historiography*, ed. A. Mallett (Turnhout: Brepols, 2020), 159.
193. For these events see Frankopan, *Call from the East*, throughout.
194. The general trend of scholarship today is in the direction of seeing religious concord on a par with conflict; for example, see Samuel Noble and Constantine A. Panchenko, *Orthodoxy and Islam in the Middle East: The Seventh to the Sixteenth Centuries* (Jordanville, NY: Holy Trinity Publications, 2021).

Chapter III Ankle-deep Blood: 1098 and 1099

1. There are huge literatures on the so-called notions of Islamic *dhimmitude* and the laws and customs it imposed, as well as, on the opposite side of the spectrum, *La convivencia* in Iberia during the Middle Ages—and then everything in between. As the present study does not pretend to be a "history of tolerance" per se, see as a useful primer Glenn W. Olsen, "The Middle Ages in the History of Toleration: a Prolegomena," *Mediterranean Studies* 16 (2007): 1–20.
2. See Stuart Soroka, Patrick Fournier, and Lilach Nir, "Cross-National Evidence of a Negativity Bias in Psychophysiological Reactions to News," *Proceedings of the National Academy of Sciences of the United States of America* 116:38 (2019): 18888–18892.
3. *Gesta Francorum et Aliorum Hierosolimitanorum*, ed. and trans. R. Hill (London: Oxford University Press, 1962), 98–101.
4. For select books oriented on the First Crusade, see Frankopan, *Call From the East*; Rubenstein, *Armies of Heaven*; Thomas Asbridge, *The First Crusade: A New History* (London: Free Press, 2004); Jonathan Riley-Smith, *The First Crusaders, 1095-1131* (Cambridge: Cambridge University Press, 1997); Jonathan Phillips (Ed.), *The First Crusade: Origins and Impacts* (Manchester: Manchester University Press, 1997); John France, *Victory in the East: A Military History of the First Crusade* (Cambridge: Cambridge University Press, 1996); Marcus Bull, *Knightly Piety and the Lay Response to the First Crusade: The Limousin and Gascony, c. 970–c. 1130* (Oxford: Oxford University Press, 1993); and Jonathan Riley-Smith, *The First Crusade and the Idea of Crusading* (Philadelphia: University of Pennsylvania Press, 1986). Earlier examples include Paul Rousset, *Les origines et les caractères de la première croisade* (Neuchâtel: LaBaconnière, 1945), and the subject dominates crusades studies in journals and edited collections of essays.
5. Frankopan, *Call From the East*, is the best run-through of these overtures. Oddly, while Frankopan is routinely cited *pro forma* his arguments are typically ignored, perhaps because of the implications. If Byzantium was truly being conquered and the western magnates were recruited explicitly to stop it, one could deem the First Crusade a "defensive" war. But as defensiveness is a virtue in "Just War" traditions, this raises the uncomfortable specter of "justifying" crusading itself. Arguing against defensiveness is Matthew G. Gabriele, "Islamophobes want to recreate the Crusades, but they don't understand them at all," *Washington Post* (June 6, 2017); and against Gabriele, Andrew Holt, "The First Crusade as a 'Defensive War': a Response to Prof. Gabriele," *Andrew Holt, PhD* (June 6, 2017), https://apholt.com/2017/06/06/the-first-crusade-as-a-defensive-war-a-response-to-prof-gabriele/#more-11147; accessed July 13, 2021, and the other blog posts he cites

within. On general contours of the debate, see Andrew Holt, "The First Crusade as a Defensive War? Four Historians Respond," *Andrew Holt, PhD* (April 15, 2018), https://apholt.com/2018/04/15/the-first-crusade-as-a-defensive-war-four-historians-respond/; accessed July 13, 2021. See also Frederick Russell, *The Just War in the Middle Ages* (Cambridge: Cambridge University Press, 1975).

6. Much has been written about Urban's sermon, but for a lucid account of its themes and dissemination, see Penny J. Cole, *The Preaching of the Crusades to the Holy Land, 1095-1270* (Cambridge, MA: Medieval Academy Books, 1991), 1–36.

7. For the major crusade surveys, see: Runciman, *History of the Crusades*; Hillenbrand, *Islamic Perspectives*; Cobb, *Race for Paradise*; Jonathan Phillips, *The Crusades, 1095-1204*, 2nd ed. (New York and London: Routledge, 2014); Thomas Asbridge, *The Crusades: The Authoritative History of the War for the Holy Land* (New York: HarperCollins, 2010); Jill N. Claster, *Sacred Violence: The European Crusades to the Middle East, 1095-1396* (Toronto: University of Toronto Press, 2009); Adrian Boas (Ed.), *The Crusader World* (New York and London: Routledge, 2015); Helen Nicholson, *The Crusades* (Indianapolis: Hackett, 2009); Jonathan Phillips, *Holy Warriors: A Modern History of the Crusades* (New York: Random House, 2009); Norman Housley, *Fighting for the Cross: Crusading to the Holy Land* (New Haven: Yale University Press, 2008); Thomas F. Madden, *The New Concise History of the Crusades* (Lanham: Rowman & Littlefield, 2006); Christopher Tyerman, *God's War: A New History of the Crusades* (Cambridge, MA: Harvard University Press, 2006); John France, *The Crusades and the Expansion of Catholic Christendom, 1000-1714* (London and New York: Routledge, 2005); Jonathan Riley-Smith, *The Crusades: A History* (New Haven: Yale University Press, 2005); Jonathan Harris, *Byzantium and the Crusades* (London: Hambledon and London, 2003); Jonathan Riley-Smith (Ed.), *The Oxford History of the Crusades* (Reprint, Oxford: Oxford University Press, 2002); Jean Richard, *The Crusades, c. 1071-c. 1291* (Cambridge: Cambridge University Press, 1999); K. Setton et al. (Ed.), *A History of the Crusades*, 6 vols. (Madison: University of Wisconsin Press, 1969–1989); Hans E. Mayer, *The Crusades* (Oxford: Oxford University Press, 1988); Jonathan Riley-Smith, *A Short History of the Crusades* (New Haven: Yale University Press, 1987); Jean Michaud, *Histoire des croisades*, 4 vols. (Paris, 1814); as well as J. Riley-Smith (Ed.), *Atlas of the Crusades* (London: Facts on File, 1990); Christopher Tyerman, *How to Plan a Crusade: Reason and Religious War in the High Middle Ages* (London: Allen Lane, 2015); and Christopher Tyerman, *The World of the Crusades: An Illustrated Guide* (New Haven and London: Yale University Press, 2019). Reference works include A. Murray (Ed.), *The Crusades: An Encyclopedia*, 4 vols. (Santa Barbara: ABC-CLIO, 2006); A.J. Andrea (Ed.), *Encyclopedia of the Crusades* (Westport: Greenwood Press, 2003); A. Holt (Ed.), *The World of the Crusades: A Daily Life Encyclopedia*, ed. A. Holt (Westport: Greenwood Press, 2019); and C. Slack (Ed.), *Historical Dictionary of the Crusades* (Lanham: Scarecrow Press, 2013).

8. On the topic see Michael Markowski, "*Crucesignatus*: its Origins and Early Usage," *Journal of Medieval History* 10 (1984): 157–65.

9. As succinctly outlined in A.J. Andrea and A. Holt (Ed.), *Seven Myths of the Crusades* (Indianapolis: Hackett, 2015), xix–xx. Although, as we have seen from the Muslim perspective it certainly appeared, to them, to have been part of a grand anti-Muslim strategy in three theaters.

10. The classic essay on this is Marcus Bull, "The Roots of Lay Enthusiasm for the First Crusade," in *History* 78:254 (1993): 353–72. For a withering critique of crusades historians' tendency to superimpose Urban's blueprint not only on the First Crusade but on successive crusades, see Paul E. Chevedden, "The View of the Crusades from Rome and Damascus: the Geo-Strategic and Historical Perspectives of Pope Urban II and ʿAlī ibn Ṭāhir al-Sulamī," *Oriens* 39:2 (2011): 257–329. A newer take on Urban is chapter three of Boyadjian, *City Lament*, which nonetheless still follows the Urban-centric theme critiqued by Chevedden.

11. On the doubtful motivation of money, see Jonathan Riley-Smith, "Early Crusaders to the East and the Costs of Crusading, 1095-1130," in *Cross Cultural Convergences in the Crusader Period: Essays Presented to Aryeh Grabois on his Sixty-Fifth Birthday*, ed. M. Goodich, S. Menache, and S. Schein (New York: Peter Lang, 1995), 237–57.
12. Susanna A. Throop, *Crusading as an Act of Vengeance, 1095-1216* (Farnham: Ashgate, 2011), 43–71.
13. Tyerman, *God's War*, 81. Pilgrims did not have full access to the city and had to pay fees for entry; for a romantic old rendering of the challenge, see Estelle Blyth, *Jerusalem and the Crusades* (London: T.C. & E.C. Jack, 1913), 8–16.
14. See William J. Purkis, *Crusading Spirituality in the Holy Land and Iberia, c. 1095–c. 1187* (Woodbridge: Boydell and Brewer, 2008), 30–58; as well as Jonathan Riley-Smith, "An Army on Pilgrimage," in *Jerusalem the Golden: The Origins and Impact of the First Crusade*, ed. S. Edgington and L. García-Guijarro Ramos (Brepols: Turnhout, 2014), 103–116. For the broad reach of this call to pilgrimage, see Nikolas Jaspert, "Eleventh-Century Pilgrimage from Catalonia to Jerusalem: New Sources on the Foundations of the First Crusade," *Crusades* 14 (2015): 1–49.
15. See the influential essay by Jonathan Riley-Smith, "Crusading as an Act of Love," *History* 65:214 (1980): 177–92.
16. Lars Kjær, "Conquests, Family Traditions and the First Crusade," *Journal of Medieval History* 45:5 (2019): 553–79.
17. Ane Bysted, *The Crusade Indulgence: Spiritual Rewards and the Theology of the Crusades, c. 1095-1216* (Leiden and Boston: Brill, 2015), 69. Bysted makes clear this was the promise for the First Crusade only—successive crusades added other sorts of rewards to the indulgence formula. On the history of the indulgence back to the eighth century, see Paul E. Chevedden, "Canon 2 of the Council of Clermont (1095) and the Goal of the Eastern Crusade: 'To Liberate Jerusalem' or 'To Liberate the Church of God?'" *Annuarium Historiae Conciliorum* 37:1 (2005): 57–108.
18. All these developments are broadly surveyed in David S. Bachrach, *Religion and the Conduct of War, c. 300–c. 1215* (Woodbridge: Boydell, 2003); see also M. Cecilia Gaposchkin, *Invisible Weapons: Liturgy and the Making of Crusade Ideology* (Ithaca: Cornell University Press, 2017), 41–53 and 67–72.
19. Cf. Stanton, "Battle of Civitate"; David C. Douglas, *William the Conqueror: The Norman Impact upon England* (Berkeley: University of California Press, 1964), 87–8.
20. On the Peace of God, see Dominique Barthélemy, *L'an mil et la paix de Dieu: La France chrétienne et féodale, 980–1060* (Paris: Fayard, 1999); the essays in T. Head and R. Landes (Ed.), *The Peace of God: Social Violence and Religious Response in France Around the Year 1000* (Ithaca: Cornell University Press, 1992); and a coherent attempt to stitch the movements to the later crusading period in Thomaž Mastnak, *Crusading Peace: Christendom, the Muslim World, and Western Political Order* (Berkeley: University of California Press, 2002). Casting much doubt on the premise and perhaps striking it a fatal blow, however, is Bull's *Knightly Piety*. Even so, the enthusiasm generated by the movements may have empowered westerners to choose their own crusade leaders by acclamation; see Jason MacLeod, "Peace, Popular Empowerment and the First Crusade," *Journal of Medieval Military History* 18 (2020): 37–79.
21. A brilliant point made in Paul E. Chevedden, "Pope Urban II and the Ideology of the Crusades," in *The Crusader World*, ed. A.J. Boas (London and New York: Routledge, 2015), 9–10 and throughout.
22. Cf. Callahan, "The Cross, the Jews, and the Destruction of the Church of the Holy Sepulchre."
23. Apocalyptic interpretations tend to draw their evidence from narrative sources, as opposed to dispositive and dating clauses within charters, and this has been a simmering argument for some time now. For the latter, see Giles Constable, "Medieval Charters

as a Source for the History of the Crusades," in *Crusaders and Crusading in the Twelfth Century*, ed. G. Constable (Farnham: Ashgate, 2008), 93–116; and Jonathan Riley-Smith, "The Idea of Crusading in the Charters of Early Crusaders, 1095-1102," *Actes du Colloque Universitaire International de Clermont-Ferrand (23-25 juin 1995)* 236 (1997): 155–66.

24. Revelation 21:2: "And I saw a new Jerusalem, coming down out of heaven from God, made ready as a bride adorned for her husband." On the notion in the late eleventh century but beforehand and in memory later on, see Suzanne M. Yeager, "The Earthly and Heavenly Jerusalem," in *The Cambridge Companion to the Literature of the Crusades*, ed. A. Bale (Cambridge: Cambridge University Press, 2019), 121–35; and Callahan, *Jerusalem and the Cross*, 120–24. Tying in pilgrimage to these notions is Gaposchkin, *Invisible Weapons*, 31–41.

25. Rubenstein, *Armies of Heaven*, 20 and 27–8; Benjamin Z. Kedar, *Crusade and Mission: European Approaches Towards the Muslims* (Princeton: Princeton University Press, 1984), 57–58. For the eschatological elements specifically in the chronicle of Raymond of Aguilers, see Thomas Lecacque, "Reading Raymond: the Bible of Le Puy, the Cathedral Library and the Literary Background of the *Liber* of Raymond of Aguilers," in *Uses of the Bible in Crusader Sources*, 105–32.

26. Georg Strack has some doubts on how Jerusalem figured into Urban's propaganda but admits his limited evidence; see "Pope Urban II and Jerusalem: a Re-Examination of his Letters on the First Crusade," *Journal of Religious History, Literature and Culture* 2:1 (2016): 51–70.

27. *Gesta Francorum*, 1. On the place of Jerusalem in Christian spirituality, see Sylvia Schein, *Gateway to the Heavenly City: Crusader Jerusalem and the Catholic West (1099-1187)* (Burlington: Ashgate, 2005).

28. Imam Hamid al-Ghazali (d. 1111); Hunt Janin, *The Pursuit of Learning in the Islamic World, 610-2003* (Jefferson and London: McFarland, 2005), 83. On al-Ghazali's connection to the intellectual development of the idea of *jihad*, see Osman Latiff, *The Cutting Edge of the Poet's Sword: Muslim Poetic Responses to the Crusades* (Leiden and Boston: Brill, 2018), 27–30.

29. Benjamin Z. Kedar, "Some New Sources on Palestinian Muslims Before and During the Crusades," in *Die Kreuzfahrerstaaten als multikulturelle Gesellschaft Einwanderer und Minderheiten im 12. und 13. Jahrhundert*, ed. H.E. Mayer (Munich: R. Oldenbourg, 1997), 130; Hillenbrand, *Islamic Perspectives*, 49–50, cautions, however, that there is a report of Christian pilgrims being held at the Levantine ports. So while those in Jerusalem were tolerated, this principle does not apply to the entire region.

30. *Annals of the Saljuq Turks*, 293. For the general context of the different Syrian states, see Michael A. Köhler, *Alliances and Treaties Between Frankish and Muslim Rulers in the Middle East: Cross-Cultural Diplomacy in the Period of the Crusades*, trans. P.M. Holt, ed. K. Hirschler (Leiden and Boston: Brill, 2013), 8–19.

31. This event is hardly ever referenced in literature on the Crusades or surveys of Jerusalem's history, academic or otherwise. It is missed completely in Cline, *Jerusalem Besieged*, 160-164; and similarly in Karen Armstrong, *Jerusalem: One City, Three Faiths* (New York: Harper Perennial, 2005), 269–70.

32. *Annals of the Saljuq Turks*, 294.

33. *Annals of the Saljuq Turks*, 294.

34. Qiwam al-Dawla abu Saʿid Kerbogha (d. 1102); *Annals of the Saljuq Turks*, 286–87.

35. France, *Victory in the East*, 136, 142.

36. David Nicolle, *Crusader Warfare, Volume I: Byzantium, Western Europe, and the Battle for the Holy Land* (London: Bloomsbury, 2007), 130. Albert of Aachen's story that the patriarch of Jerusalem personally asked Peter to raise soldiers has been discounted; see Jostischky, "Christians of Jerusalem," 36–7.

37. Tyerman, *God's War*, 96–8.
38. Rubenstein, *Armies of Heaven*, 84.
39. Rubenstein, *Armies of Heaven*, 86–9.
40. Matthew Gabriele, "Against the Enemies of Christ: The Role of Count Emicho in the Anti-Jewish Violence of the First Crusade," in *Christian Attitudes Towards the Jews*, 61, and on eschatology throughout.
41. From the "L" text of the Hebrew Crusade Chronicle, as translated in Robert Chazan, *European Jewry and the First Crusade* (Berkeley University of California Press, 1987), 243–44; the quote is from Psalm 83:4.
42. The year 1000 was considered to have been a hotbed of apocalyptic activity by seventeenth- to nineteenth-century historians. Modern scholarship has recast this as not so much terror at the approaching years but rather significant hope surrounding the Second Coming. See the various essays in Michael Frassetto (Ed.), *The Year 1000: Religious and Social Response to the Turning of the First Millennium* (New York: Palgrave Macmillan, 2002); and R. Landes, A. Gow, and D.C. Van Meter (Ed.), *The Apocalyptic Year 1000: Religious Expectation and Social Change, 950-1050* (Oxford: Oxford University Press, 2003).
43. That the apocalyptic dominated is held by adherents of the "popularist" school of thought, but see Norman Housley, *Contesting the Crusades* (Malden, MA: Blackwell, 2006), 10–12; as well as the review by John France, "Rubenstein: Armies of Heaven," *The Medieval Review* (12.06.05), https://scholarworks.iu.edu/journals-playground/index.php/tmr/article/view/17575/23693; accessed June 30, 2021. Jay Rubenstein has lately doubled down on the apocalyptic interpretation; see *Nebuchadnezzar's Dream: The Crusades, Apocalyptic Prophecy, and the End of History* (Oxford: Oxford University Press, 2019), 215.
44. See in general Daniel P. Franke, "The Crusades and Medieval Anti-Judaism: Cause or Consequence?" in *Seven Myths of the Crusades*, 48–69.
45. On the latter point, see Eva Haverkamp, "What Did the Christians Know? Latin Reports on the Persecutions of Jews in 1096," *Crusades* 7 (2008): 84: "Doubtless, an essential explanation is that the persecutions were part of the First Crusade."
46. For a breakdown of the social groups that went on the First Crusade (*paupers*—the poor, *milites*—warrior members of the nobility, *iuvenes*—youthful knights, *principes*—upper-class landowners) see Conor Kostick, *The Social Structure of the First Crusade* (Leiden and Boston: Brill, 2008).
47. Again, there is a large literature on the relations between the crusade leaders and Alexios, but for an atypical account from the Byzantine perspective, see Frankopan, *Call from the East*, 126–37.
48. *The Damascus Chronicle of the Crusades, Extracted and Translated from the Chronicle of Ibn al-Qalansi*, trans. H.A.R. Gibb (Mineola, NY: Dover, 2002), 41; as noted in Cobb, *Race for Paradise*, 75–6.
49. Yehoshua Frenkel, "Muslim Responses to the Frankish Dominion in the Near East, 1098-1291," in *The Crusades and the Near East: Cultural Histories*, ed. C. Kostick (London and New York: Routledge, 2011), 29.
50. France, *Victory in the East*, 165–6.
51. R.W. Southern, *Western Views of Islam in the Middle Ages* (Cambridge, MA: Harvard University Press, 1962), 14; and see the essays in C.F. Hernández and J. Tolan (Ed.), *The Latin Qur'an, 1143-1500: Translation, Transition, Interpretation* (Berlin and Boston: De Gruyter, 2021).
52. Nicholas Morton, *Encountering Islam on the First Crusade* (Cambridge: Cambridge University Press, 2016), 135, 149. On political expediency, see Yvonne Friedman, "Peacemaking in an Age of War: When Were Cross-religious Alliances in the Latin East Considered Treason?" in *The Crusader World*, 98–107.

53. Niall Christie, "An Illusion of Ignorance? The Muslims of the Middle East and the Franks before the Crusades," in *The Crusader World*, 311–23.
54. Hillenbrand, *Islamic Perspectives*, 274–82.
55. Hillenbrand, *Islamic Perspectives*, 296.
56. Movements taken from Tyerman, *God's War*, 131–2.
57. On trying to sort the myriad issues confronting an army moving through nonpermissive environments, see John F. Haldon et al., "Marching Across Anatolia," 209–35.
58. France, *Victory in the East*, 211. The direct testimony of this is that of Count Stephen of Blois; see "Stephen, Count of Blois and Chartres, to his Wife, Adele," in *The First Crusade: The Chronicle of Fulcher of Chartres and Other Source Materials*, ed. E. Peters, 2nd ed. (Philadelphia: University of Pennsylvania Press, 1998), 288. The history of medieval ambassadors is insufficiently studied. See the recent J.M.N. Soria and Ó.V. González (Ed.), *El embajador: evolución en la Edad Media peninsular* (Gijón: Ediciones Trea, S. L., 2021), for Iberian examples.
59. *Chronicles of the Investiture Contest: Frutolf of Michelsberg and his Continuators*, trans. T.J.H. McCarthy (Manchester: Manchester University Press, 2014), 156 and on Ekkehard's identity, 46–47; doubting this identification is T.J.H. McCarthy, "Scriptural Allusion in the Crusading Accounts of Frutolf of Michelsberg and his Continuators," in *Uses of the Bible in Crusader Sources*, 159–60. This account is corroborated by the letter of Count Stephen of Blois to his wife, the chronicle of Raymond of Aguilers, and also the later chronicle of Albert of Aachen.
60. *Deeds of God Through the Franks*, 114.
61. As argued in Köhler, *Alliances and Treaties*, 47–8.
62. *Robert the Monk's History of the First Crusade: Historia Iherosolimitana*, trans. C. Sweetenham (Aldershot: Ashgate, 2005), 136–7.
63. There is an enormous literature on the Latin sources of the First Crusade. For a handy comparison of three major ones, see John France, "The Anonymous *Gesta Francorum* and the *Historia Francorum qui ceperunt Iherusalem* of Raymond of Aguilers and the *Historia de Hierosolymitano itinere* of Peter Tudebode: An Analysis of the Textual Relationship between Primary Sources for the First Crusade," in *The Crusades and Their Sources: Essays Presented to Bernard Hamilton*, ed. J. France and W.G. Zajac (Aldershot: Ashgate, 1998), 39–69. An updated set of essays is M. Bull and D. Kempf (Eds.), *Writing the Early Crusades: Text, Transmission, and Memory* (Woodbridge: Boydell, 2014).
64. The envoys' departure is also in Ekkehard, in *Chronicles of the Investiture Contest*, 156.
65. Hillenbrand, *Islamic Perspectives*, 43–4.
66. *Gesta Francorum*, 30–31. On the Lake Battle, see France, *Victory in the East*, 245–51, 250 n. 45; he identifies the lake as Amikgölu, which has today vanished.
67. *Letters of the Crusaders*, ed. and trans. D.C. Munro (Philadelphia: University of Pennsylvania, 1902), 5–8. This letter was composed by Stephen's chaplain, Alexander, with a personal note from the count to Adele at the end; see Simon Thomas Parsons, "The Letters of Stephen of Blois Reconsidered," *Crusades* 17 (2019): 17 and, for a new Latin edition of the letter, 27–29. On the veracity of other letters purportedly from the campaign, see Thomas W. Smith, "First Crusade Letters and Medieval Scribal Cultures," *Journal of Ecclesiastical History* 71:3 (2019): 484–501.
68. *Chronicle of Ibn al-Athir*, I.16; *Gesta Francorum*, 30–31. On the foraging battle, see France, *Victory in the East*, 237–41.
69. *Chronicle of Ibn al-Athir*, I.17.
70. In what was probably an apocryphal story, Kerbogha's mother warned him against fighting the crusaders at Antioch but he refused to listen to her advice. See Natasha Hodgson, "The Role of Kerbogha's Mother in the *Gesta Francorum* and Selected Chronicles of the First Crusade," in *Gendering the Crusades*, eds. S.B. Edgington and S. Lambert (Cardiff: University of Wales Press, 2001), 163–76.

71. *Itti'āz al-ḥunafā bi-akhbār al-a'immah al-Fāṭimīyīn al-khulafā*, ed. J. al-Dīn al-Shayyāl and M.H.M. Ahmad, 3 vols. (Cairo, 1996), III.22; *Damascus Chronicle of the Crusades*, 45.

72. *Chronicle of Ibn al-Athir*, I.21. On the siege, see Michael Fulton, *Artillery in the Era of the Crusades: Siege Warfare and the Development of Trebuchet Technology* (Leiden and Boston: Brill, 2018), 72–73.

73. Svetlana Luchitskaya, "Muslim Political World," in *Crusader World*, 349–50.

74. *Chronicle of Ibn al-Athir*, I.21.

75. *Deeds of God Through the Franks*, 114. Once the crusaders entered in 1099, Fulcher of Chartres wrote of "Arabs and Ethiopians" joining those already in the tower; see *Chronicle of Fulcher of Chartres*, 91.

76. This was one Ibn Sallar, who served in the professional 5,000-man-strong Hujaria corps; see William J. Hamblin, "Fāṭimid Army During the Early Crusades" (Ph.D. thesis, University of Michigan, 1985), 45–6.

77. *Chronicle of Fulcher of Chartres*, 93.

78. *Muslim Principality in Crusader Times*, 30–31.

79. *Muslims Principality in Crusader Times*, 30–31 and n.12.

80. As explored in Hillenbrand, *Islamic Perspectives*, 44–7.

81. Hamblin, "Fāṭimid Army During the Early Crusades," 201–2.

82. *Albert of Aachen's History of the Journey to Jerusalem, Volume 1*, trans. S.B. Edgington (Farnham: Ashgate, 2017), 59.

83. France, *Victory in the East*, 358. See also Conor Kostick, *The Siege of Jerusalem: Crusade Conquest in 1099* (London: Continuum, 2009), 55–56, whose analysis suggests a naivete on al-Afdal's part in thinking the Latins would behave like a Byzantine army.

84. Ekkehard, in *Chronicles of the Investiture Contest*, 156.

85. "Admonitio in sequentem historiam belli sacri," in *Recueil des historiens des croisades occidentaux* (Paris: Imprimerie nationale, 1864), III.214–215; see also France, *Victory in the East*, 325. This is a later source; on its contours, see Luigi Russo, "The Monte Cassino Tradition of the First Crusade: From the *Chronica monasterii Casinensis* to the *Hystoria de via et recuperatione Antiochiae atque Ierusolymarum*," in *Writing the Early Crusades*, 53–62.

86. Luchitskaya, "Muslim Political World," 349–50.

87. The multiple damage points are noted in *Chronicle of Ibn al-Athir*, I.21.

88. France, *Victory in the East*, 297–8.

89. Köhler, *Alliances and Treaties*, 37–38.

90. France argues that he did so not to betray the crusaders, as was their common understanding, but rather because he could not risk losing his army and leaving the Turkish route to Constantinople unopposed; see *Victory in the East*, 302.

91. Ma'arra's defenders resisted the tower until another group of crusader sappers distracted them by undermining the wall with their tunnels; see R. Rogers, *Latin Siege Warfare in the Twelfth Century* (Oxford: Oxford University Press, 1992), 39–43.

92. Cobb, *Race for Paradise*, 97.

93. *Robert the Monk*, 193; Baldric of Bourgueil, *History of the Jerusalemites: A Translation of the Historia Ierosolimitana*, trans. S.B. Edgington (Woodbridge: Boydell, 2020), 138–39. This was not the only truce agreed upon by the antagonists; see John France, "The Fall of Antioch During the First Crusade," in *Dei gesta per Francos: Etudes sur les croisades dédiées à Jean Richard*, eds. M. Balard, B.Z. Kedar, and J. Riley-Smith (Aldershot: Ashgate, 2001), 119–20. A text celebrating Jerusalem's fall suggests Tripoli assisted the army directly; see John France, "The Text of the Account of the Capture of Jerusalem in the Ripoll Manuscript, Bibliothèque Nationale (Latin) 5132," *English Historical Review*, 103: 408 (1988): 642.

94. France, *Victory in the East*, 327.

95. *Robert the Monk*, 196.
96. *The Gesta Tancredi of Ralph of Caen: A History of the Normans on the First Crusade*, trans. B.S. Bachrach and D.S. Bachrach (Farnham: Ashgate, 2005), 130 and 134.
97. Kostick, *Siege of Jerusalem*, 62–3.
98. Galor and Bloedhorn, *Archaeology of Jerusalem*, 177.
99. Monasteries sitting outside the main walls were apparently destroyed to make room for the forewall; see Joshua Prawer, "The Jerusalem the Crusaders Captured: A Contribution to the Medieval Topography of the City," in *Crusade and Settlement: Papers Read at the First Conference of the Society for the Study of the Crusades and the Latin East and Presented to R.C. Smail*, ed. P.W. Edbury (Cardiff: University College Cardiff Press, 1985), 2.
100. *Gesta Tancredi*, 133–4, gives the disposition, in which Robert Curthose and Robert of Flanders camped before St. Stephen's Gate (today, Damascus Gate) with Tancred "to their right"; soldiers then set their ladder against the wall by which towers lay "to their left."
101. Adrian J. Boas, *Jerusalem in the Time of the Crusades* (London and New York: Routledge, 2001), 46.
102. Peter Tudebode, in *Chronicle of Fulcher of Chartres*, 245; Raymond of Aguilers, in *Chronicle of Fulcher of Chartres*, 250, *Gesta Francorum*, 88. The common translation in the latter is problematic, reading "curtain wall" when the Latin reads "minorem murum." Bad weather may have been a factor, too; see France, "Ripoll Manuscript," 642.
103. *Gesta Francorum*, 87; France, *Victory in the East*, 348.
104. Kostick, *Siege of Jerusalem*, 64.
105. On Sidon, see France, *Victory in the East*, 329.
106. Armenian elites such as Prince Constantine and his chiefs Oshin and Bazuney had sent supplies to the crusaders at Antioch, but many Armenian merchants fled the vicinity during the siege; see Ghazarian, *Armenian Kingdom of Cilicia*, 49; and Conor Kostick, "Courage and Cowardice on the First Crusade, 1096-1099," *War in History* 20:1 (2013): 36. On Armenian sources, see Robert W. Thomson, "The Crusades through Armenian Eyes," in *The Crusades From the Perspective of Byzantium and the Muslim World*, eds. A.E. Laiou and R.P. Mottahedeh (Washington D.C.: Dumbarton Oaks Research Library and Collection, 2001), 71–82.
107. France, *Victory in the East*, 131 and 142.
108. France, *Victory in the East*, 336–7.
109. For the most recent tactical analysis, see Fulton, *Artillery in the Era of the Crusades*, 72–86; a shorter summary is Peter Purton, *A History of the Early Medieval Siege, c. 450-1200* (Woodbridge: Boydell & Brewer, 2009), 216–18.
110. Housley, *Fighting for the Cross*, 193. On this procession and the one at Antioch, see Gaposchkin, *Invisible Weapons*, 110–21.
111. France, *Victory in the East*, 348–9.
112. Kostick, *Siege of Jerusalem*, 107–8, narrates this in evocative fashion. On the Muslim use of naphtha incendiaries, see John D. Hosler, "Countermeasures: The Destruction of Siege Equipment at Acre, 1189-1191," in *The Art of Siege Warfare and Military Architecture From the Classical World to the Middle Ages*, eds. M. Eisenberg and R. Khamisy (Oxford and Philadelphia: Oxbow Books, 2021), 166–9. [165–73]
113. The sole opening there in 1099 was the St. Mary's Magdalene's Postern, which was passable only one by one.
114. Boas, *Jerusalem in the Time of the Crusades*, 72; Joshua Prawer, *The History of the Jews in the Latin Kingdom of Jerusalem* (Oxford: Oxford University Press, 1988), 18. The closest textual evidence for Jewish participation in the city's defense is from Guibert of Nogent, who writes of them showering the crusaders with "a rain of stones"; see *Deeds*

of God Through the Franks, 115. Muslim townsfolk were pressed into defense as well; Alan V. Murray, "A Race Against Time—A Fight to the Death: Combatants and Civilians in the Siege and Capture of Jerusalem, 1099," in *Civilians Under Siege From Sarajevo to Troy*, eds. A. Dowdall and J. Horne (New York: Palgrave Macmillan, 2018), 170.

115. See the synopsis in Benjamin Z. Kedar, "The Jerusalem Massacre of July 1099 in the Western Historiography of the Crusades," *Crusades* 3 (2004): 62–4.

116. Galor and Bloedhorn, *Archaeology of Jerusalem*, 180. The streets' narrowness and steepness can easily be observed today, especially in the modern Christian quarter.

117. Though not an eyewitness, Ralph possessed an astute military mind that should give his descriptions additional credence; see Bernard S. Bachrach and David S. Bachrach, "Ralph of Caen as a Military Historian," in *Crusading and Warfare in the Middle Ages, Representations and Realities: Essays in Honour of John France*, eds. S. John and N. Morton (Farnham: Ashgate, 2014), 87–99.

118. *Gesta Tancredi*, 147–8.

119. The verse may have been taken from a letter from September 1099; see Luigi Russo, "The Sack of Jerusalem in 1099 and Crusader Violence Viewed by Contemporary Chronicles," in *Uses of the Bible in Crusader Sources*, 69–70. For a comparison of the sources, see the fourth chapter, "Crusader Massacre of the Inhabitants of Jerusalem—1099," in *Competing Voices from the Crusades*, eds. A. Holt and J. Muldoon (Westport: Greenwood, 2008).

120. Thomas F. Madden, "Rivers of Blood: an Analysis of One Aspect of the Crusader Conquest of Jerusalem in 1099," *Revista Chilena de Estudios Medievales* 1 (2012): 25–37. The New Testament passage is Revelation 14:20: "And the wine press was trodden outside the city, and there came forth blood out of the wine press, up to the horses' bridles, for a thousand and six hundred stadia." Kedar questions whether Raymond of Aguilers, who wrote of the bridles, borrowed the passage entirely or rather employed it because it accurately described what he saw; see "Jerusalem Massacre," 65. A fuller treatment of how the narrative accounts of the First Crusade utilized biblical passages is in general is Katherine Allen Smith, *The Bible and Crusade Narrative in the Twelfth Century* (Woodbridge: Boydell Press, 2020).

121. *Gesta Francorum*, 91–2

122. *Chronicle of Fulcher of Chartres*, 92.

123. The now-standard treatments of this issue are Kedar, "Jerusalem Massacres," and Hirschler, "Jerusalem Conquest of 492/1099," 37–76.

124. On strategy, see Alan V. Murray, "The Siege of Jerusalem in Narrative Sources," in *Jerusalem the Golden*, 212–15, wherein he accepts Kedar's argument for the third day massacre.

125. Prawer, "Settlement of the Latins," 492.

126. Boas, *Jerusalem in the Time of the Crusades*, 9. Thus the 70,000 stated confidently in *Jerusalem in History*, 129, is well-nigh impossible.

127. Espionage activities reveal that many remained inside; see Kostick, *Siege of Jerusalem*, 87–90; and Murray, "Race Against Time," 167–8.

128. Hamblin, "Fāṭimid Army During the Early Crusades," 215–16.

129. France, *Victory in the East*, 360; Hamblin, "Fāṭimid Army During the Early Crusades," 88–9.

130. *Chronicle of Fulcher of Chartres*, 88.

131. *Gesta Francorum*, 91; Fulcher, Peter Tudebode, and Raymond of Aguilers, in *Chronicle of Fulcher of Chartres*, 93, 248, and 260, respectively.

132. *Deeds of God Through the Franks*, 114–115. On the other hand, Guibert is known for adding original details of military events; see Jay Rubenstein, *Guibert of Nogent: Portrait of a Medieval Mind* (New York and London: Routledge, 2002), 97.

133. *Gesta Francorum*, 92. On the dating, see Kedar, "Jerusalem Massacre," 61.

134. In Kedar, "Jerusalem Massacre," 21; and France, *Victory in the East*, 334.

135. *Chronicle of Fulcher of Chartres*, 91; Kostick, "Courage and Cowardice," 34.

136. Peter Tudebode, in *Chronicle of Fulcher of Chartres*, 248–49; *Gesta Francorum*, 92. On the issue of which author borrowed from which, see Jay Rubenstein, "What is the *Gesta Francorum*, and who was Peter Tudebode?" *Revue Mabillon* 16 (2005): 179–204.

137. *Deeds of God Through the Franks*, 119; *History of the Jerusalemites*, 148; *Robert the Monk*, 201. Robert pulled much of his description from the verse account of Gilo of Toucy/Paris; see *The Historia Vie Hierosolimitane of Gilo of Paris*, eds. and trans. C.W. Grocock and J.E. Siberry (Oxford: Oxford University Press, 1997).

138. Daniella Talmon-Heller and Benjamin Z. Kedar, "Did Muslim Survivors of the 1099 Massacre of Jerusalem Settle in Damascus? The True Origins of the al-Ṣāliḥyya Suburb," *Al-Masaq* 17:2 (2005): 165–69. The scholar Abu'l-Qasim Makki al-Rumayli was stoned near Beirut in December 1099; see Kedar, "Some New Sources," 133.

139. Goitein, "Geniza Sources," 311.

140. *History of the Jerusalemites*, 172.

141. Jewish possessions captured within the synagogue, which Mayer identifies as 330 manuscripts and eight Torah rolls, were eventually sold back to the Jewish community at Ascalon; see Mayer, *The Crusades*, 56.

142. "Now, among those who have reached safety (26) are some who escaped on the second and third days following the battle and left with the governor who was granted safe conduct"; from a *genizah* letter translated in S.D. Goitein, "Contemporary Letters on the Capture of Jerusalem by the Crusaders," *Journal of Jewish Studies* 3 (1952): 172. See also Kedar, "Jerusalem Massacre," 59–61.

143. Goitein, "Contemporary Letters," 171–2.

144. See the analysis in Brendan G. Goldman, "Arabic-Speaking Jews in Crusader Syria: Conquest, Continuity and Adaptation in the Medieval Mediterranean" (Ph.D. thesis, Johns Hopkins University, 2018), 42–58; Goldman suggests that the *genizah* letters regarding the sack should be read typologically, not literally.

145. Rogers, *Latin Siege Warfare*, 43–4.

146. Phrase from Jim Bradbury, *The Medieval Siege* (Woodbridge: Boydell & Brewer, 1992), 317. For a more expansive exploration across medieval warfare, see Andrzej Niewiński, "*Inter arma enim silent leges* (In Times of War, the Laws Fall Silent): Violence in Medieval Warfare," *Teka Komisji Historycznej* 1:16 (2019): 9–31.

147. *Gesta Tancredi*, 57; this line is noted by Laurence W. Marvin, "Medieval and Modern C²: Command and Control in the Field during Western Europe's Long Twelfth Century (1095-1225)," *War & Society* 35:3 (2016): 176.

148. *Robert the Monk*, 200.

149. *History of the Jerusalemites*, 172.

150. Peter Tudebode, in *Chronicle of Fulcher of Chartres*, 248

151. Raymond of Aguilers, in *Chronicle of Fulcher of Chartres*, 259; translated from "qui quantum sanguinis ea die fuderit, vix credibile est," in "Raimundi de Aguilers, canonici podiensis, historia Francorum qui ceperunt Iherusalem," in *Recueil des historiens des croisades: historiens occidentaux* (Paris: Imprimerie impériale, 1866), III.300.

152. As defined in "Pursuit," *Field Manual 3-90-1: Offense and Defense, Volume 1* (Washington D.C.: Department of the Army, 2013), 5–1.

153. All noted as practical considerations in Robert W. Jones, *Bloodied Banners: Martial Display on the Medieval Battlefield* (Woodbridge: Boydell & Brewer, 2010), 4.

154. Murray, "Race Against Time," 172.

155. On the second cleansing, see Katherine Allen Smith, "The Crusader Conquest of Jerusalem and Christ's Cleansing of the Temple," in *The Uses of the Bible in Crusader Sources*, eds. E. Lapina and N. Morton (Leiden and Boston: Brill, 2017), 19–41.

156. Examples abound, but two obvious ones are the near-complete elimination of Carthage's population (in the hundreds of thousands) during the Roman sack of 146 B.C., and the imperial sack of Magdeburg on 20–24 May 1631 A.D., in which close to 80% (20,000) of its residents were killed. See respectively Adrian Goldsworthy, *The Punic Wars* (London: Cassell, 2000), 346–56; and Peter H. Wilson, *The Thirty Years' War: Europe's Tragedy* (Cambridge, MA: Harvard University Press, 2009), 467–70.
157. Latiff, *Cutting Edge of the Poet's Sword*, 5.
158. Suleiman A. Mourad, "A Critique of the Scholarly Outlook of the Crusades: The Case for Tolerance and Coexistence," in *Syria in Crusader Times: Conflict and Co-Existence*, ed. C. Hillenbrand (Edinburgh: Edinburgh University Press, 2020), 144–5.
159. Barber, "Al-Afḍal B. Badr Al-Jamālī," 62.
160. Al-Afḍal's outreach to the crusaders is often blamed for the loss of Jerusalem; see Maher Y. Abu-Munshar, "Fāṭimids, Crusaders and the Fall of Islamic Jerusalem: Foes or Allies?" *Al-Masāq* 22:1 (2010): 45–56.
161. Hirschler has noted that the identical figure of 3,000 is given by Arabic sources for the 1077 and 1099 events, which raises suspicions; see "Jerusalem Conquest of 492/1099," 50–51.
162. On this revolt, see Menahem Mor, *The Second Jewish Revolt: The Bar Kokhba War, 132-136 CE* (Leiden and Boston: Brill, 2016).
163. On the propaganda value of this image, see Dan Jones, "What the Far Right Gets Wrong about the Crusades," *Time* (October 10, 2019); on crusaders' genocidal intent, see Susan Jacoby, "The First Victims of the First Crusade," *New York Times* (February 13, 2015), and, for a sample of the type, "The Crusades Don't Get a 'Bum Rap,' They Were Genocide," *beliefnet.com* https://www.beliefnet.com/faiths/2005/05/the-crusades-dont-get-a-bum-rap-they-were-genocide.aspx; accessed July 13, 2021. A more sober analysis of "ideological slaughter" is Alan V. Murray, "The Demographics of Urban Space in Crusade-Period Jerusalem (1099-1187)," in *Urban Space in the Middle Ages and the Early Modern Age*, ed. A. Classen (Berlin: de Gruyter, 2009), 205–24.
164. Bernard Lewis, "The Roots of Muslim Rage," *The Atlantic* (September 1990).

Chapter IV Saladin the Merciful: The 1100s and 1187

1. Prawer, "Settlement of the Latins in Jerusalem," 494.
2. See chapter 2 of Boyadjian, *City Lament*.
3. For broad treatments on them, see Andrew Jotischky, *Crusading and the Crusader States* (Harlow: Longman, 2004), and Malcolm Barber, *The Crusader States* (New Haven and London: Yale University Press, 2012).
4. For example, in Nablus prayer in mosques was allowed under Latin rule, and Muslims were permitted to maintain their laws and statutes; see Kedar, "Some New Sources," 137.
5. Saladin's full name, including honorifics, was Al-Malik al-Nasir Salah al-Din Abu'l Muzaffar Yusuf ibn Ayyub al-Tikriti al-Kurdi; see Jonathan Phillips, *The Life and Legend of the Sultan Saladin* (New Haven and London: Yale University Press, 2019), xv.
6. On the election of Godfrey, see the fifth chapter of Simon John, *Godfrey of Bouillon: Duke of Lower Lotharingia, Ruler of Latin Jerusalem, c. 1060-1100* (New York and London: Yale University Press, 2017).
7. Adrian Boas, "Domestic Life in the Latin East," in *The Crusader World*, 547–50.
8. Boas, *Jerusalem in the Time of the Crusades*, 90–91.
9. Boas, *Jerusalem in the Time of the Crusades*, 91, 110. Regarding the names, the crusaders referred to the Dome of the Rock by the biblical name of the spot, rather than the Muslim one, and al-Aqsa was probably thought of as Solomon's former palace.

10. Jaroslav Folda, "The South Transept Façade of the Church of the Holy Sepulchre in Jerusalem: An Aspect of 'Rebuilding Zion,'" in *The Crusades and Their Sources: Essays Presented to Bernard Hamilton*, eds. J. France and W.G. Zajac (Aldershot: Ashgate, 1998), 239–57; Boas, *Jerusalem in the Time of the Crusades*, 105–106. A detailed history of improvement to the church from 1009 through the crusades is Charles Coüasnon, *The Church of the Holy Sepulchre in Jerusalem* (London: Oxford University Press, 1974), 54–62. Recent updates are in John Seligman and Gideon Avni, "New Excavations and Studies in the Holy Sepulcher Compound," in *Ancient Jerusalem Revealed: Archaeological Discoveries, 1998-2018*, ed. H. Geva (Jerusalem: Israel Exploration Society, 2019), 244–46. A standard treatment of the ancient and medieval structure is Colin Morris, *The Sepulchre of Christ and the Medieval West: From the Beginning to 1600* (Oxford: Oxford University Press, 2005).
11. Bartłomiej Dźwigała, "Constantine, Helena and Heraclius in the Latin Kingdom of Jerusalem," *Journal of Ecclesiastical History* 72:1 (2020): 18–35.
12. Gaposchkin, *Invisible Weapons*, 156–60. See also Ammon Linder, "'Like Purest Gold Resplendent': the Fiftieth Anniversary of the Liberation of Jerusalem," *Crusades* 8 (2009): 31–51.
13. On the routes of pilgrimage from Europe, see David Jacoby, "Evolving Routes of Western Pilgrimage to the Holy Land, Eleventh to Fifteenth Century: An Overview," in *Unterwegs im Namen der Religion II: Wege und Ziele in vergleichender Perspektive–das mittelalterliche Europa und Asien*, eds. K. Herbers and H.C. Lehner (Stuttgart: Franz Steiner, 2017), 75–100. On Jerusalem as a Christian city, see Iris Shagrir, "Urban Soundscape: Defining Space and Community in Twelfth-Century Jerusalem," in *Communicating the Middle Ages: Essays in Honour of Sophia Menache*, eds. I. Shagrir, B.Z. Kedar, and M. Balard (London and New York: Routledge, 2018), 103–120. For early travel accounts, see Denys Pringle, "Itineraria Terrae Sanctae minora III: Some Early Twelfth-Century Guides to Frankish Jerusalem, *Crusades* 20 (2021): 3–63.
14. On this notion see Benjamin Z. Kedar, "An Early Muslim Reaction to the First Crusade?" in *Crusading and Warfare in the Middle Ages*," 69–74.
15. Cobb calls these the five principal zones; see *Race for Paradise*, 106.
16. Hillenbrand, *Islamic Perspectives*, 77. On the various perspectives at play among the different ethnicities, see Aharon Ben-Ami, *Social Change in a Hostile Environment: The Crusaders' Kingdom of Jerusalem* (Princeton: Princeton University Press, 1969), 20–46.
17. Susan B. Edgington, "The Capture of Acre, 1104, and the Importance of Sea Power in the Conquest of the Littoral," in *Acre and Its Falls: Studies in the History of a Crusader City*, ed. J. France (Leiden and Boston: Brill, 2018), 17.
18. Nicholas Morton, *The Crusader States and Their Neighbours: A Military History, 1099-1187* (Oxford: Oxford University Press, 2020), 22–3.
19. One example is the granting of money-fiefs to reward warriors; see Alan V. Murray, "The Origin of Money-Fiefs in the Latin Kingdom of Jerusalem," in *Mercenaries and Paid Men: The Mercenary Identity in the Middle Ages*, ed. J. France (Leiden and Boston: Brill, 2008), 275–86.
20. *Damascus Chronicle of the Crusades*, 49–50. Bohemond has long been a topic of interest in military history circles; see most recently Georgios Theotokis, *Bohemond of Taranto: Crusader and Conqueror* (London: Pen & Sword Military, 2021).
21. Bohemond was captured at Malatya (northeast of Antioch) in the fall of 1100; see *Chronicle of Ibn al-Athir*, I.32.
22. Summarized in Tyerman, *God's War*, 170–75.
23. R.C. Smail, *Crusading Warfare, 1097-1193*, 2nd ed. (Cambridge: Cambridge University Press, 1995), 23.
24. He was only legate until the death of Urban II on 29 July.

25. The controversy is narrated in Guibert, *Deeds of God Through the Franks*, 124–5. On his career, see Michael Matzke, *Daibert von Pisa: Zwischen Pisa, Papst und erstem Kreuzzug* (Sigmaringen: Thorbecke, 1998).
26. Taken from the table in Morton, *Crusader States and Their Neighbours*, 156–7.
27. On these groups, see Jonathan Riley-Smith, "Families, Crusades and Settlement in the Latin East, 1102-1131," in *Die Kreuzfahrerstaaten*, 1–12.
28. Steve Tibble, *The Crusader Strategy: Defending the Holy Land* (New Haven and London: Yale University Press, 2020), 30–31.
29. Nicholas Morton, *The Field of Blood: The Battle for Aleppo and the Remaking of the Medieval Middle East* (New York: Basic Books, 2018), 29. On Baldwin's rule, see Alan V. Murray, *Baldwin of Bourcq: Count of Edessa and King of Jerusalem (1100-1131)* (New York: Routledge, 2021).
30. William, Archbishop of Tyre, *Deeds Done Beyond the Sea*, II.12–13.
31. *Deeds Done Beyond the Sea*, II, II.215–17; Barber, *The Crusader States*, 204–205. The incident goes unmentioned in the Artuqid chronicle of Ibn al-Azraq.
32. *Deeds Done Beyond the Sea*, II.205–7.
33. Edgington, "Capture of Acre," 28–9, argues that the attack succeeded because of the naval assets. I would counter that it succeeded because, unlike the later and more-famous siege of Acre during the Third Crusade, in which the crusaders also had ships, there was no Muslim relief army to pressure the besiegers from without. See in general John D. Hosler, *The Siege of Acre, 1189-1191: Saladin, Richard the Lionheart, and the Battle that Decided the Third Crusade* (London and New Haven: Yale University Press, 2018).
34. Albert of Aachen, *Historia Ierosolimitana: History of the Journey to Jerusalem*, ed. and trans. S.B. Edington (Oxford: Oxford University Press, 2007), 675.
35. This point on regularity is made in France, *Victory in the East*, 355–6; a retort is Kedar, "Jerusalem Massacre," 67–68.
36. Edgington, "Capture of Acre," 22.
37. In 1168, King Amalric took Bilbais in Egypt, and despite orders to the contrary his soldiers sacked it, massacred its Jewish population, and took away as many as 12,000 slaves; see Yaacov Lev, *Saladin in Egypt* (Leiden and Boston: Brill, 1999), 59–60; and Tibble, *Crusader Strategy*, 193–4.
38. *Damascus Chronicle of the Crusades*, 100.
39. *Chronicle of Ibn al-Āthir*, I.148–9.
40. *Gesta Tancredi*, 162–3.
41. Bradbury, *The Medieval Siege*, 327.
42. Prawer, *Latin Kingdom of Jerusalem*, 49. Individual acts of torture and mutilation notwithstanding; see Nicolle, *Crusader Warfare*, 48–9. For the sieges of Ascalon and Tyre, see *Deeds Done Beyond the Sea*, II.5–20 and II.217–34.
43. Translation of the "Eracles" recension, *The Conquest of Jerusalem and the Third Crusade: Sources in Translation*, trans. P. Edbury (Aldershot: Ashgate, 1998), 58; in the Ernoul recension, see *Chronique d'Ernoul, et de Bernard le trésorier*, ed. M.L. de Mas Latrie (Paris: Libraire de la société de l'histoire de France, 1871), 215. On these problematic continuations of William of Tyre, see Philip Handyside, *The Old French William of Tyre* (Leiden: Brill, 2015).
44. This according to Peter Tudebode; see *Chronicle of Fulcher of Chartres*, 247. On spies during the campaign, see Susan B. Edgington, "Espionage and Military Intelligence during the First Crusade, 1095-1099," in *Crusading and Warfare in the Middle Ages*, 75–85.
45. On ransom, see Yvonne Friedman, *Encounter Between Enemies: Captivity and Ransom in the Latin Kingdom of Jerusalem* (Leiden and Boston: Brill, 2002).
46. As argued in Ian Wilson, "By the Sword or by an Oath: Siege Warfare in the Latin East 1097-1131," in *A Military History of the Mediterranean Sea: Aspects of War, Diplomacy,*

and Military Elites, eds. G. Theotokis and A. Yilduz (Leiden and Boston: Brill, 2018), 249–50.

47. On the Jerusalem market, see Prawer, "Settlement of the Latins," 499.
48. Joshua Prawer, *Crusader Institutions* (Oxford: Oxford University Press, 1980), 89–90.
49. Prawer, "Settlement of the Latins," 496–7; Jaroslav Folda, "Crusader Art in the Twelfth Century: Reflections on Christian Multiculturalism in the Levant," in *Intercultural Contacts in the Mediterranean*, ed. B. Arbel (London: Frank Cass, 1996), 85–86. This did not necessarily mean cordial relations between Latin and eastern Christians, however; see, for example, the accusations of heresy at the Council of Jerusalem in 1141 in MacEvitt, *Rough Tolerance*, 162–3.
50. Prawer, "Settlement of the Latins," 494, and *Latin Kingdom of Jerusalem*, 95.
51. See in general Benjamin Z. Kedar, "On the Origins of the Earliest Laws of Frankish Jerusalem: the Canons of the Council of Nablus, 1120," *Speculum* 74:2 (1999): 310–35.
52. Alan V. Murray, "Franks and Indigenous Communities in Palestine and Syria (1099-1187): A Hierarchical Model of Social Interaction in the Principalities of Outremer," in *East Meets West in the Middle Ages and Early Modern Times: Transcultural Experiences in the Premodern World*, ed. A. Classen (Berlin: De Gruyter, 2013), 294.
53. Joshua Prawer, *The Crusaders' Kingdom: European Colonialism in the Middle Ages* (New York: Praeger, 1972). Much of Prawer's research in this regard has been challenged, by his own students, no less; see Sophia Menache, "After Twenty-Five Years: Joshua Prawer's Contribution to the Study of the Crusades and the Latin Kingdom of Jerusalem Reconsidered," in *The Crusader World*, 678–9; and in general, Corliss Slack, "The Quest for Gain: Were the First Crusaders Proto-Colonists?" in *Seven Myths of the Crusades*, 70–90. On Daesh's recent use of similar rhetoric, see Jason T. Roche, " 'Crusaders' and the Islamic State Apocalypse," in *International Journal of Military History and Historiography* (August 2021): 1–35.
54. Boas, *Jerusalem in the Time of the Crusades*, 14, 40; Jean Richard, *The Latin Kingdom of Jerusalem*, trans. J. Shirley, 2 vols. (Amsterdam: North-Holland, 1979), I.133.
55. See Daniella Talmon-Heller, "Arabic Sources on Muslim Villagers Under Frankish Rule," in *From Clermont to Jerusalem: The Crusaders and Crusader Societies, 1095-1500*, ed. A.V. Murray (Turnhout: Brepols, 1998), 103–18.
56. *Assises de Jérusalem, tome II: assises de la cour des bourgeois* (Paris: Académie Royal des Inscriptions et Belles-Lettres, 1843), 173–8.
57. On Muslim Turcopoles, see Alan Forey, "Paid Troops in the Service of Military Orders During the Twelfth and Thirteenth Centuries," in *The Crusader World*, 90.
58. Sketched broadly in Frankopan, *Silk Roads*, 141–2.
59. Such as in the writings of Abbot Peter the Venerable of Cluny and other western ecclesiastics; see Mastnak, *Crusading Peace*, 168–73.
60. On this see Morton, *Crusader States and Their Neighbours*, 204–5, referencing Köhler, *Alliances and Treaties*.
61. On Usama's visits to Jerusalem and other biographical information, see Paul M. Cobb, *Usama ibn Munqidh: Warrior-Poet of the Age of the Crusades* (Oxford: Oneworld, 2005).
62. For example, see Adam Bishop, "Usāma ibn Munqidh and Crusader Law in the Twelfth Century," *Crusades* 12 (2013): 53–65: "Usāma seems to be a reliable witness for the legal system of crusader Jerusalem" (64).
63. On the debate over whether or not Usama was Shia or Sunni, see Paul M. Cobb, "Hunting Crusaders with Usama ibn Munqidh," *Crusades* 6 (2007): 59–61.
64. This may have been in the cluster of new buildings built by the Templars to the west of al-Aqsa, of which only one (the Jami al-Nisa) survives today; see Galor and Bloedhorn, *Archaeology of Jerusalem*, 199–200. The construction is detailed in *Theoderich's Description of the Holy Places (circa 1172 A.D.)*, trans. A. Stewart (London: Palestine Pilgrims Text Society, 1891), 31–2. Today, the Jami al-Nisa contains the Al-Aqsa mosque library and

museum; see Katharina Galor, *Finding Jerusalem: Archaeology Between Science and Ideology* (Berkeley: University of California Press, 2017), 73–74. Other prayer spaces were evidently built into church structures outside of Jerusalem, for Ibn Jubayr saw one outside of Acre; see Mourad, "A Critique of the Scholarly Outlook," 149–50. Evidence of Jews, Muslims, and Christians worshipping in close proximity is most famously indicated at Nablus; see Pamela Berger, "Jewish-Muslim Veneration at Pilgrimage Places in the Holy Land," *Religion and the Arts* 15 (2011): 16–23.

65. *An Arab-Syrian Gentleman and Warrior in the Period of the Crusades: Memoirs of Usāmah ibn-Munqidh*, trans. P.K. Hitti (Reprint, New York: Columbia University Press, 1957), 163–4.

66. Boas, *Jerusalem in the Time of the Crusades*, 91.

67. Mu'in ad-Din Unur al-Atabeki, d. 1149. *Memoirs of Usāmah ibn-Munqidh*, 168. On Edessa, see Jonathan Phillips, *The Second Crusade: Extending the Frontiers of Christendom* (New Haven and London: Yale University Press, 2007), 38; the primary account of the siege is *Deeds Done Beyond the Sea*, II.140–3, and for the West's reaction, II.163–4.

68. *Deeds Done Beyond the Sea*, II.105–6. William has been heavily studied; see Peter W. Edbury and Gordon Rowe, *William of Tyre: Historian of the Latin East* (Cambridge: Cambridge University Press, 1988); and the essays in *Deeds Done Beyond the Sea: Essays on William of Tyre, Cyprus and the Military Orders Presented to Peter Edbury*, eds. S.B. Edgington and H.J. Nicholson (New York: Routledge, 2016).

69. See Andrew Bolinger, "Baktash the Forgotten: the Battle of Tell Bashir (1108) and the Saljuq Civil Wars," *Journal of Medieval Military History* 17 (2019): 1–19.

70. *Memoirs of Usāmah ibn-Munqidh*, 93–4, 110. On Fulk's local roles, see Hans Eberhard Mayer, "King Fulk of Jerusalem as City Lord," in *The Experience of Crusading, Volume 2: Defining the Crusader Kingdom*, eds. P. Edbury and J. Phillips (Cambridge: Cambridge University Press, 2003), 179–88.

71. Shlomo Goitein, "Formal Friendship in the Medieval Near East," *Proceedings of the American Philosophical Society* 115:6 (1971): 484–9.

72. Exploring this issue more fully and with reference to Usama's case is Nicholas Morton, "Templar and Hospitaller Attitudes towards Islam in the Holy Land during the 12th and 13th Centuries: Some Historiographical Reflections," *Levant* 47:3 (2015): 316–27. On Usama's knowledge of vernacular and ability to speak with the Franks, see Bogdan C. Smarandache, "Re-Examining Usama ibn Muqidh's Knowledge of 'Frankish': a Case of Medieval Bilingualism during the Crusades," *The Medieval Globe* 3:1 (2017): 47–75. The conclusion of Yvonne Friedman is that Usama was treated with respect due to his diplomatic status; see "The Templars as Peacemongers," in *Communicating the Middle Ages: Essays in Honour of Sophia Menache*. Eds. I. Shagrir, B.Z. Kedar, and M. Balard (London and New York: Routledge, 2018*)*, 16.

73. Cobb, "Hunting Crusaders," 67. On *amicitia*, see A. Classen and M. Sandidge (Eds.), *Friendship in the Middle Ages and Early Modern Age: Explorations of a Fundamental Ethical Discourse* (Berlin: De Gruyter, 2010).

74. *Memoirs of Usāmah ibn-Munqidh*, 26–7, 42, 60–61.

75. *Description of the Holy Land by John of Würzburg*, trans. A. Stewart (London: Palestine Pilgrims Text Society, 1890), 15; as noted in Benjamin Z. Kedar, "Convergences of Oriental Christians, Muslims and Frankish Worshippers: The Case of Saydnaya and the Knights Templar," in *The Crusades and the Military Orders: Expanding the Frontiers of Medieval Latin Christianity*, eds. Z. Hunyadi and J. Laszlovsky (Budapest: Dept. of Medieval Studies, Central European University, 2001), 91. This sundial is mentioned by neither al-Maqdisi nor Nasir in their otherwise very detailed accounts of the Dome of the Rock and its surrounds; see *Description of Syria*, 42–6; and *Book of Travels*, 50. Today, there is still a sundial south of the Dome of the Rock, "The Sundial of the South Trials." Sitting high up in the center of the south arched (*Qibla*) gate, through which one passes

when walking north to the shrine from al-Aqsa, it was made in the twentieth century by Rushdi Imam, the architect for the Supreme Muslim Council.

76. Mourad, "Tolerance and Coexistence," 150.

77. On this see Adrian Boas, "The Acclimatization of the Frankish Population to Life in the Latin East: Some Examples from Daily Life," in *Cultural Transfers Between France and Latin Orient (xiie-xiiie centuries)*, eds. M. Aurell, M. Galvez, and E. Ingrand-Varenne (Paris: Classiques Garnier, July 2021), 361–86.

78. *Description of the Holy Land*, 18.

79. *Description of the Holy Land*, 19.

80. *Description of the Holy Land*, 69. On the Caphetirici, see Bernard Hamilton, "Rebuilding Zion: the Holy Places of Jerusalem in the Twelfth Century," *Studies in Church History* 14 (1977): n. 81.

81. See Francis M. Rogers, *The Quest for Eastern Christians: Travel and Rumor in the Age of Discovery* (Minneapolis: University of Minnesota Press, 1962), 19.

82. Such as Baldwin II's use of a Muslim interpreter in the 1140s; see K.A. Tuley, "A Century of Communication and Acclimatization: Interpreters and Intermediaries in the Kingdom of Jerusalem," in *East Meets West*, 320.

83. Piers Mitchell, *Medicine in the Crusades: Warfare, Wounds and the Medieval Surgeon* (Cambridge: Cambridge University Press, 2004), 61. On earlier Christian and Muslim hospitals in the city, see Ahmed Ragab, *The Medieval Islamic Hospital: Medicine, Religion, and Charity* (Cambridge: Cambridge University Press, 2015), 59–69.

84. Benjamin Z. Kedar, "A Twelfth-Century Description of the Jerusalem Hospital," in *The Military Orders, Volume 2: Welfare and Warfare*, ed. H. Nicholson (London and New York: Routledge, 1998), 6–7, 12.

85. See Jonathan Rubin, *Learning in a Crusader City: Intellectual Activity and Intercultural Exchanges in Acre, 1191-1291* (Cambridge: Cambridge University Press, 2018), throughout.

86. Boas, *Jerusalem in the Time of the Crusades*, 40.

87. This point is made by Joseph Shatzmiller, "Jews, Pilgrimage, and the Christian Cult of Saints: Benjamin of Tudela and his Contemporaries," in *After Rome's Fall: Narrators and Sources of Early Medieval History. Essays Presented to Walter Goffart*, ed. A.C. Murray (Toronto: University of Toronto Press, 1998), 344–7. Benjamin is the most-famous Jewish traveler of the Middle Ages; on his travels, see David Jacoby, "Benjamin of Tudela and his 'Book of Travels,'" in *Venezia incrocio di culture: Percezioni di viaggiatori europei e non europei a confront: Atti del convegno Venezia, 26-27 gennaio 2006*, eds. K. Herbers and F. Schmieder (Rome: Edizioni di storia e letteratura, 2008), 134–64. For its textual history, see Marci Freedman, "The Transmission and Reception of Benjamin of Tudela's Book of Travels from the Twelfth Century to 1633" (Ph.D. thesis, University of Manchester, 2016).

88. *Itinerary of Rabbi Benjamin of Tudela*, 69. This translation states "200 of which," which Prawer notes is a mistranslation; see *Crusader Institutions*, 90–91. On such journeys in general, see Martin Jacobs, *Reorienting the East: Jewish Travelers to the Medieval Muslim World* (Philadelphia: University of Pennsylvania Press, 2014).

89. *Itinerary of Rabbi Benjamin of Tudela*, 85.

90. *Travels of Rabbi Petachia of Ratisbon*, trans. A. Benisch (London: Trubner, 1856), 61. There has been some argument about his and Benjamin's numbers, however: whether they represent counted individuals or, rather, groups of Jews.

91. *Itinerary of Rabbi Benjamin of Tudela*, 70.

92. Kobi Cohen-Hattab and Doron Bar, *The Western Wall: The Dispute over Israel's Holiest Jewish Site, 1967-2000* (Leiden and Boston: Brill, 2020), 19–20.

93. Prawer, *History of the Jews*, 142–43; Joel L. Kraemer, *Maimonides: The Life and World of One of Civilization's Greatest Minds* (New York: Doubleday, 2008), 137.

94. This passage contradicts the argument in Rashid Khalidi, "The Future of Arab Jerusalem," *British Journal of Middle Eastern Studies* 19:2 (1992): 135–36, which claims that Jews have only worshipped at the Western Wall for the last three centuries.
95. On this see Talmon-Heller, "Arabic Sources," 103–18.
96. *Chronicle of Fulcher of Chartres,* 281.
97. Folda, "Crusader Art," 82–4.
98. Steve Tibble, *The Crusader Armies, 1099-1187* (New Haven and London: Yale University Press, 2018), 118. Routed Turcopoles played a major role in Antioch's disaster at Ager Sanguinis; see Morton, *The Field of Blood,* 110.
99. Benjamin Z. Kedar, "The Eastern Christians in the Frankish Kingdom of Jerusalem: An Overview," in *Crusaders and Franks: Studies in the History of the Crusades and the Frankish Levant,* ed. B.Z. Kedar (New York and London: Routledge, 2016), 140–42. As Kedar notes, this was paradoxical because some of them, such as the Jacobites, were considered heretical by Rome. On St. James Cathedral, see Denys Pringle, *The Churches of the Crusader Kingdom of Jerusalem, Vol. III: the Kingdom of Jerusalem* (Cambridge: Cambridge University Press, 2007), 168–81.
100. Kedar, "Eastern Christians," 144–5; and in more depth the literature he cites: Ronnie Ellenblum, *Frankish Rural Settlement in the Latin Kingdom of Jerusalem* (Cambridge: Cambridge University Press, 1998); and Johannes Pahlitzsch, *Graeci und Suriani im Palästina der Kreuzfahrerzeit: Beiträge und Quellen zur Geschichte des griechisch-orthodoxen Patriarchats von Jerusalem* (Berlin: Duncker & Humblot, 2001).
101. Alex Mallett, *Popular Muslim Reactions to the Franks in the Levant, 1097-1291* (Farnham: Ashgate, 2014), 78–9.
102. See Andrew Jostischky, "Ethnographic Attitudes in the Crusader States: The Franks and the Indigenous Orthodox People," in *East and West in the Crusader States III: Context, Contacts, Confrontations,* eds. K. Ciggaar and H. Teule (Leuven: Peeters, 2003), 1–3. The regional treatment has been uneven as well; until recently there was little concerted study on the issue in Antioch, for example, but now see Andrew D. Buck, *The Principality of Antioch and its Frontiers in the Twelfth Century* (Woodbridge: Boydell, 2017), 164–88.
103. Exploring the matter further is Benjamin Z. Kedar, "The Subjected Muslims of the Frankish Levant," in *Muslims under Latin Rule, 1100-1300,* ed. J.M. Powell (Princeton: Princeton University Press, 1990), 135–76.
104. *The Divine Comedy of Dante Alighieri: Inferno,* trans. A. Mandelbaum (New York: Bantam Books, 1982), IV.127–29
105. Phillips, *The Life and Legend of the Sultan Saladin,* 324.
106. "Adoption" is Carole Hillenbrand's term; see "The Evolution of the Saladin Legend in the West," *Mélanges de l'Université Saint-Joseph* 58 (2005): 1–13.
107. Carole Hillenbrand, "Saladin's Spin Doctors," *Transactions of the Royal Historical Society* 29 (2019): 65–77.
108. One activity in an 8th-grade textbook requires students to "mention an instance of jihad carried out by commander Saladin al-Ayyubi, God rest his soul"; see "The 2020–21 Palestinian School Curriculum Grades 1–12: Selected Examples" (Ramat-Gan: Impact-se, 2021), 38.
109. Shawar ibn Mujir al-Saʿid (d. 1167).
110. This sequence of events is narrated in Malcolm Cameron Lyons and D.E.P. Jackson, *Saladin: The Politics of the Holy War* (Cambridge: Cambridge University Press, 1982), 6–9.
111. Anne-Marie Eddé, *Saladin,* trans. J.M. Todd (Cambridge, MA: Harvard University Press, 2011), 28–29. On the battle, see Mahmoud Said Omran, "King Amalric and the Siege of Alexandria, 1167," in *Crusade and Settlement,* 191–6. On Shirkuh's apparent appeal to Shawar to unify Muslims against the Franks, see Andrew S. Ehrenkreutz, *Saladin* (Albany: State University of New York Press, 1972), 39–41.

112. Harris, *Byzantium and the Crusades*, 118–19.
113. On the campaign, see Tibble, *Crusader Strategy*, 191–4.
114. Saladin sent a personal letter to King Baldwin IV of Jerusalem, consoling him over Amalric's death; see Elon Harvey, "Saladin Consoles Baldwin IV Over the Death of his Father," *Crusades* 15 (2016): 27–33.
115. Al-Adid li-Din Allah (d. 1171).
116. For a detailed discussion of their letters of appointment, see Yaacov Lev, *Saladin in Egypt*, 66–76.
117. The eunuch was Mu'tamin al-Khilafa.
118. The primary account is *Chronicle of Ibn al-Athir*, II.179–80; for a recent narrative see Phillips, *Saladin*, 61–2.
119. Hassan al-Mustadi Ibn Yusuf al-Mustanjid (d. 1180); on these events see Phillips, *Saladin*, 66–72; Eddé, *Saladin*, 47–49; Lyons and Jackson, *Saladin*, 44–47. The event was undersold by William of Tyre, who saw Saladin taking power by clubbing the caliph to death, eliminating his family, and then seizing the Egyptian treasury; see *Deeds Done Beyond the Sea*, II.358–59.
120. On these events, see Eddé, *Saladin*, 44–6.
121. On the campaign, see Hillenbrand, *Islamic Perspectives*, 76.
122. Eddé, *Saladin*, 42–3.
123. Hosler, *Siege of Acre*, 155.
124. Phillips, *Saladin*, 212–14.
125. Phillips, *Saladin*, 80. Al-Maqrizi notes that several Turkish managers refused to let the Jews and Christians go, in the interest of keeping the Egyptian bureaucracy functioning; see *A History of the Ayyubid Sultans of Egypt, Translated from the Arabic of al-Maqrīzī*, trans. R.J.C. Broadhurst (Boston: Twayne, 1980), 40–41.
126. *Memoirs of Usāmah ibn-Munqidh*, 189–90.
127. Phillips, *Saladin*, 124.
128. Phillips, *Saladin*, 131.
129. On sorting out the chronology, see William Facey, "Crusaders on the Red Sea: Renaud de Châtillon's Raids of AD 1182-83," in *People of the Red Sea: Proceedings of Red Sea Project II Held in the British Museum October 2004*, ed. J.C.M. Starkey (Oxford: Archaeopress, 2005), 87–98.
130. John France, *Great Battles: Hattin* (Oxford: Oxford University Press, 2015), 103–4; Phillips, *Saladin*, 183–5.
131. Friedman, *Encounter Between Enemies*, 107.
132. The holder of an *iqta* had the right to extract revenues from a specific piece of land; see Cobb, *Islamic Perspectives*, 27.
133. *Damascus Chronicle of the Crusades*, 53.
134. Hadia Dajani-Shakeel, "Jihād in Twelfth-Century Arabic Poetry: a Moral and Religious Force to Counter the Crusades," *Muslim World* 66 (1976): 108.
135. See Suleiman A. Mourad and James E. Lindsay, *The Intensification and Reorientation of Sunni Jihad Ideology in the Crusader Period: Ibn 'Asākir of Damascus (1105-1176) and His Age, with an Edition and Translation of Ibn 'Asākir's* The Forty Hadiths for Inciting Jihad (Leiden and Boston: Brill, 2013), 3–12.
136. For Saladin's unification of Egypt and Syria, see the narrative in chapters 6–8 of Phillips, *Saladin*.
137. Hillenbrand, *Islamic Perspectives*, 103–4 and 107 on the distinctions between "greater *jihad*," or personal spiritual struggle, and "lesser *jihad*," or holy war as borne out in the writings of the famous jurist Ali ibn Tahir al-Sulami (d. 1106), who nonetheless saw the former as a necessary prerequisite to legitimate the latter on an individual basis. On him, see *The Book of the Jihad of 'Ali ibn Tahir al-Sulami (d. 1106): Text, Translation and Commentary*, trans. N. Christie (Farnham: Ashgate, 2015); and Niall Christie, "Motivating Listeners in the *Kitab al-Jihad* of 'Ali ibn Tahir al-Sulami," *Crusades* 6

(2007): 1–14. On the subject in greater detail, see David Cook, *Understanding Jihad* (Berkeley: University of California Press, 2005), 32–48.

138. Hillenbrand, *Islamic Perspectives*, 188, and 180–6 on the various aspects of Saladin's particular *jihad*.

139. On the repairs, see Adrian J. Boas, *Crusader Archaeology: The Material Culture of the Latin East* (London and New York: Routledge, 2017), 15–17

140. On Ayyubid human resources, see Tibble, *Crusader Armies*, 296–9.

141. On the distinctions between offering, threatening, and seeking battle, see Stephen Morillo, "Battle Seeking: the Contexts and Limits of Vegetian Strategy," *Journal of Medieval Military History* 1 (2002): 21–42.

142. As argued in Michael Ehrlich, "The Battle of Hattin: a Defeat Foretold?" *Journal of Medieval Military History* 5 (2007): 32.

143. On Guy's decision process and early movements, see France, *Hattin*, 83–91.

144. Morton charts the different figures for the Jerusalem army in the source material, which range from 19,200 to over 40,000; see *Crusader States and Their Neighbors*, 158. For analysis of these, see Tibble, *Crusader Armies*, 323–4.

145. *Conquest of the Holy Land*, 149.

146. France, *Hattin*, 100. A dissenting voice is Morton, who has defended Guy's decisions in light of operational norms for Frankish armies in the decades previous; see *Crusader States and Their Neighbours*, 184–9.

147. For narratives of the siege, whose details are well-known, see Fulton, *Artillery in the Era of the Crusades*, 155–8; and Purton, *Early Medieval Siege*, 300–301.

148. Phillips, *Saladin*, 195.

149. France, *Hattin*, 111. Much of this money had come from the Angevin realms and various donations made by Henry II of England; see Christopher Tyerman, *England and the Crusades, 1095-1588* (Chicago: University of Chicago Press, 1988), 46–7. On the orders' own resources, see Karl Borchardt, "The Military-Religious Orders in the Crusader West," in *Crusader World*, 114–17, 121–2.

150. Modern military practitioners have fallen deeply for this version of Saladin. In one rendering he was a "great" Muslim leader who sought no vengeance at Jerusalem, instead taking its residents "prisoners" but then ransoming them for "a token amount"; see William D. Wunderle, *Through the Lens of Cultural Awareness: A Primer for US Armed Forces Deploying to Arab and Middle Eastern Countries* (Fort Leavenworth: US Govt. Printing Office, 2006), 31.

151. Al-Maqrizi simply relates that they were imprisoned; see *Ayyubid Sultans of Egypt*, 85. Lyons and Jackson, *Saladin*, 276–7, are silent on consequences; Ehrenkreutz, *Saladin*, 205, avoids the subject completely. Eddé and Phillips have commented on the fates of only the elite women; see *Saladin*, 220, and *Saladin*, 196–7, respectively.

152. *Arab Historians of the Crusades*, trans. F. Gabrieli (Berkeley: University of California Press, 1969), 162–3.

153. One of the few attempts to critique Saladin on this event is a blog post by Andrew P. Holt, "Saladin's Legacy: Some Thoughts," *Andrew Holt, Ph.D.*, https://apholt. com/2017/07/25/saladins-legacy-some-thoughts/?fbclid=IwAR3DSQlxybOdWYps bzxTXTSeQ01iNl44he9UsmrGl22GmiIlsZK1rxXI08o; accessed August 22, 2021.

154. *Arab Historians of the Crusades*, 204–207. Hillenbrand, "Saladin's Spin Doctors," 73, wittily observes, "He was one of those authors who would never use three words when 300 would do."

155. For example, Tyerman, *God's War*, 373–4; Mayer, *Crusades*, 135–6; Riley-Smith, *Short History of the Crusades*, 86–7; Madden, *Concise History of the Crusades*, 78, at least mentions the slavery; Cobb, *Race for Paradise*, 190, questions the numbers of enslaved but does not mention rape; Purton, *Early Medieval Siege*, 301, judges the whole event as "carried out in a rather more civilised fashion than the Christian conquest of 1099."

The event is mentioned but then glossed over in Yvonne Friedman, "Women in Captivity and their Ransom During the Crusader Period," in *Cross Cultural Convergences in the Crusader Period: Essays Presented to Aryeh Grabois on his Sixty-Fifth Birthday*, eds. M. Goodich, S. Menache, and S. Schein (New York: Peter Lang, 1995), 81. John Gillingham has surveyed studies on enslavement practices but for the 1187 event does not mention rape; see "Crusading Warfare, Chivalry, and the Enslavement of Women and Children," in *The Medieval Way of War: Studies in Medieval Military History in Honor of Bernard S. Bachrach*, ed. G.I. Halfond (Farnham: Ashgate, 2015), 134.

156. Amin Maalouf, *The Crusades Through Arab Eyes* (New York: Schocken Books, 1984), 200.
157. Hillenbrand, *Islamic Perspectives*, 298.
158. D.S. Richards, "A Consideration of Two Sources for the Life of Saladin," *Journal of Semitic Studies* 25:1 (1980): 61; M. Hilmy M. Ahmad, "Some Notes on Arabic Historiography During the Zengid and Ayyubid Periods (521/1127–648/1250)," in *Historians of the Middle East*, ed. B. Lewis (London: Oxford University Press, 1962), 87. On his accuracy, see H.R. Gibb, *Studies on the Civilization of Islam*, eds. S.J. Shaw and W.R. Polk (Boston: Beacon Press, 1962), 93.
159. Gillingham, "Crusading Warfare," 134; in a later piece, Gillingham notes that Islamic jurists held that owners could have sex with their slaves but not in a war zone; see "The Treatment of Male and Female Prisoners of War During the Third Crusade," in *Military Cultures and Martial Enterprises in the Middle Ages: Essays in Honour of Richard P. Abels*, eds. J.D. Hosler and S. Isaac (Woodbridge: Boydell), 200. Friedman has noted that some Muslims sought to breed stronger warriors by mating with Frankish women; see *Encounter Between Enemies*, 227–8, but she does not examine the 1187 event in this sense. On rape in warfare in general, see Jonathan Gottschall, "Explaining Wartime Rape," *Journal of Sex Research* 41:2 (2004): 129–36; and Claudia Card, "Rape as a Weapon of War," *Hypatia* 11:4 (1996): 5–18.
160. The *jizya* was a tax exacted on non-Muslims. *Arab Historians of the Crusades*, 163.
161. *The Rare and Excellent History of Saladin by Bahāʾ al- Dīn Ibn Shaddād*, trans. D.S. Richards (Farnham: Ashgate, 2002), 214–15.
162. Johannes Pahlitzsch, "The People of the Book," in *Ayyubid Jerusalem: The Holy City in Context, 1187-1250*, eds. R. Hillenbrand and S. Auld (London: Altajir Trust, 2009), 435; Richard B. Rose, "The Native Christians of Jerusalem, 1187-1260," in *The Horns of Hattin: Proceedings of the Second Conference of the Society for the Study of the Crusades and the Latin East, Jerusalem and Haifa 2–6 July 1987*, ed. B.J. Kedar (Jerusalem and London: Society for the Study of the Crusades and the Latin East, 1992), 239–49. There were no Ethiopians in the city, as has previously been alleged; see E. Van Donzel, "Were there Ethiopians in Jerusalem at the Time of Saladin's Conquest in 1187?" in *East and West in the Crusader States*, 125.
163. Al-Malik al-Muzaffar Taqi al-Din ʿUmar (d. 1191).
164. Mahmoud K. Hawari, *Ayyubid Jerusalem (1187-1250): An Architectural and Archaeological Study* (Oxford: Archaeopress, 2007), 20–21.
165. *Arab Historians of the Crusades*, 164–8 and 173–5.
166. ʿImad al-Din claims it was Patriarch Heraclius who actually did this, not Saladin; see *The Conquest of the Holy Land by Ṣalāḥ al-Dīn: A Critical Edition and Translation of the Anonymous* Libellus de expugnatione terrae sanctae per Saladinum, eds. and trans. K. Brewer and J.H. Kane (London and New York: Routledge, 2020), 221.
167. This was the Khanaqh al-Salahiyya madrasa. For the descriptions of Saladin's endowment in Jerusalem, see "The Endowment Deed of the Khānqāh al-Ṣalāḥiyya in Jerusalem Founded by Saladin on 17 October 1189," trans. J. Pahlitzsch, in *The Crusades: An Encyclopedia*, IV.1301–1305. For analysis, see Yehoshua Frenkel, "Political and Social Aspects of Endowments (*awqāf*): Saladin in Cairo (1169–73) and Jerusalem

(1187–93)," *Bulletin of the School of Oriental and African Studies* 62: 1 (1999), 5. *Rare and Excellent History*, 230, notes a certain request in 1192 from Georgian Christians about the return of their seized facilities in the city.

168. *Chronicle of Ibn al-Athir*, II.402; Carole Hillenbrand, "Ayyubid Jerusalem: A Historical Introduction," in *Ayyubid Jerusalem*, 8. On the specific alterations to the Temple Mount under Saladin, see in the same volume Sabri Jarrah, "From Monastic Cloisters to *Sahn*: The Transformation of the Open Space of the Masjid al-Aqsa under Saladin," 374–6; and, in more detail, Sabri Jarrar, "Two Islamic Construction Plans for al-Haram al-Sharif," in *City of the Great King: Jerusalem from David to the Present*, ed. N. Rosovsky (Cambridge, MA: Harvard University Press, 1996), 380–416.

169. Latiff, *Cutting Edge of the Poet's Sword*, 112, 123. Ibn Jubayr was deeply impressed by Saladin's reputation, although he never met the sultan personally; see Jonathan Phillips, "The Travels of Ibn Jubayr and his View of Saladin," in *Cultural Encounters During the Crusades*, eds. K.V. Jensen, K. Salonen, and H. Vogt (Odense: University Press of Southern Denmark, 2013), 79–80.

170. Latiff, *Cutting Edge of the Poet's Sword*, 170–72.

171. Latiff, *Cutting Edge of the Poet's Sword*, 110, 116, 126, 179–80.

172. This connection is missed by Latiff.

173. *Arab Historians of the Crusades*, 152; Phillips, *Saladin*, 201.

174. Saladin often focused his attacks on weak targets for rhetorical and morale purposes; see William J. Hamblin, "Saladin and Muslim Military Theory," in *Horns of Hattin*, 228–38

175. Michael Angold, "The Fall of Jerusalem (1187) as Viewed from Byzantium," 297–8. For important corrections to the traditional story of a full alliance, see Savvas Neocleous, "The Byzantines and Saladin: Opponents of the Third Crusade?" *Crusades* 9 (2010): 87–106.

176. Boyadjian, *City Lament*, 106.

177. See Miriam Rita Tessera, "The Use of the Bible in Twelfth-Century Papal Letters to Outremer," in *Uses of the Bible in Crusader Sources*, 202; and chapter five of Boyadjian, *City Lament*.

178. For the bull, see "Pope Gregory VIII, *Audita tremendi*, October 29, 1187," in *Crusade and Christendom: Annotated Documents in Translation from Innocent III to the Fall of Acre, 1187-1291*, eds. J. Bird, E. Peters, and J.M. Powell (Philadelphia: University of Pennsylvania Press, 2013), 5–9.

179. This was echoed in a letter to the Hospitallers in Italy, which described the defeat and warned that "Saracens and Turks . . . like an innumerable army of ants" now threatened the other Christian cities in the Levant; see "Letter from the East to the Master of Hospitalers, 1187," in *Letters of the Crusaders*, 20.

180. On the composition of the forces, see Stephen Bennett, *Elite Participation in the Third Crusade* (Woodbridge: Boydell & Brewer, 2021).

181. On the facets of the siege, see Hosler, *Siege of Acre*.

182. On the battle, see the updates in Michael Ehrlich, "The Battle of Arsur: a short-lived victory," *Journal of Medieval Military History* 12 (2014), 109–18; and Benjamin Z. Kedar, "King Richard's Plan for the Battle of Arsūf/Arsur, 1191," in *The Medieval Way of War: Studies in Medieval Military History in Honor of Bernard S. Bachrach*, ed. G.I. Halfond (Aldershot: Ashgate, 2015), 117–32.

183. Hosler, *Siege of Acre*, 86–8.

184. On the various works, see Hawari, *Ayyubid Jerusalem*, 22–3.

185. John Gillingham, *Richard I* (New Haven and London: Yale University Press, 1999), 218.

186. On the formalities of signing treaties in the period, see Yvonne Friedman, "Learning the Religious Concepts of the Other: Muslim-Christian Treaties in the Latin East," in *Religion and Peace: Historical Aspects*, ed. Y. Friedman (New York: Routledge, 2017), 67–83.

187. Cobb, *Race for Paradise*, 203.

188. *Rare and Excellent History*, 231.
189. Tyerman, *God's War*, 471–2.
190. *The History of the Holy War: Ambroise's Estoire de la Guerre Sainte*, ed. and trans. M. Ailes and M. Barber, 2 vols (Woodbridge: Boydell Press, 2003), 189–90. On Ambroise's stay in the East, see John D. Hosler, "Embedded Reporters: Ambroise, Richard de Templo, and Roger of Howden on the Third Crusade," in *Military Cultures and Martial Enterprises*, 177–91.
191. E. Ashtor-Strauss, "Saladin and the Jews," *Hebrew Union College Annual* 27 (1956): 324–5.
192. Ashtor-Strauss, "Saladin and the Jews," 308.
193. Ashtor-Strauss, "Saladin and the Jews," 313–17.
194. Boas, *Jerusalem in the Time of the Crusades*, 37; Eddé, *Saladin*, 411.
195. *Rare and Excellent History*, 233–6.
196. Al-Afdal ibn Salah ad-Din (d. 1225). The school was bulldozed during the 1967 war; see Benjamin Z. Kedar, Shlomit Weksler-Bdolah, and Tawfiq Da'ādli, "The Madrasa Afḍaliyya/Maqām Al-shaykh 'Īd: an Example Of Ayyubid Architecture In Jerusalem," *Revue Biblique* 119:2 (2012): 271–87; and Şerife Eroğlu Memiş, "Between Ottomanization and Local Networks: Appointment Registers as Archival Sources for Waqf Studies. The Case of Jerusalem's Maghariba Neighborhood," in *Ordinary Jerusalem, 1840-1940: Opening New Archives, Revisiting a Global City*, eds. A. Dalachanis and V. Lemire (Leiden and Boston: Brill, 2018), 82.
197. Eddé, *Saladin*, 221.

Chapter V Alliances and Antichrists: 1229 and 1244

1. By the time of Saladin, Egypt could provide over 8,000 soldiers for duty, although half of these were typically kept in Egypt as a strategic reserve; see Gibb, *Studies on the Civilisation of Islam*, 81.
2. See in general Alan V. Murray, "The Place of Egypt in the Military Strategy of the Crusades, 1099-1221," in *The Fifth Crusade in Context: The Crusading Movement in the Early Thirteenth Century*, eds. G. Perry, T.W. Smith, and J. Vandeburie (New York: Routledge, 2016), 117–34; and, more recently, Laurence W. Marvin, "The Battle of Fariskur (29 August 1219) and the Fifth Crusade: Causes, Course, and Consequences," *Journal of Military History* 85:3 (2021): 600–604.
3. Al-Malik al-Kamil Nasir ad-Din Abu al-Ma'ali Muhammad, d. 1238.
4. And even among scholars; the development is ignored completely and Frederick's reign written off as an "ephemeral and ineffective rule of Jerusalem" in Magen Broshi, "The Inhabitants of Jerusalem," in *City of the Great King*, 23.
5. Norman F. Cantor, *Inventing the Middle Ages: The Lives, Works, and Ideas of the Great Medievalists of the Twentieth Century* (New York: William Morrow, 1991), 84.
6. Al-Malik al-Aziz Uthman ibn Salah ad-Din Yusuf (d. 1198); Al-Malik al-'Adil Sayf al-Din Abu Bakr ibn Ayyub (d. 1218). For a summary of their and contemporaries' careers, see Michael Chamberlain, "The Crusader Era and the Ayyūbid Dynasty," in *The Cambridge History of Egypt, Volume I: Islamic Egypt, 640-1517*, ed. C.F. Petry (Cambridge: Cambridge University Press, 2008), 219–22.
7. *Chronicle of Ibn al-Athir*, III.16. The author was apparently in Damascus himself when these events transpired.
8. *Chronicle of Ibn al-Athir*, III, 23–4. On al-Afdal's reign, see Gerald Hawting, "Al-Afḍal, the Son of Saladin, and His Reputation," *Journal of the Royal Asiatic Society* 26:1–2 (2016): 19–32.
9. On this whole sequence of events, see R. Stephen Humphreys, *From Saladin to the Mongols: The Ayyubids of Damascus, 1193-1260* (Albany: State University of New York Press, 1977), 93–104.

10. Tyerman, *God's War*, 488–94.
11. *The History of Jerusalem by Jacques de Vitry*, trans. A. Stewart (London: Palestine Pilgrims' Text Society, 1896), 119.
12. I.S. Robinson, *The Papacy, 1073-1198: Continuity and Change* (Cambridge: Cambridge University Press, 1990), 20.
13. On his rule, see John Clare Moore, *Pope Innocent III (1160/61-1216): To Root Up and to Plant* (Leiden: Brill, 2003); Jane E. Sayers, *Innocent III: Leader of Europe, 1198-1216* (London: Longman, 1994); and the essays in J.M. Powell (Ed.), *Innocent III Vicar of Christ or Lord of the World?*, 2nd ed. (Washington D.C.: Catholic University of America Press, 1994).
14. *The Deeds of Pope Innocent III, by an Anonymous Author*, trans. J.M. Powell (Washington D.C.: Catholic University of America Press, 2004), 61.
15. Whether this diversion was intentional (the "treason" theory) or by happenstance (the "accident" theory) has been a central debate; see Thomas F. Madden, "Food and the Fourth Crusade: A New Approach to the Divergence Question," in *Logistics of Warfare in the Age of the Crusades*, ed. J.H. Pryor (Aldershot: Ashgate, 2006), 209–28. For the crusade in general, see Jonathan Phillips, *The Fourth Crusade and the Sack of Constantinople* (London: Pimlico, 2005); on the sources, see *Contemporary Sources for the Fourth Crusade*, eds. Alfred J. Andrea and Brett E. Whalen (Leiden and Boston: Brill, 2008).
16. For a description of the sack, see Donald E. Queller and Thomas F. Madden, *The Fourth Crusade: The Conquest of Constantinople*, 2nd ed. (Philadelphia: University of Pennsylvania Press, 1997), 193–200.
17. On various aspects, see the contributions in Thomas F. Madden (Ed.), *The Fourth Crusade: Event, Aftermath, and Perceptions. Papers from the Sixth Conference of the Society for the Study of the Crusades and the Latin East, Istanbul, Turkey, 25-29 August 2004* (New York: Routledge, 2016).
18. Harris, *Byzantium and the Crusades*, 177. On the Latin empire, see Filip van Tricht, *The Latin Renovatio of Byzantium: The Empire of Constantinople (1204-1228)* (Leiden and Boston: Brill, 2011); the chief source for the Latin Empire is George Akropolites, *The History: Introduction, Translation and Commentary*, ed. R. Macrides (Oxford: Oxford University Press, 2007).
19. Laurence W. Marvin, *The Occitan War: A Military and Political History of the Albigensian Crusade, 1209-1218* (Cambridge: Cambridge University Press, 2008), 1–2. There is significant debate over the identities of the Cathars; see Mark Gregory Pegg, *A Most Holy War: The Albigensian Crusade and the Battle for Christendom* (Oxford and New York: Oxford University Press, 2007); and Jessalynn Bird's excellent contrastive review of both books in *Crusades* 9 (2010): 208–13.
20. On the preparations, see James M. Powell, *Anatomy of a Crusade, 1213-1221* (Philadelphia: University of Pennsylvania Press, 1986), 15–18. On fundraising, a recent study argues that private funds could be more important in the period than those raised by the institutional church; see Daniel Edwards, *Finance and the Crusades: England c. 1213-1337* (Abingdon: Routledge, 2022). Interest in the council surged around its 800th anniversary in 2015. See M.C. Ferrari and K. Herbers (Eds.), *Europe 1215: Politics, Culture and Literature at the Time of the IV Lateran Council* (Cologne: Böhlau, 2018); and A. Massironi and A. Larson (Eds.), *The Fourth Lateran Council and the Development of Canon Law and the ius commune* (Turnhout: Brepols, 2018).
21. "The Fourth Lateran Council, Canon 71: *Ad liberandam*, 1215," in *Crusade and Christendom*, 127–8. On the Jewish element, see John Tolan, "Of Milk and Blood: Innocent III and the Jews, Revisited," in *Jews and Christians in Thirteenth-Century France*, eds. E. Baumgarten and J.D. Galinsky (New York: Palgrave Macmillan, 2015), 139–49. *Ad liberandum* in the council canons was distinct from his crusade encyclical, *Quia maior*; see Gaposchkin, *Invisible Weapons*, 203–5.

22. A notorious act that was nonetheless preceded by centuries in the Near East through restrictions of the caliphs Mutawwakil and al-Hakim in the ninth and eleventh centuries; see chapter 2 of the present book.

23. On how a lack of such nuance made for better crusade appeals, see Thomas W. Smith, "Not Sharing the Holy Land: Attitudes Towards Sacred Space in Papal Crusade Calls, 1095–1234," *al-Masaq* 33:4 (2021): 1–22.

24. As characterized by K.S. Parker, "The Indigenous Christians of the Ayyūbid Sultanate at the Time of the Fifth Crusade," in *Fifth Crusade in Context*, 140. The dynamics were simply different in the East, where familiarity could breed less—or at least less antagonistic—contempt. For the West, see the foundational R.I. Moore, *Formation of a Persecuting Society: Authority and Deviance in Western Europe, 950-1250*, 2nd ed. (Oxford: Blackwell, 2007); more specialist studies like Sara Lipton, *Images of Intolerance: The Representation of Jews and Judaism in the Bible moralisée* (Berkeley: University of California Press, 1999); and the recent source collection, *The Intolerant Middle Ages: A Reader*, ed. E. Smelyansky (Toronto: University of Toronto Press, 2020).

25. H.A.R. Gibb, "The Aiyūbids," in *A History of the Crusades, Volume II: the Later Crusades, 1189-1311*, eds. R.L. Wolff, H.W. Hazard, and K.M. Setton (Madison: University of Wisconsin Press, 1969), 697.

26. Stefan Heidemann, "Economic Growth and Currency in Ayyubid Palestine," in *Ayyubid Jerusalem: The Holy City in Context*, 289.

27. Cobb, *Race for Paradise*, 215.

28. As argued in Shlomo Sand, *The Invention of the Land of Israel: From Holy Land to Homeland*, trans. G. Forman (London and New York: Verso, 2012), 126–9. For a thematic treatment of pilgrimage in general, see Nicole Chareyon, *Pilgrims to Jerusalem in the Middle Ages*, trans. W.D. Wilson (New York: Columbia University Press, 2005).

29. On these topics see Ram Ben-Shalom, "The Messianic Journey of Jonathan ha-Kohen of Lunel to the Land of Israel Re-Examined," *Mediterranean Historical Review* 33:1 (2018): 1–25; and Ashtor-Strauss, "Saladin and the Jews," 317–23.

30. Ben-Shalom, "Messianic Journey," 5–7.

31. The standard biography is Guy Perry, *John of Brienne: King of Jerusalem, Emperor of Constantinople, C.1175-1237* (Cambridge: Cambridge University Press, 2013).

32. Prawer, *History of the Jews*, 217, 264.

33. "Itinerary of Rabbi Samuel ben Samson in 1210," in *Jewish Travellers (801-1755)*, ed. E.N. Adler (London: Routledge, 1930), 104: "The gate opposite is in the western wall. At the base of this wall there is to be observed a kind of arch placed at the base of the Temple. It is by a subterranean passage that the priests reach the fount of Etam, the spot where the baths were."

34. "Itinerary of Rabbi Samuel ben Samson," 104. On other related elements, see Ben-Shalom, "Messianic Journey," 10–13. The passage on the heifer, which some messianic thought sees as a necessary sacrifice before the rebuilding of the Temple, is Numbers 19.2: "This is the regulation which the law of the Lord prescribes. Tell the Israelites to procure for you a red heifer that is free from every blemish and defect and on which no yoke has ever been laid."

35. Ashtor-Strauss, "Saladin and the Jews," 326. On medieval Jewish travel literature of the period, see Ayelet Oettinger, "Making the Myth Real: the Genre of Hebrew Itineraries to the Holy Land in the 12th-13th Century," *Folklore* 36 (2007): 41–66.

36. "James of Vitry's Sermon to Pilgrims," in *Crusade and Christendom*, 146–7. For analysis and an edition of the sermons, see Jessalynn Bird, "James of Vitry's Sermons to Pilgrims," *Essays in Medieval Studies* 25 (2008): 81–113.

37. *History of Jerusalem by Jacques de Vitry*, 64. On Jacques's history writing, see Jessalynn Bird, "The *Historia Orientalis* of Jacques de Vitry: Visual and Written Commentaries as Evidence of a Text's Audience, Reception, and Utilization," *Essays in Medieval Studies* 20 (2003): 56–74.

38. *History of Jerusalem by Jacques de Vitry*, 64–7.
39. Robert E. Lerner, "Frederick II, Alive, Aloft, and Allayed, in Franciscan-Joachite Eschatology," in *The Use and Abuse of Eschatology in the Middle Ages*, eds. W. Verbeke, D. Verhelst, and A. Welkenhuysen (Leuven: Leuven University Press, 1988), 362–4.
40. On this theme, see Lydia M. Walker, "Living in the Penultimate Age: Apocalyptic Thought in James of Vitry's *ad status* Sermons," in *Uses of the Bible in Crusader Sources*, 297–315. On Joachim, see Anna Sapir Abulafia, "The Conquest of Jerusalem: Joachim of Fiore and the Jews," in *The Experience of Crusading, Volume One: Western Approaches*, eds. M. Bull and N. Housley (Cambridge: Cambridge University Press, 2003), 127–46. On apocalypticism in the region in general, see chapter 8 in John V. Tolan, *Saracens: Islam in the Medieval European Imagination* (New York: Columbia University Press, 2002).
41. *History of Jerusalem by Jacques de Vitry*, 86–8. The interplay between Jews, Muslims, and Christians was much more complex, as evidenced by the complex sets of laws appearing in Acre in the period, which were often set across the kingdom and in Jerusalem when Christians possessed it. See in general Marwan Nader, *Burgesses and Burgess Law in the Latin Kingdoms of Jerusalem and Cyprus (1099-1325)* (Aldershot: Ashgate, 2006).
42. Pahlitzsch, "People of the Book," 440.
43. Bysted, *Crusade Indulgence*, 267–71.
44. Matthew C. Phillips, "The Typology of the Cross and Crusade Preaching," in *Crusading in Art, Thought and Will*, eds. M.E. Parker, B. Halliburton, and A. Romine (Leiden and Boston: Brill, 2019), 178–80.
45. Powell, *Anatomy of a Crusade*, 67–8.
46. See Thomas W. Smith, *Curia and Crusade: Pope Honorius III and the Recovery of the Holy Land, 1216-1227* (Turnhout: Brepols, 2017).
47. Pierre-Vincent Claverie, "'Totius populi Christiani regotium': The Crusading Conception of Pope Honorius III, 1216-21," in *Fifth Crusade in Context*, 27.
48. On Philip's last decade, see John W. Baldwin, *The Government of Philip Augustus: Foundations of French Royal Power in the Middle Ages* (Berkeley: University of California Press, 1986), 331–9.
49. Karol Polejowski, "The Teutonic Order During the Fifth Crusade and Their Rise in Western Europe: The French Case Study (1218-58)," in *Fifth Crusade in Context*, 195–6.
50. For numbers, the best treatment is the in-progress Laurence W. Marvin, *The Damietta Crusade, 1217-1221: A Military History*, which the author was kind enough to let me consult; otherwise, see Christopher Marshall, *Warfare in the Latin East, 1192-1291* (Cambridge: Cambridge University Press, 1994), 71–2. Many of the soldiers who fought in the Albigensian Crusade also participated in the Fifth; see G.E.M. Lippiatt, "Worse Than all the Infidels: The Albigensian Crusade and the Continuing Call of the East," in *Crusading Europe: Essays in Honour of Christopher Tyerman*, eds. G.E.M. Lippiatt and J.L. Bird (Turnhout: Brepols, 2020), 119–46.
51. Claverie, "Crusading Conception," 33. On the role of miracles, see Beth C. Spacey, *The Miraculous and the Writing of Crusade Miracle* (Woodbridge: Boydell & Brewer, 2020); and Elizabeth Lapina, *Warfare and the Miraculous in the Chronicles of the First Crusade* (University Park: Pennsylvania State University Press, 2015).
52. Powell, *Anatomy of a Crusade*, 138.
53. *Roger of Wendover's Flowers of History, Comprising the History of England From the Descent of the Saxons to A.D. 1235*, 2 vols., trans. J.A. Giles (London: Henry G. Bohn, 1849), II.406.
54. As noted in Powell, *Anatomy of a Crusade*, 140–41. Oliver also authored a short history of Jerusalem in Christian possession from the First Crusade to Lateran IV; see "Historia regum Terre sanctae," in *Die Schriften des Kölner Domscholasters, Späteren Bischofs von*

Paderborn und Kardinal-Bischofs von S. Sabina Oliverus, ed. D. Hoogeweg (Tübingen: Litterarischer Verein, 1894), 83–158. For analysis, see Megan Cassidy-Welch, *War and Memory at the Time of the Fifth Crusade* (University Park: Pennsylvania State University Press, 2019), 113–15.

55. On these siegeworks, see Fulton, *Artillery in the Era of the Crusades*, 207–16.
56. Marvin, "Battle of Fariskur," 607–13. Jacques was a witness to much of the fighting during the Fifth Crusade; on aspects, see Cassidy-Welch, *War and Memory*, 42–58. This particular battle was immediately preceded by the famous meeting between St. Francis of Assisi and al-Kamil, in which the former attempted to convert the latter; see John Tolan, *Saint Francis and the Sultan: The Curious History of a Christian-Muslim Encounter* (Oxford: Oxford University Press, 2009); on missionary activities in general, see Barbara Bombi, "The Fifth Crusade and the Conversion of the Muslims," in *Fifth Crusade in Context*, 68–91. Suggesting a climate of missionary activity is a story told by the Dominican preacher Stephen of Bourbon, in which a Muslim converted to Christianity but was brought before a Muslim judge; *The Exempla, or Illustrative Stories from the Sermons vulgares of Jacques de Vitry*, ed. T.F. Crane (London: David Nutt, 1890), 175.
57. For the terms of the deals, see "Oliver of Paderborn, *The Capture of Damietta*, ca. 1217-1222," in *Crusade and Christendom*, 185.
58. Mourad, "A Critique of the Scholarly Outlook," 154.
59. Powell, *Anatomy of a Crusade*, 160.
60. Tyerman, *God's War*, 639.
61. Sharaf ad-Din al-Muʾazzam Isa (d. 1227); Perry, *John of Brienne*, 111–14. John's claim came through his marriage to Stephanie, the daughter of Leon I of Armenia; on how it fits into the longer tradition, see Natasha Hodgson, "Conflict and Cohabitation: Marriage and Diplomacy Between Latins and Cilician Armenians, c. 1097-1253," in *Crusades and the Near East*, 96–7.
62. Housley, *Fighting for the Cross*, 16–17; Tyerman, *God's War*, 640–42.
63. Tyerman, *God's War*, 640.
64. *Chronicle of Ibn al-Athir*, III.179.
65. *Ayyūbid Sultans of Egypt*, 181 and 200; *Flowers of History*, 410.
66. "Oliver of Paderborn," 178.
67. Galor and Bloedhorn, *Archaeology of Jerusalem*, 189.
68. Guy Perry, "From King John of Jerusalem to the Emperor-Elect Frederick II: A Neglected Letter from the Fifth Crusade," in *Fifth Crusade in Context*, 44.
69. *History of Jerusalem by Jacques de Vitry*, 84.
70. Pahlitzsch, "People of the Book," 437.
71. Latiff, *Cutting Edge of the Poet's Sword*, 215–16.
72. Hawari, *Ayyubid Jerusalem*, 18.
73. Prawer, *History of the Jews*, 86–90.
74. Nehemiah 1:3. Some would return later, after 1244, but they, too, would flee again once the Mongols invaded the region in 1260; see *Encyclopedia of the Crusades*, II.684.
75. *Ayyūbid Sultans of Egypt*, 185.
76. From the poet Sharaf al-Din ibn ʾUnayn, as quoted in *Ayyūbid Sultans of Egypt*, 189.
77. David Abulafia, *Frederick II: A Medieval Emperor* (London: Allen Lane, 1988), 120–21.
78. Ernst Kantorowicz, *Frederick the Second, 1194-1250* (New York: Richard R. Smith, 1931), 108; Powell, *Anatomy of a Crusade*, 122.
79. Abulafia, *Frederick II*, 128.
80. *Roger of Wendover's Flowers of History*, 434–5.
81. Powell, *Anatomy of a Crusade*, 190–91.
82. William Chester Jordan, *Europe in the High Middle Ages* (New York: Penguin Putnam, 2003), 250–51.

83. Abulafia, *Frederick II*, 318–19. The label has stuck in some ways, in both scholarly and literary circles; see Ernst Wilhelm Wies, *Friedrich II. von Hohenstaufen: Messias oder Antichrist* (Esslingen: Bechtle, 1994); and Cecelia Holland, *Antichrist: A Novel of the Emperor Frederick II* (New York: Atheneum, 1970).
84. Kantorowicz, *Frederick the Second*, 137–8. This work was monumental and, despite its age, remains one of the better accounts of Frederick's life. Kantorowicz was skewered by Norman Cantor, who pointed out that he not only joined the *Freikorps* but that his book was used as Nazi propaganda and had originally been published with a swastika on its cover; Cantor, *Inventing the Middle Ages*, 96–7. For a robust defense, however, see the essays in R.L. Benson and J. Fried, Eds., *Ernst Kantorowicz: Erträge der Doppeltagung Institute for Advanced Study, Princeton, Johann Wolfgang Goethe-Universität, Frankfurt* (Stuttgart: F. Steiner, 1997).
85. On the pope's role in the proceedings, see Thomas W. Smith, "Between Two Kings: Pope Honorius III and the Seizure of the Kingdom of Jerusalem by Frederick II in 1225," *Journal of Medieval History* 41 (2015): 41–59. Smith suggests that Honorius himself knew about the plot in advance, possibly through Jacques of Vitry.
86. John went on to war against imperial forces while in papal service in 1228; he thereafter became emperor of Constantinople in 1229.
87. Kantorowicz, *Frederick the Second*, 171.
88. James M. Powell, "Frederick II and the Muslims: The Making of an Historiographical Tradition," in *Iberia and the Mediterranean World of the Middle Ages, Volume I: Proceedings from Kalamazoo. Studies in Honor of Robert I. Burns, S.J.*, ed. L.J. Simon (Leiden: Brill, 1995), 263.
89. *Flowers of History*, 507.
90. Abulafia, *Frederick II*, 146. His policies towards Jews were not always so welcoming, and in Sicily he confirmed the regulations of the Fourth Lateran Council concerning distinctive attire; see Kantorowicz, *Frederick the Second*, 121.
91. Kantorowicz, *Frederick the Second*, 173–4.
92. On the muster at Brindisi, see Kantorowicz, *Frederick the Second*, 168–9.
93. See in general Peter W. Edbury, *John of Ibelin and the Kingdom of Jerusalem* (Woodbridge: Boydell Press, 1997).
94. Philip de Novare, *The Wars of Frederick II Against the Ibelins in Syria and Cyprus*, trans. J.L. La Monte and M.J. Hubert (New York: Columbia University Press, 1936), 73–4.
95. *Flowers of History*, 511.
96. On the indirect nature of such negotiations, see William S. Murrell, "Interpreters in Franco-Muslim Negotiations," *Crusades* 20 (2021): 131–50.
97. On the negotiations, see Philip de Novare, 33–6.
98. Philip de Novare, 73, specifies the number of vessels; on their type, see John H. Pryor, "Transportation of Horses by Sea During the Era of the Crusades: Eighth Century to 1285 A.D. Part I: to c. 1225," *Mariner's Mirror* 68 (1982): 23–4. On the knights, see Marshall, *Warfare in the Latin East*, 71.
99. Thomas C. Van Cleve, "The Crusade of Frederick II," in *History of the Crusades, Volume II*, 447–8.
100. Helen J. Nicholson, *The Knights Hospitaller* (Woodbridge: Boydell Press, 2001), 31. On the substance of Templar support in the period, see Malcolm Barber, "Supplying the Crusader States: The Role of the Templars," in *Horns of Hattin*, 322–6.
101. *Ayyūbid Sultans of Egypt*, 198.
102. On the nature of this crown-wearing, see Abulafia, *Frederick II*, 187; on the invocation of the Davidic line, Kantorowicz, *Frederick the Second*, 201–2.
103. Prawer, *History of the Jews*, 90–91. A Jewish traveler from the Yeshiva in Paris may have alluded to prayer at the Western Wall; see "Rabbi Jacob, the Messenger of Rabbi

Jechiel of Paris (1238-1244)," in *Jewish Travellers*, 117: "... when we reach Jerusalem we go on one of the ruins and look at the Temple Mount and the wall of the Court of Women, and the Court of Israel, the site of the Altar, and the site of the Temple, and the Sanctuary, and we make a second rent in our garments for the Temple."

104. *Rare and Excellent History*, 198.
105. "Letter from Frederick II to Henry III of England, 1229: The Imperial Achievement," in *Crusade and Christendom*, 252.
106. Björn K.U. Weiler, *Henry III of England and the Staufen Empire, 1216-1272* (Woodbridge: Boydell & Brewer, 2006), 39–40.
107. David Carpenter, *Henry III: The Rise to Power and Personal Rule, 1207-1258* (New Haven and London: Yale University Press, 2020), 80–81; on Bouvines, see the reconstructions in John France, "The Battle of Bouvines, 27 July 1214," in *The Medieval Way of War: Studies in Honor of Bernard S. Bachrach*, ed. G.I. Halfond (Farnham: Ashgate, 2015), 251–71; and J.F. Verbruggen, *The Art of Warfare in Western Europe During the Middle Ages: From the Eighth Century to 1340*, trans. S. Willard and Mrs. R.W. Southern, 2nd ed. (Woodbridge: Boydell & Brewer, 1997), 239–60.
108. "Ibn Wasil (ca. 1282) and Ibn al-Jauzi (ca. 1250) on the Loss of Jerusalem," in *Crusade and Christendom*, 256; Konrad Hirschler, *Medieval Arabic Historiography: Authors as Actors* (New York: Routledge, 2006), 20. Al-Maqrizi's account is very similar; see *Ayyūbid Sultans of Egypt*, 206. On Ibn Wasil's career and works, see Konrad Hirschler, "Ibn Wāṣil: An Ayyūbid Perspective on Frankish Lordships and Crusades," in *Medieval Muslim Historians and the Franks in the Levant*, ed. A. Mallett (Leiden and Boston: Brill, 2014), 136–60.
109. "Letter from Gerold, Patriarch of Jerusalem, to the Christian Faithful: The Coming of Antichrist, ca. 1230," in *Crusade and Christendom*, 262.
110. *Ayyūbid Sultans of Egypt*, 207.
111. As identified in Elizabeth J. Mylod, "Latin Christian Pilgrimage in the Holy Land, 1187-1291" (Ph.D. thesis, University of Leeds, 2013), 154–5.
112. "The Holy Pilgrimages (1229-39)," "Anonymous IX and Anonymous X (c. 1229-39)," and "The Ways and Pilgrimages of the Holy Land (1244-65)," in *Pilgrimage to Jerusalem and the Holy Land*, ed. D. Pringle (Burlington: Ashgate, 2012), 169–70, 174–7, 217–19.
113. "All the Land that the Sultan Retains (c. 1239)," in *Pilgrimage to Jerusalem*, 181–85.
114. "Greek Anonymous I (1253-54): A Partial Account of the Holy Places of Jerusalem relating to the Sufferings of Our Lord Jesus Christ and Certain Other Persons," in *Pilgrimage to Jerusalem*, 194.
115. See on this change E.J. Mylod, "Pilgrimage, the Holy Land and the Fifth Crusade," in *Fifth Crusade in Context*, 146–59.
116. Abulafia, *Frederick II*, 189–90.
117. *Ayyūbid Sultans of Egypt*, 208–9.
118. Mallet, *Popular Muslim Reactions to the Franks*, 62; "Ibn Wasil and Ibn al-Jauzi," 260.
119. *Ayyūbid Sultans of Egypt*, 207–8.
120. Mourad, "A Critique of the Scholarly Outlook," 154–5.
121. "Ibn Wasil and Ibn al-Jauzi," 259; Daniella Talmon-Heller, "Islamic Preaching in Syria During the Counter-Crusade (Twelfth-Thirteenth Centuries)," in *In Laudem Hierosolymitani: Studies in Crusades and Medieval Culture in Honour of Benjamin Z. Kedar*, eds. I. Shagrir, R. Ellenblum, and J. Riley-Smith (Aldershot: Ashgate, 2007), 71–2.
122. "Letter from Gerold," 261, 264–5.
123. Kantorowicz, *Frederick the Second*, 205.
124. Nicolle, *Crusader Warfare*, 22–3.

125. On the Lucera colony, see Kantorowicz, *Frederick the Second*, 130–32; and Abulafia, *Frederick II*, 146–8.
126. Abulafia, *Frederick II*, 189–90.
127. Kantorowicz, *Frederick the Second*, 88–9. On their gifts in Acre, see Adrian J. Boas and Georg Philipp Melloni, "New Evidence for Identifying the Site of the Teutonic Compound in Acre," in *Acre and Its Falls*, 75.
128. Philip de Novare, 89.
129. "Letter from Gerold," 263.
130. Philip de Novare, 90–91. On the roles of these orders in crusading, see Christopher T. Maier, *Preaching the Crusades: Mendicant Friars and the Cross in the Thirteenth Century* (Cambridge: Cambridge University Press, 1998).
131. "Letter from Gerold," 264–4; Philip de Novare, 91.
132. Hillenbrand, "Ayyubid Jerusalem," 12–13.
133. Powell, "Frederick II and the Muslims," 265–9.
134. Rivka Gonen, *Contested Holiness: Jewish, Muslim, and Christian Perspectives on the Temple Mount in Jerusalem* (Jersey City: KTAV, 2003), 153.
135. Philip de Novare, 93–4.
136. Tyerman, *God's War*, 764.
137. Thomas W. Smith, "The Use of the Bible in the *Arengae* of Pope Gregory IX's Crusade Calls," in *Use of the Bible in Crusader Sources*, 217. On the subject more specifically, see Richard Taylor Spence, "Pope Gregory IX and the Crusade" (Ph.D. thesis, Syracuse University, 1978).
138. Tyerman, *God's War*, 763–7. On the diversions, see in general Michael Lower, *The Barons' Crusade: The Call to Arms and its Consequences* (Philadelphia: University of Pennsylvania Press, 2003).
139. *Ayyūbid Sultans of Egypt*, 251.
140. "The Aiyūbids," 706.
141. Fulton, *Artillery in the Era of the Crusades*, 223–4.
142. *Crusader Syria in the Thirteenth Century: The Rothelin Continuation of the History of William of Tyre with Part of the Eracles or Acre Text*, trans. J. Shirley (London and New York: Routledge, 2016), 40; Marshall, *Warfare in the Latin East*, 231.
143. On the tower's construction, see Dennis Pringle, "Crusader Jerusalem," in *Fortification and Settlement in Crusader Palestine*, ed. D. Pringle (Aldershot: Ashgate, 2000), 112.
144. Boas, *Jerusalem in the Time of the Crusades*, 76.
145. For details, see Galor and Bloedhorn, *Archaeology of Jerusalem*, 236–40.
146. Tyerman, *God's War*, 767.
147. "Matthew Paris: Richard of Cornwall on Crusade," in *Crusade and Christendom*, 292.
148. "Richard of Cornwall on Crusade" 295–7. Tyerman notes that the heavy lifting was really done in Theobald's, not Richard's, treaty, and the fame the latter gathered was due more to the earl's own propaganda than reality; see Tyerman, *England and the Crusades*, 101–2.
149. Al-Malik al-Salih Najm al-Din Ayyub (d. 1249).
150. *Rothelin Continuation*, 63.
151. Ilya Berkovich, "The Battle of Forbie and the Second Frankish Kingdom of Jerusalem," *Journal of Military History* 75 (2011): 35.
152. On this theme, see Björn Weiler, "The 'Negotium Terrae Sanctae' in the Political Discourse of Latin Christendom, 1215-1311," *International History Review* 25:1 (2003): 1–36.
153. *Ayyūbid Sultans of Egypt*, 272; Hawari, *Ayyubid Jerusalem*, 18.
154. Al-Maqrizi's accusation that the Christians desecrated the sites with wine and music seems an unfounded flourish; see Mourad, "A Critique of the Scholarly Outlook," 147–8.

155. *Rothelin Continuation*, 63–4.
156. *Ayyubids, Mamlukes and Crusaders: Selections from the Tārīkh al-Duwal wa 'l-Mulūk of Ibn al-Furāt*, trans. U. and M.C. Lyons, 2 vols. (Cambridge: Heffer, 1971), I.3. The William of Tyre continuator adds other details, such as the beheading of the sepulchre priests and the shipping of the church's columns to Mecca; see *Rothelin Continuation*, 64.
157. "The Final Capture of Jerusalem," in *Letters of the Crusaders*, 33.
158. Cobb, *Race for Paradise*, 213.
159. Nasir ad-Din al-Malik al-Mansur Ibrahim bin Asad ad-Din Shirkuh, d. 1246.
160. These convoluted events are untangled in Berkovich, "The Battle of Forbie," 18–19, 21–2.
161. *Ibn al-Furat*, 4-5; *Ayyūbid Sultans of Egypt*, 274; *Rothelin Continuation*, 63. The former claims that "the Frankish kings ... and the counts" were present, but in reality the Jerusalem king, Conrad IV (d. 1254) never actually visited the region.
162. Marshall, *Warfare in the Latin East*, 200; "The Aiyūbids," 709.
163. On La Forbie in general, see Marie-Luis Bulst-Thiele, "Zur Geschichte de Ritterorden und des Konigreichs Jerusalem im 13. Jahrhundert bis zue Schlacht bei La Forbie am 17 Oktober 1244," *Deutsches Achiv fur Erforschung des Mittelalters* 22 (1966): 197–226.
164. Berkovich, "Battle of Forbie," 26 and 30.
165. *Ibn al-Furat*, 5; *Ayyūbid Sultans of Egypt*, 274.
166. *Ibn al-Furat*, 5; *Rothelin Continuation*, 64.
167. *Ibn al-Furat*, 5.
168. *Rothelin Continuation*, 64; *Ayyūbid Sultans of Egypt*, 274, 180. The latter's numbers are hard to judge because while al-Maqrizi claims 30,000 were slain at Forbie he elsewhere claimed the army of the Fifth Crusade had 200,000 infantry and 10,000 cavalry, which are preposterous numbers.
169. Calculated from the figures in Shlomo Lotan, "The Battle of La Forbie (1244) and its Aftermath: Re-Examination of the Military Orders' Involvement in the Latin Kingdom of Jerusalem in the Mid-Thirteenth Century," *Ordines militares colloquia Tournensia historica: Yearbook for the Study of the Military Orders* 17 (2012), 59. On the leper order of St. Lazarus, see Rafaël Hyacinthe, *L'Ordre de Saint-Lazare de Jérusalem au Moyen Age* (Millau: Conservatoire Larzac Templier et Hospitalier, 2003).
170. Lotan, "Battle of La Forbie," 60–63. On Montfort in particular, see A.J. Boas and R.G. Khamisy (Eds.), *Montfort: History, Research and Recent Studies of the Principal Fortress of the Teutonic Order in the Latin East* (Leiden and Boston: Brill, 2017).
171. On the Seventh Crusade, see William C. Jordan, *Louis IX and the Challenge of the Crusade* (Princeton: Princeton University Press, 2016); W.B. Bartlett, *The Last Crusade: The Seventh Crusade and the Final Battle for the Holy Land* (Cheltenham: History Press, 2006). On the Eighth Crusade, see Michael Lower, *The Tunis Crusade of 1270: A Mediterranean History* (Oxford: Oxford University Press, 2018).
172. Details from *Ayyūbid Sultans of Egypt*, 280–83.
173. Harawi, *Ayyubid Jerusalem*, 26.
174. Al-Malik al-Zahir Rukn al-Din Baybars al-Bunduqdari (d. 1277).
175. On Ayn-Jalut, see the works of Reuven Amitai-Preiss, especially *Mongols and Mamluks: The Mamluk-Ilkhanid War, 1260-1281* (Cambridge: Cambridge University Press, 1995); and "Ayn Jālūt Revisited," *Tārīh* 2 (1992): 119–50.
176. Hawari, *Ayyubid Jerusalem*, 18.
177. Yehoshua Frenkel, "Jews and Muslims in the Latin Kingdom of Jerusalem," in *A History of Jewish-Muslim Relations*, 160.
178. The original structure was mentioned in Rabbi Joseph Schwartz's *A Descriptive Geography and Brief Historical Sketch of Palestine* (Philadelphia: A. Hart, 1850), 277–8.
179. Michael Prestwich, *Edward I* (Berkeley: University of California Press, 1988), 77.

180. Mylod, "Latin Christian Pilgrimage," 59. On these and other treaties of the period, see Peter Malcolm Holt, *Early Mamluk Diplomacy, 1260-1290: Treaties of Baybars and Qalāwūn with Christian Rulers* (Leiden: Brill, 1995).
181. See Pierre Moukarzel, "The European Embassies to the Court of the Mamluk Sultans in Cairo," in *Mamluk Cairo: A Crossroads for Embassies*, eds. F. Bauden and M. Dekkiche (Leiden and Boston: Brill, 2019), 685–710. On the temporary truces, see Jonathan Riley-Smith, "Peace Never Established: the Case of the Kingdom of Jerusalem," *Transactions of the Royal Historical Society* 28 (1978): 100–102. On the fall of Acre in 1291, see Roger Crowley, *The Accursed Tower: The Fall of Acre and the End of the Crusades* (New Haven and London: Yale University Press, 2019).
182. Peter Jackson, *The Mongols and the Islamic World: From Conquest to Conversion* (New Haven and London: Yale University Press, 2017), 378.
183. Ora Limor, "Sharing Sacred Space: Holy Places in Jerusalem between Christianity, Judaism, and Islam," in *In Laudem Hierosolymitani*, 220–21.

Conclusion

1. Khalidi, "Future of Arab Jerusalem," 133.
2. There are too many examples to count, but for some major treatments see for example: Fred J. Kouri, *The Arab-Israeli Dilemma*, 3rd ed. (Syracuse: Syracuse University Press, 1985); Mark A. Tessler, *A History of the Israeli-Palestinian Conflict* (Bloomington: Indiana University Press, 1994); Menachem Klein, *Jerusalem: The Contested City* (New York: New York University Press, 2001); Kirsten E. Schulze, *The Arab-Israeli Conflict* (New York and London: Routledge, 2006); Avi Shlaim, *The Iron Wall: Israel and the Arab World* (London: Penguin, 2015); Ian J. Bickerton and Carla L. Klausner, *A History of the Arab-Israeli Conflict* (New York and London: Routledge, 2016); Alan Dowty, *Israel/Palestine* (Cambridge: Polity, 2017); George J. Mitchell, *A Path to Peace: A Brief History of Israeli-Palestinian Negotiations and a Way Forward in the Middle East* (New York: Simon and Schuster, 2017); and Neil Caplan, *The Israel-Palestine Conflict: Contested Histories* (Hoboken: Wiley-Blackwell, 2019). Michael Zank, *Jerusalem: A Brief History* (Hoboken: Wiley-Blackwell, 2018), is broader in coverage but lacks analysis. Charles Smith, *Palestine and the Arab-Israeli Conflict: A History with Documents* (New York: Bedford/St Martin's, 2020), dispenses with the pre-Ottoman years in its prologue. Much better is Alan G. Jamieson, *Faith and Sword: A Short History of Christian-Muslim Conflict*, 2nd ed. (London: Reaktion Books, 2016), which devotes nearly half of its chapters to pre-1500 history.
3. Karen Armstrong, *Jerusalem: One City, Three Faiths* (New York: Harper Perennial, 2005), x.
4. See the conclusion in Tannous, *Making of the Medieval Middle East*, 491–504.
5. These nuances are completely ignored in many histories. As just one example, any hint of tolerance under either the Fatimids or Christians is skated over in Sharif Amin Abu Shammalah, "Bayt al-Maqdis: A Short History from Ancient to Modern Times," in *Al-Quds: History, Religion, and Politics*, eds. A. al-Fattah El-Awaisim and M. Ataman (Istanbul: Turkuvaz Haberleşme, 2019), 43–70.
6. F.E. Peters, "The Holy Places," in *City of the Great King*, 59.
7. "Protection of Holy Places Law 5727 (1967)," *The Knesset*, https://www.knesset.gov.il/laws/special/eng/holyplaces.htm#:~:text=Protection%20of%20Holy%20Places%20Law%205727%20(1967)&text=The%20Holy%20Places%20shall%20be,with%20regard%20to%20those%20places; accessed November 14, 2021.
8. Michael Dumper, *The Politics of Sacred Space*, 20.
9. Marshall J. Breger and Leonard Hammer, "The Legal Regulation of Holy Sites," in *Holy Places in the Israeli-Palestinian Conflict: Confrontation and Co-existence*, eds. L. Hammer, M.J. Breger, and Y. Reiter (New York and London: Routledge, 2009), 30–32. Jewish sites such as the Western Wall were added in 1981.

10. A point missed in the "Historical Chronology" in former U.S. President Jimmy Carter's book, *Palestine: Peace, Not Apartheid* (New York: Simon & Schuster, 2006), 2, which only lists two medieval events: 1099 and 1187. On overemphasis on 1099 and its purported role as "the founding moment of a systematic ideological violence," see Philippe Buc, *Holy War, Martyrdom, and Terror: Christianity and Violence in the West* (Philadelphia: University of Pennsylvania Press, 2015), 8.
11. Dumper, *Politics of Sacred Space*, 44.
12. In the fall of 2021, an Israeli court ruled that "silent" Jewish prayers on the mount were not criminal, thus stoking fears of a slippery slope into full-blown Jewish devotions in the space. See Hanan Greenwood and Nadav Shragai, "In First, Court Backs 'Silent' Jewish Prayer on Temple Mount," *Israel Hayom* (October 7, 2021); and "Judge's Approval of Jewish Man's 'Quiet Prayer' on Temple Mount Stirs Arab Anger," *The Times of Israel* (October 8, 2021). That said, pressure remains for Jews not to even ascend the Temple Mount. Halakhah guidelines prohibit it for a variety of practical and spiritual reasons and local rabbis forbid entrance, lest the faithful err by treading upon the ground of the Holy of Holies; moreover, of course, not all Jews are messianic.
13. Suzanne Goldenberg, "Rioting as Sharon Visits Islam Holy Site," *The Guardian* (September 28, 2000).
14. Notwithstanding the fact that said Jews are routinely arrested as soon as their lips form the first prayerful phrase by members of the IDF, who are on hand to enforce the prohibitions.
15. See Lihi Ben Shitrit, *Women and the Holy City: The Struggle Over Jerusalem's Sacred Space* (Cambridge: Cambridge University Press, 2020), 122–3; Yitzhak Reiter, *Jerusalem and Its Role in Islamic Solidarity* (London: Palgrave Macmillan, 2008), 12–15; and the essays in A. Pedahzur and C. Jones, Eds., *Between Terrorism and Civil War: The Al-Aqsa Intifada* (London and New York: Routledge, 2013). President Tayyip Erdogan of Turkey, has vowed to free al-Aqsa from Israeli control; see Seth J. Frantzman, "Turkey Vows to 'Liberate Al-Aqsa' after Turning Hagia Sophia to Mosque," *Jerusalem Post* (August 12, 2020).
16. On the 1967 war, see Michael B. Oren, *Six Days of War: June 1967 and the Making of the Modern Middle East* (New York: Oxford University Press, 2002); Guy Laron, *The Six Day War: The Breaking of the Middle East* (New Haven and London: Yale University Press, 2017); and Jeremy Bowen, *Six Days: How the 1967 War Shaped the Middle East* (New York: St Martin's, 2013).
17. As quoted in Mordechai Bar-On, *Moshe Dayan: Israel's Controversial Hero* (New Haven and London: Yale University Press, 2012), 135.
18. Moshe Dayan, *Story of My Life* (New York: Morrow, 1976).
19. Stressing it as rather a modern tradition is Khalidi, "Future of Arab Jerusalem," 135–6; see also Gudrun Krämer, *A History of Palestine: From the Ottoman Conquest to the Founding of the State of Israel*, trans. G. Harman and G. Krämer (Princeton: Princeton University Press, 2011), 25. F.M. Loewenberg, a professor of social work, has tried to explain away all of these references but does not contend with the secondary literature on the subject and is not convincing; see "Is the Western Wall Judaism's Holiest Site?," *Middle East Quarterly* (Fall 2017), https://www.meforum.org/6898/is-the-western-wall-judaism-holiest-site, accessed November 15, 2021; for studies, see Ruth Goldschmidt-Lehmann, "The Western Wall: Selected Bibliography," *Cathedra* 12 (1979): 207–26.
20. That prayer predated Suleiman's *firman* by centuries seems unknown even to the editors of the Jewish Virtual Library: see "Sites and Places in Jerusalem: the Temple Mount," https://www.jewishvirtuallibrary.org/the-temple-mount; accessed November 11, 2021.
21. Cohen-Hattab and Bar, *The Western Wall*, 21; Hunt Janin, *Four Paths to Jerusalem: Jewish, Christian, Muslim, and Secular Pilgrimages, 1000 BCE to 2001 CE* (Jefferson: McFarland, 2015), 150; Nazmi al-Jubeh, "The Jews in Jerusalem and Hebron during the Ottoman

Era," in *A History of Jewish-Muslim Relations*, 213. On the broader relationship between the Ottoman sultans and Jews under their governance, see Salo Wittmayer Baron, *A Social and Religious History of the Jews: Late Middle Ages and Era of European Expansion, 1200-1650. Volume XVIII: the Ottoman Empire, Persia, Ethiopia, India, and China*, 2nd ed. (New York: Columbia University Press, 1983).

22. Dror Ze'evi, *An Ottoman Century: The District of Jerusalem in the 1600s* (Albany: SUNY Press, 2012), 23.
23. For a review of some recent Palestinian Authority announcements to this effect, see Donna Rachel Edmunds, "PA Tells Palestinians: the Western Wall Belongs only to Muslims," *Jerusalem Post* (January 22, 2020).
24. Shitrit, *Women and the Holy City*, 122. On the numerous issues involved with sharing the site, see Wendy Pullan et al., *The Struggle for Jerusalem's Holy Places* (New York and London: Routledge, 2013).
25. For numerous examples, see the introduction to Yitzhak Reiter and Dvir Dimant, *Islam, Jews and the Temple Mount: The Rock of Our/Their Existence* (New York: Routledge, 2020).
26. See "Item 25: Occupied Palestine," *United Nations: The Question of Palestine* (October 12, 2016), https://www.un.org/unispal/document/auto-insert-199847/; accessed November 18, 2021; and "Israel to Join US in Quitting Unesco," *BBC* (October 12, 2017), https://www.bbc.com/news/world-us-canada-41598991; accessed November 18, 2021.
27. Archaeologists continue to carry out myriad excavations in the city; for a recent summation see Kay Prag, *Re-Excavating Jerusalem: Archival Archaeology* (Oxford: Oxford University Press, 2019).
28. Examples include the Old Testament roots of Jewish claims to Jerusalem or the depth of spiritual connections between Judaism and the city; the British Mandate, the Balfour Agreement, territorial exchanges in the 1948–1949, 1967, and 1973 wars, Palestinian statehood, residential settlements in the West Bank, the First Intifada, the blockade of the Gaza Strip, accusations of Israel as "an apartheid state" and the corresponding BDS (Boycott, Divestment, Sanctions) movement in response, and so on. A useful summary of current Palestinian complaints against the State of Israel is Yehoshafat Harkabi, *Arab Attitudes to Israel* (New York and London: Routledge, 2017).

BIBLIOGRAPHY

Primary Sources

Abi 'Ubayd al-Qasim Ibn Sallam. *The Book of Revenue: Kitab al-Amwal.* Trans. I.A.K. Nyazee (Reading: Garnet, 2005).

"Admonitio in sequentem historiam belli sacri," in *Recueil des historiens des croisades occiden-taux* (Paris: Imprimerie nationale, 1864), III.

Agapios, *Kitāb al-'Unvan: Histoire universelle écrite par Agapius,* trans. A. Vasiliev, 2 vols. (Paris: Firmin Didot, 1909), II.1; English translation Agapius, *Universal History, Tertullian.org,* trans. R. Pearse, https://www.tertullian.org/fathers/agapius_history_02_part2.htm; accessed March 3, 2022.

Albert of Aachen, *Historia Ierosolimitana: History of the Journey to Jerusalem.* Ed. and trans. S.B. Edgington (Oxford: Oxford University Press, 2007).

Albert of Aachen's History of the Journey to Jerusalem, Volume 1. Trans. S.B. Edgington (Farnham: Ashgate, 2017).

Al-Muqtaqi bi-amr Allah. *The History of the Seljuq State: A Translation with Commentary of the Akhbār al-dawla al-saljūqiyya.* Trans. C.E. Bosworth (London and New York: Routledge, 2011).

Al-Qur'ān: A Contemporary Translation. Trans. Ahmed Ali (Princeton, 1993), 266.

"Annales Altahenses maiores: pars altera auctore monacho Altahensi a. 1033-1073." In *Monumenta Germaniae Historica.* Ed. G.H. Pertz. SS, vol. XX (Hannover, 1868), III.

The Annals of the Saljuq Turks: Selections from al-Kāmil fīl-Ta 'īkh of 'Izz al-Dīn ibn al-Athīr. Trans. D.S. Richards (London and New York: Routledge, 2002).

"'Antiochus Strategos' Account of the Sack of Jerusalem in A.D. 614," *English Historical Review* 25:99 (1910): 502–17.

Arab Historians of the Crusades. Trans. F. Gabrieli (Berkeley: University of California Press, 1969).

An Arab-Syrian Gentleman and Warrior in the Period of the Crusades: Memoirs of Usāmah ibn-Munqidh. Trans. P.K. Hitti (Reprint, New York: Columbia University Press, 1957).

The Armenian History Attributed to Sebeos. Trans R.W. Thompson (Liverpool: Liverpool University Press, 1999).

Assises de Jérusalem, tome II: assises de la cour des bourgeois (Paris: Académie Royal des Inscriptions et Belles-Lettres, 1843).

Ayyubids, Mamlukes and Crusaders: Selections From the Tārīkh al-Duwal wa 'l-Mulūk of Ibn al-Furāt. Trans. U. and M.C. Lyons, 2 vols. (Cambridge: Heffer, 1971).

Baldric of Bourgueil, *History of the Jerusalemites: A Translation of the Historia Ierosolimitana.* Trans. S.B. Edgington (Woodbridge: Boydell, 2020).

The Book of the Jihad of 'Ali ibn Tahir al-Sulami (d. 1106): Text, Translation and Commentary. Trans. N. Christie (Farnham: Ashgate, 2015).

Byzantium in the Time of Troubles: The Continuation of the Chronicle of John Skylitzes (1057-1079). Ed. and trans. E. McGeer and J.W. Nesbitt (Leiden and Boston: Brill, 2020).

"Cairo Genizah." *Cambridge Digital Library.* <https://cudl.lib.cam.ac.uk/collections/genizah/1>. (Accessed May 19, 2021).

The Chronicle of Ibn al-Athir for the Crusading Period, From al-Kamil fi'l-Ta 'rikh. Trans. D.S. Richards. 3 vols. (Farnham: Ashgate, 2005).

The Chronicle of John, Bishop of Nikiu, Translated from Zotenberg's Ethiopic Text. Trans. R.H. Charles (London and Oxford: Text and Translation Society, 1913).

The Chronicle of Michael the Great, Patriarch of the Syrians. Trans. R. Bedrosian (Long Branch, NJ: Sources of the Armenian Tradition, 2013).

The Chronicle of Theophanes: Anni Mundi 6095-6305 (A.D. 602-813). Ed. and trans. H. Turtledove (Philadelphia: University of Pennsylvania Press, 1982).

Chronicles of the Investiture Contest: Frutolf of Michelsberg and his Continuators. Trans. T.J.H. McCarthy (Manchester: Manchester University Press, 2014).

"Chronicon anonymum." In *Chronica minora, pars prior.* Ed. I. Guidi (Leipzig: Otto Harrassowitz, 1903).

Chronicon Pascale, 284-628 AD. Trans. M. Whitby and M. Whitby (Liverpool: Liverpool University Press, 1989).

Chronique d'Ernoul, et de Bernard le trésorier. Ed. M.L. de Mas Latrie (Paris: Libraire de la société de l'histoire de France, 1871).

La chronographie d'Élie Bar-Šinaya, métropolitain de Nisibe. Ed. L.J. Delaporte (Paris: H. Champion, 1910).

The Chronography of Gregory Abu 'l Faraj, the Son of Aaron, the Hebrew Physician, Commonly Known as Bar Hebraeus: Being the First Part of his Political History of the World. Trans. E.A.W. Budge. 2 vols. (London: Oxford University Press, 1932).

Competing Voices from the Crusades. Eds. A. Holt and J. Muldoon (Westport: Greenwood, 2008).

The Conquest of the Holy Land by Ṣalāḥ al-Dīn: A Critical Edition and Translation of the Anonymous Libellus de expugnatione terrae sanctae per Saladinum. Ed. and trans. K. Brewer and J.H. Kane (London and New York: Routledge, 2020).

The Conquest of Jerusalem and the Third Crusade: Sources in Translation. Trans. P. Edbury (Aldershot: Ashgate, 1998).

Constantine Porphyrogenitus. *De administrando imperio.* Ed. G. Moravcsik. Trans. R.J.H. Jenkins (Washington D.C.: Dumbarton Oaks Center for Byzantine Studies, 1967).

Contemporary Sources for the Fourth Crusade. Eds. A.J. Andrea and B.E. Whalen (Leiden and Boston: Brill, 2008).

The Conquest of Syria, Persia, and Egypt by the Saracens, Containing the Lives of Abubeker, Omar and Otham, the Immediate Successors of Mahomet. Trans. S. Ockley (London: R. Knaplock, 1708).

Crusade and Christendom: Annotated Documents in Translation from Innocent III to the Fall of Acre, 1187-1291. Eds. J. Bird, E. Peters, and J.M. Powell (Philadelphia: University of Pennsylvania Press, 2013).

Crusader Syria in the Thirteenth Century: The Rothelin Continuation of the History of William of Tyre with Part of the Eracles or Acre Text. Trans. J. Shirley (London and New York: Routledge, 2016).

The Damascus Chronicle of the Crusades, Extracted and Translated from the Chronicle of Ibn al-Qalansi. Trans. H.A.R. Gibb (Mineola, NY: Gibb, 2002).

The Deeds of Pope Innocent III, by an Anonymous Author. Trans. J.M. Powell (Washington D.C.: Catholic University of America Press, 2004).

Description of the Holy Land by John of Würzburg. Trans. A. Stewart (London: Palestine Pilgrims Text Society, 1890).

Description of Syria (Including Palestine) by Mukaddasi. Trans. Guy Le Strange (London: Palestine Pilgrims' Text Society, 1886).

The Divine Comedy of Dante Alighieri: Inferno. Trans. A. Mandelbaum (New York: Bantam Books, 1982).

"The Endowment Deed of the Khānqāh al-Ṣalāḥiyya in Jerusalem Founded by Saladin on 17 October 1189." Trans. J. Pahlitzsch. In *The Crusades: An Encyclopedia.* Ed. A. Murray. 4 vols. (Santa Barbara: ABC-CLIO, 2006), IV.1301–1305.

Eutychius. *Annals.* Trans. R. Pearse. <https://www.roger-pearse.com/weblog/eutychius-annals-my-posts-containing-the-translation/>. (Accessed January 14, 2021)

The Exempla, or Illustrative Stories from the Sermons Vulgares of Jacques de Vitry. Ed. T.F. Crane (London: David Nutt, 1890).

The First Crusade: The Chronicle of Fulcher of Chartres and Other Source Materials. Ed. E. Peters. 2nd ed. (Philadelphia: University of Pennsylvania Press, 1998).

The Fotooh Al-Sham, Being an Account of the Moslim Conquests in Syria, by Aboo Asma'ail Mohammad bin 'Abd Allah al-Azdi al-Bacri. Ed. E.W.N. Lees (Calcutta: Baptist Mission Press, 1854).

The Founder of Cairo: The Fatimid Imam-Caliph al-Mu'izz and His Era, an English Translation of the Text on al-Mu'izz from Idrīs 'Imād al-Dīn's 'Uyūn al-akhbār. Trans. S. Jiwa (London: I.B. Tauris, 2013).

George Akropolites. *The History: Introduction, Translation and Commentary.* Ed. R. Macrides (Oxford: Oxford University Press, 2007).

Gesta Francorum et Aliorum Hierosolimitanorum. Ed. and trans. R. Hill (London: Oxford University Press, 1962).

The Gesta Tancredi of Ralph of Caen: A History of the Normans on the First Crusade. Trans. B.S. Bachrach and D.S. Bachrach (Farnham: Ashgate, 2005).

Guibert of Nogent, *The Deeds of God Through the Franks.* Trans. R. Levine (Teddington: Echo, 2008).

Ha-Kohen, Solomon ben Joseph and Julius H. Greenstone. "The Turkoman Defeat at Cairo." *American Journal of Semitic Languages and Literatures* 22:2 (1906): 144–75.

"Historia regum Terre sanctae." In *Die Schriften des Kölner Domscholasters, Späteren Bischofs von Paderborn und Kardinal-Bischofs von S. Sabina Oliverus.* Ed. D. Hoogeweg (Tübingen: Litterarischer Verein, 1894), 83–158.

The Historia Vie Hierosolimitane of Gilo of Paris. Ed. and trans. C.W. Grocock and J.E. Siberry (Oxford: Oxford University Press, 1997).

"Histoire de Yahya-ibn-Sa'id d'Antioche, continuateur de Sa'id-ibn-Bitriq." In *Patrologia Orientalis.* Trans. I. Kratchkovsky and A. Vasiliev. Vol. 18 (Paris: Firmin-Didot, 1924).

"Histoire de Yahya-ibn-Sa'id d'Antioche, continuateur de Sa'id-ibn-Bitriq." In *Patrologius Orientalis.* Trans. I. Kratchkovsky and A. Vasiliev. Vol. 23 (Paris: Firmin-Didot, 1932).

Histoire Nestorienne inédite (Chronique de Séert), première partie. Trans. A. Scher (Paris: Fermin Didot, 1907).

History of al-Ṭabarī, Volume XII: The Battle of al-Qadisiyyah and the Conquest of Syria and Palestine. Trans. Y. Friedmann (Albany: State University of New York Press, 1991).

The History of al-Ṭabari, Volume V: The Sāsānids, the Byzantines, the Lakmids, and Yemen. Trans. C.E. Bosworth (Albany: State University of New York Press, 1999).

The History of Alexander the Great, Being the Syriac Version of the Pseudo-Callisthenes. Ed. and trans. E.A. Wallis Budge (Cambridge: Cambridge University Press, 1889).

A History of the Ayyubid Sultans of Egypt, Translated from the Arabic of al-Maqrīzī. Trans. R.J.C. Broadhurst (Boston: Twayne, 1980).

History of Churches and Monasteries of Egypt, and Some Neighbouring Countries, Attributed to Abû Salih, the Armenian. Ed. and trans. B.T.A. Evetts (Oxford: Clarendon, 1895).

History of Ghevond: The Eminent Vardapet of the Armenians (VIII Century). Trans. Z. Arzoumanian. 2nd ed. (Burbank: Western Diocese of the Armenian Church of North America, 2008).

The History of the Holy War: Ambroise's Estoire de la Guerre Sainte. Ed. and trans. M. Ailes and M. Barber. 2 vols. (Woodbridge: Boydell Press, 2003).

The History of Jerusalem by Jacques de Vitry. Trans. A. Stewart (London: Palestine Pilgrims' Text Society, 1896).

The History of Leo the Deacon: Byzantine Expansion in the Tenth Century. Eds. D. Sullivan and A-M. Talbot (Washington D.C.: Dumbarton Oaks Studies, 2005).

"History of the Patriarchs of the Coptic Church of Alexandria (S. Mark to Benjamin I)." Ed. and trans. B. Evetts. In *Patrologia Orientalis*, 49 vols. (Paris: Firmin-Didot, 1907), I–II.

Homilies: Sophronios of Jerusalem. Ed. and trans. J.M. Duffy (Washington D.C.: Dumbarton Oaks Medieval Library, 2020).

Ibn el-Athir, *Annales du Maghreb & de l'Espagne*. Ed. and trans. E. Fagnán (Algiers: A. Jourdan, 1898).

Ibn Khaldun, *The Muqaddimah: An Introduction to History, the Classic Islamic History of the World*. Trans. F. Rosenthal, ed. N.J. Dawood (Princeton and Oxford: Princeton University Press, 2005).

The Intolerant Middle Ages: A Reader. Ed. E. Smelyansky (Toronto: University of Toronto Press, 2020)

The Itinerary of Rabbi Benjamin of Tudela. Trans. and ed. A. Asher. 2 vols. (New York: Hakesheth, 1938).

Itti ʿāz al-ḥunafā bi-akhbār al-a ʾimmah al-Fāṭimīyīn al-khulafā. Ed. J. al-Dīn al-Shayyāl and M.H.M. Ahmad, 3 vols. (Cairo, 1996).

Jewish Travellers. Ed. E.A. Adler (London: Routledge, 1930).

John the Persian and Rabban bar ʿIdta, *The Histories of Rabban Hormizd the Persian and Rabban bar-ʿIdta*. Ed. and trans. E.A. Wallis Budge. 2 vols. (London: Luzac, 1902).

John Skylitzes, *A Synopsis of Byzantine History, 811-1057*. Trans. J. Wortlet (Cambridge: Cambridge University Press, 2010).

Kitâb futûḥ al-Buldân of al-Imâm abu-l ʿAbbâs Aḥmad ibn-Jâbir al-Balâhuri. Trans. P.K. Hitti (New York: Columbia University Press, 1916).

Letters of the Crusaders. Ed. and trans. D.C. Munro (Philadelphia: University of Pennsylvania, 1902).

Les livre de la Chasteté composé par Jésusdenah, évêque de Baçrah. Ed. J.B. Chabot (Rome: Ecole Française de Rome, 1896).

Matthew of Edessa's Chronicle. Trans. R. Bedrosian (Sophene, 2020).

Mourad, Suleiman A. and James E. Lindsay, *The Intensification and Reorientation of Sunni Jihad Ideology in the Crusader Period: Ibn ʿAsākir of Damascus (1105-1176) and His Age, with an Edition and Translation of Ibn ʿAsākir's* The Forty Hadiths for Inciting Jihad (Leiden and Boston: Brill, 2013).

Muhammad Ibn Saʿd, *Kitab at-Tabaqat al-Kabir, Volume III: The Companions of Badr*. Trans. A. Bewley (London: Ta-Ha, 2013).

Muhammad ibn Saʿd, *The Men of Medina (Volume 1)*. Trans. A. Bewley (London Ta-Ha, 1997).

A Muslim Principality in Crusader Times: The Early Artuqid State. Ed. and trans. C. Hillenbrand (Istanbul: Nederlands Historisch-Archaeologisch Institut, 1990).

Nāṣer-e Khosraw's Book of Travels (Safarnāma). Trans. W.M. Thackston (Albany: The Persian Heritage Foundation, 1986).

Nikephoros, *Short History*. Trans. C. Mango (Washington D.C.: Dumbarton Oaks Research Library and Collection, 1990).

Orations of the Fatimid Caliphs: Festival Sermons of the Ismaili Imams. Ed. and trans. P.E. Walker (London: I.B. Tauris, 2009).

Philip de Novare, *The Wars of Frederick II Against the Ibelins in Syria and Cyprus*. Trans. J.L. La Monte and M.J. Hubert (New York: Columbia University Press, 1936).

Pilgrimage to Jerusalem and the Holy Land. Ed. D. Pringle (Burlington: Ashgate, 2012).

Pilgrimage in the Middle Ages: A Reader. Ed. B.E. Whalen (Toronto: University of Toronto Press, 2011).

"Raimundi de Aguilers, canonici podiensis, historia Francorum qui ceperunt Iherusalem." In *Recueil des historiens des croisades: historiens occidentaux*. Vol. 3. (Paris: Imprimerie impériale, 1866).

The Rare and Excellent History of Saladin by Bahā' al- Dīn Ibn Shaddād. Trans. D.S. Richards (Farnham: Ashgate, 2002).

The Register of Pope Gregory VII, 1073-1085: An English Translation. Trans. H.E.J. Cowdrey (Oxford: Oxford University Press, 2002).

Robert the Monk's History of the First Crusade: Historia Iherosolimitana. Trans. C. Sweetenham (Aldershot: Ashgate, 2005).

Rodulfus Glaber. *The Five Books of the Histories and The Life of St. William*. Ed. N. Bust. Trans. J. France and P. Reynolds (Oxford: Oxford University Press, 1989).

Roger of Wendover's Flowers of History, Comprising the History of England From the Descent of the Saxons to A.D. 1235. Trans. J.A. Giles. 2 vols. (London: Henry G. Bohn, 1849).

Schwartz, Joseph. *A Descriptive Geography and Brief Historical Sketch of Palestine* (Philadelphia: A. Hart, 1850).

The Seventh Century in West-Syrian Chronicles. Trans. A. Palmer (Liverpool: Liverpool University Press, 1993).

The Taktika of Leo VI. Trans. G.T. Dennis (Washington D.C.: Dumbarton Oaks Texts, 2014).

Taxation in Islam. Ed. and trans. A. Ben Shemesh. 2 vols. (Leiden: Brill, 1958).

Theoderich's Description of the Holy Places (circa 1172 A.D.). Trans. A. Stewart (London: Palestine Pilgrims Text Society, 1891).

Theophilus of Edessa's Chronicle and the Circulation of Historical Knowledge in Late Antiquity and Early Islam. Trans. R.G. Hoyland (Liverpool: Liverpool University Press, 2011).

Three Byzantine Military Treatises. Trans. G.T. Dennis (Washington D.C.: Dumbarton Oaks Texts, 2008).

Towards a Shi'i Mediterranean Empire: Fatimid Egypt and the Founding of Cairo, the Reign of the Imam-Caliph al-Mu'izz from al-Maqīrī's Itti'āz al-ḥunafā. Trans. S. Jiwa (London: I.B. Tauris, 2009).

Trajectories in Near Eastern Apocalyptic: A Postrabbinic Jewish Apocalypse Reader. Ed. J.C. Reeves (Atlanta: Society of Biblical Literature, 2005).

Travels of Rabbi Petachia of Ratisbon. Trans. A. Benisch (London: Trubner, 1856).

United Nations. "Item 25: Occupied Palestine." *United Nations: The Question of Palestine* (October 12, 2016). <https://www.un.org/unispal/document/auto-insert-199847/> (accessed November 18, 2021).

William, Archbishop of Tyre, *A History of Deeds Done Beyond the Sea*. Trans. E.A. Babcock and A.C. Krey. 2 vols. (New York: Columbia University Press, 1943).

Secondary Sources

Abu-Izzeddin, Nejla M. *The Druzes: A New Study of their History, Faith and Society* (Leiden: Brill, 1993).

Abulafia, Anna Sapir. "The Conquest of Jerusalem: Joachim of Fiore and the Jews." In *The Experience of Crusading, Volume One: Western Approaches*. Eds. M. Bull and N. Housley (Cambridge: Cambridge University Press, 2003), 127–46.

Abulafia, David. *Frederick II: A Medieval Emperor* (London: Allen Lane, 1988).

Abu-Munshar, Maher Y. "Fāṭimids, Crusaders and the Fall of Islamic Jerusalem: Foes or Allies?" *Al-Masāq* 22:1 (2010): 45–56.

Abun-Nasr, Jamil M. *A History of the Maghrib in the Islamic Period* (Cambridge: Cambridge University Press, 1987).

Ahmad, M. Hilmy M. "Some Notes on Arabic Historiography During the Zengid and Ayyubid Periods (521/1127–648/1250)." In *Historians of the Middle East*. Ed. B. Lewis (London Oxford University Press, 1962), 77–97.

Ahrweiler, Hélène. "L'Asie Mineure et les invasions arabes (VIIe – IXe siècles)." *Revue Historique* 227 (1962): 1–32.

Al-Jubeh, Nazmi. "The Jews in Jerusalem and Hebron During the Ottoman Era." In *A History of Jewish-Muslim Relations from the Origins to the Present Day*. Eds. A. Meddeb and B. Stora (Princeton: Princeton University Press, 2013), 211–17.

Al-Tel, Othman Ismael. "Umar ibn al-Khattab's Visits to Bayt al-Maqdis: A Study on Its Reasons and Objectives." *Journal of Al-Tamaddun* 12:1 (2017): 79–91.

Amitai-Preiss, Reuven. "Ayn Jālūt Revisited," *Tārih* 2 (1992): 119–50.

Amitai-Preiss, Reuven. *Mongols and Mamluks: The Mamluk-Ilkhanid War, 1260-1281* (Cambridge: Cambridge University Press, 1995).

Andrea, A. (Ed.). *Encyclopedia of the Crusades*. (Westport: Greenwood Press, 2003).

Andrea, A. and A. Holt (Eds.). *Seven Myths of the Crusades* (Indianapolis: Hackett, 2015).

Andrews, Tara L. *Matt'ēos Urhayec'i and His Chronicle: History as Apocalypse in a Crossroads of Cultures* (Leiden and Boston: Brill, 2017).

Andrews, Tara L. "Matthew of Edessa (Matt'eos Urhayec'i)." In *Franks and Crusades in Medieval Eastern Christian Historiography*. Ed. A. Mallett (Turnhout: Brepols, 2020), 153–78.

Angold, Michael. "The Fall of Jerusalem (1187) as Viewed from Byzantium." *The Crusader World*. Ed. A. Boas (New York and London: Routledge, 2015), 289–308.

Argárate, Pablo. "Islam from an Eighth-Century Christian Perspective." *Orientalia Patristica: Papers of the International Patristic Symposium, April 23 – 27, 2018* (Drohbeta-Turnu-Severin: Didahia Severin, 2019), 57–84.

Armstrong, Karen. *Jerusalem: One City, Three Faiths* (New York: Harper Perennial, 2005).

Asbridge, Thomas. *The Crusades: The Authoritative History of the War for the Holy Land* (New York: HarperCollins, 2010).

Asbridge, Thomas. *The First Crusade: A New History* (London: Free Press, 2004).

Ashtor-Strauss, E. "Saladin and the Jews," *Hebrew Union College Annual* 27 (1956): 305–26.

Avni, Gideon. "The Persian Conquest of Jerusalem (614 c.e.) —An Archaeological Assessment." *Bulletin of the American Schools of Oriental Research* 357 (2010): 35–40.

Bacharach, Jere L. "African Military Slaves in the Medieval Middle East: the Cases of Iraq (869-955) and Egypt (868-1171)." *International Journal of Middle East Studies* 13:4 (1981): 471–95.

Bachrach, Bernard S. and David S. Bachrach, "Ralph of Caen as a Military Historian." In *Crusading and Warfare in the Middle Ages, Representations and Realities: Essays in Honour of John France*. Eds. S. John and N. Morton (Farnham: Ashgate, 2014), 87–99.

Bachrach, David S. *Religion and the Conduct of War, c. 300-c. 1215* (Woodbridge: Boydell, 2003).

Baldwin, John W. *The Government of Philip Augustus: Foundations of French Royal Power in the Middle Ages* (Berkeley: University of California Press, 1986).

Barber, Malcolm. *The Crusader States* (New Haven and London: Yale University Press, 2012).

Barber, Malcolm. "Supplying the Crusader States: The Role of the Templars," In *The Horns of Hattin: Proceedings of the Second Conference of the Society for the Study of the Crusades and the Latin East, Jerusalem and Haifa 2–6 July 1987*. Ed. B.Z. Kedar (Jerusalem and London: Society for the Study of the Crusades and the Latin East, 1992), 314–26.

Barber, Mathew. "Al-Afḍal B. Badr Al-Jamālī: The Vizierate and the Fatimid Response to the First Crusade: Masculinity in Historical Memory." In *Crusading and Masculinities*. Eds. N.R. Hodgson, K.J. Lewis, and M.M. Mesley (London and New York: Routledge, 2020), 53–71.

Bar-On, Mordechai. *Moshe Dayan: Israel's Controversial Hero* (New Haven and London: Yale University Press, 2012).

Baron, Salo Wittmayer. *A Social and Religious History of the Jews: Late Middle Ages and Era of European Expansion, 1200-1650. Volume XVIII: The Ottoman Empire, Persia, Ethiopia, India, and China*. 2nd ed. (New York: Columbia University Press, 1983).

Bartal, Renana. "Relics of Place: Stone Fragments of the Holy Sepulchre in Eleventh-Century France." *Journal of Medieval History* 44:4 (2018): 406–21.

Barthélemy, Dominique. *L'an mil et la paix de Dieu: La France chrétienne et féodale*, 980–1060 (Paris: Fayard, 1999).

Bartlett, W.B. *The Last Crusade: The Seventh Crusade and the Final Battle for the Holy Land* (Cheltenham: History Press, 2006).

Basan, Osman Aziz. *The Great Seljuqs: A History* (New York: Routledge, 2010).

Baynes, Norman H. "The Military Operations of Emperor Heraclius." *United Service Magazine* 46–47 (1913): 526–33 and 659–66.

Beihammer, Alexander Daniel. *Byzantium and the Emergence of Muslim-Turkish Anatolia, ca. 1040-1130* (London and New York: Routledge, 2017).

Ben-Ami, Aharon. *Social Change in a Hostile Environment: The Crusaders' Kingdom of Jerusalem* (Princeton: Princeton University Press, 1969).

Ben-Ami, Doron, Yana Tchekhanovets, and Gabriela Bijovsky. "New Archaeological and Numismatic Evidence for the Persian Destruction of Jerusalem in 614 CE." *Israel Exploration Journal* 60:2 (2010): 204–21.

Ben-Shalom, Ram. "The Messianic Journey of Jonathan ha-Kohen of Lunel to the Land of Israel Re-Examined." *Mediterranean Historical Review* 33:1 (2018): 1–25.

Bennett, Stephen. *Elite Participation in the Third Crusade* (Woodbridge: Boydell & Brewer, 2021).

Benson, R.L. and J. Fried, Eds., *Ernst Kantorowicz: Erträge der Doppeltagung Institute for Advanced Study, Princeton, Johann Wolfgang Goethe-Universität, Frankfurt* (Stuttgart: F. Steiner, 1997).

Berend, N. (Ed.), *Minority Influences in Medieval Society* (London and New York: Routledge, 2021).

Berger, Pamela. "Jewish-Muslim Veneration at Pilgrimage Places in the Holy Land." *Religion and the Arts* 15 (2011): 1–60.

Berkovich, Ilya. "The Battle of Forbie and the Second Frankish Kingdom of Jerusalem." *Journal of Military History* 75 (2011): 9–44.

Besant, Walter and Edward Henry Palmer. *Jerusalem: City of Herod and Saladin* (London: Chatto & Windus, 1908).

Beshir, B.J. "Fatimid Military Organization." Zeitschrift Geschichte und Kultur des Islamischen Orients 55 (1978): 37–49.

Bickerton, Ian J. and Carla L. Klausner. *A History of the Arab-Israeli Conflict* (New York and London: Routledge, 2016).

Biddle, Martin. *The Tomb of Christ* (Stroud: Sutton, 1999).

Bird, Jessalynn. "The *Historia Orientalis* of Jacques de Vitry: Visual and Written Commentaries as Evidence of a Text's Audience, Reception, and Utilization." *Essays in Medieval Studies* 20 (2003): 56–74.

Bird, Jessalynn. "James of Vitry's Sermons to Pilgrims." *Essays in Medieval Studies* 25 (2008): 81–113.

Bird, Jessalynn. "Review of Laurence W. Marvin and Mark Gregory Pegg." *Crusades* 9 (2010): 208–13.

Bishop, Adam. "Usāma ibn Munqidh and Crusader Law in the Twelfth Century." *Crusades* 12 (2013): 53–65.

Bliss, Frederick Jones and Archibald Campbell Dickie. *Excavations at Jerusalem, 1894-1897* (London: Committee of the Palestine Exploration Fund, 1898).

Blumenthal, Uta-Renate. *The Investiture Controversy: Church and Monarchy from the Ninth to the Twelfth Century* (Philadelphia: University of Pennsylvania Press, 1988).

Blyth, Estelle. *Jerusalem and the Crusades* (London: T.C. & E.C. Jack, 1913).

Boas, Adrian J. "The Acclimatization of the Frankish Population to Life in the Latin East: Some Examples from Daily Life." In *Cultural Transfers Between France and Latin Orient (xiie-xiiie centuries)*. Eds. M. Aurell, M. Galvez, and E. Ingrand-Varenne (Paris: Classiques Garnier, July 2021), 361–86.

Boas, Adrian J. *Crusader Archaeology: The Material Culture of the Latin East* (London and New York: Routledge, 2017).

Boas, Adrian J. (Ed.). *The Crusader World*. (New York and London: Routledge, 2015).

Boas, Adrian J. "Domestic Life in the Latin East." In *The Crusader World*. Ed. A. Boas (New York and London: Routledge, 2015), 544–67.

Boas, Adrian J. *Jerusalem in the Time of the Crusades* (London and New York: Routledge, 2001).

Boas, Adrian J. and R.G. Khamisy (Eds.). *Montfort: History, Research and Recent Studies of the Principal Fortress of the Teutonic Order in the Latin East*. (Leiden and Boston: Brill, 2017).

Boas, Adrian J. and Georg Philipp Melloni. "New Evidence for Identifying the Site of the Teutonic Compound in Acre." In *Acre and Its Falls: Studies in the History of a Crusader City*. Ed. J. France (Leiden and Boston: Brill, 2018), 69–89.

Bolinger, Andrew. "Baktash the Forgotten: the Battle of Tell Bashir (1108) and the Saljuq Civil Wars." *Journal of Medieval Military History* 17 (2019): 1–19.

Bombi, Barbara. "The Fifth Crusade and the Conversion of the Muslims." In *The Fifth Crusade in Context: The Crusading Movement in the Early Thirteenth Century*. Eds. G. Perry, T.W. Smith, and J. Vandeburie (New York: Routledge, 2016), 68–91.

Booth, Phil. "The Muslim Conquest of Egypt Reconsidered." *Travaux et mémoires* 17 (2013): 639–70.

Borchardt, Karl. "The Military-Religious Orders in the Crusader West." *The Crusader World*. Ed. A. Boas (New York and London: Routledge, 2015), 111–27.

Bosworth, C.E. "The City of Tarsus and the Arab-Byzantine Frontier in Early and Middle 'Abbāsid Times." *Oriens* 23 (1992): 268–86.

Bowen, Jeremy. *Six Days: How the 1967 War Shaped the Middle East* (New York: St Martin's, 2013).

Bowersock, G.W. "Polytheism and Monotheism in Arabia and the Three Palestines." *Dumbarton Oaks Papers* 51 (1997): 1–10.

Boyadjian, Tamar M. *The City Lament: Jerusalem Across the Medieval Mediterranean* (Ithaca and London: Cornell University Press, 2018).

Bradbury, Jim. *The Medieval Siege* (Woodbridge: Boydell & Brewer, 1992).

Bramoullé, David. *Les Fatimides et la mer (909-1171)* (Leiden and Boston: Brill, 2019).

Bramoullé, David. "The Fatimids and the Red Sea (969-1171)." In *Navigated Spaces, Connected Places*. Eds. D. Agius et al. BAR International Series (Oxford Archaeopress, 2012), 127–36.

Breger, Marshall J. and Leonard Hammer. "The Legal Regulation of Holy Sites." In *Holy Places in the Israeli-Palestinian Conflict: Confrontation and Co-existence*. Eds. L. Hammer, M.J. Breger, and Y. Reiter (New York and London: Routledge, 2009), 20–49.

Brett, Michael. "Fatimid Historiography: A Case Study–the Quarrel with the Zirgids, 1048-58." In *Medieval Historical Writing in the Christian and Islamic Worlds*. Ed. D.O. Morgan (London: School of Oriental and African Studies, 1982), 47–59.

Brett, Michael. *The Fatimid Empire* (Edinburgh: Edinburgh University Press, 2017).

Brock, Sebastian P. "Syriac Historical Writing: a Survey of the Main Sources." *Journal of the Iraq Academy, Syriac Corporation* 5 (1979): 1–30.

Brock, Sebastian P. "Syriac Sources for Seventh-Century History." *Byzantine and Modern Greek Studies* 2 (1976): 17–36.

Brooks, E.W. "The Arabs in Asia Minor (641–750), from Arabic Sources." *Journal of Hellenic Studies* 18 (1898): 182–208.

Brooks, E.W. "The Chronological Canon of James of Edessa." *Zeitschrift der Deutschen Morgenlädischen Gesellschaft* 53 (1899): 261–327; 54 (1900): 100–102.

Broshi, Magen. "The Inhabitants of Jerusalem." In *City of the Great King: Jerusalem From David to the Present*. Ed. N. Rosovsky (Cambridge, MA: Harvard University Press, 1996), 9–34.

Buc, Philippe. *Holy War, Martyrdom, and Terror: Christianity and Violence in the West* (Philadelphia: University of Pennsylvania Press, 2015).

Buck, Andrew D. *The Principality of Antioch and its Frontiers in the Twelfth Century* (Woodbridge: Boydell, 2017).

Bull, Marcus. *Knightly Piety and the Lay Response to the First Crusade: The Limousin and Gascony, c. 970-c. 1130* (Oxford: Oxford University Press, 1993).

Bull, Marcus. "The Roots of Lay Enthusiasm for the First Crusade." *History* 78:254 (1993): 353–72.

Bull, Marcus and Damien Kempf (Eds). *Writing the Early Crusades: Text, Transmission, and Memory.* (Woodbridge: Boydell, 2014).

Bulst-Thiele, Marie-Luis. "Zur Geschichte de Ritterorden und des Konigreichs Jerusalem im 13. Jahrhundert bis zue Schlacht bei La Forbie am 17 Oktober 1244." *Deutsches Achiv fur Erforschung des Mittelalters* 22 (1966): 197–226.

Bysted, Ane. *The Crusade Indulgence: Spiritual Rewards and the Theology of the Crusades, c. 1095-1216* (Leiden and Boston: Brill, 2015).

Cahen, Claude. "The Turkish Invasion: The Selchükids." In *A History of the Crusades, Volume 1: The First Hundred Years.* Eds. M.W. Baldwin and K.M. Setton (Madison: University of Wisconsin Press, 1958), 135–76.

Cahen, Claude and M. Cahen. "La première pénétration Turque en Asie-mineure (seconde soitié du xi e S)." *Byzantion* 18 (1946-1948), 5–67.

Callahan, Daniel F. "The Cross, the Jews, and the Destruction of the Church of the Holy Sepulchre in the Writings of Ademar of Chabannes." In *Christian Attitudes Toward the Jews in the Middle Ages.* Ed. M. Frassetto (New York and London: Routledge, 2007), 15–23.

Callahan, Daniel F. "Heresy and the Antichrist in the Writings of Ademar of Chabannes." In *Where Heaven and Earth Meet: Essays on Medieval Europe in Honor of Daniel F. Callahan.* Eds. M. Frassetto, M. Gabriele, and J.D. Hosler (Leiden and Boston, 2014), 178–226.

Callahan, Daniel F. *Jerusalem and the Cross in the Life and Writings of Ademar of Chabannes* (Leiden and Boston: Brill, 2016).

Cameron, Alan. *Circus Factions: Blues and Greens at Rome and Byzantium* (Oxford: Oxford University Press, 1976).

Cameron, Averil. "Blaming the Jews: the Seventh-Century Invasions of Palestine in Context." *Travaux et mémoires 14* (2002): 57–78.

Cameron, Averil. "Late Antique Apocalyptic: A Context for the Qurʾan?" In *Apocalypticism and Eschatology in Late Antiquity: Encounters in the Abrahamic Religions, 6th-8th Centuries.* Eds. H. Amirav, E. Grypeou, and G. Stroumsa (Leuven: Peeters, 2017), 1–19.

Canard, Marius. "Destruction de l'Église de la Résurrection." *Byzantion* 35 (1965): 16–43.

Canard, Marius. "Les sources arabes de l'histoire Byzantine aux confins des Xe et XIe siècles." *Revue des études byzantines* 19 (1961): 284–314.

Cantor, Norman F. *Inventing the Middle Ages: The Lives, Works, and Ideas of the Great Medievalists of the Twentieth Century* (New York: William Morrow, 1991).

Caplan, Neil. *The Israel-Palestine Conflict: Contested Histories* (Hoboken: Wiley-Blackwell, 2019).

Card, Claudia. "Rape as a Weapon of War." *Hypatia* 11:4 (1996): 5–18.

Carey, Brian Todd. *The Road to Manzikert: Byzantine and Islamic Warfare, 527-1071* (Barnsley: Pen & Sword, 2012).

Carpenter, David. *Henry III: The Rise to Power and Personal Rule, 1207-1258* (New Haven and London: Yale University Press, 2020).

Carter, Jimmy. *Palestine: Peace, Not Apartheid* (New York: Simon & Schuster, 2006).

Cassidy-Welch, Megan. *War and Memory at the Time of the Fifth Crusade* (University Park: Pennsylvania State University Press, 2019).

Chamberlain, Michael. "The Crusader Era and the Ayyūbid Dynasty." In *The Cambridge History of Egypt, Volume I: Islamic Egypt, 640-1517*. Ed. C.F. Petry (Cambridge: Cambridge University Press, 2008), 211–41.

Champagne, M.-T. and I.M. Resnick (Eds.). *Jews and Muslims Under the Fourth Lateran Council: Papers Commemorating the Octocentenary of the Fourth Lateran Council (2125)*. (Turnhout: Resnick, 2018).

Chareyon, Nicole. *Pilgrims to Jerusalem in the Middle Ages*. Trans. W.D. Wilson (New York: Columbia University Press, 2005).

Chazan, Robert. "1007-1012: Initial Crisis for Northern-European Jewry." *Proceedings of the American Academy for Jewish Research* 18–19 (1970–1971): 101–17.

Chazan, Robert. "Crusading in Christian-Jewish Polemics." In *The Medieval Crusade*. Ed. S.J. Ridyard (Woodbridge: Boydell Press, 2004), 33–52.

Chazan, Robert. *European Jewry and the First Crusade* (Berkeley: University of California Press, 1987).

Chevedden, Paul E. "Canon 2 of the Council of Clermont (1095) and the Goal of the Eastern Crusade: 'To Liberate Jerusalem' or 'To Liberate the Church of God?'" *Annuarium Historiae Conciliorum* 37:1 (2005): 57–108.

Chevedden, Paul E. "A Crusade from the First: the Norman Conquest of Islamic Sicily, 1060-1091." *Al-Masaq* 22 (2010): 191–225.

Chevedden, Paul E. "The Islamic Interpretation of the Crusades: a New (Old) Paradigm for Understanding the Crusades." *Der Islam* 83 (2006): 90–136.

Chevedden, Paul E. "The Islamic View and the Christian View of the Crusades: a New Synthesis." *History* 93:2 (2008): 181–200.

Chevedden, Paul E. "Pope Urban II and the Ideology of the Crusades." In *The Crusader World*. Ed. A.J. Boas (New York and London: Routledge, 2015), 17–53.

Chevedden, Paul E. "The View of the Crusades from Rome and Damascus: the Geo-Strategic and Historical Perspectives of Pope Urban II and ʿAlī ibn Ṭāhir al-Sulamī." *Oriens* 39:2 (2011): 257–329.

Christie, Niall. "An Illusion of Ignorance? The Muslims of the Middle East and the Franks Before the Crusades." In *The Crusader World*. Ed. A.J. Boas (New York and London: Routledge, 2015), 311–23.

Christie, Niall. "Motivating Listeners in the Kitab al-Jihad of ʿAli ibn Tahir al-Sulami," *Crusades* 6 (2007): 1–14.

Classen, C. and M. Sandidge (Eds.). *Friendship in the Middle Ages and Early Modern Age: Explorations of a Fundamental Ethical Discourse*. (Berlin: De Gruyter, 2010).

Claster, Jill N. *Sacred Violence: The European Crusades to the Middle East, 1095-1396* (Toronto: University of Toronto Press, 2009).

Claverie, Pierre-Vincent. "'Totius populi Christiani regotium': The Crusading Conception of Pope Honorius III, 1216-21." In *The Fifth Crusade in Context: The Crusading Movement in the Early Thirteenth Century*. Eds. G. Perry, T.W. Smith, and J. Vandeburie (New York: Routledge, 2016), 27–39.

Cline, Eric H. *Jerusalem Besieged: From Ancient Canaan to Modern Israel* (Ann Arbor: University of Michigan Press, 2005).

Cobb, Paul M. "Hunting Crusaders with Usama ibn Munqidh." *Crusades* 6 (2007): 59–68.

Cobb, Paul M. *The Race for Paradise: An Islamic History of the Crusades* (Oxford: Oxford University Press, 2014).

Cobb, Paul M. *Usama ibn Munqidh: Warrior-Poet of the Age of the Crusades* (Oxford: Oneworld, 2005).

Cohen, Mark R. "New Light on the Conflict over the Palestinian Gaonate, 1038-1042, and on Daniel b. 'Azarya: a Pair of Letters to the Nagid of Qayrawan." *AJS Review* 1 (1976): 1–39.

Cohen, Mark R. *Under Crescent and Cross: The Jews in the Middle Ages* (Princeton: Princeton University Press, 1994).

Cohen-Hattab, Kobi and Doron Bar. *The Western Wall: The Dispute over Israel's Holiest Jewish Site, 1967–2000* (Leiden and Boston: Brill, 2020).

Cole, Penny J. *The Preaching of the Crusades to the Holy Land, 1095-1270* (Cambridge, MA: Medieval Academy Books, 1991).

Constable, Giles. "Medieval Charters as a Source for the History of the Crusades." In *Crusaders and Crusading in the Twelfth Century*. Ed. G. Constable (Farnham: Ashgate, 2008), 93–116.

Constantelos, Demetrios J. "The Moslem Conquests of the Near East as Revealed in the Greek Sources of the Seventh and Eighth Centuries." *Byzantion* 42 (1972): 325–57.

Cook, David. *Understanding Jihad* (Berkeley: University of California Press, 2005).

Cortese, Delia and Simonetta Calderini. *Women and the Fatimids in the World of Islam* (Edinburgh: Edinburgh University Press, 2006).

Coüasnon, Charles. *The Church of the Holy Sepulchre in Jerusalem* (London: Oxford University Press, 1974).

Cowdrey, H.E.J. "Pope Gregory VII's 'Crusading Plans' of 1074." In *Outremer: Studies in the History of the Crusading Kingdom of Jerusalem Presented to Joshua Prawer*. Eds. B.Z. Kedar et al. (Jerusalem: Yad Izhak Ben-Zvi Institute, 1982), 27–40.

Cowdrey, H.E.J. "Pope Gregory VII and the Bearing of Arms." In *Montjoie: Studies in Crusade History in Honour of Hans Eberhard Mayer*. Eds. B.Z. Kedar, J. Riley-Smith, and R. Hiestand (Aldershot: Variorum, 1997), 21–36.

Cowdrey, H.E.J. *Pope Gregory VII, 1073-1085* (Oxford: Oxford University Press, 1998).

Crone, Patricia and Michael Cook. *Hagarism: The Making of the Islamic World* (Cambridge: Cambridge University Press, 1977).

Crowley, Roger. *The Accursed Tower: The Fall of Acre and the End of the Crusades* (New Haven and London: Yale University Press, 2019).

Cuffel, Alexandra. "Conversion and Religious Polemic Between Jews and Christians in Egypt from the Fatimid Through the Mamluk Periods." In *Minorities in Contact in the Medieval Mediterranean*. Eds. C.A. Vidal, J. Tearney-Pearce, and L. Yarbrough (Turnhout: Brepols, 2020), 71–103.

Cust, L.G.A. *The Status Quo in the Holy Places* (London: HMSO, 1929).

Dajani-Shakeel, Hadia. "Jihād in Twelfth-Century Arabic Poetry: a Moral and Religious Force to Counter the Crusades." *Muslim World* 66 (1976): 96–113.

Dayan, Moshe. *Story of My Life* (New York: Morrow, 1976).

De Lange, Nicholas. "Jews in the Age of Justinian." In *The Cambridge Companion to the Age of Justinian*. Ed. M. Maas (Cambridge: Cambridge University Press, 2005), 401–26.

Decter, Jonathan. *Dominion Built of Praise: Panegyric and Legitimacy Among the Jews in the Medieval Mediterranean* (Philadelphia: University of Pennsylvania Press, 2018).

Den Heijer, Johannes and Joachim Yeshaya. "Solomon ben Joseph ha-Kohen on Fāṭimid Victory: a Hebrew Ode to al-Mustanṣir Billāh and Badr al-Jamālī Reconsidered." *Al-Masaq* 25:2 (2013): 155–83.

Den Heijer, Johannes, Yaacov Lev, and Mark N. Swanson. "The Fatimid Empire and its Population." *Medieval Encounters* 21 (2015): 323–44.

Dennis, George T. "Defenders of the Christian People: Holy War in Byzantium." In *The Crusades from the Perspective of Byzantium and the Muslim World*. Eds. A.E. Laiou and R.P. Mottahedeh (Washington D.C.: Dumbarton Oaks Research Library and Collection, 2001), 31–9.

Déroche, Vincent. "Doctrina Jacobi Nuper Baptizati." *Travaux et mémoires* 11 (1991): 47–229.

Devreesse, Robert. "La fin inédite d'une lettre de saint Maxime: Un baptême forcé de juifs et samaritains à Carthage en 632." *Revue de sciences religieuses* 17.1 (1937): 34–5.

Di Segni, Leah, and Yoram Tsafrir. "The Ethnic Composition of Jerusalem's Population in the Byzantine Period (312-638 CE)," *Liber Annus* 62 (2012): 405–54.

Donner, Fred M. *The Early Islamic Conquests*. Rev. ed. (Princeton: Princeton University Press, 2014).

Douglas, David C. *William the Conqueror: The Norman Impact Upon England* (Berkeley: University of California Press, 1964).

Dowty, Alan. *Israel/Palestine* (Cambridge: Polity, 2017).

Drijvers, Jan Willem. "Heraclius and the *Restitutio crucis*." In *The Reign of Heraclius (610-641): Crisis and Confrontation*. Eds. G.J. Reinink and B.H. Stolte (Leuven: Peeters, 2002), 175–90.

Dumper, Michael. *The Politics of Sacred Space: The Old City of Jerusalem in the Middle East Conflict* (Boulder and London: Lynne Rienner, 2002).

Duri, Abdul Aziz. "Jerusalem in the Early Islamic Period, 7th-11th Centuries AD." In *Jerusalem in History*. Ed. K.J. Asali (Buckhurst Hill: Scorpion, 1989), 105–29.

Duri, Abd al-Aziz. *The Rise of Historical Writing Among the Arabs*. Ed. and trans. L.I. Conrad (Princeton: Princeton University Press, 2014).

Dussaud, René. *La pénétration des Arabes en Syrie avant l'Islam* (Paris: Geuthner, 1955).

Dźwigała, Bartłomiej. "Constantine, Helena and Heraclius in the Latin Kingdom of Jerusalem." *Journal of Ecclesiastical History* 72:1 (2020): 18–35.

Edbury, Peter W. *John of Ibelin and the Kingdom of Jerusalem* (Woodbridge: Boydell Press, 1997).

Edbury, Peter W. and Gordon Rowe, *William of Tyre: Historian of the Latin East* (Cambridge: Cambridge University Press, 1988).

Eddé, Anne-Marie. *Saladin*. Trans. J.M. Todd (Cambridge, MA: Harvard University Press, 2011).

Edgington, Susan B. "The Capture of Acre, 1104, and the Importance of Sea Power in the Conquest of the Littoral." In *Acre and Its Falls: Studies in the History of a Crusader City*. Ed. J. France (Leiden and Boston: Brill, 2018), 13–29.

Edgington, Susan B. "Espionage and Military Intelligence During the First Crusade, 1095-1099," In *Crusading and Warfare in the Middle Ages, Representations and Realities: Essays in Honour of John France*. Eds. S. John and N. Morton (Farnham: Ashgate, 2014), 75–85.

Edgington, Susan B. and H.J. Nicholson (Eds.). *Deeds Done Beyond the Sea: Essays on William of Tyre, Cyprus and the Military Orders Presented to Peter Edbury*. (New York: Routledge, 2016).

Edwards, Daniel. *Finance and the Crusades: England c. 1213-1337* (Abingdon: Routledge, 2022).

Ehrenkreutz, Andrew S. *Saladin* (Albany: State University of New York Press, 1972).

Ehrlich, Michael. "The Battle of Arsur: a short-lived victory." *Journal of Medieval Military History* 12 (2014), 109–18.

Ehrlich, Michael. "The Battle of Hattin: a Defeat Foretold?" *Journal of Medieval Military History* 5 (2007): 16–32.

El-Awaisi, Abd al-Fattah. "Umar's Assurance of Safety to the People of Aelia (Jerusalem): a Critical Analytical Study of the Historical Source." *Journal of Islamic Jerusalem Studies* 3:2 (2000), 47–89.

El-Azhari, Taef Kamal. *The Saljūqs of Syria During the Crusades, 463-549 A.H./1070-1154 A.D.* Trans. C.E. Bosworth (Berlin: Schwartz, 1997).

Elad, Amikam. *Medieval Jerusalem and Islamic Worship: Holy Places, Ceremonies, Pilgrimage* (Leiden and Boston: Brill, 1999).

Ellenblum, Ronnie. *The Collapse of the Eastern Mediterranean: Climate Change and the Decline of the East, 950-1072* (Cambridge: Cambridge University Press, 2012).

Ellenblum, Ronnie. *Frankish Rural Settlement in the Latin Kingdom of Jerusalem* (Cambridge: Cambridge University Press, 1998).

Esders, Stefan. "The Merovingians and Byzantium: Diplomatic, Military, and Religious Issues, 500-700." In *The Oxford Handbook of the Merovingian World*. Eds. B. Effros and I. Moreira (Oxford: Oxford University Press, 2020), 347–69.

Facey, William. "Crusaders on the Red Sea: Renaud de Châtillon's Raids of AD 1182-83." In *People of the Red Sea: Proceedings of Red Sea Project II Held in the British Museum October 2004*. Ed. J.C.M. Starkey (Oxford: Archaeopress, 2005), 87–98.

Famin, César. *Histoire de la rivalité et du protectorat des églises Chrétiennes en Orient* (Paris: Firmin Didot, 1853).

Ferrari, M.C. and K. Herbers (Eds.). *Europe 1215: Politics, Culture and Literature at the Time of the IV Lateran Council.* (Cologne: Böhlau, 2018).

Folda, Jaroslav. "Crusader Art in the Twelfth Century: Reflections on Christian Multiculturalism in the Levant." *Intercultural Contacts in the Mediterranean*. Ed. B. Arbel (London: Frank Cass, 1996), 80–91.

Folda, Jaroslav. "The South Transept Façade of the Church of the Holy Sepulchre in Jerusalem: An Aspect of 'Rebuilding Zion.'" In *The Crusades and Their Sources: Essays Presented to Bernard Hamilton*. Eds. J. France and W.G. Zajac (Aldershot: Ashgate, 1998), 239–57.

Forey, Alan. "Paid Troops in the Service of Military Orders during the Twelfth and Thirteenth Centuries." In *The Crusader World*. Ed. A. Boas (New York and London: Routledge, 2015), 84–97.

Fowden, Garth. *Before and After Muhammad: The First Millennium Refocused* (Princeton: Princeton University Press, 2013).

France, John. "The Anonymous *Gesta Francorum* and the *Historia Francorum qui ceperunt Iherusalem* of Raymond of Aguilers and the *Historia de Hierosolymitano itinere* of Peter Tudebode: An Analysis of the Textual Relationship Between Primary Sources for the First Crusade." In *The Crusades and Their Sources: Essays Presented to Bernard Hamilton*. Eds. J. France and W.G. Zajac (Aldershot: Ashgate, 1998), 39–69.

France, John. "The Battle of Bouvines, 27 July 1214." In *The Medieval Way of War: Studies in Honor of Bernard S. Bachrach*. Ed. G.I. Halfond (Farnham: Ashgate, 2015), 251–71.

France, John. *The Crusades and the Expansion of Catholic Christendom, 1000-1714* (London and New York: Routledge, 2005).

France, John. "Egypt, the Jazira and Jerusalem: Middle-Eastern Tensions and the Latin States in the Twelfth Century." In *Crusader Landscapes in the Medieval Levant: The Archaeology and History of the Latin East*. Eds. M. Sinibaldi et al. (Cardiff: University of Wales Press, 2016), 146–56.

France, John. "The Fall of Antioch During the First Crusade." In *Dei gesta per Francos: Etudes sur les croisades dédiées à Jean Richard*. Eds. M. Balard, B.Z. Kedar, and J. Riley-Smith (Aldershot: Ashgate, 2001), 113–20.

France, John. *Great Battles: Hattin* (Oxford: Oxford University Press, 2015).

France, John. "Rubenstein: Armies of Heaven." *The Medieval Review* (12.06.05). <https://scholarworks.iu.edu/journals-playground/index.php/tmr/article/view/17575/23693>. (Accessed June 30, 2021).

France, John. "The Text of the Account of the Capture of Jerusalem in the Ripoll Manuscript, Bibliothèque Nationale (Latin) 5132." *English Historical Review* 103:408 (1988): 640–57.

France, John. *Victory in the East: A Military History of the First Crusade* (Cambridge: Cambridge University Press, 1996).

Franke, Daniel P. "The Crusades and Medieval Anti-Judaism: Cause or Consequence?" In *Seven Myths of the Crusades*. Eds. A.J. Andrea and A. Holt (Indianapolis: Hackett, 2015), 48–69.

Franke, Daniel P. "Strategy, the Norman Conquest of Southern Italy, and the First Crusade." In *Warfare in the Norman Mediterranean*. Ed. G. Theotokis (Woodbridge: Boydell & Brewer, 2020), 211–24.

Frankopan, Peter. *The First Crusade: The Call from the East* (Cambridge: Harvard University Press, 2012).

Frankopan, Peter. *The Silk Roads: A New History of the World* (New York: Knopf, 2015).

Frassetto, Michael. *Christians and Muslims in the Middle Ages: From Muhammad to Dante* (Lanham: Lexington, 2020).

Frassetto, Michael (Ed.). *The Year 1000: Religious and Social Response to the Turning of the First Millennium*. (New York: Palgrave Macmillan, 2002).

Frenkel, Miriam. "Pilgrimage and Charity in the Geniza Society." In *Jews, Christians, and Muslims in Medieval and Early Modern Times: A Festschrift in Honor of Mark R. Cohen*. Eds. A.E. Franklin et al. (Leiden and Boston: Brill, 2014), 59–66.

Frenkel, Yehoshua. "Jews and Muslims in the Latin Kingdom of Jerusalem." In *A History of Jewish-Muslim Relations: From the Origins to the Present Day*. Eds. A. Meddeb and B. Stora (Princeton: Princeton University Press, 2013), 156–61.

Frenkel, Yehoshua. "Muslim Responses to the Frankish Dominion in the Near East, 1098-1291." In *The Crusades and the Near East: Cultural Histories*. Ed. C. Kostick (London and New York: Routledge, 2011), 27–54.

Frenkel, Yehoshua. "Political and Social Aspects of Endowments (*awqāf*): Saladin in Cairo (1169-73) and Jerusalem (1187-93)." *Bulletin of the School of Oriental and African Studies* 62: 1 (1999), 1–20.

Friedman, Yvonne. *Encounter Between Enemies: Captivity and Ransom in the Latin Kingdom of Jerusalem* (Leiden and Boston: Brill, 2002).

Friedman, Yvonne. "Learning the Religious Concepts of the Other: Muslim-Christian Treaties in the Latin East." In *Religion and Peace: Historical Aspects*. Ed. Y. Friedman (New York: Routledge, 2017), 67–83.

Friedman, Yvonne. "Peacemaking in an Age of War: When Were Cross-religious Alliances in the Latin East Considered Treason?" In *The Crusader World*. Ed. A.J. Boas (Abingdon: Routledge, 2016), 98–107.

Friedman, Yvonne. "The Templars as Peacemongers." In *Communicating the Middle Ages: Essays in Honour of Sophia Menache*. Eds. I. Shagrir, B.Z. Kedar, and M. Balard (London and New York: Routledge, 2018), 15–23.

Friedman, Yvonne. "Women in Captivity and Their Ransom During the Crusader Period." In *Cross Cultural Convergences in the Crusader Period: Essays Presented to Aryeh Grabois on his Sixty-Fifth Birthday*. Eds. M. Goodich, S. Menache, and S. Schein (New York: Peter Lang, 1995), 75–88.

Friendly, Alfred. *That Dreadful Day: The Battle of Manzikert, 1071* (London: Hutchinson, 1981).

Frizzell, Lawrence E. J. and Frank Henderson. "Jews and Judaism in the Medieval Latin Liturgy." In *The Liturgy of the Medieval Church*. Eds. T.J. Heffernan and E.A. Matter (Kalamazoo: Medieval Institute Publications, 2001), 187–214.

Fulton, Michael. *Artillery in the Era of the Crusades: Siege Warfare and the Development of Trebuchet Technology* (Leiden and Boston: Brill, 2018).

Gabriele, Matthew G. "Against the Enemies of Christ: The Role of Count Emicho in the Anti-Jewish Violence of the First Crusade." In *Christian Attitudes Toward the Jews in the Middle Ages*. Ed. M. Frassetto (New York and London: Routledge, 2007), 61–82.

Galadza, Daniel. *Liturgy and Byzantinization in Jerusalem* (Oxford: Oxford University Press, 2018).

Galor, Katharina. *Finding Jerusalem: Archaeology Between Science and Ideology* (Berkeley: University of California Press, 2017).

Galor, Katharina and Hanswulf Bloedhorn. *The Archaeology of Jerusalem: From the Origins to the Ottomans* (New Haven and London: Yale University Press, 2013).

Gaposchkin, M. Cecilia. *Invisible Weapons: Liturgy and the Making of Crusade Ideology* (Ithaca: Cornell University Press, 2017).

Gat, Shimon. "The Seljuks in Jerusalem." *Cathedra: For the History of Eretz* 101 (2001): 91–124 (in Hebrew). English translation in *Town and Material Culture in the Medieval Middle East.* Ed. Y. Lev (Leiden and Boston: Brill, 2002), 1–40.

Gervers, M. and J.M. Powell (Eds.). *Tolerance and Intolerance: Social Conflict in the Age of the Crusades.* (Syracuse: Syracuse University Press, 2001).

Ghazarian, Jacob G. *The Armenian Kingdom in Cilicia During the Crusades* (Richmond: Curzon, 2000).

Gibb, H.A.R. "The Aiyūbids," in *A History of the Crusades, Volume II: The Later Crusades, 1189-1311.* Eds. R.L. Wolff, H.W. Hazard, and K.M. Setton (Madison: University of Wisconsin Press, 1969), 693–714.

Gibb, H.A.R. *Studies on the Civilization of Islam*, eds. S.J. Shaw and W.R. Polk (Boston: Beacon Press, 1962).

Gil, Moshe. *A History of Palestine, 634-1099* (Cambridge: Cambridge University Press, 1997).

Gil, Moshe. "The Political History of Jerusalem During the Early Muslim Period." In *The History of Jerusalem: The Early Muslim Period, 638-1099.* Eds. J. Prawer and H. Ben-Shammai (New York: New York University Press, 1996), 1–37.

Gillingham, John. "Crusading Warfare, Chivalry, and the Enslavement of Women and Children." In *The Medieval Way of War: Studies in Medieval Military History in Honor of Bernard S. Bachrach.* Ed. G.I. Halfond (Farnham: Ashgate, 2015), 133–52.

Gillingham, John. *Richard I* (New Haven and London: Yale University Press, 1999).

Gillingham, John. "The Treatment of Male and Female Prisoners of War during the Third Crusade." In *Military Cultures and Martial Enterprises in the Middle Ages: Essays in Honour of Richard P. Abels.* Eds. J.D. Hosler and S. Isaac (Woodbridge: Boydell, 2019), 192–210.

Glidden, Harold W. "A Note on Early Arabian Military Organization." *Journal of the American Oriental Society* 56:1 (1936): 88–91.

Goitein, S.D. "Contemporary Letters on the Capture of Jerusalem by the Crusaders." *Journal of Jewish Studies* 3 (1952): 162–77.

Goitein, S.D. "Formal Friendship in the Medieval Near East." *Proceedings of the American Philosophical Society* 115:6 (1971): 484–9.

Goitein, S.D. "Geniza Sources for the Crusader Period: A Survey." In *Outremer: Studies in the History of the Crusading Kingdom of Jerusalem Presented to Joshua Prawer.* Eds. B.Z. Kedar et al. (Jerusalem: Yad Izhak Ben-Zvi Institute, 1982), 306–22.

Goitein, S.D. *A Mediterranean Society: The Jewish Communities of the Arab World as Portrayed in the Documents of the Cairo Genizah. An Abridgment in One Volume.* Ed. J. Lassner (Berkeley: University of California Press, 1999).

Goldschmidt-Lehmann, Ruth. "The Western Wall: Selected Bibliography." *Cathedra* 12 (1979): 207–26.

Goldstein, Miriam. *Karaite Exegesis in Medieval Jerusalem: The Judeo-Arabic Pentateuch Commentary of Yūsuf ibn Nūḥ and Abū al-Faraj Hārūn* (Tübingen: Mohr Siebeck, 2011).

Goldsworthy, Adrian. *The Punic Wars* (London: Cassells, 2000).

Gonen, Rivka. *Contested Holiness: Jewish, Muslim, and Christian Perspectives on the Temple Mount in Jerusalem* (Jersey City: KTAV, 2003).

Gordon, Matthew S. "Kindi, Al-, Philosopher." In *Medieval Islamic Civilization: An Encyclopedia*. Ed. J.W. Meri. 2 vols. (New York and London: Routledge, 2006), I.438.

Gottschall, Jonathan. "Explaining Wartime Rape." *Journal of Sex Research* 41:2 (2004): 129–36.

Grabar, Oleg. "Islamic Jerusalem or Jerusalem Under Islamic Rule." In *The City in the Islamic World*. Eds. S.K Jayyusi et al. (Leiden and Boston: Brill, 2008), I:317–27.

Grossman, Avraham. "Jerusalem in Jewish Apocalyptic Literature." In *The History of Jerusalem: The Early Muslim Period, 638-1099*. Eds. J. Prawer and H. Ben-Shammai (New York: New York University Press, 1996), 295–310.

Guilland, Rodolphe. "L'Expedition de Maslama contre Constantinople (717-718)." In *Études Byzantines* (Paris, 1959), 109–33.

Hagemann, Hannah-Lena and Peter Verkinderen, "Kharijism in the Umayyad Period." In *The Umayyad World*. Ed. A. Marsham (London and New York: Routledge, 2021), 489–517.

Haldon, John F. "Administrative Continuities and Structural Transformations in East Roman Military Organisation, c. 580-640." In *State, Army and Society in Byzantium: Approaches to Military, Social and Administrative History, 6th-12th Centuries* (Aldershot: Variorum, 1995), 1–20.

Haldon, John F. "Approaches to an Alternative Military History of the Period ca. 1025-1071." In *The Empire in Crisis? Byzantium in the Eleventh Century*. Institute for Byzantine Research International Symposium 11 (Athens, 2003), 45–74.

Haldon, John F. *Byzantium in the Seventh Century: The Transformation of a Culture* (Cambridge: Cambridge University Press, 1990).

Haldon, John F. "Eastern (Byzantine) Roman Views on Islam and Jihād, c. 900 CE: A Papal Connection?" In *Italy and Early Medieval Europe: Papers for Chris Wickham*. Eds. R. Balzaretti, J. Barrow, and P. Skinner (Oxford: Oxford University Press, 2018), 476–85.

Haldon, John F. "Information and War: Some Comments on Defensive Strategy and Information in the Middle Byzantine (*ca.* 660-1025)." In *War and Warfare in Late Antiquity*. Eds. A. Sarantis and N. Christie (Leiden and Boston: Brill, 2013), 373–93.

Haldon, John F. (Ed.). *Money, Power and Politics in Early Islamic Syria: A Review of Current Debates* (Farnham: Ashgate, 2010).

Haldon, John F. "Seventh-Century Continuities: The *Ajnād* and the 'Thematic Myth.'" In *The Byzantine and Early Islamic Near East, Volume III: States, Resources and Armies*. Ed. A. Cameron (Princeton: Darwin Press, 1995), 379–424.

Haldon, John. *Warfare, State and Society in the Byzantine World, 565-1204* (London: Routledge, 1999).

Haldon, John F. et al., "Marching Across Anatolia: Medieval Logistics and Modeling the Manzikert Campaign." *Dumbarton Oaks Papers* 65/66 (2011/12): 209–35.

Hamblin, William J. "Saladin and Muslim Military Theory." In *The Horns of Hattin: Proceedings of the Second Conference of the Society for the Study of the Crusades and the Latin East, Jerusalem and Haifa 2–6 July 1987*. Ed. B.Z. Kedar (Jerusalem and London: Society for the Study of the Crusades and the Latin East, 1992), 228–38.

Hamilton, Bernard. "Rebuilding Zion: the Holy Places of Jerusalem in the Twelfth Century." *Studies in Church History* 14 (1977): 105–16.

Handyside, Philip. *The Old French William of Tyre* (Leiden: Brill, 2015).

Harkabi, Yehoshafat. *Arab Attitudes to Israel* (New York and London: Routledge, 2017).

Harris, Jonathan. *Byzantium and the Crusades* (London: Hambledon and London, 2003).

Harvey, Elon. "Saladin Consoles Baldwin IV Over the Death of his Father." *Crusades* 15 (2016): 27–33.

Haverkamp, Eva. "What Did the Christians Know? Latin Reports on the Persecutions of Jews in 1096." *Crusades* 7 (2008): 59–86.

302

Hawari, Mahmoud K. *Ayyubid Jerusalem (1187-1250): An Architectural and Archaeological Study* (Oxford: Archaeopress, 2007).

Hawting, Gerald R. "Al-Afḍal, the Son of Saladin, and his Reputation." *Journal of the Royal Asiatic Society* 26:1–2 (2016): 19–32.

Hawting, Gerald R. *The First Dynasty of Islam: The Umayyad Caliphate, 661-750* (London: Croom Helm, 1986).

Head, T. and R. Landes (Eds.). *The Peace of God: Social Violence and Religious Response in France Around the Year 1000* (Ithaca: Cornell University Press, 1992).

Heidemann, Stefan. "Economic Growth and Currency in Ayyubid Palestine." In *Ayyubid Jerusalem: The Holy City in Context, 1187-1250*. Eds. R. Hillenbrand and S. Auld (London: Altajir Trust, 2009), 276–300.

Hennessey, Cecily. "The Theodore Psalter and the Rebuilding of the Holy Sepulchre, Jerusalem." *Electronic British Library Journal*, Article 4 (2017): 1–11.

Hernández, C.F. and J. Tolan (Eds.). *The Latin Qur'an, 1143-1500: Translation, Transition, Interpretation*. (Berlin and Boston: De Gruyter, 2021).

Hillenbrand, Carole. "Ayyubid Jerusalem: A Historical Introduction." In *Ayyubid Jerusalem: The Holy City in Context, 1187-1250*. Eds. R. Hillenbrand and S. Auld (London: Altajir Trust, 2009), 1–21.

Hillenbrand, Carole. *The Crusades: Islamic Perspectives* (Edinburgh: Edinburgh University Press, 2000).

Hillenbrand, Carole. "The Evolution of the Saladin Legend in the West." *Mélanges de l'Université Saint-Joseph* 58 (2005): 1–13.

Hillenbrand, Carole. "Saladin's Spin Doctors." *Transactions of the Royal Historical Society* 29 (2019): 65–77.

Hillenbrand, Carole. *Turkish Myth and Muslim Symbol: The Battle of Manzikert* (Edinburgh: Edinburgh University Press, 2007).

Hippos (Sussita) Excavations Project. https://www.dighippos.com/sussita/index.php/staff/2-eisenberg. Accessed November 8, 2021.

Hirschler, Konrad. "Ibn Wāṣil: An Ayyūbid Perspective on Frankish Lordships and Crusades." In *Medieval Muslim Historians and the Franks in the Levant*. Ed. A. Mallett (Leiden and Boston: Brill, 2014), 136–60.

Hirschler, Konrad. "The Jerusalem Conquest of 492/1099 in the Medieval Arabic Historiography of the Crusades: from Regional Plurality to Islamic Narrative." *Crusades* 13 (2014): 37–76.

Hirschler, Konrad. *Medieval Arabic Historiography: Authors as Actors* (New York: Routledge, 2006).

Hitti, Philip K. *History of the Arabs* (London: Palgrave Macmillan, 2002).

Hodgson, Natasha. "Conflict and Cohabitation: Marriage and Diplomacy Between Latins and Cilician Armenians, c. 1097-1253." In *Crusades and the Near East*. Ed. C. Kostick (New York: Routledge, 2010), 83–106.

Hodgson, Natasha. "The Role of Kerbogha's Mother in the *Gesta Francorum* and Selected Chronicles of the First Crusade." In *Gendering the Crusades*. Eds. S.B. Edgington and S. Lambert (Cardiff: University of Wales Press, 2001), 163–76.

Holland, Cecelia. *Antichrist: A Novel of the Emperor Frederick II* (New York: Atheneum, 1970).

Holt, A. (Ed). *The World of the Crusades: A Daily Life Encyclopedia* (Westport: Greenwood Press, 2019).

Holt, Peter Malcolm. *Early Mamluk Diplomacy, 1260-1290: Treaties of Baybars and Qalāwūn with Christian Rulers* (Leiden: Brill, 1995).

Horowitz, Elliott. "'The Vengeance of the Jews was Stronger than Their Avarice': Modern Historians and the Persian Conquest of Jerusalem in 614." *Jewish Social Studies* 4:2 (1998): 1–39.

Hosler, John D. "Countermeasures: The Destruction of Siege Equipment at Acre, 1189-1191." In *The Art of Siege Warfare and Military Architecture From the Classical World to the*

Middle Ages. Eds. M. Eisenberg and R. Khamisy (Oxford and Philadelphia: Oxbow Books, 2021), 165–73.

Hosler, John D. "Embedded Reporters: Ambroise, Richard de Templo, and Roger of Howden on the Third Crusade." In *Military Cultures and Martial Enterprises in the Middle Ages: Essays in Honour of Richard P. Abels*. Eds. J.D. Hosler and S. Isaac (Woodbridge: Boydell, 2020), 177–91.

Hosler, John D. *The Siege of Acre, 1189-1191: Saladin, Richard the Lionheart, and the Battle That Decided the Third Crusade* (London and New Haven: Yale University Press, 2018).

Hourani, Albert. *A History of the Arab Peoples* (Reprint, Cambridge, MA: Harvard University Press, 2002).

Housley, Norman. *Contesting the Crusades* (Malden, MA: Blackwell, 2006).

Housley, Norman. *Fighting for the Cross: Crusading to the Holy Land* (New Haven: Yale University Press, 2008).

Howard-Johnston, James. "Heraclius' Persian Campaigns and the Revival of the East Roman Empire, 622-630." *War in History* 6:1 (1999): 1–44.

Howard-Johnston, James. *Witnesses to a World Crisis: Historians and Histories of the Middle East in the Seventh Century* (Oxford: Oxford University Press, 2010).

Hoyland, Robert G. "Sebeos, the Jews, and the Rise of Islam." In *Medieval and Modern Perspectives on Muslim-Jewish Relations*, ed. R.L. Nettler (London and New York: Routledge, 1995), 89–102.

Hoyland, Robert G. *Seeing Islam as Others Saw It: A Survey and Evaluation of Christian, Jewish and Zoroastrian Writings on Early Islam* (Princeton: Darwin Press, 1997).

Hoyland, Robert G. *In God's Path: The Arab Conquests and the Creation of an Islamic Empire* (Oxford: Oxford University Press, 2015).

Humphreys, R. Stephen. *From Saladin to the Mongols: The Ayyubids of Damascus, 1193-1260* (Albany: State University of New York Press, 1977).

Hurbanič, Martin. *The Avar Siege of Constantinople in 626: History and Legend* (Cham: Springer, 2019).

Hyacinthe, Rafaël. *L'Ordre de Saint-Lazare de Jérusalem au Moyen Age* (Millau: Conservatoire Larzac Templier et Hospitalier, 2003).

Impact-se. "The 2020–21 Palestinian School Curriculum Grades 1–12: Selected Examples" (Ramat-Gan: Impact-se, 2021).

Isaac, Benjamin. "The Army in the Late Roman East: The Persian Wars and the Defence of the Byzantine Provinces." In *The Byzantine and Early Islamic Near East, Volume III: States, Resources and Armies*. Ed. A. Cameron (Princeton: Darwin Press, 1995), 125–56.

Jackson, Peter. *The Mongols and the Islamic World: From Conquest to Conversion* (New Haven and London: Yale University Press, 2017).

Jacobs, Martin. *Reorienting the East: Jewish Travelers to the Medieval Muslim World* (Philadelphia: University of Pennsylvania Press, 2014).

Jacoby, David. "Benjamin of Tudela and his 'Book of Travels.'" In *Venezia incrocio di culture: Percezioni di viaggiatori europei e non europei a confront: Atti del convegno Venezia, 26-27 gennaio 2006*. Eds. K. Herbers and F. Schmieder (Rome: Edizioni di storia e letteratura, 2008), 134–64.

Jacoby, David. "Evolving Routes of Western Pilgrimage to the Holy Land, Eleventh to Fifteenth Century: an Overview." In *Unterwegs im Namen der Religion II: Wege und Ziele in vergleichender Perspektive – das mittelalterliche Europa und Asien*. Eds. K. Herbers and H.C. Lehner (Stuttgart: Franz Steiner, 2017), 75–100.

Jamieson, Alan G. *Faith and Sword: a Short History of Christian-Muslim Conflict*. 2nd ed. (London Reaktion Books, 2016).

Jandora, John W. "The Battle of the Yarmūk: a Reconstruction." *Journal of Asian History* 19:1 (1985): 8–21.

Jandora, John W. "Developments in Islamic Warfare: the Early Conquests." *Studia Islamica* 64 (1986): 101–13.

Janin, Hunt. *Four Paths to Jerusalem: Jewish, Christian, Muslim, and Secular Pilgrimages, 1000 BCE to 2001 CE* (Jefferson: McFarland, 2015).

Janin, Hunt. *The Pursuit of Learning in the Islamic World, 610-2003* (Jefferson and London: McFarland, 2005).

Jankowiak, Marek. "The First Arab Siege of Constantinople." *Travaux et mémoires* 17 (2013): 237–320.

Jankowiak, M. and F. Montinaro (Eds), *Studies in Theophanes. Travaux et mémoires* 19 (2015).

Jarrah, Sabri. "From Monastic Cloisters to *Sahn*: The Transformation of the Open Space of the Masjid al-Aqsa under Saladin." In *Ayyubid Jerusalem: The Holy City in Context, 1187-1250.* Eds. R. Hillenbrand and S. Auld (London: Altajir Trust, 2009), 360–76.

Jarrar, Sabri. "Two Islamic Construction Plans for al-Haram al-Sharif." In *City of the Great King: Jerusalem from David to the Present.* Ed. N. Rosovsky (Cambridge, MA: Harvard University Press, 1996), 380–416.

Jaspert, Nikolas. "Eleventh-Century Pilgrimage From Catalonia to Jerusalem: New Sources on the Foundations of the First Crusade." *Crusades* 14 (2015): 1–49.

Jiwa, Shainool. "Historical Representations of a Fatimid Imam-caliph: Exploring al-Maqrizi's and Idris' Writings on al-Mu'izz Li Din Allah." *British Alifba: Studi Arabo-Islamici e Mediterranei*, 22 (2012): 57–70.

Jiwa, Shainool. "Governance and Pluralism Under the Fatimids (909-996 CE)." In *The Shi'i World: Pathways in Tradition and Modernity.* Eds. F. Daftary, A.B. Sajoo, and S. Jiwa (London: I.B. Tauris, 2015), 111–30.

John, Simon. *Godfrey of Bouillon: Duke of Lower Lotharingia, Ruler of Latin Jerusalem, c. 1060-1100* (New York and London: Yale University Press, 2017).

Johnson, Einar. "The Great German Pilgrimage of 1064-1065." In *The Crusades and Other Historical Essays: Presented to Dana C. Munro by His Former Students.* Ed. L.J. Paetow (Freeport, NY: Books for Libraries, 1928), 3–43.

Jones, Robert W. *Bloodied Banners: Martial Display on the Medieval Battlefield* (Woodbridge: Boydell & Brewer, 2010).

Jordan, William Chester. *Europe in the High Middle Ages* (New York: Penguin Putnam, 2003).

Jordan, William Chester. *Louis IX and the Challenge of the Crusade* (Princeton: Princeton University Press, 2016).

Jotischky, Andrew. "The Christians of Jerusalem, the Holy Sepulchre and the Origins of the First Crusade." *Crusades* 7 (2008): 35–57.

Jotischky, Andrew. *Crusading and the Crusader States* (Harlow: Longman, 2004).

Jotischky, Andrew. "Ethnographic Attitudes in the Crusader States: The Franks and the Indigenous Orthodox People." In *East and West in the Crusader States III: Context, Contacts, Confrontations.* Eds. K. Ciggaar and H. Teule (Leuven: Peeters, 2003), 1–19.

Judd, Steven C. "Medieval Explanations for the Fall of the Umayyads." In *Umayyad Legacies: Medieval Memories from Syria to Spain.* Eds. A. Borrut and P. Cobb (Leiden and Boston: Brill, 2010), 89–104.

Kaegi, Walter E. *Byzantium and the Early Islamic Conquests* (Cambridge: Cambridge University Press, 1995).

Kaegi, Walter E. "Confronting Islam: Emperors versus Caliphs (641-c. 850)." In *The Cambridge History of the Byzantine Empire, c. 500-1492.* Ed. J. Shepard (Cambridge: Cambridge University Press, 2008), 365–94.

Kaegi, Walter E. *Heraclius: Emperor of Byzantium* (Cambridge: Cambridge University Press, 2003).

Kaldellis, Anthony. "Did Ioannes I Tzimiskes Campaign in the East in 974?" *Byzantion* 84 (2014): 235–40.

Kantorowicz, Ernst. *Frederick the Second, 1194-1250* (New York: Richard R. Smith, 1931).

Kedar, Benjamin Z. "A Twelfth-Century Description of the Jerusalem Hospital." In *The Military Orders, Volume 2: Welfare and Warfare.* Ed. H. Nicholson (London and New York: Routledge, 1998), 3–26.

Kedar, Benjamin Z. "Convergences of Oriental Christians, Muslims and Frankish Worshippers: the Case of Saydnaya and the Knights Templar." In *The Crusades and the Military Orders: Expanding the Frontiers of Medieval Latin Christianity*. Eds. Z. Hunyadi and J. Laszlovsky (Budapest Dept. of Medieval Studies, Central European University, 2001), 89–100.

Kedar, Benjamin Z. *Crusade and Mission: European Approaches Towards the Muslims* (Princeton: Princeton University Press, 1984).

Kedar, Benjamin Z. "An Early Muslim Reaction to the First Crusade?" In *Crusading and Warfare in the Middle Ages, Representations and Realities: Essays in Honour of John France*. Eds. S. John and N. Morton (Farnham: Ashgate, 2014), 69–74.

Kedar, Benjamin Z. "The Eastern Christians in the Frankish Kingdom of Jerusalem: An Overview." In *Crusaders and Franks: Studies in the History of the Crusades and the Frankish Levant*. Ed. B.Z. Kedar (New York and London: Routledge, 2016), 143–53.

Kedar, Benjamin Z. "King Richard's Plan for the Battle of Arsūf/Arsur, 1191." In *The Medieval Way of War: Studies in Medieval Military History in Honor of Bernard S. Bachrach*. Ed. G.I. Halfond (Aldershot: Ashgate, 2015), 117–32.

Kedar, Benjamin Z. "The Jerusalem Massacre of July 1099 in the Western Historiography of the Crusades." *Crusades* 3 (2004): 15–76.

Kedar, Benjamin Z. "On the Origins of the Earliest Laws of Frankish Jerusalem: the Canons of the Council of Nablus, 1120." *Speculum* 74:2 (1999): 310–35.

Kedar, Benjamin Z. "Some New Sources on Palestinian Muslims Before and During the Crusades." In *Die Kreuzfahrerstaaten als multikulturelle Gesellschaft Einwanderer und Minderheiten im 12. und 13. Jahrhundert*. Ed. H.E. Mayer (Munich: R. Oldenbourg, 1997), 129–40.

Kedar, Benjamin Z. "The Subjected Muslims of the Frankish Levant." In *Muslims under Latin Rule, 1100-1300*. Ed. J.M. Powell (Princeton: Princeton University Press, 1990), 135–76.

Kedar, Benjamin Z., Shlomit Weksler-Bdolah, and Tawfiq Da'ādli, "The Madrasa Afḍaliyya/Maqām Al-shaykh 'īd: an Example of Ayyubid Architecture In Jerusalem." *Revue Biblique* 119:2 (2012): 271–87.

Kennedy, Hugh. *The Court of the Caliphs: The Rise and Fall of Islam's Greatest Dynasty* (London: Weidenfeld & Nicolson, 2004).

Kennedy, Hugh. *The Great Arab Conquests: How the Spread of Islam Changed the World We Live In* (Philadelphia: Da Capo Press, 2007).

Kennedy, Hugh. *The Prophet and the Age of the Caliphates: The Islamic Near East from the Seventh to the Eleventh Century*. 3rd ed. (London and New York: Routledge, 2016).

Kenyon, Kathleen M. *Digging Up Jerusalem* (New York: Praeger, 1974).

Khalidi, Rashid. "The Future of Arab Jerusalem." *British Journal of Middle Eastern Studies* 19:2 (1992): 133–43.

Khetia, Vinay. "The Night Journey and Ascension of Muhammad in *Tasfir* al-Tabari." *Al-Bayān* 10:1 (2012): 39–62.

Kistler, J.M. *War Elephants* (Lincoln: University of Nebraska Press, 2007).

Kjær, Lars. "Conquests, Family Traditions and the First Crusade." *Journal of Medieval History* 45:5 (2019): 553–79.

Klein, Menachem. *Jerusalem: The Contested City* (New York: New York University Press, 2001).

Klemm, Verena. *Memoirs of a Mission: The Ismaili Scholar, Statesman and Poet al-Mu'ayyad fi'l-Din al-Shīrāzī* (London and New York: I.B. Tauris, 2003).

Knesset. "Protection of Holy Places Law 5727 (1967)." <https://www.knesset.gov.il/laws/special/eng/holyplaces.htm#:~:text=Protection%20of%20Holy%20Places%20Law%205727%20(1967)&text=The%20Holy%20Places%20shall%20be,with%20regard%20to%20those%20places> (accessed November 14, 2021).

Köhler, Michael A. *Alliances and Treaties Between Frankish and Muslim Rulers in the Middle East: Cross-Cultural Diplomacy in the Period of the Crusades*. Trans. P.M. Holt. Ed. K. Hirschler (Leiden and Boston: Brill, 2013).

Kortüm, Hans-Henning. "Der Pilgerzug von 1064/65 ins Heilige Land. Eine Studie über Orientalismuskonstruktionen im 11. Jahrhundert." *Historische Zeitschrift* 277:3 (2003): 561–92.

Kostick, Conor. "Courage and Cowardice on the First Crusade, 1096-1099." *War in History* 20:1 (2013): 32–49.

Kostick, Conor. *The Siege of Jerusalem: Crusade Conquest in 1099* (London: Continuum, 2009).

Kostick, Conor. *The Social Structure of the First Crusade* (Leiden and Boston: Brill, 2008).

Kouri, Fred J. *The Arab-Israeli Dilemma*. 3rd ed. (Syracuse: Syracuse University Press, 1985).

Krämer, Gudrun. *A History of Palestine: From the Ottoman Conquest to the Founding of the State of Israel*. Trans. G. Harman and G. Krämer (Princeton: Princeton University Press, 2011).

Kraemer, Joel L. *Maimonides: The Life and World of One of Civilization's Greatest Minds* (New York: Doubleday, 2008).

Landes, R., A. Gow, and D.C. Van Meter (Eds.), *The Apocalyptic Year 1000: Religious Expectation and Social Change, 950-1050*. (Oxford: Oxford University Press, 2003).

Lapina, Elizabeth. *Warfare and the Miraculous in the Chronicles of the First Crusade* (University Park: Pennsylvania State University Press, 2015).

Laron, Guy. *The Six Day War: The Breaking of the Middle East* (New Haven and London: Yale University Press, 2017).

Lassner, Jacob. *Jews, Christians, and the Abode of Islam: Modern Scholarship, Medieval Realities* (Chicago and London: University of Chicago Press, 2012).

Lassner, Jacob. *Medieval Jerusalem: Forging an Islamic City in Spaces Sacred to Christians and Jews* (Ann Arbor: University of Michigan Press, 2017).

Latiff, Osman. *The Cutting Edge of the Poet's Sword: Muslim Poetic Responses to the Crusades* (Leiden and Boston: Brill, 2018).

Lecacque, Thomas. "Reading Raymond: The Bible of Le Puy, the Cathedral Library and the Literary Background of the *Liber* of Raymond of Aguilers." In *The Uses of the Bible in Crusader Sources*. Eds. E. Lapina and N. Morton (Leiden and Boston: Brill, 2017), 105–32.

Lerner, Robert E. "Frederick II, Alive, Aloft, and Allayed, in Franciscan-Joachite Eschatology." In *The Use and Abuse of Eschatology in the Middle Ages*. Eds. W. Verbeke, D. Verhelst, and A. Welkenhuysen (Leuven: Leuven University Press, 1988), 359–81.

Lev, Yaacov. "Army, Regime, and Society in Fatimid Egypt, 358-487/968-1094." *International Journal of Middle East Studies* 19:3 (1987): 337–65.

Lev, Yaacov. "Regime, Army and Society in Medieval Egypt, 9th-12th Centuries." In *War and Society in the Eastern Mediterranean, 7th–15th Centuries*. Ed. Y. Lev (Leiden: Brill, 1997), 115–52.

Lev, Yaacov. *Saladin in Egypt* (Leiden and Boston: Brill, 1999).

Levine, Amy-Jill. "Epilogue: Sites of Toleration." In *Tolerance, Intolerance, and Recognition in Early Christianity and Early Judaism*. Eds. O. Lehtipuu and M. Labahn (Amsterdam: Amsterdam University Press, 2021), 291–303.

Levy-Rubin, Milka. "Changes in the Settlement Pattern of Palestine Following the Arab Conquest." In *Shaping the Middle East: Jews, Christians, and Muslims in an Age of Transition, 400-800 C.E*. Eds. K.G. Holum and H. Lapin (Bethesda: University Press of Maryland, 2011), 155–72.

Levy-Rubin, Milka. "The Crusader Maps of Jerusalem." In *Knights of the Holy Land: The Crusader Kingdom of Jerusalem*. Ed. S. Rozenberg (Jerusalem: Israel Museum, 1999), 230–37.

Levy-Rubin, Milka. "New Evidence Relating to the Process of Islamization in Palestine in the Early Muslim Period–the Case of Samaria." *Journal of the Economic and Social History of the Orient* 43:3 (2000): 257–76.

Levy-Rubin, Milka. "The Reorganisation of the Patriarchate of Jerusalem During the Early Muslim Period." *ARAM Periodical* 15 (2003): 197–226.

Levy-Rubin, Milka. "Were the Jews Prohibited from Settling in Jerusalem? On the Authenticity of Al-Ṭabarī's Jerusalem Surrender Agreement." *Jerusalem Studies in Arabic and Islam* 36 (2009): 63–81.

Levy-Rubin, Milka. "Why Was the Dome of the Rock Built? A New Perspective on a Long-Discussed Question." *Bulletin of the School of Oriental and African Studies* 80:3 (2017): 441–64.

Lidov, Alex. "The Holy Fire and Visual Constructs of Jerusalem, East and West." In *Visual Constructs of Jerusalem*. Eds. B. Kühnel, G. Noga-Bannai, and H. Vorholt (Turnhout: Brepols, 2014), 241–52.

Limor, Ora. "Sharing Sacred Space: Holy Places in Jerusalem Between Christianity, Judaism, and Islam." *In Laudem Hierosolymitani: Studies in Crusades and Medieval Culture in Honour of Benjamin Z. Kedar*. Eds. I. Shagrir, R. Ellenblum, and J. Riley-Smith (Aldershot: Ashgate, 2007), 219–32.

Linder, Ammon. "'Like Purest Gold Resplendent': the Fiftieth Anniversary of the Liberation of Jerusalem." *Crusades* 8 (2009): 31–51.

Lippiatt, G.E.M. "Worse Than all the Infidels: The Albigensian Crusade and the Continuing Call of the East." In *Crusading Europe: Essays in Honour of Christopher Tyerman*. Eds. G.E.M. Lippiatt and J.L. Bird (Turnhout: Brepols, 2020), 119–46.

Lipton, Sara. *Images of Intolerance: The Representation of Jews and Judaism in the Bible moralisée* (Berkeley: University of California Press, 1999).

Loewenberg, F.M. "Is the Western Wall Judaism's Holiest Site?" *Middle East Quarterly* (Fall 2017). <https://www.meforum.org/6898/is-the-western-wall-judaism-holiest-site> (accessed November 15, 2021).

Loewenberg, Meir. "When Iran Ruled Jerusalem." *Segula: The Jewish History Magazine* (January 2013): 30–38.

Lotan, Shlomo. "The Battle of La Forbie (1244) and its Aftermath: Re-Examination of the Military Orders' Involvement in the Latin Kingdom of Jerusalem in the Mid-Thirteenth Century." *Ordines militares colloquia Tournensia historica: Yearbook for the Study of the Military Orders* 17 (2012), 53–68.

Louër, Laurence. *Sunnis and Shi'a: A Political History*. Trans. E. Rundell (Princeton: Princeton University Press, 2020).

Lower, Michael. *The Barons' Crusade: The Call to Arms and its Consequences* (Philadelphia: University of Pennsylvania Press, 2003).

Lower, Michael. *The Tunis Crusade of 1270: A Mediterranean History* (Oxford: Oxford University Press, 2018).

Luchitskaya, Svetlana. "Muslim Political World." In *The Crusader World*. Ed. A. Boas (New York and London: Routledge, 2015), 346–61.

Lynch, Ryan J. *Arab Conquests and Early Islamic Historiography: The Futuh al-Buldan of al-Baladhuri* (London: I.B. Tauris, 2020).

Lyons, Malcolm Cameron and D.E.P. Jackson. *Saladin: The Politics of the Holy War* (Cambridge: Cambridge University Press, 1982).

Maalouf, Amin. *The Crusades Through Arab Eyes* (New York: Schocken Books, 1984).

MacEvitt, Christopher. *The Crusades and the Christian World of the East: Rough Tolerance* (Philadelphia: University of Pennsylvania Press, 2008).

Mackintosh-Smith, Tim. *Arabs: A 3,000-Year History of Peoples, Tribes, and Empires* (New Haven and London: Yale University Press, 2019).

MacLeod, Jason. "Peace, Popular Empowerment and the First Crusade." *Journal of Medieval Military History* 18 (2020): 37–79.

Madden, Thomas F. "Food and the Fourth Crusade: A New Approach to the Divergence Question." In *Logistics of Warfare in the Age of the Crusades*. Ed. J.H. Pryor (Aldershot: Ashgate, 2006), 209–28.

Madden, Thomas F. (Ed.). *The Fourth Crusade: Event, Aftermath, and Perceptions. Papers from the Sixth Conference of the Society for the Study of the Crusades and the Latin East, Istanbul, Turkey, 25-29 August 2004*. (New York: Routledge, 2016).

Madden, Thomas F. *The New Concise History of the Crusades* (Lanham: Rowman & Littlefield, 2006).

Madden, Thomas F. "Rivers of Blood: an Analysis of One Aspect of the Crusader Conquest of Jerusalem in 1099." *Revista Chilena de Estudios Medievales* 1 (2012): 25–37.

Madelung, Wilferd. *The Succession to Muhammad: A Study of the Early Caliphate* (Cambridge: Cambridge University Press, 1997).

Magness, Jodi. "Archaeological Evidence for the Sasanid Invasion of Jerusalem." In *City of David Studies of Ancient Jerusalem, the Eleventh Annual Conference*, ed. E. Meiron (Jerusalem: Megalim, 2010), 40–61.

Magness, Jodi. "The Walls of Jerusalem in the Early Islamic Period." *The Biblical Archaeologist* 54:4 (1991): 208–17.

Maier, Christopher T. *Preaching the Crusades: Mendicant Friars and the Cross in the Thirteenth Century* (Cambridge: Cambridge University Press, 1998).

Mallett, Alex. *Popular Muslim Reactions to the Franks in the Levant, 1097-1291* (Farnham: Ashgate, 2014).

Mare, W. Harold. *The Archaeology of the Jerusalem Area* (Grand Rapids: Baker, 1987).

Markham, Paul. "The Battle of Manzikert: Military Disaster or Political Failure?" *deremilitari. org* (2005). <https://deremilitari.org/2013/09/the-battle-of-manzikert-military-disaster-or-political-failure/>. (Accessed June 4, 2021).

Markowski, Michael. "*Crucesignatus*: its Origins and Early Usage." *Journal of Medieval History* 10 (1984): 157–65.

Marmorstein, A. "Solomon ben Judah and Some of his Contemporaries." *Jewish Quarterly Review* 8:1 (1917): 1–29.

Marshall, Christopher. *Warfare in the Latin East, 1192-1291* (Cambridge: Cambridge University Press, 1994).

Marvin, Laurence W. "The Battle of Fariskur (29 August 1219) and the Fifth Crusade: Causes, Course, and Consequences." *Journal of Military History* 85:3 (2021): 597–618.

Marvin, Laurence W. *The Damietta Crusade, 1217-1221: A Military History* (in progress).

Marvin, Laurence W. "Medieval and Modern C²: Command and Control in the Field during Western Europe's Long Twelfth Century (1095-1225)." *War & Society* 35:3 (2016): 152–79.

Marvin, Laurence W. *The Occitan War: A Military and Political History of the Albigensian Crusade, 1209-1218* (Cambridge: Cambridge University Press, 2008).

Marx, Karl and Friedrich Engels. *Gesamtausgabe (MEGA), vierte Abteilung: Exzerpte, Notizen, Marginalien*. Ed. M. Neuhaus et al. (Amsterdam: International Institute of Social History, 2007).

Massironi, A. and A. Larson (Eds.). *The Fourth Lateran Council and the Development of Canon Law and the ius commune*. (Turnhout: Brepols, 2018).

Mastnak, Thomaž. *Crusading Peace: Christendom, the Muslim World, and Western Political Order* (Berkeley: University of California Press, 2002).

Matzke, Michael. *Daibert von Pisa: Zwischen Pisa, Papst und erstem Kreuzzug* (Sigmaringen: Thorbecke, 1998).

Mayer, Hans Eberhard. *The Crusades*. Trans. J. Gillingham. 2nd ed. (Oxford: Oxford University Press, 1990).

Mayer, Hans Eberhard. "King Fulk of Jerusalem as City Lord." In *The Experience of Crusading, Volume 2: Defining the Crusader Kingdom*. Eds. P. Edbury and J. Phillips (Cambridge: Cambridge University Press, 2003), 179–88.

Mayerson, Philip. "The First Muslim Attacks on Southern Palestine (A.D. 633-634)." *Transactions and Proceedings of the American Philological Association* 95 (1965): 155–99.

McCarthy, T.J.H. "Scriptural Allusion in the Crusading Accounts of Frutolf of Michelsberg and his Continuators." In *The Uses of the Bible in Crusader Sources*. Eds. E. Lapina and N. Morton (Leiden and Boston: Brill, 2017), 152–75.

McCormick, Michael. *Charlemagne's Survey of the Holy Land: Wealth, Personnel, and Buildings of a Mediterranean Church Between Antiquity and the Middle Ages* (Washington D.C.: Dumbarton Oaks Research Library & Collection, 2011).

Memiş, Şerife Eroğlu. "Between Ottomanization and Local Networks: Appointment Registers as Archival Sources for Waqf Studies. The Case of Jerusalem's Maghariba Neighborhood." In *Ordinary Jerusalem, 1840-1940: Opening New Archives, Revisiting a Global City*. Eds. A. Dalachanis and V. Lemire (Leiden and Boston: Brill, 2018), 75–99.

Menache, Sophia. "After Twenty-Five Years: Joshua Prawer's Contribution to the Study of the Crusades and the Latin Kingdom of Jerusalem Reconsidered." In *The Crusader World*. Ed. A. Boas (New York and London: Routledge, 2015), 675–87.

Meri, Josef (Yousef). "Critical Reflections on the Study of Muslim-Jewish Relations." In *The Routledge Handbook of Muslim-Jewish Relations*. Ed. J. Meri (New York and London: Routledge, 2016), 15–34.

Michaud, Jean. *Histoire des croisades*, 4 vols. (Paris, 1814).

Mikati, Rana. "Fighting for the Faith? Notes on Women and War in Early Islam." *Journal of Near Eastern Studies* 78:2 (2019): 201–13.

Mikhail, Maged S.A. *From Byzantine to Islamic Egypt: Religion, Identity and Politics After the Arab Conquest* (London and New York: Tauris, 2014).

Mikhail, Maged S.A. "Notes on the 'Ahl al-Dīwān': The Arab-Egyptian Army of the Seventh through the Ninth Centuries C.E." *Journal of the American Oriental Society* 128:2 (2008): 273–84.

Mitchell, George J. *A Path to Peace: A Brief History of Israeli-Palestinian Negotiations and a Way Forward in the Middle East* (New York: Simon and Schuster, 2017).

Mitchell, Piers. *Medicine in the Crusades: Warfare, Wounds and the Medieval Surgeon* (Cambridge: Cambridge University Press, 2004).

Monferrer Sala, Juan Pedro. "'And the Lord will raise a great emir in a land': Muslim Political Power Viewed by Coptic-Arabic Authors, a Case in the Arabic 'Apocalypse of Pseudo-Athanasius' II." In *Minorities in Contact in the Medieval Mediterranean*. Eds. C.A. Vidal, J. Tearney-Pearce, and L. Yarbrough (Turnhout: Brepols, 2020), 191–210.

Moore, John Clare. *Pope Innocent III (1160/61-1216): To Root Up and to Plant* (Leiden: Brill, 2003).

Moore, R.I. *Formation of a Persecuting Society: Authority and Deviance in Western Europe, 950-1250*. 2nd ed. (Oxford: Blackwell, 2007).

Mor, Menahem. *The Second Jewish Revolt: The Bar Kokhba War, 132-136 CE* (Leiden and Boston: Brill, 2016).

Morillo, Stephen. "Battle Seeking: the Contexts and Limits of Vegetian Strategy." *Journal of Medieval Military History* 1 (2002): 21–42.

Morris, Colin. *The Sepulchre of Christ and the Medieval West: From the Beginning to 1600* (Oxford: Oxford University Press, 2005).

Morton, Nicholas. *The Crusader States and Their Neighbours: A Military History, 1099-1187* (Oxford: Oxford University Press, 2020).

Morton, Nicholas. *Encountering Islam on the First Crusade* (Cambridge: Cambridge University Press, 2016).

Morton, Nicholas. *The Field of Blood: The Battle for Aleppo and the Remaking of the Medieval Middle East* (New York: Basic Books, 2018).

Morton, Nicholas. "Templar and Hospitaller Attitudes Towards Islam in the Holy Land during the 12th and 13th Centuries: Some Historiographical Reflections." *Levant* 47:3 (2015): 316–27.

Moukarzel, Pierre. "The European Embassies to the Court of the Mamluk Sultans in Cairo." In *Mamluk Cairo: A Crossroads for Embassies*. Eds. F. Bauden and M. Dekkiche (Leiden and Boston: Brill, 2019), 685–710.

Mourad, Suleiman A. "A Critique of the Scholarly Outlook of the Crusades: The Case for Tolerance and Coexistence." In *Syria in Crusader Times: Conflict and Co-Existence*. Ed. C. Hillenbrand (Edinburgh: Edinburgh University Press, 2020), 144–60.

Mourad, Suleiman A. "On Early Islamic Historiography: Abū Ismāʿīl Al-Azdī and his Futūḥ Al-Shām." *Journal of the American Oriental Society* 120:4 (2000): 577–93.

Mourad, Suleiman A. "The Symbolism of Jerusalem in Early Islam." In *Jerusalem: Idea and Reality*. Ed. T. Mayer and S.A. Mourad (Abingdon: Routledge, 2008), 86–102.

Murray, Alan V. *Baldwin of Bourcq: Count of Edessa and King of Jerusalem (1100-1131)* (New York: Routledge, 2021).

Murray, Alan V. (Ed.). *The Crusades: An Encyclopedia*, 4 vols. (Santa Barbara: ABC-CLIO, 2006).

Murray, Alan V. "The Demographics of Urban Space in Crusade-Period Jerusalem (1099-1187)." In *Urban Space in the Middle Ages and the Early Modern Age*. Ed. A. Classen (Berlin: de Gruyter, 2009), 205–24.

Murray, Alan V. "Franks and Indigenous Communities in Palestine and Syria (1099-1187): A Hierarchical Model of Social Interaction in the Principalities of Outremer." In *East Meets West in the Middle Ages and Early Modern Times: Transcultural Experiences in the Premodern World*. Ed. A. Classen (Berlin: De Gruyter, 2013), 291–310.

Murray, Alan V. "The Origin of Money-Fiefs in the Latin Kingdom of Jerusalem." In *Mercenaries and Paid Men: The Mercenary Identity in the Middle Ages*. Ed. J. France (Leiden and Boston: Brill, 2008), 275–86.

Murray, Alan V. "The Place of Egypt in the Military Strategy of the Crusades, 1099-1221." In *The Fifth Crusade in Context: The Crusading Movement in the Early Thirteenth Century*. Eds. G. Perry, T.W. Smith, and J. Vandeburie (New York: Routledge, 2016), 117–34.

Murray, Alan V. "A Race Against Time–A Fight to the Death: Combatants and Civilians in the Siege and Capture of Jerusalem, 1099." In *Civilians Under Siege From Sarajevo to Troy*. Eds. A. Dowdall and J. Horne (New York: Palgrave Macmillan, 2018), 163–84.

Murray, Alan V. "The Siege of Jerusalem in Narrative Sources." In *Jerusalem the Golden: The Origins and Impact of the First Crusade*. Eds. S.B. Edgington and L. García-Guijarro (Turnhout: Brepols, 2014), 191–215.

Murrell, William S. "Interpreters in Franco-Muslim Negotiations." *Crusades* 20 (2021): 131–50.

Mylod, Elizabeth J. "Pilgrimage, the Holy Land and the Fifth Crusade." In *The Fifth Crusade in Context: The Crusading Movement in the Early Thirteenth Century*. Eds. G. Perry, T.W. Smith, and J. Vandeburie (New York: Routledge, 2016), 146–59.

Nader, Marwan. *Burgesses and Burgess Law in the Latin Kingdoms of Jerusalem and Cyprus (1099-1325)* (Aldershot: Ashgate, 2006).

Nees, Lawrence. "Insular Latin Sources, 'Arculf,' and Early Islamic Jerusalem." In *Where Heaven and Earth Meet: Essays on Medieval Europe in Honor of Daniel F. Callahan*. Eds. M. Frassetto, M. Gabriele, and J.D. Hosler (Leiden and Boston: Brill, 2014), 79–100.

Neocleous, Savvas. "The Byzantines and Saladin: Opponents of the Third Crusade?" *Crusades* 9 (2010): 87–106.

Nicholson, Helen. *The Crusades* (Indianapolis: Hackett, 2009).

Nicholson, Helen. *The Knights Hospitaller* (Woodbridge: Boydell Press, 2001).

Nicolle, David. *Crusader Warfare, Volume I: Byzantium, Europe and the Struggle for the Holy Land 1050-1300 AD* (London: Bloomsbury, 2007).

Nicolle, David. *Manzikert 1071: The Breaking of Byzantium* (Oxford: Osprey, 2013).

Niewiński, Andrzej. "*Inter arma enim silent leges* (In Times of War, the Laws Fall Silent): Violence in Medieval Warfare." *Teka Komisji Historycznej* 1:16 (2019): 9–31.

Noble, Samuel and Constantine A. Panchenko, *Orthodoxy and Islam in the Middle East: The Seventh to the Sixteenth Centuries* (Jordanville, NY: Holy Trinity Publications, 2021).

Oettinger, Ayelet. "Making the Myth Real: the Genre of Hebrew Itineraries to the Holy Land in the 12th-13th Century." *Folklore* 36 (2007): 41–66.

Olsen, Glenn W. "The Middle Ages in the History of Toleration: a Prolegomena." *Mediterranean Studies* 16 (2007): 1–20.

Omar, Abdallah Ma'rouf. *Jerusalem in Muhammad's Strategy: The Role of the Prophet Muhammad in the Conquest of Jerusalem* (Newcastle-upon-Tyne: Cambridge Scholars Publishing, 2019).

Omran, Mahmoud Said. "King Amalric and the Siege of Alexandria, 1167." In *Crusade and Settlement: Papers Read at the First Conference of the Society for the Study of the Crusades and the Latin East and Presented to R.C. Smail.* Ed. P.W. Edbury (Cardiff: University College Cardiff Press, 1985), 191–6.

Oren, Michael B. *Six Days of War: June 1967 and the Making of the Modern Middle East* (New York: Oxford University Press, 2002).

Ousterhout, Robert. "Rebuilding the Temple: Constantine Monomachus and the Holy Sepulchre." *Journal of the Society of Architectural Historians* 48:1 (1989): 66–78.

Pahlitzsch, Johannes. *Graeci und Suriani im Palästina der Kreuzfahrerzeit: Beiträge und Quellen zur Geschichte des griechisch-orthodoxen Patriarchats von Jerusalem* (Berlin Duncker & Humblot, 2001).

Pahlitzsch, Johannes. "The People of the Book." In *Ayyubid Jerusalem: The Holy City in Context, 1187-1250.* Eds. R. Hillenbrand and S. Auld (London: Altajir Trust, 2009), 435–40.

Papastathis, Charalambos K. "A New Status for Jerusalem? An Eastern Orthodox Viewpoint." *Catholic University Law Review* 45:3 (1996): 723–31.

Parker, K.S. "The Indigenous Christians of the Ayyūbid Sultanate at the Time of the Fifth Crusade." In *The Fifth Crusade in Context: The Crusading Movement in the Early Thirteenth Century.* Eds. G. Perry, T.W. Smith, and J. Vandeburie (New York: Routledge, 2016), 135–45.

Parsons, Simon Thomas. "The Letters of Stephen of Blois Reconsidered." *Crusades* 17 (2019): 1–30.

Peacock, A.C.S. *The Great Seljuk Empire* (Edinburgh: Edinburgh University Press, 2015).

Pedahzur, A. and C. Jones (Eds.). *Between Terrorism and Civil War: The Al-Aqsa Intifada* (London and New York: Routledge, 2013).

Pegg, Mark Gregory. *A Most Holy War: The Albigensian Crusade and the Battle for Christendom* (Oxford and New York: Oxford University Press, 2007).

Penn, Michael Philip. *Envisioning Islam: Syriac Christians and the Early Muslim World* (Philadelphia: University of Pennsylvania Press, 2015).

Perry, Guy. "From King John of Jerusalem to the Emperor-Elect Frederick II: A Neglected Letter from the Fifth Crusade." In *The Fifth Crusade in Context: The Crusading Movement in the Early Thirteenth Century.* Eds. G. Perry, T.W. Smith, and J. Vandeburie (New York: Perry, 2016), 40–49.

Perry, Guy. *John of Brienne: King of Jerusalem, Emperor of Constantinople, c.1175-1237* (Cambridge: Cambridge University Press, 2013).

Peters, F.E. "The Holy Places." In *City of the Great King: Jerusalem from David to the Present.* Ed. N. Rosovsky (Cambridge, MA: Harvard University Press, 1996), 37–59.

Petersen, A. and D. Pringle (Eds.). *Ramla: City in Muslim Palestine, 715-1917.* (Oxford: Archaeopress, 2021).

Petersen, Leif Inge Ree. *Siege Warfare and Military Organization in the Successor States (400-800 AD): Byzantium, the West, and Islam* (Leiden and Boston: Brill, 2013).

Phillips, Jonathan. *The Crusades, 1095-1204.* 2nd ed. (New York and London: Routledge, 2014).

Phillips, Jonathan. (Ed.). *The First Crusade: Origins and Impacts.* (Manchester: Manchester University Press, 1997).

Phillips, Jonathan. *The Fourth Crusade and the Sack of Constantinople* (London: Pimlico, 2005).

Phillips, Jonathan. *Holy Warriors: A Modern History of the Crusades* (New York: Random House, 2009).

Phillips, Jonathan. *The Life and Legend of the Sultan Saladin* (New Haven and London: Yale University Press, 2019).

Phillips, Jonathan. *The Second Crusade: Extending the Frontiers of Christendom* (New Haven and London: Yale University Press, 2007).

Phillips, Jonathan. "The Travels of Ibn Jubayr and his View of Saladin." In *Cultural Encounters During the Crusades*. Eds. K.V. Jensen, K. Salonen, and H. Vogt (Odense: University Press of Southern Denmark, 2013), 75–90.

Phillips, Matthew C. "The Typology of the Cross and Crusade Preaching." In *Crusading in Art, Thought and Will*. Eds. M.E. Parker, B. Halliburton, and A. Romine (Leiden and Boston: Brill, 2019), 166–85.

Pipes, Daniel. *Slave Soldiers and Islam: The Genesis of a Military System* (New Haven and London: Yale University Press, 1981).

Polejowski, Karol. "The Teutonic Order During the Fifth Crusade and Their Rise in Western Europe: The French Case Study (1218-58)." In *The Fifth Crusade in Context: The Crusading Movement in the Early Thirteenth Century*. Eds. G. Perry, T.W. Smith, and J. Vandeburie (New York: Routledge, 2016), 195–204.

Polliack, Meira. "The Karaites." In *Jerusalem 1000-1400: Every People Under Heaven*. Eds. B.D. Boehm and M. Holcomb (New Haven and London: Yale University Press, 2016), 79–81.

Powell, James M. *Anatomy of a Crusade, 1213-1221* (Philadelphia: University of Pennsylvania Press, 1986).

Powell, James M. (Ed.). *Innocent III: Vicar of Christ or Lord of the World?* 2nd ed. (Washington D.C.: Catholic University of America Press, 1994).

Powell, James M. "Frederick II and the Muslims: The Making of an Historiographical Tradition." In *Iberia and the Mediterranean World of the Middle Ages, Volume I: Proceedings from Kalamazoo. Studies in Honor of Robert I. Burns, S.J.* Ed. L.J. Simon (Leiden: Brill, 1995), 261–69.

Prag, Kay. *Excavations by K.M. Kenyon in Jerusalem 1961-1967: Discoveries in Hellenistic to Ottoman Jerusalem* (Oxford: Oxford University Press, 2008).

Prag, Kay. *Re-excavating Jerusalem: Archival Archaeology* (Oxford: Oxford University Press, 2019).

Prawer, Joshua. "The Settlement of the Latins in Jerusalem." *Speculum* 27:4 (1952): 490–503.

Prawer, Joshua. *Crusader Institutions* (Oxford: Oxford University Press, 1980).

Prawer, Joshua, *The Crusaders' Kingdom: European Colonialism in the Middle Ages* (New York: Praeger, 1972).

Prawer, Joshua. *The History of the Jews in the Latin Kingdom of Jerusalem* (Oxford: Oxford University Press, 1988).

Prawer, Joshua. "The Jerusalem the Crusaders Captured: A Contribution to the Medieval Topography of the City." In *Crusade and Settlement: Papers Read at the First Conference of the Society for the Study of the Crusades and the Latin East and Presented to R.C. Smail*. Ed. P.W. Edbury (Cardiff: University College Cardiff Press, 1985), 1–16.

Prestwich, Michael. *Edward I* (Berkeley: University of California Press, 1988).

Pringle, Denys. *The Churches of the Crusader Kingdom of Jerusalem, Vol. III: The Kingdom of Jerusalem* (Cambridge: Cambridge University Press, 2007).

Pringle, Denys. "Crusader Jerusalem." In *Fortification and Settlement in Crusader Palestine*. Ed. D. Pringle (Aldershot: Ashgate, 2000), 105–113.

Pringle, Denys "Itineraria Terrae Sanctae minora III: Some Early Twelfth-Century Guides to Frankish Jerusalem." *Crusades* 20 (2021): 3–63.

Proudfoot, Ann S. "The Sources of Theophanes for the Heraclian Dynasty." *Byzantion* 44 (1974): 367–439.

Pryor, John H. "Transportation of Horses by Sea During the Era of the Crusades: Eighth Century to 1285 A.D. Part I: to c. 1225." *Mariner's Mirror* 68 (1982): 9–30.

Pullan, Wendy et al., *The Struggle for Jerusalem's Holy Places* (New York and London: Routledge, 2013).

Purkis, William J. *Crusading Spirituality in the Holy Land and Iberia, c. 1095–c. 1187* (Woodbridge: Boydell and Brewer, 2008).

Purton, Peter. *A History of the Early Medieval Siege, c. 450-1200* (Woodbridge: Boydell & Brewer, 2009).

Queller, Donald E. and Thomas F. Madden. *The Fourth Crusade: The Conquest of Constantinople*. 2nd ed. (Philadelphia: University of Pennsylvania Press, 1997).

Qureshi, E. and M. Sells (Eds.). *The New Crusades: Constructing the Muslim Enemy*. (New York: Columbia University Press, 2003).

Ragab, Ahmed. *The Medieval Islamic Hospital: Medicine, Religion, and Charity* (Cambridge: Cambridge University Press, 2015).

Rashba, Gary L. *Holy Wars: 3,000 Years of Battles in the Holy Land* (Philadelphia and Newbury: Casemate, 2011).

Reinink, Gerrit J. "Heraclius, the New Alexander: Apocalyptic Prophecies During the Reign of Heraclius." In *The Reign of Heraclius (610-641): Crisis and Confrontation*. Eds. G.J. Reinink and B.H. Stolte (Leuven: Peeters, 2002), 81–94.

Reiter, Yitzhak. *Jerusalem and its Role in Islamic Solidarity* (London: Palgrave Macmillan, 2008).

Reiter, Yitzhak and Dvir Dimant, *Islam, Jews and the Temple Mount: The Rock of Our/Their Existence* (New York: Routledge, 2020).

Richard, Jean. *The Crusades, c. 1071-c. 1291* (Cambridge: Cambridge University Press, 1999).

Richard, Jean. *The Latin Kingdom of Jerusalem*. Trans. J. Shirley. 2 vols. (Amsterdam: North-Holland, 1979).

Richards, D.S. "A Consideration of Two Sources for the Life of Saladin." *Journal of Semitic Studies* 25:1 (1980): 46–65.

Riley-Smith, Jonathan. "An Army on Pilgrimage." In *Jerusalem the Golden: The Origins and Impact of the First Crusade*. Eds. S.B. Edgington and L. García-Guijarro (Turnhout: Brepols, 2014), 103–16.

Riley-Smith, Jonathan (Ed.). *Atlas of the Crusades*. (London: Facts on File, 1990).

Riley-Smith, Jonathan. *The Crusades: A History* (New Haven: Yale University Press, 2005).

Riley-Smith, Jonathan. "Crusading as an Act of Love." *History* 65:214 (1980): 177–92.

Riley-Smith, Jonathan. "Early Crusaders to the East and the Costs of Crusading, 1095-1130." In *Cross Cultural Convergences in the Crusader Period: Essays Presented to Aryeh Grabois on his Sixty-Fifth Birthday*. Eds. M. Goodich, S. Menache, and S. Schein (New York: Peter Lang, 1995), 237–57.

Riley-Smith, Jonathan. "Families, Crusades and Settlement in the Latin East, 1102-1131." In *Die Kreuzfahrerstaaten als multikulturelle Gesellschaft Einwanderer und Minderheiten im 12. und 13. Jahrhundert*. Ed. H.E. Mayer (Munich: R. Oldenbourg, 1997), 1–12.

Riley-Smith, Jonathan. *The First Crusade and the Idea of Crusading* (Philadelphia: University of Pennsylvania Press, 1986).

Riley-Smith, Jonathan. *The First Crusaders, 1095-1131* (Cambridge: Cambridge University Press, 1997).

Riley-Smith, Jonathan. "The Idea of Crusading in the Charters of Early Crusaders, 1095-1102." *Actes du Colloque Universitaire International de Clermont-Ferrand (23-25 juin 1995)* 236 (1997): 155–66.

Riley-Smith, Jonathan (Ed.). *The Oxford History of the Crusades*. (Reprint, Oxford: Oxford University Press, 2002).

314

Riley-Smith, Jonathan. "Peace Never Established: the Case of the Kingdom of Jerusalem." *Transactions of the Royal Historical Society* 28 (1978): 87–102.

Riley-Smith, Jonathan. *A Short History of the Crusades* (New Haven: Yale University Press, 1987).

Robinson, I.S. "Gregory VII and the Soldiers of Christ." *History* 58 (1973): 169–92.

Robinson, I.S. *The Papacy, 1073-1198: Continuity and Change* (Cambridge: Cambridge University Press, 1990).

Roche, Jason T. "'Crusaders' and the Islamic State Apocalypse." In *International Journal of Military History and Historiography* (August 2021): 1–35.

Rogers, Francis M. *The Quest for Eastern Christians: Travel and Rumor in the Age of Discovery* (Minneapolis: University of Minnesota Press, 1962).

Rogers, R. *Latin Siege Warfare in the Twelfth Century* (Oxford: Oxford University Press, 1992).

Rose, Richard B. "The Native Christians of Jerusalem, 1187-1260." In *The Horns of Hattin: Proceedings of the Second Conference of the Society for the Study of the Crusades and the Latin East, Jerusalem and Haifa 2–6 July 1987*. Ed. B.Z. Kedar (Jerusalem and London: Society for the Study of the Crusades and the Latin East, 1992), 239–49.

Rosenfeld, Henry. "The Social Composition of the Military in the Process of State Formation in the Arabian Desert." *Journal of the Royal Anthropological Institute of Great Britain and Ireland* 95:1 (1965): 75–86.

Rousset, Paul. *Les origines et les caractères de la première croisade* (Neuchâtel: LaBaconnière, 1945).

Różycki, Łukasz. "Between the Old and the New: Byzantine Battle Tactics in the Time of the Battle of Manzikert." In *War in Eleventh-Century Byzantium*. Eds. G. Theotokis and M. Meško (Abingdon and New York: Routledge, 2020), 9–36.

Rubenstein, Jay. *Armies of Heaven: The First Crusade and the Quest for Apocalypse* (New York: Basic Books, 2011).

Rubenstein, Jay. *Guibert of Nogent: Portrait of a Medieval Mind* (New York and London: Routledge, 2002).

Rubenstein, Jay. *Nebuchadnezzar's Dream: The Crusades, Apocalyptic Prophecy, and the End of History* (Oxford: Oxford University Press, 2019).

Rubenstein, Jay. "What is the *Gesta Francorum*, and who was Peter Tudebode?" *Revue Mabillon* 16 (2005): 179–204.

Rubin, Jonathan. *Learning in a Crusader City: Intellectual Activity and Intercultural Exchanges in Acre, 1191-1291* (Cambridge: Cambridge University Press, 2018).

Runciman, Steven. *A History of the Crusades*. 3 vols. (Cambridge: Cambridge University Press, 1951).

Russell, Frederick. *The Just War in the Middle Ages* (Cambridge: Cambridge University Press, 1975).

Russo, Luigi. "The Monte Cassino Tradition of the First Crusade: From the *Chronica monasterii Casinensis* to the *Hystoria de via et recuperatione Antiochiae atque Ierusolymarum*." In *Writing the Early Crusades: Text, Transmission and Memory*. Eds. M. Bull and D. Kempf (Woodbridge: Boydell, 2014), 53–62.

Russo, Luigi. "The Sack of Jerusalem in 1099 and Crusader Violence Viewed by Contemporary Chronicles." In *The Uses of the Bible in Crusader Sources*. Eds. E. Lapina and N. Morton (Leiden and Boston: Brill, 2017), 63–73.

Rustow, Marina. *Heresy and the Politics of Community: The Jews of the Fatimid Caliphate* (Ithaca: Cornell University Press, 2008).

Rustow, Marina. "Jews and Muslims in the Eastern Islamic World." In *A History of Jewish-Muslim Relations: From the Origins to the Present Day*. Eds. A. Meddeb and B. Stora (Princeton: Princeton University Press, 2013), 75–110.

Rustow, Marina. *The Lost Archive: Traces of a Caliphate in a Cairo Synagogue* (Princeton: Princeton University Press, 2020).

Sahas, Daniel J. "The Face to Face Encounter between Patriarch Sophronius of Jerusalem and the Caliph 'Umar ibn al-Khaṭṭāb: Friends or Foes?" In *The Encounter of Eastern Christianity with Early Islam*. Eds. E. Grypeou, M. Swanson, and D. Thomas (Leiden and Boston: Brill, 2006), 33–44.

Sahas, Daniel J. "The Seventh Century in Byzantine-Muslim Relations: Characteristics and Forces." *Islam and Christian-Muslim Relations* 2:1 (1991): 3–22.

Sahas, Daniel J. "Why Did Heraclius not Defend Jerusalem and Fight the Arabs?" *Parole de l'Orient* 24 (1999): 79–97.

Sahner, Christian C. *Christian Martyrs Under Islam: Religious Violence and the Making of the Muslim World* (Princeton: Princeton University Press, 2018).

Salaymah, Lena. "Early Islamic Legal-Historical Precedents: Prisoners of War." *Law and History Review* 26:3 (2008): 521–44.

Sand, Shlomo. *The Invention of the Land of Israel: From Holy Land to Homeland*. Trans. G. Forman (London and New York: Verso, 2012).

Sanders, Paula A. "The Fāṭimid State, 969-1171." In *The Cambridge History of Egypt, Volume I: Islamic Egypt, 640-1517*. Ed. C.F. Petry (Cambridge: Cambridge University Press, 1998), 151–74.

Sayers, Jane E. *Innocent III: Leader of Europe, 1198-1216* (London: Longman, 1994).

Schein, Sylvia. *Gateway to the Heavenly City: Crusader Jerusalem and the Catholic West (1099-1187)* (Burlington: Ashgate, 2005).

Schick, Robert. "Jerusalem in the Roman and Byzantine Periods in Mujīr al-Dīn's Fifteenth-Century History of Jerusalem and Hebron." In *Radical Traditionalism: The Influence of Walter Kaegi in Late Antique, Byzantine, and Medieval Studies*. Ed. C. Raffensberger and D. Olster (Lanham: Rowman & Littlefield, 2019), 23–34.

Schwartz, Seth. *The Ancient Jews from Alexander to Muhammad* (Cambridge: Cambridge University Press, 2014).

Schulze, Kirsten E. *The Arab-Israeli Conflict* (New York and London: Routledge, 2006).

Seligman, Jon. "The Hinterland of Jerusalem During the Byzantine Period." In *Unearthing Jerusalem: 150 Years of Archaeological Research in the Holy City*. Eds. K. Galor and G. Avni (University Park: Penn State University Press, 2011), 361–83.

Seligman, Jon and Gideon Avni. "New Excavations and Studies in the Holy Sepulcher Compound." In *Ancient Jerusalem Revealed: Archaeological Discoveries, 1998-2018*. Ed. H. Geva (Jerusalem: Israel Exploration Society, 2019), 238–46.

Setton, K. et al. (Eds.). *A History of the Crusades*. 6 vols. (Madison: University of Wisconsin Press, 1969–1989).

Shagrir, Iris. "Urban Soundscape: Defining Space and Community in Twelfth-Century Jerusalem." In *Communicating the Middle Ages: Essays in Honour of Sophia Menache*. Eds. I. Shagrir, B.Z. Kedar, and M. Balard (London and New York: Routledge, 2018), 103–20.

Shammalah, Sharif Amin Abu. "Bayt al-Maqdis: A Short History from Ancient to Modern Times." In *Al-Quds: History, Religion, and Politics*. Eds. A. al-Fattah El-Awaisim and M. Ataman (Istanbul: Turkuvaz Haberleşme, 2019), 43–70.

Shatzmiller, Joseph. "Jews, Pilgrimage, and the Christian Cult of Saints: Benjamin of Tudela and his Contemporaries." In *After Rome's Fall: Narrators and Sources of Early Medieval History. Essays Presented to Walter Goffart*. Ed. A.C. Murray (Toronto: University of Toronto Press, 1998), 337–347.

Shitrit, Lihi Ben. *Women and the Holy City: The Struggle Over Jerusalem's Sacred Space* (Cambridge: Cambridge University Press, 2020).

Shlaim, Avi. *The Iron Wall: Israel and the Arab World* (London: Penguin, 2015).

Shoemaker, Steven. *The Death of a Prophet: The End of Muhammad's Life and the Beginnings of Islam* (Philadelphia: University of Pennsylvania Press, 2012).

Shūfānī, Ilyās. *Al-Riddah and the Muslim Conquest of Arabia* (Toronto: University of Toronto Press, 1973).

"Sites and Places in Jerusalem: the Temple Mount." <https://www.jewishvirtuallibrary.org/the-temple-mount> (accessed November 11, 2021).

Slack, Corliss (Ed.). *Historical Dictionary of the Crusades*. (Lanham: Scarecrow Press, 2013).

Slack, Corliss. "The Quest for Gain: Were the First Crusaders Proto-Colonists?" In *Seven Myths of the Crusades*. Eds. A.J. Andrea and A. Holt (Indianapolis: Hackett, 2015), 70–90.

Smail, R.C. *Crusading Warfare, 1097-1193*. 2nd ed. (Cambridge: Cambridge University Press, 1995).

Smarandache, Bogdan C. "Re-Examining Usama ibn Muqidh's Knowledge of 'Frankish': a Case of Medieval Bilingualism during the Crusades." *The Medieval Globe* 3:1 (2017): 47–75.

Smith, Charles. *Palestine and the Arab-Israeli Conflict: A History with Documents* (New York: Bedford/St Martin's, 2020).

Smith, Katherine Allen. *The Bible and Crusade Narrative in the Twelfth Century* (Woodbridge: Boydell Press, 2020).

Smith, Katherine Allen. "The Crusader Conquest of Jerusalem and Christ's Cleansing of the Temple." In *The Uses of the Bible in Crusader Sources*. Eds. E. Lapina and N. Morton (Leiden and Boston: Brill, 2017), 19–41.

Smith, Thomas W. "Between Two Kings: Pope Honorius III and the Seizure of the Kingdom of Jerusalem by Frederick II in 1225." *Journal of Medieval History* 41 (2015): 41–59.

Smith, Thomas W. *Curia and Crusade: Pope Honorius III and the Recovery of the Holy Land, 1216-1227* (Turnhout: Brepols, 2017).

Smith, Thomas W. "First Crusade Letters and Medieval Scribal Cultures." *Journal of Ecclesiastical History* 71:3 (2019): 484–501.

Smith, Thomas W. "Not Sharing the Holy Land: Attitudes Towards Sacred Space in Papal Crusade Calls, 1095-1234." *Al-Masaq* 33:4 (2021): 1–22.

Smith, Thomas W. "The Use of the Bible in the *Arengae* of Pope Gregory IX's Crusade Calls." In *The Uses of the Bible in Crusader Sources*. Eds. E. Lapina and N. Morton (Leiden and Boston: Brill, 2017), 206–35.

Soria, J.M.N. and Ó.V. González (Eds.). *El embajador: evolución en la Edad Media peninsular*. (Gijón: Ediciones Trea, S. L., 2021).

Soroka, Stuart, Patrick Fournier, and Lilach Nir. "Cross-National Evidence of a Negativity Bias in Psychophysiological Reactions to News." *Proceedings of the National Academy of Sciences of the United States of America* 116:38 (2019): 18888–18892.

Southern, R.W. *Western Views of Islam in the Middle Ages* (Cambridge, MA: Harvard University Press, 1962).

Spacey, Beth C. *The Miraculous and the Writing of Crusade Miracle* (Woodbridge: Boydell & Brewer, 2020).

Stanton, Charles D. "The Battle of Civitate: a Plausible Account." *Journal of Medieval Military History* 11 (2013): 25–56.

Starr, Joshua. "Notes on the Byzantine Incursions into Syria and Palestine (?)." *Archiv oritentální* 8:1 (1936): 91–5.

Stephenson, Paul. "The Imperial Theology of Victory." In *A Companion to the Byzantine Culture of War, ca. 300-1204*. Ed. Y. Stouraitis (Leiden and Boston: Brill, 2018), 23–58.

Stoyanov, Yuri. *Defenders and Enemies of the True Cross: The Sasanian Conquest of Jerusalem in 614 and Byzantine Ideology of Anti-Persian Warfare* (Vienna: Austrian Academy of Sciences Press, 2011).

Strack, Georg. "Pope Urban II and Jerusalem: a Re-Examination of his Letters on the First Crusade." *Journal of Religious History, Literature and Culture* 2:1 (2016): 51–70.

Sullivan, Denis. "Byzantine Fronts and Strategies, 300-1204." In *A Companion to the Byzantine Culture of War, ca. 300-1204*. Ed. Y. Stouraitis (Leiden and Boston: Brill, 2018), 259–307.

Sweet, Louise E. "Camel Raiding of North Arabian Bedouin: a Mechanism of Ecological Adaptation." *American Anthropologist* 67:5 (Oct 1965): 1132–50.

Talmon-Heller, Daniella. "Arabic Sources on Muslim Villagers Under Frankish Rule." In *From Clermont to Jerusalem: The Crusades and Crusader Societies, 1095-1500*. Ed. A.V. Murray (Turnhout: Brepols, 1998), 103–18.

Talmon-Heller, Daniella. "Islamic Preaching in Syria During the Counter-Crusade (Twelfth-Thirteenth Centuries)." In *In Laudem Hierosolymitani: Studies in Crusades and Medieval Culture in Honour of Benjamin Z. Kedar*. Eds. I. Shagrir, R. Ellenblum, and J. Riley-Smith (Aldershot: Ashgate, 2007), 61–76.

Talmon-Heller, Daniella and Benjamin Z. Kedar. "Did Muslim Survivors of the 1099 Massacre of Jerusalem Settle in Damascus? The True Origins of the al-Ṣāliḥyya Suburb." *Al-Masaq* 17:2 (2005): 165–9.

Talmon-Heller, Daniella and Miriam Frenkel. "Religious Innovation under Fatimid Rule: Jewish and Muslim Rites in Eleventh-Century Jerusalem." *Medieval Encounters* 25:3 (2019): 203–26.

Tannous, Jack. *The Making of the Medieval Middle East* (Princeton: Princeton University Press, 2013).

Tchekhanovets, Yana. "Recycling the Glory of Byzantium: New Archaeological Evidence of Byzantine-Islamic Transition in Jerusalem." *Studies in Late Antiquity* 2:2 (2018): 215–37.

Tchekhanovets, Yana. "Ring with Resurrection Scene from Umayyad Jerusalem." *Electrum* 26 (2019): 177–85.

Tessera, Miriam Rita. "The Use of the Bible in Twelfth-Century Papal Letters to Outremer." In *The Uses of the Bible in Crusader Sources*. Eds. E. Lapina and N. Morton (Leiden and Boston: Brill, 2017), 179–205.

Tessler, Mark A. *A History of the Israeli-Palestinian Conflict* (Bloomington: Indiana University Press, 1994).

Theodoropoulos, Panagiotis. "Did the Byzantines Call Themselves Byzantines? Elements of Eastern Roman Identity in the Imperial Discourse of the Seventh Century." *Byzantine and Modern Greek Studies* 45:1 (2021): 25–41.

Theotokis, Georgios. *Bohemond of Taranto: Crusader and Conqueror* (London: Pen & Sword Military, 2021).

Theotokis, Georgios. "The Norman Invasion of Sicily, 1061-1072: Numbers and Military Tactics." *War in History* 17:4 (2010): 381–402.

Thomson, Robert W. "The Crusades Through Armenian Eyes." In *The Crusades from the Perspective of Byzantium and the Muslim World*. Eds. A.E. Laiou and R.P. Mottahedeh (Washington D.C.: Dumbarton Oaks Research Library and Collection, 2001), 71–82.

Throop, Susanna A. *Crusading as an Act of Vengeance, 1095-1216* (Farnham: Ashgate, 2011).

Tibble, Steve. *The Crusader Armies, 1099-1187* (New Haven and London: Yale University Press, 2018).

Tibble, Steve. *The Crusader Strategy: Defending the Holy Land* (New Haven and London: Yale University Press, 2020).

Tierney, Brian. *The Crisis of Church and State, 1050-1300* (Toronto: University of Toronto Press, 1988).

Tolan, John. "Of Milk and Blood: Innocent III and the Jews, Revisited." In *Jews and Christians in Thirteenth-Century France*. Eds. E. Baumgarten and J.D. Galinsky (New York: Palgrave Macmillan, 2015), 139–49.

Tolan, John V. *Saint Francis and the Sultan: The Curious History of a Christian-Muslim Encounter* (Oxford: Oxford University Press, 2009).

Tolan, John V. *Saracens: Islam in the Medieval European Imagination* (New York: Columbia University Press, 2002).

Toral-Niehoff, Isabel. "Justice and Good Administration in Medieval Islam: *The Book of the Pearl of the Ruler* by Ibn ʿAbd Rabbih (860–940)." In *The Good Christian Ruler in the First*

Millennium. Eds. P.M. Forness, A. Hasse-Ungeheuer, and H. Leppin (Berlin: De Gruyter, 2021), 383–96.

Treadgold, Warren. *A History of the Byzantine State and Society* (Stanford: Stanford University Press, 1997).

Treadgold, Warren. "Review of Geoffrey Regan, *First Crusader: Byzantium's Holy Wars* (New York: Palgrave Macmillan, 2003)." *Catholic Historical Review* 90:1 (2004): 94–95.

Tucker, Spencer (Ed.). *Battles That Changed History: An Encyclopedia of World Conflict.* (Santa Barbara: ABC-CLIO, 2011).

Tuley, K.A. "A Century of Communication and Acclimatization: Interpreters and Intermediaries in the Kingdom of Jerusalem." In *East Meets West in the Middle Ages and Early Modern Times: Transcultural Experiences in the Premodern World.* Ed. A. Classen (Berlin: De Gruyter, 2013), 311–40.

Tyerman, Christopher. *England and the Crusades, 1095-1588* (Chicago: University of Chicago Press, 1988).

Tyerman, Christopher. *God's War: A New History of the Crusades* (Cambridge, MA: Harvard University Press, 2006).

Tyerman, Christopher. *How to Plan a Crusade: Reason and Religious War in the High Middle Ages* (London: Allen Lane, 2015).

Tyerman, Christopher. *The World of the Crusades: An Illustrated Guide* (New Haven and London: Yale University Press, 2019).

United States Government US Army. *Field Manual 3-90-1: Offense and Defense, Volume 1* (Washington D.C.: Department of the Army, 2013).

Van Cleve, Thomas C. "The Crusade of Frederick II." In *A History of the Crusades, Volume II: The Later Crusades, 1189-1311.* Eds. R.L. Wolff, H.W. Hazard, and K.M. Setton (Madison: University of Wisconsin Press, 1969), 429–62.

Van der Horst, Pieter W. "A Short Note on the Doctrina Jacobi nuper baptizati." In *Studies in Ancient Judaism and Early Christianity* (Leiden and Boston: Brill, 2014): 203–8.

Van Donzel, E. "Were there Ethiopians in Jerusalem at the Time of Saladin's Conquest in 1187?" In *East and West in the Crusader States: Context, Contacts, Confrontations, II.* Ed. K. Ciggaar and H. Teule (Leuven: Peeters, 1999), 125–30.

Van Tricht, Filip. *The Latin Renovatio of Byzantium: The Empire of Constantinople (1204-1228)* (Leiden and Boston: Brill, 2011).

Vassis, Ioannis. "George of Pisidia: The Spring of Byzantine Poetry?" In *A Companion to Byzantine Poetry.* Eds. W. Hörandner, A. Rhoby, and N. Zagklas (Leiden and Boston: Brill, 2019), 149–65.

Verbruggen, J.F. *The Art of Warfare in Western Europe During the Middle Ages: From the Eighth Century to 1340.* Trans. S. Willard and Mrs. R.W. Southern. 2nd ed. (Woodbridge: Boydell & Brewer, 1997).

Vidal, C.A., J. Tearney-Pearce and L. Yarbrough (Eds.). *Minorities in Contact in the Medieval Mediterranean* (Turnhout: Brepols, 2020).

Vratimos, Antonios. "Revisiting the Role of the Armenians in the Battle of Manzikert," *Reti Medievali Rivista* 21:1 (2020): 1–17.

Walker, Lydia M. "Living in the Penultimate Age: Apocalyptic Thought in James of Vitry's *ad status* Sermons." In *The Uses of the Bible in Crusader Sources.* Eds. E. Lapina and N. Morton (Leiden and Boston: Brill, 2017), 297–315.

Walker, Paul E. "Al-Maqrīzī and the Fatimids," *Mamlūk Studies Review* 7:2 (2003): 83–97.

Walker, Paul E. *Caliph of Cairo: Al-Hakim bi-Amr Allah, 996-1021* (Cairo and New York: American University in Cairo Press, 2009).

Walker, Paul E. "The 'Crusade' of John Tzimiskes in the Light of New Arabic Evidence." *Byzantion* 47 (1977): 301–27.

Weiler, Björn K. *Henry III of England and the Staufen Empire, 1216-1272* (Woodbridge: Boydell & Brewer, 2006).

Weiler, Björn K. "The 'Negotium Terrae Sanctae' in the Political Discourse of Latin Christendom, 1215-1311." *International History Review* 25:1 (2003): 1–36.

Wekler-Bdolah, Shlomit. "The Fortifications of Jerusalem in the Byzantine Period." *ARAM* 18–19 (2006–2007): 85–112.

Whatley, Conor. *Procopius on Soldiers and Military Institutions in the Sixth-Century Roman Empire* (Leiden and Boston: Brill, 2021).

Whitby, Mary. "George of Pisidia's Presentation of Emperor Heraclius and His Campaigns: Variety and Development." In *The Reign of Heraclius (610-641): Crisis and Confrontation*. Eds. G.J. Reinink and B.H. Stolte (Leuven: Peeters, 2002), 157–74.

Wies, Ernst Wilhelm. *Friedrich II. von Hohenstaufen: Messias oder Antichrist* (Esslingen: Bechtle, 1994).

Wilson, Ian. "By the Sword or by an Oath: Siege Warfare in the Latin East 1097-1131." In *A Military History of the Mediterranean Sea: Aspects of War, Diplomacy, and Military Elites*. Eds. G. Theotokis and A. Yilduz (Leiden and Boston: Brill, 2018), 235–52.

Wilson, Peter H. *The Thirty Years' War: Europe's Tragedy* (Cambridge, MA: Harvard University Press, 2009).

Wood, Philip. *The Chronicle of Seert: Christian Historical Imagination in Late Antique Iraq* (Oxford: Oxford University Press, 2013).

Woods, David. "The 60 Martyrs of Gaza and the Martyrdom of Bishop Sophronius of Jerusalem." In *Arab-Byzantine Relations in Early Islamic Times*. Ed. M. Bonner (Aldershot: Ashgate, 2004), 129–50.

Wunderle, William D. *Through the Lens of Cultural Awareness: A Primer for US Armed Forces Deploying to Arab and Middle Eastern Countries* (Fort Leavenworth: US Govt. Printing Office, 2006).

Yahalom, Joseph. "The Temple and the City in Liturgical Hebrew Poetry." In *The History of Jerusalem: The Early Muslim Period, 638-1099*. Eds. J. Prawer and H. Ben-Shammai (New York: New York University Press, 1996), 270–94.

Yarbrough, Luke. *Friends of the Emir: Non-Muslim State Officials in Premodern Islamic Thought* (Cambridge: Cambridge University Press, 2019).

Yarbrough, Luke. "Muslim Rulers, Christian Subjects." In *Christian-Muslim Relations: A Bibliographical History*. Eds. D. Pratt and C.L. Tieszen (Leiden and Boston: Brill, 2020), 359–87.

Yeager, Suzanne M. "The Earthly and Heavenly Jerusalem." In *The Cambridge Companion to the Literature of the Crusades*. Ed. A. Bale (Cambridge: Cambridge University Press, 2019), 121–35.

Yusuf, Sayyid Muhammad. "The Battle of al-Qadisiyya." *Islamic Culture* 19 (1945): 1–28.

Yuval, Israel Jacob. *Two Nations in Your Womb: Perceptions of Jews and Christians in Late Antiquity and the Middle Ages* (Berkeley: University of California Press, 2008).

Zaman, Md Saifuz. "Yarmouk—the Necessity of Studying the Battle in Early Medieval Military Historiography." *Journal of Military and Strategic Studies* 16:2 (2015): 160–78.

Zank, Michael. *Jerusalem: A Brief History* (Hoboken: Wiley-Blackwell, 2018).

Ze'evi, Dror. *An Ottoman Century: The District of Jerusalem in the 1600s* (Albany: SUNY Press, 2012).

Zelinger, Yehiel. "The Line of the Southern City Wall of Jerusalem in the Early Periods." In *Ancient Jerusalem Revealed: Archaeological Discoveries, 1998-2018*. Ed. H. Geva (Jerusalem: Israel Exploration Society, 2019), 285–88.

Zouache, Abbès. "Remarks on the Blacks in the Fatimid Armies, Tenth-Twelfth Century CE," *Northeast African Studies* 19:1 (2019): 23–60.

Zukerman, Constantin. "Heraclius and the Return of the Holy Cross." *Travaux et mémoires* 17 (2013): 197–218.

BIBLIOGRAPHY

Theses

Al-Tel, Othman Ismael. "The First Islamic Conquest of Aelia (Islamic Jerusalem)." (Ph.D. thesis, University of Abertay Dundee, 2002).

Elagina, Daria. "The Textual Tradition of the Chronicle of John of Nikiu: Towards the Critical Edition of the Ethiopic Version." (Ph.D. thesis, Universität Hamburg, 2018).

Freedman, Marci. "The Transmission and Reception of Benjamin of Tudela's Book of Travels from the Twelfth Century to 1633." (Ph.D. thesis, University of Manchester, 2016).

Goldman, Brendan G. "Arabic-Speaking Jews in Crusader Syria: Conquest, Continuity and Adaptation in the Medieval Mediterranean." (Ph.D. thesis, Johns Hopkins University, 2018).

Hamblin, William J. "Fāṭimid Army During the Early Crusades." (Ph.D. thesis, University of Michigan, 1985).

Harris, Andrew. "'Save thy people and bless thine inheritance': Consolidation of Gains, the Roman-Persian War, and the Rashidun Conquest, A.D. 622-637." (Master's thesis, School of Advanced Military Studies, 2020).

Kazmouz, Mahmoud Mataz. "Multiculturalism in Islam: The Document of Madīnah & 'Umar's Assurance of Safety as Two Case Studies." (Ph.D. thesis, University of Aberdeen, 2011).

Mylod, Elizabeth J. "Latin Christian Pilgrimage in the Holy Land, 1187-1291." (Ph.D. thesis, University of Leeds, 2013).

Spence, Richard Taylor. "Pope Gregory IX and the Crusade." (Ph.D. thesis, Syracuse University, 1978).

News Media and Blogs

Edmunds, Donna Rachel. "PA Tells Palestinians: the Western Wall Belongs only to Muslims." *Jerusalem Post* (January 22, 2020).

Frantzman, Seth J. "Turkey Vows to 'Liberate Al-Aqsa' after Turning Hagia Sophia to Mosque." *Jerusalem Post* (August 12, 2020).

Holt, Andrew. "The First Crusade as a 'Defensive War': a Response to Prof. Gabriele." *Andrew Holt, PhD* (June 6, 2017). <https://apholt.com/2017/06/06/the-first-crusade-as-a-defensive-war-a-response-to-prof-gabriele/#more-11147>. (Accessed July 13, 2021).

Holt, Andrew. "Saladin's Legacy: Some Thoughts." *Andrew Holt, Ph.D.*, <https://apholt.com/2017/07/25/saladins-legacy-some-thoughts/?fbclid=IwAR3DSQlxybOdWYpsbzx TXTSeQ01iNl44he9UsmrGl22GmiIlsZK1rxXI08o>. (Accessed August 22, 2021).

Holt, Andrew. "The First Crusade as a Defensive War? Four Historians Respond." *Andrew Holt, PhD* (April 15, 2018), <https://apholt.com/2018/04/15/the-first-crusade-as-a-defensive-war-four-historians-respond/>. (Accessed July 13, 2021).

Gabriele, Matthew G. "Islamophobes Want to Recreate the Crusades, but They Don't Understand Them At All." *Washington Post* (June 6, 2017).

Goldenberg, Suzanne. "Rioting as Sharon Visits Islam Holy Site." *Guardian* (September 28, 2000).

Greenwood, Hanan and Nadav Shragai. "In First, Court Backs 'Silent' Jewish Prayer on Temple Mount." *Israel Hayom* (October 7, 2021).

"Israel to Join US in Quitting Unesco." *BBC* (October 12, 2017). <https://www.bbc.com/news/world-us-canada-41598991> (accessed November 18, 2021).

Jacoby, Susan. "The First Victims of the First Crusade," *New York Times* (February 13, 2015).

Jones, Dan. "What the Far Right Gets Wrong about the Crusades," *Time* (October 10, 2019).

"Judge's Approval of Jewish Man's 'Quiet Prayer' on Temple Mount Stirs Arab Anger." *The Times of Israel* (October 8, 2021).

Lewis, Bernard, "The Crusades Don't Get a 'Bum Rap,' They Were Genocide," *beliefnet.com*. <https://www.beliefnet.com/faiths/2005/05/the-crusades-dont-get-a-bum-rap-they-were-genocide.aspx>. (Accessed July 13, 2021).

Lewis, Bernard. "The Roots of Muslim Rage," *The Atlantic* (September 1990).

Winer, Stuart. "Building Project Unearths Ancient History in Tel Aviv Suburb." *Times of Israel* (August 18, 2021).

INDEX